# Cross-Border Pipeline Arrangements

# Cross-Border Pipeline Arrangements

## What Would a Single Regulatory Framework Look Like?

Chowdhury Ishrak Ahmed Siddiky

Wolters Kluwer
Law & Business

*Published by:*
Kluwer Law International
PO Box 316
2400 AH Alphen aan den Rijn
The Netherlands
Website: www.kluwerlaw.com


*Sold and distributed in North, Central and South America by:*
Aspen Publishers, Inc.
7201 McKinney Circle
Frederick, MD 21704
United States of America
Email: customer.service@aspenpublishers.com


*Sold and distributed in all other countries by:*
Turpin Distribution Services Ltd.
Stratton Business Park
Pegasus Drive, Biggleswade
Bedfordshire SG18 8TQ
United Kingdom
Email: kluwerlaw@turpin-distribution.com




*Printed on acid-free paper.*


ISBN 978-90-411-3844-6

Printed and Bound by CPI Group (UK) Ltd, Croydon, CR0 4YY.

To My Parents

# About the Author

Chowdhury Ishrak Ahmed Siddiky obtained his PhD in Energy Law and policy from the Centre for Energy Petroleum Mineral Law and Policy (CEPMLP) at the University of Dundee. He also completed his LLM in Energy Law and Policy from the same institution. The author holds an LLB (Hons) from the University of Kent at Canterbury and was called to the English Bar from Middle Temple London. He is also an advocate at the Supreme Court of Bangladesh. Ishrak has also worked in the oil and gas industry and is a lawyer and consultant, advising and taking part in negotiations on behalf of the governments and the private clients.

# Table of Contents

# List of Tables

# List of Figures

# List of Abbreviations

| | |
|---|---|
| BIT | Bilateral Investment Treaty |
| BTC | Baku–Tblisi–Ceyhan Pipeline |
| BTU | British Thermal Unit |
| CPC | Caspian Pipeline Consortium |
| ECT | Energy Charter Treaty Energy Charter Treaty Protocol |
| FSU | Former Soviet Union |
| GATT | General Agreement on Tariffs and Trade |
| HGA | Host Government Agreement |
| IAEA | International Atomic Energy Agency |
| IGA | Intergovernmental Agreement |
| IPA | International Pipeline Agency |
| LNG | Liquefied Natural Gas |
| NPT | Non-proliferation Treaty |
| NREP | Northern Route Export Pipeline |
| SCP | South Caucasus Pipeline/South Caspian Pipeline |
| VRA | Volta River Authority |
| WAGP | West African Gas Pipeline |
| WTO | World Trade Organization |
| WREP | Western Route Export Pipeline |

# Acknowledgements

I am deeply indebted to my parents Chowdhury Tanbir Ahmed Siddiky and Khurshid Azim Siddiky for their love and encouragement during this process. They deserve all the credit for this work as I can only aspire to be like them but can never match their accomplishments! I would also like to thank my sister for always being there for me and for her love and encouragement. I also acknowledge my brother's support.

I am heavily indebted to Stephen Dow for the colossal role he has played during the entire research. Without his guidance it would have been difficult to finish this work – supervisor, friend and confidant. I also wish to thank Chris Rogers for the role he played for helping me with this work. I would like to acknowledge the help of Professor Philip Andrew Speed during my research.

I would also like to convey my gratitude to all my past and present colleagues for sharing their knowledge and for providing me with a great learning experience. Among these are Dr Ekpen Omonbude, Dr Ali Zahrani, Dr Mohammad Yusuf, Dr Garba, Dr Ji Chen, Dr Zhanibek Saurbek, Dr Fuad Animashoun, Abubakar Coco, Omotola Adu, Saleh Saleh, Panos Ghikas and Rebecca Cree. I wish to especially thank Homagni Choudhury for his unflinching loyalty and support while doing this research.

Chowdhury Ishrak Ahmed Siddiky
August 2011

# Chapter 1

# Introduction

## 1.1.       THE ISSUES

This book deals with the problem which occurs when stakeholders involved in a pipeline do not abide by the obligations agreed between the different partners at the beginning of the project, resulting in the breach of a legitimate expectation[1] of the stakeholders involved. Although the stakeholders involved in the pipeline project are already legally bound by the contracts and agreements signed by them, the problem arises when governments intervene[2] due to geo-political, legal and economic factors. This intervention by governments due to these three factors results in the breach of a legitimate expectation and is more frequent in pipelines with a weak enforcement and regulatory mechanism.

The incentive by governments to get involved in order to protect their geo-political, legal and economic interests is quite natural as they either want to protect their sovereignty and have a firm grip over the pipeline passing through their

---

1. The concept of legitimate expectation arises from administrative law and it applies to 'fairness and reasonableness to the situation where a person has an expectation or interest in a public body retaining a long standing practice or keeping a promise' (See P.G. Osborne, *Osborne's Law Dictionary* (London: Sweet and Maxwell, 2009)). However, for the purpose of this book, the concept of legitimate expectation means that the stakeholder's interests in the pipeline are respected and protected based on the agreements signed between the different stakeholders in a pipeline project.

2. The term 'intervention' means an action affecting the parties to that arrangement but which is contrary to the existing contractual/legal terms for that pipeline regime. For the purpose of this book 'interference' could also mean the government involving itself in a dispute or when the government intends to use its position in the pipeline agency by forcefully and deliberately involving itself to protect its own economic, geo-political and legal interest and hence affect the function of the pipeline regime and its regulatory capacity to work independently to protect everyone's interest in the pipeline. Footnote 7 of s. 1.2 also uses the term intervention, and has similar meaning.

country or they are relying on the pipeline to export or import their hydro-carbon resources. Government intervention for legal, geo-political and economic reasons in any pipeline project is controversial because the government itself is one of the parties in the project and based upon its stature and reassurance other companies or entities become part of that project. As a result, when the government intervenes to protect its own interest it is not only disregarding its existing agreed position but also breaching the legitimate expectation of the stakeholders involved in the pipeline project.

The members of a government[3] in a pipeline regime tend to try to negotiate with the other partners in the pipeline regime when they intervene due to geo-political, legal and economic interests. If the pipeline regime is strong, in that there are strong enforcement mechanisms to ensure that the members abide by their contractual obligations, the government will have to go through the enforcement agency in order to attempt to fulfil their demands.

In the case of a weak regime – where there is little or no enforcement mechanism – the government or any other strong member within the regime can intervene whenever they feel their interest needs to be protected. In that situation, other members of the regime will feel vulnerable as there is no one to protect their interest. It is also important to note that governments or other strong members might intervene to renegotiate the existing nature of the contract, not breach it, if they want to have favourable terms to suit their changing needs.

This book will analyse the problem of a government or other member's intervention in a pipeline regime in order to protect their interest. This will be done through case studies and will determine whether there can be any other mechanism or 'safety net' available for the parties involved in the pipeline regime once a government or any other strong party intervenes, breaching the legitimate expectation of others involved in the pipeline.

1.2.         THE EXISTING POSITION OF
             CROSS-BORDER PIPELINES

The legal framework for cross-border pipelines is rather complex. Each pipeline is considered as a separate entity because different members are part of each pipeline project, and since their interests differ, so does the agreement signed by them. As a result, there is no single regulation or legal process controlling their operation. There are two types of cross-border pipeline arrangements. One is the domestic pipeline model, which is governed under the national laws of the country through which the pipeline is passing. Since such pipelines can pass through different countries,[4] a pipeline chain can have several operators or owners at the same time. Furthermore, 'the regulation of transnational pipeline issues is based on

---

3.   The government is also a member of a pipeline regime together with other members. These could include other governments, private companies, international oil companies or others who have invested in the pipeline project.
4.   In each country, the pipeline would be under the subject of those countries' domestic laws.

contracts between owners or operators of national sections, or by agreements with respective governments'.[5]

Although a sound legal framework with respect to pipelines can help lower disputes between various contractual parties within the transnational pipeline chain, 'the most durable would be bilateral and multilateral treaties that provide the legal foundation on which commercial agreements relating to cross-border pipelines would be based'.[6]

The second cross-border pipeline model is the international model, where the entire pipeline chain is considered as a single integrated entity. Such pipelines tend to have a legal regime through the signing of various intergovernmental agreements (IGAs) and commercial contracts between the parties involved in the pipeline project. This kind of project is 'protected by inter-governmental agreements proscribing unwarranted disruption of the flow and undue burdens of excessive transit fees or taxes'.[7] These sorts of pipeline projects have operated in areas known for their political volatility and, as a result, active participation[8] of the government is required for the smooth operation of the project.

International legal agreements like the Energy Charter Treaty (ECT), World Trade Organization (WTO) and 1921 Barcelona Convention are also relevant to cross-border pipelines, however, their objectives are different[9] and are not aligned to the needs of cross-border pipelines.[10] There is, however, a difference between offshore and land-based pipelines. Offshore pipelines have a legal framework under international law in the form of 1982 UNCLOS (United Nations Convention on the Law of the Sea).[11] There is a clear framework under UNCLOS with regard to the construction, operation and protection of pipelines.[12]

Land-based pipelines do not have any status under international law, and the pipelines are operated under bilateral or multilateral agreements signed between the various parties involved in the pipeline project. Although such international treaties do not directly specify anything with regard to cross-border pipelines, they

---

5. See S. Vinogradov, *Cross-Border Oil and Gas pipelines: International Legal and Regulatory Regimes* (Houston: AIPN study, 2001).
6. See The World Bank, *Russian Oil Transport and Export Study, Strategic Export Expansion Options and Legal, Contractual and Regulatory framework*, Washington D.C., 1997.
7. See R. Lagoni, 'Pipelines', *Encyclopedia of Public International Law* (1997): 3.
8. There can be confusion between 'active participation' and 'interference' from the government. In this case, active participation means the involvement of the government in starting the project, as without their involvement the project might not go ahead. It only amounts to interference when government involves itself in a dispute or when the government intends to use its position in the pipeline agency by forcefully and deliberately protecting its own economic, geopolitical and legal interest. This kind of interference affects the function of the pipeline regime and its regulatory capacity to work independently to protect everyone's interest in the pipeline. Footnote 1 under s. 1.1 of this chapter also defines what intervention means and in both scenarios the term can be used interchangeably to mean the explanation above.
9. Different here means that these legal instruments are more geared towards investment and trade, not specifically directed towards pipelines or its problems.
10. See Vinogradov, *supra* n. 5, 20–28.
11. See *ibid.*, 29–35.
12. See *ibid.*

contain principles and rules applicable to the various ways of transport and communication. The principles of 'freedom of transit', 'non-interference', 'non-discrimination' and 'equal treatment' are vital for cross-border pipelines projects.[13]

The legal framework for cross-border pipelines can be divided into four tiers.[14] They are:

- The country to country relationship.[15]
- The country/pipeline company relationship.[16]
- The pipeline consortium relationship.[17]
- The pipeline company/commercial contractor relationship.[18]

All four aspects of the legal framework are extremely important and are dependent on each other. In fact, for successful cross-border pipelines, all four tiers of the legal framework have to work efficiently and properly. The working of these legal tiers depends upon the various intergovernmental and multilateral agreements and treaties signed between the various parties involved in the project. For example, in a pipeline project there is first an agreement between the different governments involved in the pipeline.[19] After that is completed, there are individual agreements signed between the different companies involved in the project and respective governments.[20] Next, all of the parties within the pipeline chain sign different agreements between themselves, which ties them to the project. Finally, there are contracts signed between the pipeline company which acts as one entity comprising all of the companies, partners and individual contractors or third parties. All these aspects have to work smoothly for the pipeline to operate without any disruption.

## 1.3. THE REASON FOR GOVERNMENT PARTICIPATION

A government participates in the entire process of a pipeline project because without its direct and indirect help[21] the pipeline project might not see the light

---

13. See *ibid.*, 24–28.
14. The main reason for dividing them up is to show the different legal structures available in a pipeline. All of them have to function together for a pipeline to work properly. In the later chapters of this book, all of these four tiers are discussed together and are not broken up into different tiers.
15. An example of this would be the agreement between the UK and Belgium over the building of the Interconnector pipeline.
16. For example, the agreement signed between the Government of Azerbaijan with BP with regard to the BTC pipeline.
17. This is the agreement signed between the different partners including BP, Statoil, Socar and other shareholders of the pipeline regime.
18. For example, the agreement signed between the BTC pipeline company with any other third parties providing services.
19. This is known as the IGAs.
20. These are commonly known as HGAs.
21. Here it means government assistance in order to get the pipeline project off the ground; it still cannot be termed as interference.

of day. Direct help from the government involves its active participation[22] in the form of signing intergovernmental and Host Government Agreements (HGAs) which allow the other partners to start building the pipeline. The government also helps by providing reassurances with regard to the legal and infrastructural aspects of the pipeline. Indirect help from the government stems from the provision of security and stability to ensure that the investors can invest in the project without any hesitation or risk.

The government also participates because without its participation the other companies and financiers who are interested in the project might not join in the implementation of the project. The government, in this instance, provides the credibility needed for the implementation of the project. The government also participates because of economic reasons as it wants to increase its economic power. A pipeline project not only creates jobs for people but also improves the overall transport infrastructure within a country or region which can indirectly benefit the country as a whole. If a country is dependent upon hydro-carbon resources then its government would particularly want to be a part of the project as it would want to channel the profit earned from the pipeline towards other economic activities within the country.

The government is also interested in being part of a pipeline regime if it can use the pipeline as a strategic asset. This is especially the case with transit countries that are an integral part of the entire pipeline chain. This is because without their participation the pipeline project might not be implemented. Transit governments, knowing this fact, would want to be a part of the project in order to earn valuable foreign exchange without providing much investment towards the project. It would also be used for strategic purposes and the geo-strategic position would be used to its benefit in times of any conflict with other countries that are dependent upon the hydro-carbon resources flowing through the pipeline.

Energy security is also a reason for government participation in a pipeline project. Most governments want to ensure that the country gets an uninterrupted supply of hydro-carbon resources which, in turn, would provide the energy security needed for its citizens. Government participation ensures that security, as energy security is fundamental to domestic and foreign policy.[23]

## 1.4.  INTERVENTION FROM THE GOVERNMENT

The problem with cross-border pipelines lies with the intervention of the government for geo-political, economic and legal reasons.[24] Although there are

---

22. This is explained in n. 7 in s. 1.2 of this chapter.
23. There can be a debate about pipeline and commodity, but this book is only focused on pipelines. However, both pipeline and commodity play a role in government participation in a pipeline project because both are reciprocal for the government in order to earn money.
24. This statement ties in with the problem discussed before regarding the intervention of the government in pipeline projects due to these three incentives.

agreements signed between the various parties involved in the pipeline project, the three factors mentioned give incentive to the government to intervene in order to protect their interest.[25] Despite agreements and the preventive measures present in those agreements, there are disruptions in the pipeline which cause problems for all the parties involved in the project.

The legal aspect of cross-border pipelines involves the pipeline passing through various countries. However, since each country has a different legal jurisdiction there is no overarching legal framework for cross-border pipelines.[26] Moreover, there is also the question of regulating pipelines. The stronger players in pipeline projects want to have control over the pipeline operation, as a result, it might sometimes act as a hindrance if all the parties' interests are not taken into account.[27] Other issues that the agreements have to address are third party access, transit tariffs and fees, environmental and safety standards, liability if accidents take place and so on.[28]

Agreements for cross-border pipelines work in a complex manner. There are many treaties and contracts[29] involved between the parties and these involve both multilateral and bilateral agreements between the various players in the pipeline regime.[30] The agreements also consist of dispute resolution clauses, environmental standards that need to be maintained, the role each country has to play to safeguard the pipeline and various other financial and regulatory measures.[31] Although all the players sign off their rights to form a single company which looks after the pipeline on their behalf, the actual enforcement of the various clauses of the agreement is carried out by the respective countries, as individual pipeline regimes might not have enough enforcement capacity to ensure that the members abide by their contractual obligations.[32] Governments tend to intervene when there is a contradiction between local laws or if any citizens bring claims against the pipeline and the government due to the company not acquiring their land properly or not giving

---

25. Although all the parties sign the agreement as they are happy with their respective position, the disagreements and unhappiness starts to creep in with the changing economic, legal and geopolitical landscape. The government intervenes due to the changes in these factors which prompts it to disregard its original position.
26. See P. Stevens, *Cross-Border Oil and Gas Pipelines: Problems and Prospects* (Washington DC: ESMAP, 2003).
27. There is a need for compromise in order for all the parties in the pipeline regime to benefit. If the stronger party forces its way in the pipeline regime the other members might disagree resulting in conflict, which will cause disruption as the stronger party gets its way. Ch. 8 of this book has a section entitled 'the purpose of joining the regime' which deals with this aspect of why the interests of all the parties should be taken into account and it sheds some light on this area.
28. See Vinogradov, *supra* n. 5.
29. This involves IGAs and HGAs, discussed in the previous section of this chapter.
30. There can also be bilateral agreements signed between the different members in a pipeline regime and others which might also protect the investment of the investors.
31. See M. Mugaroby (2000).
32. This happens when the pipeline regime is weak which means that the level of enforcement capacity is either not there or extremely weak. This links in with the problem that this book is trying to answer in that the regulatory capacity of a pipeline might not be enough when the government or any other influential regime member intervenes in the pipeline.

them appropriate compensation or if there is any environmental damage caused by the pipeline project. Some countries also have a weak legal framework which allows the government to intervene if its domestic agenda or policies are contradicted within the agreements signed.

The economic aspect of the pipeline can also be a factor in government intervention. The economic viability of any pipeline is important not only for the parties involved in the project but also to the energy exporting and importing countries. Most of the investors in the project want a steady return on their investment while the energy exporting country wants to maximize its profit. The function of energy transit countries is also important as they play a vital role in ensuring that there is no disruption in the supply chain. They, in return, get transit tariffs. A government tends to intervene when its economic interest gets overshadowed by the other parties involved in the project. This intervention can come either from the exporting, importing or even the transit country.

Government intervention, in this respect, comes in the form of increased taxes and increased tariff.[33] It might also ask for a greater stake or leverage from the other shareholders involved in the pipeline project. The government of the transit country might want a greater transit tariff for letting the pipeline pass through its country. Another form of government intervention can be a change in the legal framework which might increase its economic return but lower the profit made by others. This can be done through new oil and gas legislation which advocates for greater participation of state run oil and gas companies.

Geo-politics is another reason government tends to intervene in pipeline projects. Most pipelines pass through various countries and involve participants from different backgrounds. Some pipelines are built because of geo-political reasons in order to foster greater cooperation between a number of countries while others are built because of better transit or a secured route.[34] The incentive for a government to intervene arises when it wants to use the pipeline as a political weapon or as leverage to get what it wants from other countries or parties involved in the project.[35] This results in increased disruption and cause for concern by the

---

33. The government might want to increase its income from the pipeline and also from the commodity that is being transferred through the pipeline. The transit country might want to increase its tariff while the exporter might want to make more profit from the commodity. Sometimes the exporting country might increase the price for one of two reasons: in order to pay the increased tariff demanded by the transit country or to earn more foreign exchange in order to take advantage of the market.

34. This means that pipelines are built taking into account the geo-political dimension without thinking about the financial viability of the project. The BTC pipeline is an example of that as it was not financially viable at the beginning although there was a lot of political interest from Western countries. Ultimately it was built because all of the parties involved in the project wanted to build it to bypass Russia in order to lower its pipeline dominance. Sometimes countries are landlocked with huge energy resources and it requires geo-political manoeuvring for all the parties to benefit.

35. They might use the pipeline as leverage for getting increased rent out of it, which is in their economic interest, or they could use the pipeline for other geo-political intentions which might not have anything to do with the pipeline, using it as a bargaining chip for something else.

exporting and importing countries, and might even cause problems within the pipeline project if the government is one of the stakeholders in the project.

1.5.                    THE PROBLEM WITH GOVERNMENT INTERVENTION

The above section discussed the three incentives for a government to intervene in cross-border pipelines, despite there being various mechanisms present in the form of agreements and contracts to ensure that there is a secured supply of hydro-carbon resources. One of the problems with government intervention is that it is in breach of the contract[36] signed by that government and others involved in the project. This might force the other parties to take them to court or seek other arbitration mechanisms which may be available. However, the parties in cross-border pipeline projects do not take on the government because of the financial costs involved and also because of the disruption that the lawsuit might bring. As a result, most government intervention, or any conflict with a government, is solved through forced negotiation on the part of the government.[37] The evidence for this, up to the present, is that no big disputes between the parties involved in a pipeline have been solved through going to courts or arbitration. The strength of the government and the parties involved in the project determine who has the upper hand in the conflict and in the negotiation. The parties in the contract, especially the private parties and companies have to be flexible and ready for this sort of situation in cross-border pipeline projects. However, for the government, this kind of intervention lowers their credibility in terms of respecting the sanctity of a contract.

Another problem with government intervention is that it loses credibility in the eyes of the investors. This might result in investors being unwilling to invest in good projects because they are sceptical of the government's role in the project they would be investing in. There might be a situation where the government is not able to find enough investors to invest in a cross-border pipeline project despite the project being financially viable because of its previous interventions. Moreover, this sort of intervention might make the government less stable in the eyes of both the business and the international community.

The third problem that government intervention might cause is greater concern with regard to the aspect of security of supply. Security of supply for both exporters and importers of hydro-carbon resources is of great importance

---

36. There can be an argument regarding whether the government is actually in breach of the contract. From the government perspective, it is simply renegotiation and they are forcefully increasing their demand; while from the perspective of the other stakeholders it is a breach because the government cannot demand to renegotiate whenever they want.
37. Although the aggrieved parties have the option of going for arbitration, as is normally mentioned in a contract, the parties tend to go for negotiation. The reason is that arbitration procedures take longer to solve a dispute and every minute of disruption is costly for them. As a result, the parties would rather go for negotiation over their respective position. The party with bigger and better leverage, in this case the government, is able to dictate terms. Moreover, negotiations take place even after the contract has been renegotiated several times.

because both parties are dependent upon an uninterrupted supply of gas and oil. Any disruption in the supply of resources might cause considerable suffering to the people in those countries, especially during winter. As a result, a government which intervenes to serve its own interest might not be looked at favourably by other countries due to their lack of stability and frequent intervention. This might cause diplomatic problems between them. Such a government might also lose its standing in the wider world because of its intervention and also for not being a partner considerate of others' needs.

The factors mentioned above, including the geo-political, legal and economic aspects, play a part in government intervention, which ultimately causes it to shift from its original position in the contract. Although it causes many problems, as discussed, a government is willing to take those risks because it believes the three factors, mentioned above, are important enough for it to intervene to protect its own interest in the pipeline and support its other domestic or foreign polices which might be related to that pipeline.

## 1.6.  STRUCTURE OF THE BOOK

The analytical framework is covered under Chapter 2, highlighting the use of regime theory in order to analyse the behaviour of the members in a pipeline regime. The reason for doing so is to understand why the pipeline members behave in a particular way to protect their interests and how this could be interpreted from the perspective of international relations. It also mentions the four criteria that would be used to analyse the case studies, together with the reasons for choosing those case studies and how these case studies would be analysed through using these criteria.

Chapter 3 highlights the different aspects of cross-border pipelines including the geo-political, legal and economic sides. The chapter also discusses the technical aspects of the pipelines and the differences between gas and oil pipelines. The purpose of the chapter is to highlight the different roles of the pipelines and the different level of infrastructure and logistics that is required in order for the pipeline to be built from start to completion.

Chapter 4 discusses two pipelines in a strong regime and the behaviour of the members in those regimes. It highlights that the implications of being in a strong regime are that the level of enforcement in the regime is robust and the members tend to abide by their various obligations as agreed at the start of the project. Due to a strong enforcement mechanism, the level of intervention from the government and other members is constrained resulting in increased strength of the regime, benefiting all the members who are part of it. There are both neo-liberal and neo-realist tendencies present in the regime and despite its strength it is still not adept at dealing with all pipeline problems or interventions.

Chapter 5 analyses two pipelines in a moderately strong regime and how the members within these regimes function under this kind of regime category. The enforcement capacity of the pipeline is still quite strong but the regulators enforcing the various rules and regulations are not as independent and robust as those in a strong regime. As a result, government or some other members in the regime can intervene more for their own geo-political, legal and economic reasons which might not serve everyone's interest. The behaviour of the members is a mixture of neo-liberalism and neo-realism, depending upon their interest at the time.

Chapter 6 covers three pipeline case studies in the weak regime category and shows that the level of enforcement of various rules and regulations within the pipeline regime is minimal or non-existent. The reason for this is that some of the pipelines do not have the regulatory mechanisms available and even if they are available they cannot work independently. The implication of this is frequent government intervention due to geo-political, legal and economic reasons which causes frequent disruption in the pipeline. The behaviour of the members displays a mixture of neo-liberal and neo-realist tendencies although the neo-realists (governments or other strong members) have the upper hand as they try to implement their agenda of absolute gain, which is not beneficial for all the actors in a regime.

Chapter 7 discusses the role of ECT, the WTO mechanism and Bilateral Investment Treaties (BITs) and how they are not able to deal with cross-border pipeline problems. The role of International Atomic Energy Agency (IAEA) is also discussed in order to use its regulatory and enforcement features for the building of a new agency or unifying mechanism. The chapter concludes that the current regulatory and enforcement mechanisms are not ideal for dealing with cross-border pipeline issues as they fail to deal with the issues mentioned in Chapter 1 of the book.

Chapter 8 highlights the formation of a new agency or unifying mechanism to deal with cross-border problems. There is an in-depth analysis of the purpose of joining this new unifying mechanism in the form of an agency and how it would help to stop the level of intervention by government or other parties in the pipeline regime, without interfering in the sovereignty of any particular country. The chapter also provides the process through which the agency would work together with its enforcement capabilities. It concludes that this new agency would go further and provide more regulatory features than the ECT, WTO or the IAEA, as discussed in the previous chapter.

Chapter 9 is the concluding chapter and it also analyses the role a new agency would play in regulating different cross-border pipelines through lowering the level of intervention by government or other participants for their own benefit. It then goes on to explain how the different economic, geo-political and legal issues would be dealt with by the agency. Finally, it discusses different options available other than a new agency.

# Chapter 2
# The Analytical Framework

## 2.1. INTRODUCTION

The purpose of this analytical framework is to use it as a tool in analysing the case studies. This chapter begins with a discussion about regime theory because it is used as a theoretical framework in trying to analyse the behaviour of the parties, especially governments, in cross-border pipeline projects.[1] This section leads with an in-depth discussion about regime theory and the two schools of thought within this theory. This theory is then used to formulate the four criteria that will be used in analysing the seven case studies in the following chapters.

There is also discussion about the four criteria and how they are going to be used in analysing the different behaviour of the parties in cross-border pipeline projects. These four criteria will also help in the understanding of the different problems faced by parties in a pipeline project. The chapter also provides a short synopsis of the case studies together with the reasons they were chosen for analysis.

## 2.2. REGIME THEORY

Although there is considerable debate regarding the definition of regime theory and about its role and importance in the study of international relations, this research will avoid all debates regarding the theory and will simply use the theory in providing an analysis of cross-border oil and gas pipelines. However, the

---

1. Regime theory is used to analyse the behaviour of the parties and the government in this regard. There will be a discussion regarding whether their behaviour is neo-realistic or neo-liberal as they intervene due to geo-political, legal and economic reasons. The definition of a regime for the purpose of this book is also provided as each pipeline is considered as a separate regime and the government is one of the players or, in certain instances, the main player in that regime.

observations of all the scholars and the strengths and weaknesses of the regime theory, and its various facets will be highlighted in order to give a holistic view of the subject and the role it has played and can play in the future. In fact, the main purpose is not to use the term 'regime' in a vague and ambiguous way but to treat it from the perspective of international relations.

The original definition of a regime was formulated by Stephen Krasner who considered regime as:

> implicit or explicit principles, norms, rules, and decision making procedures around which actors' expectations converge in a given area of international relations.

Further:

> Principles are beliefs of fact, causation, and rectitude, norms are standards of behaviour defined in terms of rights and obligations, rules are specific pre-scriptions or proscriptions for action and decision making procedures are prevailing practices for making and implementing collective choice.[2]

According to Robert Keohane, regimes are 'institutions with explicit rule, agreed upon by governments that pertain to particular sets of issues in international issues'.[3] While Oran Young, however, considered regimes as 'social institutions governing the actions of those involved in specifiable activities or sets of activities'.[4]

A regime for the purpose of this study would be defined as:

> an institution, framework or an autonomous body with unambiguous rules and principles which regulates the behaviour of states and other national and private entities involved in the issue area of cross-border pipelines.[5]

This definition has been formulated because it is issue specific and provides a comprehensive outlook on the various issues that a pipeline regime needs to cover in order to create an institutional framework or an autonomous regime for cross-border oil and gas pipelines.[6] Although regimes are created through the signing of various agreements, both bilateral and multilateral, the definition

---

2. See S. Krasner, 'Structural Causes and Regime Consequences: Regime as Intervening Vari-ables', in *International Regimes*, ed. Stephen Krasner (Ithaca: Cornell University Press, 1983).
3. See R. Keohane, 'Neoliberal Institutionalism: A Perspective on World Politics', in *International Institutions and State Power: Essays in International Relations Theory*, ed. Robert Keohane (Boulder, CO: Westview Press, 1989).
4. See O. Young, *International Cooperation: Building Regimes for Natural Resources and the Environment* (Ithaca and London: Cornell University Press, 1989), 12.
5. The above definition includes all the players involved in the operation of the cross-border pipeline project. These players include the governments, the private parties who have invested in the project and have a substantial stake in them, and also users of the pipeline who, despite not being owners, also play an important role in the operation of the pipeline.
6. Chapters 4, 5 and 6 of this book use this in order to analyse the different pipeline case studies.

above was created to be more comprehensive and issue specific so that a regime based on a unique set of rules and principles could be set up.

Rules for the purpose of this book are norms of conduct which are precise, unambiguous and binding upon the actors and thus can either be fulfilled or not.[7] For example, the various articles of the agreements and treaties signed by the stakeholders involved in the pipeline will be considered as rules. The agreement obligates them to follow these and is the framework based upon which a regime is formed because it mentions the roles of all the parties involved in the pipeline project.

Principles, however, are norms which establish that something be carried out to the greatest possible degree in relation to legal or factual possibilities.[8] For example, each agreement and treaty signed by the stakeholders includes objectives or goals which they strive to achieve. These would be considered as principles based upon which the agreement or treaty is formulated. As a result, principles are important ingredients based upon which a regime is formed and also provide the framework based upon which parties sign agreements.

Therefore, for the purpose of this book, any pipeline project would be considered to have regime ingredients and credentials if they have either of the two. However, all the pipeline agreements have both principles and rules in those agreements as signed by all parties and thus have regime ingredients. For example, in the West African Gas Pipeline Treaty, Article II2(2) mentions that 'the West African Gas pipeline shall be an open access transporter to the extent contemplated in the International Project Agreement'.[9] This is an example of a principle, whereas a typical rule would be Article IV2(a)(ii) which says that 'the West African Gas Pipeline Authority will monitor compliance by the company of its obligations under the International Project Agreement'.[10]

However, what makes a regime strong, moderately strong or weak is whether the principles and rules of a particular pipeline regime are enforced by the regulatory bodies of those regimes and complied with by all the stakeholders involved. The strength of the regulatory bodies in implementing the various principles and rules of a regime is an indication of how the regime functions.

The regime theory is the most appropriate theory in analysing cross-border pipelines because although many agreements are signed between various members in the field of cross-border oil and gas pipelines, there are still many disputes which take place between the various participants that can jeopardize the entire pipeline chain. These reasons include a lack of compliance with the various agreement clauses, lack of monitoring and transparency and economic and geo-political problems. As a result, an institutional legal regime with ideas and an ethos taken from

---

7. J. Grant, *Encyclopaedic Dictionary of International Law* (USA: Oceana Publications, 2004).
8. *Ibid.*
9. See the WAGP Treaty between the Federal Republic of Nigeria, Republic of Ghana, Benin and Togo. Can be accessed at <www.wagpa.org>.
10. See the WAGP Treaty between the Federal Republic of Nigeria, Republic of Ghana, Benin and Togo. Can be accessed at <www.wagpa.org>.

regime theory can be used to formulate a framework for an autonomous body, which can help deal with these problems to some extent. In fact, the main purpose is not to use the term 'regime' in a vague and ambiguous way but to treat it from the perspective of international relations.

The purpose of the institutional framework or new regime would be to ensure that all the participants within the pipeline chain are abiding by their various rules and regulations and the regime would ensure that they are complying with their obligations. A regime where all the members are aware of their obligations and which strives to ensure that all members achieve their respective goals as set out when joining this regime is one of the main objectives of this cross-border pipeline regime. As a result, this regime would also try to ensure that those joining it could avail themselves of all the facilities provided and were able to obtain equal access to its different mechanisms.

2.3.          THE REALIST AND NEO-REALIST SCHOOLS[11]

The Realist perspective of regime theory could be associated with power-based theories including hegemony, relative gains and distributional conflict. According to the Realists there are many obstacles to having international cooperation which in turn causes difficulty in forming international regimes. For the Realists, power is the ultimate source for forming and maintaining regimes.[12] Moreover, they think that without power it is difficult for any regime to last in the long run and without hegemonic power there would be no formation of regimes in the first place. They believe certain regimes could be formed for mutual interest which include the security and sovereignty of states. The concept of political autonomy is also compatible with Realist views.[13]

However, the Realists also believe that cooperation is not possible and there are many obstacles towards achieving it, because each and every single state wants to have sovereignty over their needs and therefore is reluctant to depend for their needs on others. In fact, autonomy is extremely important for them in the anarchic world and interdependency goes against that philosophy even if it provides short term gains.[14]

Neo-realists, however, point out that states are more interested in relative gains than absolute gains because larger gains by other states can in the long

---

11.  The reason for placing this school under the regime theory is because it would help in further analysing the behaviour of the members or the government in a pipeline from a regime theory perspective. The members of a pipeline regime act like a hegemony and are more interested in benefiting from the regime, which is neo-realist in nature.

12.  See R. Vernon, *Sovereignty at Bay: The Multinational Spread of U.S Enterprises* (Boston, USA: Basic Books, 1979).

13.  See *ibid.*

14.  See P. Stevens, *Cross-Border Oil and Gas Pipelines: Problems and Prospects* (Washington DC: ESMAP Study, 2003).

run lead to confrontation.[15] In a regime, there is always a possibility of some states gaining more than the other which, in turn, will reduce support for the regime. The problem with cooperation is that some states within a regime can cheat and get away with it because there is no effective monitoring. Even if there is a breach and a member is caught, there is no effective way of sanctioning them, resulting in states losing their faith in that regime. Fritz Scharpf also points out that:

> while the benefits of cooperation are more attractive than the outcomes expected in the case of non-agreement, cooperation is seriously threatened by distributive conflict over the choice among cooperative solutions. . . . It is probably fair to say that in the majority of ongoing relationships that is the major obstacle to cooperative solution.[16]

Grieco, however, points out in his analysis that 'international regimes can be used not only to get rid of the cheating problem but the relative gain problem as well. Regimes may also be used to affect both the variables that determine the severity of relative gain concerns: The size in the gap of pay-offs and the sensitivity of actors to relative losses'.[17] Grieco also highlights the fact that often regimes could help mitigate the gaps between stronger and weaker partners in a regime by providing weak actors with preferential treatment, as done under the General Agreement on Tariffs and Trade (GATT) regime.

However, neo-realists also believe that some regimes may be of mutual benefit if it concerns security aspects of states but overall these regimes will tend to have a very limited impact on world politics. This is because the hegemonic states with their sheer power and influence would be able to achieve the relative gains according to their wish with little or no effort at all and can make their position stronger in the regime. They, in fact, see the regime as a place to protect their existing strength. This is shown through the Pareto optimality curve, 'which is a set of points where the amount of goods available to two states is greater than at any other point on the inside of the curve, but where one part may enjoy more good than the other'.[18] As a result, some Realists believe the notion that some states enjoy that position because of their power. It also affects whether the powerful hegemony accepts the regime.

In a cooperative setting, states would not only focus on whether or not they are willing to forgo certain policy-making autonomies but would also be worried about the gains that other partners might make. Waltz points out that 'when faced with the possibility of cooperating for mutual gain, states that feel insecure must ask how the gain will be divided. They are compelled to ask not "will both of us gain? But who will gain more?" Even the prospect of large absolute gains for both parties

15. See Vernon, *supra* n. 12.
16. See F. Scharpf, 'Decision Rules, Decision Styles and Policy Choices', *Journal of Theoretical Politics* 1 (1989): 149–176, at 162.
17. See J. Grieco, 'Realist Theory, and the Problem of International Cooperation: Analysis with an Amended Prisoner's Dilemma', *Journal of Politics* 50 (1988): 600–624.
18. See W. Zacher, & A. Sutton, *Governing Global Networks: International Regimes for Transportation and Communications* (Cambridge: Cambridge University Press, 1996).

does not elicit their cooperation as long as each fears how the other will use its increased capabilities'.[19]

However, Grieco points out three important aspects regarding this matter. He indicates that:

(1)  states sensitive to the distribution of gains are not really relative gain seekers;

(2)  states are not only relative gain seekers but also want absolute gains. As a result they do not have problems going for cooperation at least in the short run;

(3)  although states are never completely indifferent to differences in gains, their sensitivity to relative losses varies.[20]

He also points out that the greater a state's expectation of relative gains the greater is its interest in cooperation, no matter how well others do.

The Realists also believe that some regimes which protect the political autonomy of states are compatible with their theory because it relates to autonomy of states to control the business and political environment within their boundary or adjacent to it. However, this does not cause any problem for cooperation because states are not depending upon others for help as they can monitor the activities through their own security agencies and it does not affect the state's power in any way.[21]

In fact, Krasner highlights the fact that the Prisoners' Dilemma (PD) game used by Keohane to prove his argument about cooperation serves the neo-liberals well, as it helps them to support their argument on cooperation because actors in the game adjust their policies accordingly to cooperate. However, this is inapplicable in the Sexes game[22] because cooperation is not achieved by mutual adjustment among the actors but by one actor adjusting according to the other's wishes.[23] According to Krasner, although the neo-liberals do not disregard the importance of power in their analysis, they fail to comprehend that power can dictate the rules of the game and if the actor with more power moves first then the other would be bound to follow him if they understand that his rules are irrevocable. However, Krasner believes that the role of regimes is quite important. In fact, 'regimes are necessary because of the common aversion to uncoordinated action and to establish stability'.[24]

---

19.  See K. Waltz, *Theory of International Politics* (New York: Random House, 1979), 179.
20.  See J. Grieco, *Cooperation among Nations: Europe, America and Non-Tariff Barriers to Trade* (Ithaca: Cornell University Press, 1990).
21.  See Krasner, *supra* n. 2.
22.  The Battle of Sexes game is a coordination game coined by the Realists. Here the problem is not associated with the danger of defection to a competitive strategy, but the possibility of failing to coordinate strategies, with the consequence that a mutually desired goal is unintentionally missed.
23.  The Battles of Sexes game also points out that in real world politics, states tend to agree with each other and can have common goals but have different routes in attaining those goals.
24.  See S. Krasner, 'Sovereignty, Regimes, and Human Rights', in *Regime Theory and International Relations*, ed. Volker Rittberger et al. (Clarendon: Oxford University Press, 1991).

Krasner also enhances his argument by explaining how the formation of a regime has helped to coordinate the actions of different actors in the allocation of electromagnetic spectrums.[25] He also believes that institutions, to some extent, have helped to coordinate the actions of states and mentions that 'Whereas previous institutional choices have not imposed much constraint, new interest and power capabilities conferred by new technologies have led to new institutional arrangements'.[26] According to Krasner, the regime itself can be a source of power. Although states with more power will have more say, even weaker states can have a say in the forum with their voting rights and other regime facilities.[27]

## 2.4.       THE NEO-LIBERAL SCHOOL[28]

The neo-liberals advocate for collaboration among actors. They consider states as rational egoists who are interested in their own goals and gains. The neo-liberals believe that a regime promotes common good and is best suited when its participants or members include benign hegemonies. According to them, power might be necessary for the formation and maintenance of a regime but it is not the only criteria because different members within a regime have different interests and all these interests, and expectations too, play a big part in a regime and should not be overlooked.

The neo-liberals also use the concept of rationality and market failure to explain their theory of regimes including its formation. In an anarchic world system there is even more competition among actors than collaboration. For example, in the free market economy, one state wants to outdo the other in terms of producing goods or market power and all these actions are taken because one state believes that the other will do the same.[29] The neo-liberals also believe that a regime could survive without a hegemony because states are more interested in gain and they will need to achieve that through cooperation than anything else.

States might not also be overly bothered about a decision-making autonomy once they see they are making some gains from the regime. As a result, they will be willing to trade off their decision-making and other political autonomy in order to make those gains which will serve their interest more. According to them, there are not that many issue areas which might make states feel threatened if other states gained more than them.[30] In fact, Keohane mentions the fact that opposition to

---

25.   See *ibid.*
26.   See Grieco, *supra* n. 20.
27.   See Krasner, *supra* n. 24.
28.   This school of regime theory is also important to know because it would help us to analyse the behaviour of the government or other members who are part of the regime. Every regime has actors who are powerful and want to gain the maximum from joining a regime, they are neo-realist while neo-liberals are more interested in forging cooperation and this is one of the behaviour traits of actors in a pipeline regime.
29.   See Keohane, *supra* n. 3.
30.   See *ibid.*

cooperation due to some actors getting more relative gain than others 'is theoretically implausible when applied to situations in which substantial mutual gains can be realized through cooperation and in which governments do not expect others to threaten them with force'.[31] States will, as a result, cooperate where there is mutual gain and even if they gain less than others in the regime they will stay because it serves their purpose. However, neo-liberals do accept the fact that sometimes powerful states might gain more than other states but all states gain to some extent from the regime. Keohane also mentions that reciprocity is the most important aspect of cooperation among egoistic states.

The neo-liberalists also believe that there are some formal and informal institutions which help in facilitating cooperation among countries. These institutions also play a role during negotiations and help to monitor and provide transparency between various actors within a regime. They also help to sanction members if they fail to abide by the rules and procedures. As a result, there is little chance of cheating, as argued by the Realists. The neo-liberalist believes that although there are certain obstacles towards cooperation, this is nothing to worry about as long as states have mutual interest and understanding in an issue area, which will facilitate further cooperation. This in turn would also help overcome any obstacles towards cooperation. As mentioned before, according to the neo-liberals there is no need for a hegemony for regime formation and survival as advocated by the Realists. In fact, Oran Young mentions that:

> there is nothing in theories of bargaining or negotiation as such to justify the conclusion that hegemony is needed to produce agreement, so long as a contract zone or a zone of agreement exists. In fact, rational actors will find a way to realize feasible joint gains.[32]

Some modern institutional concepts like contractualism and situation structuralism are used by neo-liberals to explain international regimes. Contractualism studies the 'effects of international regimes on the ability of actors to cooperate in situations resembling the Prisoner's Dilemma and develops a functional approach to explain the creation and function of regimes'.[33] Situation structuralism, however, further enhances the concept of contractualism by taking into account the various scenarios where actors will cooperate through regimes and analyses the 'implications of different constellations of interests (or games) for the likelihood of regime formation as well as the institutional form of regimes'.[34]

Keohane also mentions the fact that the contractualist theory is extremely important because it operates under the assumption that the states that are actively concerned in an issue area must share a common interest which they can then

---

31. See J. Grieco, *supra* n. 20.
32. See Young, *supra* n. 4, 200.
33. A. Hasenclever, et al., *Theories of International Regimes*, Cambridge Studies in International Relations. Cambridge University Press, London, 1997, 27.
34. See *ibid.*

realize through cooperation.[35] However, Keohane was also careful to mention that states having mutual interest does not guarantee cooperation. Moreover, in factors regarding what makes regimes unique and their functions, Keohane uses the rationality model to explain the problems involved. According to him the main problems of states are uncertainty and the reaction of others in return for the actions they are taking. As a result, the government might sometimes be hesitant in striking mutually beneficial agreements which would have helped them in the long run. This problem can be solved by a regime that provides the information with little or no cost at all and by doing this they will facilitate cooperation between states and make the regime more credible and stronger.[36]

Cooperation, as mentioned before, is also an important ingredient in neo-liberal ethos as it helps in balancing the interests of all the actors gaining from a regime. However, this evolution of cooperation is a process and cannot be taken for granted. Axelrod mentions that 'an important way to promote cooperation is to arrange that the same two individuals will meet each other again, be able to recognize each other from the past, and recall how the other has behaved until now'.[37] In other words, it means that in order to cooperate with each other, two countries would not only evaluate their past interactions but would also take into account whether in the future they have a chance of working towards a common goal.

Axelrod also mentions that cooperation can still be possible in a world of unconditional defection.[38] This means that cooperation is not possible if it is undertaken by actors who are far away from each other and have no chance to meet and interact. However, 'cooperation can evolve from small clusters of individuals who base their cooperation on reciprocity and have even a small proportion of their interactions with each other'.[39] In a regime sense this is important because a regime cannot be formed by actors who do not have common interest and do not have any chance of meeting or interacting. Therefore, in order to form a regime there needs to be some form of interaction and the possibility of working in the same area.

Reciprocity is also important for cooperation to thrive. In a regime with a neo-liberal ethos, every actor has their own interest but for all the actors to have some form of gain, there needs to be reciprocity from all the actors present in the regime. Once there is a culture of reciprocity between different actors, the regime could protect itself from attack by less cooperative actors within the regime who have different intentions.[40]

The potential for cooperation increases when each player is willing to help the other. The dilemma arises when a player realizes that cooperating could be

---

35. See R. Keohane, *After Hegemony: Cooperation and Discord in the World Political Economy* (Princeton, New Jersey: Princeton University Press, 1984).
36. See *ibid.*, 97 and 245.
37. See R. Axelrod, *The Evolution of Cooperation* (USA: Basic Books, 1984).
38. See *ibid.*
39. See *ibid.*
40. See *ibid.*

costly.[41] Axelrod mentions that 'the opportunity for mutual gain from cooperation comes into play when the gains from the other's cooperation are larger than the costs of one's own cooperation and, in that case, mutual cooperation is preferred by both to mutual non-cooperation'.[42] Moreover, getting what one wants in a cooperative setting is not always easy. The reason for this is twofold as: (i) one would need the help of another actor to help and cooperate although the other actor might be in a better position in the short run by not helping; and (ii) an actor would be tempted to get all the cooperation and help without providing any costly cooperation or help in return.[43]

The durability of a relationship between two actors is important in cooperation rather than the trust between them. When the conditions are right for both parties they would come to cooperate with each other and learn through trial and error about the possibilities they have for mutual gain and the strategies which are not helpful for their cooperation.[44] In fact, 'whether the actors trust each other or not is less important in the long run than whether the conditions are ripe for them to build a stable pattern of cooperation with each other'.[45]

According to the neo-liberals, the Prisoner's Dilemma game makes states less inclined to join a regime. This is because states become worried about being double crossed. However, a regime where there is a strong monitoring system, has transparency and, issues sanctions to actors who go against the regime's norms and principles would make states interested in joining them.[46] It would also make other states wanting to cheat more careful because they might receive sanctions for their behaviour. All these factors might lower the fear factor among states and could also lower the level of cheating, resulting in states trusting the regime more and this would in turn enhance the level of cooperation. Another interesting feature is that different regimes have different norms and principles in different issue areas. Some regimes can be nested under other bigger regimes with greater norms and principles and in 'these ways regimes produce connections or linkages between issues and with agreements dealing with particular issues'.[47]

Regimes, according to neo-liberals, also allow states to sign agreements more easily or with limited or no cost. Most agreements are not signed simply on an ad hoc basis or randomly, they are part of a larger framework which is 'nested' within other agreements covering other important issues. For example, a trade agreement between the EU, the US and Japan can be signed to lower the rate of tariff between the countries, but this agreement is under the bigger umbrella of GATT, and the agreement signed by them has to follow the norms, rules and principles of GATT because they are part of it. The GATT trade regime is further

---

41. See *ibid.*
42. See *ibid.*
43. See *ibid.*
44. See R. Axelrod, *Conflicts of Interest, A Theory of Divergent Goals with Application to Politics* (Chicago: Markham, 1970).
45. See *ibid.*
46. See Krasner, *supra* n. 24.
47. See Scharpf, *supra* n. 16.

nested with other areas like monetary, foreign and other issues. According to Keohane, 'within a multilayered system, a major function of international regimes is to facilitate the making of specific agreements on matters of substantive significance within the issue area covered by the regime'.[48]

Finally, regimes can also provide some sort of framework for rules and principles in order to sign agreements according to neo-liberal beliefs. Keohane mentions the fact that there are other outside factors including domestic or foreign policies of state and, political and economic philosophies which also influence governments while signing agreements.[49] However, Keohane also points out that regimes do not establish binding and enforceable legal liabilities in any strict or ultimately reliable sense, although the lack of hierarchical structure or regime does not prevent the development of any form of law.[50] Furthermore, regimes are much more important 'in providing established negotiating frameworks and in helping to coordinate actor's expectations'.[51]

## 2.5. THE CRITERIA FOR ANALYSING THE BEHAVIOUR OF PARTIES IN THE CASE STUDIES

The seven pipeline cases will be divided according to strong regimes, moderately strong regimes and weak regimes.[52] This is done to look at various evidences in the pipeline regimes in order to understand their regime strength and also to find out how the problems faced by these pipelines affect the regime itself. It would also allow an understanding of the reasons why the parties within the pipeline chain behave as they do, especially the behaviour of government and their incentives for doing so from the regime theory perspective. The pipelines of the Former Soviet Union (FSU) and the Interconnector falls under the strong regime category, the Baku–Tblisi–Ceyhan Pipeline (BTC) and the West African Gas Pipeline (WAGP) are considered a moderately strong regime while the Caspian Pipeline Consortium (CPC) pipeline, the Maghreb–Europe pipeline and the Shah-Deniz pipeline fall under the weak regime category.

There are four different criteria that will be used in analysing the various pipelines from different regions. The purpose of these criteria are to provide an in-depth and systematic analysis of the evidences found in the case studies in order to get results which would enable us to understand the various states of the pipelines in the three different regime categories mentioned above and also the

---

48. See R. Keohane, 'The Demand for International Regimes', in *International Regimes*, ed. Stephen D Krasner. Cornell University Press, 1983, 150.
49. See *ibid.*
50. See *ibid.*
51. See Grieco, *supra* n. 31.
52. The definitions of strong, moderately strong and weak regimes are provided in Chs 4, 5 and 6 where each pipeline case study is divided according to its regime strength.

behaviour of the different parties involved in the project, especially government. The four different criteria that will be used are as follows:

- the nature and characteristics of the regime of cross-border pipelines;
- the nature and characteristics of the problems in cross-border pipelines;
- common interests of the parties;
- the enforcement and compliance of the various cross-border pipeline agreements or framework.

2.5.1.     THE NATURE AND CHARACTERISTICS OF THE REGIME
           OF CROSS-BORDER PIPELINES[53]

The nature and characteristics of the regime of cross-border pipelines are analysed for the different characteristics of cross-border pipelines and whether or not there are any regime norms present in these pipelines. There will be analysis of the objective and purpose of building these pipelines and their functioning capacity with regard to the various norms of a regime or whether the activities of the various parties match the thinking of the neo-realist or neo-liberal school of thought.[54]

2.5.2.     THE NATURE AND CHARACTERISTICS OF THE PROBLEMS
           IN CROSS-BORDER PIPELINES[55]

The nature and characteristics of the problems in cross-border pipelines include economic, legal and political problems. The economic problem stems from the fact that due to the changing interests of the parties, the transit country wants a greater share of the profit earned by the exporting country which might lead to disruption of the supply if the parties within the pipeline chain fail to reach a consensus. There are instances where the transit country might hold the exporting and importing country hostage if they do not abide by their demand for increased tariff.[56] Cross-border pipelines offer considerable economic benefits for the people involved and

---

53. This criterion would also enable an understanding of the type of regime a cross-border pipeline is and whether this causes the actors involved in it to behave in a certain way which ties-in with the original problem this book tries to investigate.
54. See Krasner, *supra* n. 48 and Keohane, *supra* n. 3.
55. This criterion links back to the problem for cross-border pipelines discussed earlier which this book is trying to analyse. The incentive for government intervention and its behaviour towards other parties and vice versa is also taken into account. The geo-political, legal and economic aspects discussed here are the incentives for the government to intervene or the issues which cause the problem, and this has been mentioned before in an earlier section. However, this criterion would be used in the case studies to analyse the three incentives from a regime perspective in order to understand the nature of the problems which cause the actors to behave differently.
56. An example of this is Belarus, as the country disrupted supply for increased tariff in order to let Russian gas pass through the country to Europe. See Ch. 4 of this book for details.

are thus an important source of income for the stakeholders indirectly involved in the construction and maintenance of the pipelines.

The stakeholders involved in the pipeline project invest a vast sum of money for the implementation of the project. However, there are instances when the pipelines lack proper infrastructure in transit countries which is a cause of disruption in the pipeline.[57] This not only results in government intervention but also results in economic loss for the investors. There are also situations where countries fail to abide by their obligation to supply gas as agreed, resulting in disruption to the pipeline supply. All these economic problems can result in government intervention.

Legal problems involve the lack of an overarching legal framework present in cross-border pipelines causing problems to the stakeholders involved in the project. Since each and every single country has a separate legal jurisdiction of their own, it becomes difficult and sometimes impossible to abide by the various contracts signed between the parties as they tend to interpret it according to their own national laws. Although the agreements bring all the laws of different countries together under one accord, problems tend to arise when disputes between the parties take place as they try to solve a dispute according to their own interpretation of the laws.[58]

There are also countries with a weak legal system which cannot deal with the problems which might arise during a pipeline dispute. There can be environmental or property right cases brought to the local court which might have an adverse impact on the pipeline.[59] This can also be a reason for government intervention, as it would try to protect its position in the pipeline by ensuring that these cases do not disrupt the flow of the pipeline by changing domestic legislations or by providing compensation to the victims.

Geo-politics also play a crucial role in the building of pipelines. Some pipelines are built under political consideration rather than economic consideration. However, without political stability even pipelines with great economic prospect might end up not working effectively.[60] The main cause of political disputes within the pipeline chain is due to the change of interests between the various

---

57. An example of this is Benin and Togo in the WAGP pipeline, as both the transit countries lacked sufficient infrastructure to supply Nigerian gas to Ghana. See Ch. 5 of this book for details.
58. An example of this is Russia in the CPC pipeline, where they claimed back taxes from the stakeholders involved in the pipeline, although they were not supposed to under the agreement signed between them and the stakeholders involved in the pipeline. However, Russia claimed that according to their interpretation of the agreement, they were allowed to ask the international oil and gas companies involved in the project for taxes. See Ch. 6 of this book for further details in the area.
59. An example of this is the BTC pipeline, where claims were brought against the pipeline in Georgia. The court in Georgia asked the pipeline operators to pay compensation causing problems for the pipeline stakeholders. It was later resolved through government intervention.
60. The evidence for this is the BTC pipeline, which is sometimes known as a political pipeline. This is because initially it was not considered financially viable to build this pipeline. However, due to the strong political will of all the actors involved in the pipeline, it was built and is running smoothly.

players within the project. As a result, they might use the pipeline as a weapon to fulfil their demands. In fact, the players within the pipeline chain look after their national interests first and these interests may differ, resulting in disputes taking place.

A lack of political stability, overdependence on the transport of energy resources and a lack of democratic process in certain regions are also responsible for political disputes in the cross-border pipeline chain.[61] There are instances when a change in government caused a change in government policy towards certain pipeline projects resulting in conflicts between the various parties within the project. Resource nationalism together with political instability in certain countries has also created disputes, which interrupted the flow of energy between countries, resulting in government intervention.[62]

As a result, the problems discussed above all have neo-realist or neo-liberal dimensions and depending upon the interests of various countries their attitude also changes.[63] Some of the economic and political problems arise due to the countries' better bargaining position and their objective of gaining something through cooperating with others, which the neo-liberalists also advocate.[64] However, they also reinforce the neo-realist view that, in certain circumstances, international regimes can have an influence on the anarchic world.[65] The purpose of this criterion would be to highlight these factors from the case studies and to make an in-depth analysis along these lines to understand the true nature of the disputes in cross-border pipelines.

2.5.3.       COMMON INTERESTS OF THE PARTIES[66]

In cross-border pipelines, cooperation among different parties is extremely important for the successful implementation of the project. The reason why parties

---

61. The evidence for this is the Caspian region and the newly independent CIS states. There have been constant disputes between Russia, Ukraine and Belarus which has disrupted the flow of hydro-carbon resources in the past.

62. An example of this is the Russia–Ukraine gas dispute, where Russia stopped the supply of gas to Europe after Ukraine diverted some of the gas from the pipeline meant for Europe for their own use in order to force Russia into an increased tariff. As a result, both countries have used their position to fulfil their own interests. Moreover, a brief war between Russia and Georgia also caused disruption in the BTC pipeline and part of the pipeline was badly damaged due to Russian bombing. The BTC is the only pipeline which does not involve Russia and according to some commentators, Russia intentionally damaged the pipeline, when the pipeline was far from the war zone. See Ch. 5 of this book for more details in the area.

63. This distinction helps us to analyse the behaviour of the parties involved in a pipeline regime and how they react to the various problems in a pipeline from a regime theory perspective.

64. See Young, *supra* n. 4 and Keohane, *supra* n. 3.

65. See Grieco, *supra* n. 17.

66. This criterion allows us to better evaluate the interests of the parties which in turn gives incentive for the parties in the pipeline project to act in a certain way. This also helps us to evaluate the problem regarding the interference of parties, especially government, in their own interest.

cooperate is because they have common interests, which fosters close relationships among the different players involved. There are three parties involved in cross-border pipeline projects. They are the exporting, transit and importing countries.

The growing need for energy to increase economic growth and the scarcity of it has caused both the exporting and importing countries to cooperate in order to fulfil their own interests. The transit country, however, wants to earn transit fees by allowing the pipeline to pass through their country. The interests of all parties involved in the project are, therefore, different, although all their interests are interlinked with the pipeline project.

At the beginning of the project, different actors come together under a common platform because they feel they would be able to gain by cooperating with each other as their interests are similar. This involves the three players and the other private parties and investors involved in the project. At this stage there is harmony amongst all the players involved because they are relatively satisfied with their positions.

However, once the cross-border pipeline project starts to function, all the parties try to gain from it. Although they might be happy with their current position as their interests are satisfied, there might be a tendency on the part of certain players to ask for a greater stake in the pipeline if they see that other parties are gaining significantly more than them.[67] Their interest changes dramatically and they want a greater stake or to earn more from the pipeline chain.[68] From a neo-realist perspective, relative gain is more important than absolute gain and players who are in this group would change their interest accordingly because they believe in that philosophy.[69] Neo-liberals, however, believe that relative gain is important but not the ultimate priority, as long as the common interests of the parties involved in the project are satisfied.[70] Therefore, players falling into this group in cross-border pipeline projects would not change their interest dramatically. They believe in the common good of the players involved rather than guarding their own self interest.[71]

Another scenario where parties grow apart from their common interest is when one of the parties in the pipeline chain has a greater bargaining power than the rest. This particular player can act like a hegemony and due to its size, power and strategic location can exert greater leverage from the parties involved in the project. Although the hegemony cooperated with the other players because it had common interests, the interest changes once their priority changes and they see

---

67. See Young, *supra* n. 4.
68. See Hasenclever et al., *supra* n. 33.
69. See Krasner, *supra* n. 24.
70. See Keohane, *supra* n. 35.
71. It might be in everyone's interest to be under one common regulator because it would allow them to follow one set of rules and regulations, which in turn would lead to greater coordination and cooperation among the members of the regime. For example, in the Interconnector pipeline there are too many regulators within the pipeline regime which causes confusion and a lack of coordination among the parties involved in the pipeline, as they have a hard time following everyone's criteria which in turn results in the parties not abiding by their obligations.

a situation they can gain from.[72] Unstable governance and resource nationalism can also play a part in the hegemony's change in attitude towards fellow players involved in the project.

The purpose of this criterion would be to analyse all these factors and to highlight the major interests of the various stakeholders involved in the project. This would enable the actual motive of the different players in the pipeline regime to be revealed. It would also help in the understanding of the role a regime could play to lower the level of disputes arising from the change of interests between the various actors.

2.5.4.      THE ENFORCEMENT OF AND COMPLIANCE WITH THE VARIOUS CROSS-BORDER PIPELINE AGREEMENTS OR FRAMEWORK[73]

One of the problems with cross-border pipelines is that some of the clauses of the agreements or contracts are not fully enforced or complied with.[74] Therefore, in times of disputes, most parties are not willing to cooperate with each other or abide by the various norms and regulations of the contract, resulting in a deadlock and disruption of supply. Both the neo-liberal and neo-realist schools of regime theory advocate for proper enforcement and regulation of the various agreements signed between the parties.[75] Cheating is one of the main problems that makes a regime ineffective, according to the neo-realists.[76]

The purpose of this criterion would be to analyse whether the parties are actually complying with the various clauses of the agreements and, if not, whether they are properly enforced by the respective parties involved. Both enforcement and compliance mechanisms are important parts of a regime and are also important for cross-border pipelines because they reduce the amount of disputes taking place between the various actors involved, resulting in the smooth operation of cross-border pipelines.

It is also important to distinguish between the different forms of regime based upon the evidence found in the case studies. Actors in a strong regime tend to abide by their obligations due to the presence of a strong enforcement mechanism. The enforcement mechanism in a moderately strong regime might not be as robust as a strong regime resulting in a lack of compliance and enforcement. A weak

---

72. This change in behavioural pattern from the regime theory perspective leads a government to intervene in terms of geo-political, legal or economic issues and can be linked to the problem that this book is trying to answer. See Ch. 1.
73. This criterion would enable whether the agreements are enforced properly by the parties to be understood which in turn would also help in understanding the costs of intervention from certain parties as there is a link between the intervention from government and the enforcement capabilities of the pipeline regime which is a problem this book is trying to look at.
74. See S. Vinogradov, 'Cross-Border Oil and Gas Pipelines: International Legal and Regulatory Regimes', AIPN (2001).
75. See R. Keohane, *supra* n. 49 and Krasner, *supra* n. 24.
76. See Grieco, *supra* n. 31.

regime would lack a strong regulatory mechanism as the enforcement mechanism is too weak to combat the various interventions from the members within the pipeline regime.

2.6.     THE DIFFERENT DIMENSIONS OF A REGIME
         AND THE MOTIVE BEHIND THE FOUR CRITERIA

The purpose of setting up any sort of regime or arrangement is judged according to the ways in which it has been able to deal with the various problems and whether the arrangement or the regime that was created has been successful in mitigating those problems. A regime can be termed as effective if it carries out its various functions or solves the problems that originally motivated its establishment.[77]

The legal aspect from a regime perspective would involve whether a contract is being enforced and complied with properly and whether the parties are aware of their various roles within the legal framework. The problem with this is that although from a legal perspective a regime can be termed as effective, in other fields it may be ineffective or the regime itself may be termed as ineffective because it might not be able to work effectively to solve the main problem which originally motivated its creation.[78] However, from a legal perspective the measurement of the legal aspect is quite straightforward as, depending upon the attitude of different parties towards their contractual obligation and their compliance, it can be understood whether a regime can be termed as legally effective.

The economic aspect would include whether a regime is efficient enough.[79] Economists would want to focus on how much outcome is generated and at what costs. The lower the cost in achieving the actual result and with greater efficiency, the higher would be the chance of a regime being termed as effective.[80] However, there might be problems in the measurement of efficiency if it is based on empirical evidence from other regimes or on some other models, and as a result the true test of efficiency can produce different results, causing confusion and lack of understanding regarding its economic aspects.[81] It has also been said that 'in solving or managing international problems, we are seldom able to determine how efficient a regime is'.[82]

The geo-political approach of a regime can be totally different. The purpose of setting up regimes is to bring the various actors' interests to the fore so that they can come together and discuss their problems to try to find ways in breaking the

---

77. See A. Underdal, et al., 'The Study of Regime Effectiveness: Agenda-Setting Paper for the Concerted Action Workshop', 16–18 Oct. 1998.
78. See *ibid.*
79. See *ibid.*
80. See *ibid.*
81. See *ibid.*
82. See O. Young, et al., *The Effectiveness of International Environmental Regimes*. The MIT Press, 1999.

deadlock between them.[83] Geo-political effectiveness, in this case, will be measured not in whether the regime was successful in solving the various problems but whether it has changed the actions and behaviours of the various political actors to create a situation conducive to negotiation and discussion.[84] A regime's role or its effectiveness lies in trying to change the attitudes of the different parties. For example, the objective of the 1985 Vienna Convention was to protect the ozone layer, the objective of the 1992 Framework Convention on Climate Change and the 1997 Kyoto Protocol was to stabilize greenhouse gas levels to an acceptable limit.[85] Thus, a regime from a geo-political sense 'means spurring actions towards achieving these objectives and specific regulatory rules, protocols, and operational targets are means to these ends rather than ends in themselves'.[86]

Therefore, legal, geo-political and economic dimensions in respect of cross-border pipelines vary from project to project. One of the reasons for this is that the motivation for pipeline projects differs between different actors. Some pipelines are built for political gain while others are built for economic reasons, and their level of expectation varies. Although it is claimed by some experts in the field that pipelines built without economic considerations cannot be sustained in the long run, there are ample examples where economic considerations were not the sole criteria for building a pipeline.[87]

The four criteria chosen will help to analyse the different case studies in this book, as they are focused on the nature and characteristics of the regime, together with how the behaviour of the actors within those regimes shape the way a regime changes due to geo-political, legal and economic dimensions.[88]

Although it might seem that the analysis in the case studies is focused only on the nature of the regime and the behaviour of the actors on a spectrum that runs from neo-liberal to neo-realist, the four criteria are important steps in understanding the actual workings of a pipeline regime. The first criterion helps in the identification of whether an individual pipeline has the characteristics of a regime and if it does, what kind of regime it is. This is followed by the problems a regime faces and how the behaviour of the actors changes once their interest

---

83. See *ibid.*
84. See *ibid.*
85. See *ibid.*
86. See *ibid.*
87. A good example of this is the BTC pipeline, which was first thought to be costly and not economically viable.
88. It is also quite interesting to note that Vinod Aggarwal used Strength, Scope and Nature as the criteria in assessing the regime of International Textile Trade. By using these criteria, he was able to conclude whether a regime is working effectively and also the amount of transformation that a regime has gone through. It should also be noted, however, that a regime for international trade is different to a regime for natural resources. More can be read at: *Liberal Protectionism: The International Politics of Organized Textile Trade*. Berkeley: University of California Press, 1986.

   Oran Young also used five criteria namely, institutional character, jurisdictional boundary, conditions for operation, consequences of operation and regime dynamics as his analytical tool in explaining various regimes. This can be found at: Young, *supra* n. 4.

changes and how their actions affect other actors in the regime and their legitimate expectations. Establishing the common interests of the parties then helps to understand the individual interests of each stakeholder in the pipeline regime and the motive for the decision they take which then causes problems. Finally, the enforcement mechanism helps in understanding the strength of the regime and whether all the actors are abiding by their regime obligations and, if not, what is the reason behind it.

A regime can either have neo-realist or neo-liberal tendencies and their actions can affect the way a regime can be perceived, however, this does not change the overall function of the regime. The four criteria also help in the understanding of the legal, economic and geo-political dimensions of a pipeline regime, as all three dimensions cause the government to intervene to protect their interest in the pipeline. However, this intervention might affect the legitimate expectations of others in the pipeline. As a result, the four criteria should be seen as four steps that are required to find out about the regime and its strength in meeting the expectations of the stakeholders involved.

## 2.7.        THE CASE STUDIES

The purpose of the case studies would be to analyse the causes of the problems faced by each pipeline and how the various disputes are dealt with within the confinement of the agreements signed between the various parties and their regime framework. The four criteria mentioned in the above section would be used to judge the problems of the pipeline projects. The theoretical framework developed by using regime theory would also be used in trying to understand the regime implications of the current framework of cross-border pipelines and the behaviour of the parties involved in the project. The case studies would also test the assumption made before, that an autonomous body with a regulatory framework and strong regime principles may help to minimize and address conflicts in cross-border pipelines. The case studies that will be analysed are as follows:[89]

- The BTC Pipeline.
- The CPC Pipeline.
- The Shah-Deniz Pipeline.
- The WAGP Pipeline.
- The Interconnector Pipeline.
- Pipelines in the FSU.
- The Maghreb–Europe Gas Pipeline.

---

89. The case studies provide an in-depth discussion about each pipeline and they can be representative of the problems faced by pipeline regimes. This is because they represent different regions of the world and some of them are considered as important pipelines transporting hydro-carbon resources to different parts of the world including, Europe, Asia, Central Asia, the Caspian region and Northern and West Africa.

The main criteria for choosing the case studies are: (i) Reliable published data;[90] (ii) Geo-political scenario and economic implications;[91] and (iii) Historical aspects.[92] The reason for analysing so many cross-border pipeline agreements is to understand the trend of disputes between them and to find out how effective they are in resolving disputes within the frameworks that are currently in place. Some of the pipelines might work properly because of economic reasons while others for political and legal reasons. The main focus of this book would be to understand these factors and how these factors affect all these pipelines and whether they play any role in the overall pipeline project.

## 2.8.        CONCLUSION

In order to have a successful cross-border pipeline, there has to be a balance of all the parties' interests. This might involve political will, economic and legal aspects and other ulterior motives of all the parties involved. As a result, by using regime theory as one of the analytical tools, the geo-political aspect of cross-border pipelines and the impact of the regime can be analysed more thoroughly and the behaviour of the parties could be understood. Furthermore, it would provide a multidimensional view of the pipeline projects. The different schools of regime theory also help us to understand the changing interests of government and other members when they intervene in a pipeline project to protect their own interest.

The use of regime theory would also help in understanding the relationship between different members involved in a pipeline regime and how their relationship changes once there is a conflict of interest. The four criteria mentioned before have a strong link with regime theory as the first and fourth criteria are used to understand the nature of each pipeline regime and their enforcement capabilities. The strength of each pipeline regime either strong, moderately strong or weak[93] can also be an important marker in understanding the nature of the regime and whether it has any bearing on the problems faced by cross-border pipeline regimes.

---

90. This refers to all published data relevant to pipelines, including various legal agreements, official reports, journal articles, pipeline websites and reports, individual websites and data from the stakeholders involved in the pipeline, such as international oil companies or state oil and gas companies.
91. This refers to the geo-political and economic implications that the pipeline brings to a particular region. In some pipelines, geo-political aspects play an important role in deciding whether to build the pipeline or whether it would be safe for a pipeline to pass through a particular region. Economic implications are also crucial in understanding whether the pipeline is financially viable. Both these criteria help in understanding the economic and geo-political motives in building the pipeline.
92. This refers to whether the pipeline has any history of disruption and if there are disruptions in those pipelines, what are the reasons and what has been done to resolve those disputes?
93. The case studies have been classified under strong, moderately strong and a weak regime. The definition of the three types of regimes are provided at the beginning of each chapter and then it is analysed to see the individual strengths and weaknesses of each individual regime, if it is strong, what makes it strong and if it is weak then the reasons for it.

The theory is also used in analysing the different enforcement mechanisms currently available for cross-border pipelines like the ECT and the WTO dispute settlement mechanisms. The purpose of using regime theory was to analyse them and find out the regime capabilities of these mechanisms in dealing with cross-border pipeline disputes.[94] Finally, the theory is also used in advocating for a new International Pipeline Agency (IPA), which would act like a unifying mechanism in dealing with cross-border pipeline disputes.[95] Regime theory will be crucial from this aspect, as it would help to analyse the reasons why states or actors would join this new agency and the benefit cooperation could bring to all the actors from joining this new pipeline agency. The regime theory is not only used to analyse the individual cross-border pipelines and the behaviour of the actors involved in those pipelines, but also helps build a new agency or a mechanism to deal with cross-border pipeline disputes.

---

94. This is done in Ch. 8 of this book.
95. This is done in Ch. 9 of this book.

# Chapter 3

# The Characteristics of Cross-Border Pipelines

## 3.1. INTRODUCTION

The nature and characteristics of cross-border pipelines are quite complex as they require not just financing and planning but a whole raft of other factors such as geo-political and legal input as well as the cooperation of all the actors involved in building the pipeline. The role of all the actors has to be coordinated in order for this type of multi-billion dollar investment to succeed.[1] The objective of this chapter is to investigate the various factors that need to be taken into account before the building of a pipeline.

The first part of the chapter deals with the different technical aspects of cross-border pipelines together with the various stages of building a pipeline. There is then a discussion about the difference between oil and gas pipelines as they are different and require different expertise in order to be built. The chapter then focuses on the economic aspects of cross-border pipelines and the different factors that have to be taken into account by the stakeholders involved in the project. This aspect of the pipeline is extremely important because without investors securing the finance and being confident about the return, it is difficult for the pipeline building process to start. There then follows a discussion about the legal aspects of cross-border pipelines as without a stable legal regime it is difficult for the investors to invest in the pipeline project. The geo-political aspects[2] of pipelines are then highlighted because without the will of the various governments and their

---

1. See ESMAP, *Cross-Border Oil and Gas Pipelines: Problems and Prospects*, technical paper 035, UNDP/World Bank/ESMAP, 15–22, 2003.
2. The geo-political aspect here means the political interests of the stakeholders involved in the pipeline.

cooperation, a cross-border pipeline cannot be built. Political will is an important ingredient for the successful building and operation of a pipeline.

The next part of the chapter deals with the transit issue of pipelines. The role of transit countries is extremely important especially if the producing countries are landlocked. As a result, this issue is discussed in detail followed by some of the important indicators that need to be taken into account while building a pipeline.


3.2.　　　　　THE TECHNICAL ASPECTS OF PIPELINES[3]

Oil and gas pipeline networks each have different aspects. In the case of natural gas, the whole process involves gathering, transmitting and then passing the gas through the distribution lines. For oil pipelines, the process is to gather, trunk and distribute the oil through the pipelines. These are basically the core functions of a gas or an oil pipeline. It is important to note that the technical specification of a pipeline might change with the terrain through which it is passing. For example, a pipeline passing through a city or under the sea will have different engineering specifications and aspects than one passing through rough mountain terrain. A transmission system tends to have a larger diameter if it is to travel longer distances and supplies oil or gas to the distribution lines at high pressure. A distribution system passing through the city and going on to other distant locations tend to be smaller in diameter and have low pressure.[4] Other important technical aspects of pipelines are pipeline sizing,[5] load factor, whether the pipeline is oil or gas, operating cost[6] and compressor cost.[7]

Load factor plays an important part in pipelines. It is defined 'as the relationship between the daily throughput averaged over a year and the maximum throughput on any day in that particular year, expressed as a percentage'.[8] This definition is applied to a specific stream of product passing through the pipelines.[9] It is normal for a pipeline to carry two or more such streams and each stream would have its own load factor.[10] The terms load factor and utilization factor are used interchangeably. However, utilization factor is defined 'as the ratio of average throughput capacity of the pipeline built'.[11] As a result the

---

3. Although this part does not have any significance towards the arguments provided in the book, the purpose of this section is to familiarize the reader with the different technical aspects of the pipelines which will come up in some of the case studies in the following chapters.
4. See J. Vincent-Genod, *Fundamentals of Pipeline Engineering* (Houston: Gulf Publishing, 1984).
5. Pipeline sizing refers to the capacity of the pipeline to carry the hydro-carbon resources. Cost plays an important role in the sizing of the pipeline. The bigger the pipeline, the greater will be the cost.
6. Operating cost refers to the cost of operating the pipeline including maintenance.
7. See Vincent-Genod, *supra* n. 4.
8. See *ibid.*
9. See *ibid.*
10. See *ibid.*
11. See J.L. Kennedy, *Oil and Gas Pipeline Fundamentals* (Tulsa: Pennwell, 1993).

utilization factor can be termed as the load factor for the streams of gas or oil passing through the pipeline (Figure 3.1).[12]

*Figure 3.1    The Process of Oil and Natural Gas reaching from Producer to the Consumer*

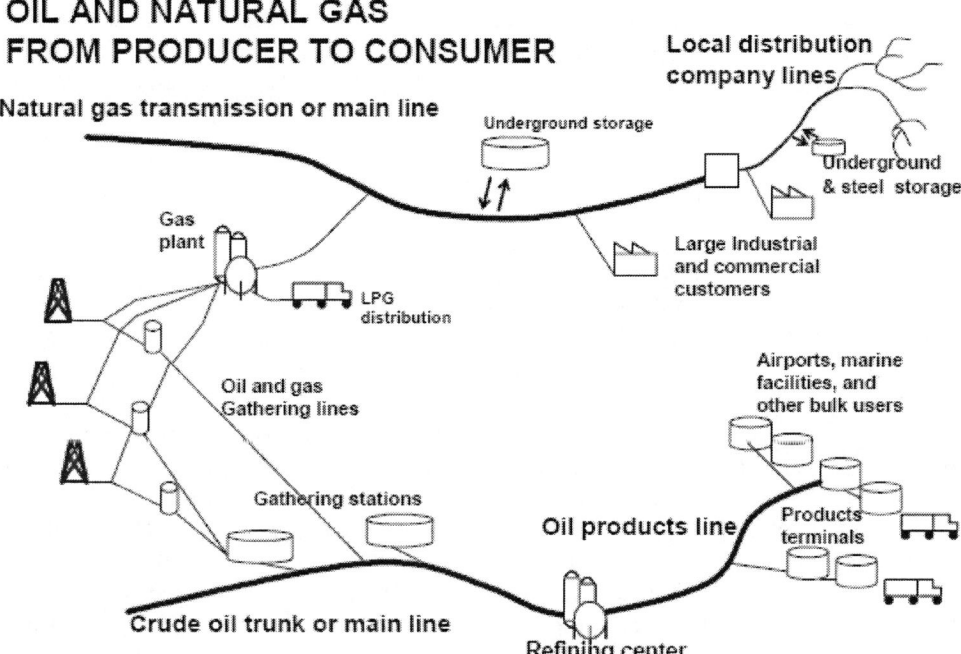

Source: Miesner and Leffer, *Oil and Gas Pipelines in Non-technical Language*, Penwell Corporation, 2006.

The size of the pipeline is also an important consideration for the stakeholders involved in the pipeline project. This is because most stakeholders would expect the pipeline to utilize its maximum capacity. Some important factors that need to be considered in choosing the pipeline size are as follows:[13]

1.    'Reliability that the additional volumes of gas or oil would be carried by the pipeline

2.    The features of the fiscal regime relevant to the pipeline and its various party users

---

12.   See *ibid.*
13.   The purpose of highlighting these technical specifications is to show the factors that are taken into account while deciding on a pipelines size. The bigger the pipeline, the greater the revenue for the stakeholders involved in the pipeline.

3.    The business motive of the investors and how they want to use the pipeline

4.    Environmental objectives, the addition of pumping, compression stations and the policy implication of the relevant regulatory authorities'.[14]

There are some other technical factors which are also important in the building of the pipeline. These include *'whether the costs of oil and gas meet the entry specifications of the pipeline system, the cost of reducing the quality of oil and gas due to the composition of fluids in the pipeline, the cost to the third parties who are involved in the pipeline connection'.*[15]

## 3.3.    THE DIFFERENCE BETWEEN OIL AND GAS PIPELINES

One of the main differences between oil and gas pipelines is the way both commodities are transported through the pipelines. The physical state of natural gas is gas while that of oil is liquid. Due to this difference there is an impact on the design of the pipelines. Since natural gas is transported in a gaseous state it is compressible.[16] As it is compressible this means that more natural gas can be put in one end than taken out from the other end, and this is known as packing the line.[17] Packing the line can be a challenge because if the pressure is too high then it becomes hard to force in the gas while if it is low the end users would not be able to get as much gas as they require.[18] Oil, however, is not compressible meaning whatever is put inside the pipeline will come out in the same volume from the other side. There is also a leak detection system in pipelines to ensure that the entire volume of oil passes through the pipelines without any shortages.[19] As a result, a volume-based leak detection system is more important for oil pipelines than gas pipelines.[20]

There is also less environmental damage in the case of a rupture in a gas pipeline than an oil pipeline. Due to its compressibility, more natural gas can be stored as energy in the pipeline than oil. In the event of any leak, the stored gas or energy tears the pipeline apart and the gas gets released into the air causing minimal damage. However, since oil is liquid it does not dissipate into the air and causes more environmental damage.

Security of supply is more important for gas than oil as gas disruption requires reconnection and this has different characteristics to oil pipelines.[21] There is also

---

14.  See Kennedy, *supra* n. 11.
15.  See *ibid.*
16.  See ESMAP, *supra* n. 1.
17.  See *ibid.*
18.  See *ibid.*
19.  See *ibid.*
20.  See *ibid.*
21.  See B. McLellan, 'Transporting Oil and Gas – the background to the Economics', *Oil and Gas Finance and Accounting* 7 no. 2 (1992).

volume risk[22] for gas since the supply of gas requires market consumption.[23] In the case of oil, however, there is greater flexibility in transportation which lowers its volume risk. In the case of gas, these risks are covered through take or pay clauses.

The transportation of oil is also flexible and costs less than gas. It can be easily moved from one place to another which means the cost, freight and insurance of oil are lower which also makes the final price low.[24] In the case of gas, the choice is only between Liquefied Natural Gas (LNG) and pipelines, which makes the cost higher. Consumers and producers of gas are more closely linked due to the nature of the commodity and therefore any disruption in the pipeline would affect the entire chain, both upstream and downstream.[25] In the case of oil, the producer can sell it elsewhere if there is any problem or disruption.[26]

## 3.4. THE ECONOMIC ASPECTS OF CROSS-BORDER PIPELINES

There are five main factors behind the economics of cross-border pipelines. They are: economies of scale of the pipeline, the life of the pipeline, the involvement of governments, the place of the pipelines in the value chain and the vulnerability of the pipeline with regard to market failure.[27]

The case studies in the following chapters will analyse how government or other actors in a pipeline regime intervene due to economic interest. For example, in the CPC pipeline, the Russian government used the economic interest of other members who wanted to increase the size of the pipeline leverage for their own interest in the pipeline. The Shah-Deniz and WAGP pipelines are also examples where government intervened due to economic interest.

### 3.4.1. THE ECONOMIES OF SCALE OF THE PIPELINE

The building of a pipeline requires considerable investment as it is a fixed object. The bigger the pipeline the lower would be the cost of transport. This is because as the capacity of the pipeline increases the average fixed costs fall, assuming there is a certain level of supply.[28] Cross-border pipelines are therefore characterized by a

---

22. Volume risks are normally borne by the buyer meaning the seller has the guarantee that it is going to sell all the gas it brings to the market. See *ibid.*
23. See McLellan, *supra* n. 21.
24. See T.O. Miesner & W.L. Leffler, *Oil and Gas Pipelines in Non-technical Language* (Penwell Corporation, 2006).
25. See *ibid.*
26. See *ibid.*
27. See *ibid.*
28. See R. Soligo & A. Jaffe, *The Economics of Pipeline Routes: the Conundrum of Oil Exports from the Caspian Basin*, Baker Institute for Public Policy, Rice University, Working Paper, April 1998.

high fixed cost and low variable costs. The main cost of the pipeline occurs when the pipeline is actually being built along with the construction of pumping stations. However, the cost also depends upon where the pipeline is being built. If it is built in rough terrain the costs would be considerably higher than building on a flat piece of land.

A pipeline has the characteristics of a natural monopoly and it is therefore more economically viable to build large pipelines than small ones.[29] However, once the pipeline is built it is difficult to increase its overall capacity because it would require further construction which would drive up the cost of the project.[30] The high fixed costs in cross-border pipelines imply that even if the project is not profitable it would still continue provided the variable cost is covered and there is some sort of contribution towards the fixed cost.[31] The operators of the pipeline would continue to operate the pipeline until they are able to earn back their investment or if there is still a profit to be earned. Due to the high fixed costs of the pipeline it is important for the pipeline to maximize its entire capacity. This is because if the pipeline is operating below its capacity it would spread the fixed cost over its low throughput, which in turn would lower the profit of the stakeholders involved in the pipeline.[32]

### 3.4.2.    THE LIFE OF THE PIPELINE

The average life of any pipeline could be in excess of twenty years. It is a long-term investment which requires cooperation, dedication and flexibility from all the stakeholders involved in the project. Once the pipeline is built there is less flexibility in terms of moving the pipeline, since it is a fixed project. It is possible that the pipeline may become hostage to the strongest partner in the pipeline chain. This can happen in the form of increased rent seeking by one of the partners to take advantage of the situation and reap the profits available. The other partners might have to follow the demand of the influential partner, as very little could be done due to the nature of cross-border pipelines.[33]

It is important therefore to ensure that agreements that govern pipelines cover all necessary grounds for stakeholders to rely on during any time of conflict. These agreements should also contain provisions for any unforeseeable changes and have the flexibility to accommodate the needs of all the parties involved. The longer the life of the pipelines, the greater the chance of the parties diverging in their interests. However, the investors involved in the pipeline would want the pipeline to have a

---

29. See P. Stevens, *A History of Transit Pipelines in the Middle East: Lessons for the Future*, University of Dundee, CEPMLP Seminar Paper SP23, 1996.
30. See *ibid.*
31. See Soligo & Jaffe, *supra* n. 28.
32. See T.R. Stauffer, 'Caspian Fantasy: The Economics of Political Pipelines', *The Brown Journal of World Affairs* VII, no. 2 (2000).
33. See *ibid.*

long life as it would enable them to spread their risks and recuperate their investments over a period of time.

### 3.4.3. THE INVOLVEMENT OF GOVERNMENTS

The involvement of governments is crucial in the successful operation of a pipeline. Most pipelines, as a result, are under government control. A government has the responsibility to acquire the land, provide infrastructural facilities and ensure other cooperation in the building of pipelines. Most governments see the pipeline as having national and strategic importance. This causes them to be an integral part of the project. Too much government interference might not be desirable, however, because there would be other private stakeholders who would want to recover their profits early whilst the government has interests other than to make profit. These can be either political or social. Furthermore, the dual role of the government as both a guardian to its citizens and a commercial partner in a pipeline project might have an impact on the overall efficiency of the pipeline project as there might be a conflict of interest.[34]

### 3.4.4. THE PLACE OF PIPELINES IN THE VALUE CHAIN

The value of the commodity passing through the pipelines is intricately linked with the pipeline itself. The control of a pipeline can have major implications for the other competing parties, for example, the producers, consumers and even some third parties.[35] The reason for this is that some parties can be involved in both the upstream and downstream part of the project. In addition, a pipeline has also to make a profit in order to be economically viable.[36] Sometimes the sharing of profits among various stakeholders can be problematic because there is no set way of dividing these profits, resulting in conflicts between the parties.

Pipelines are also vulnerable because any part of the pipeline not operating would also disrupt the supply of commodities in the pipelines.[37] This would cause disruption in the entire pipeline chain and would also jeopardize the chances of parties earning rent from the pipeline.[38] There is also a chance that government might interfere if there is any form of market failure due to excessive competition between the stakeholders in the project.[39]

---

34. See Soligo & Jaffe, *supra* n. 28.
35. See *ibid.*
36. See *ibid.*
37. See ESMAP, *supra* n. 1.
38. See *ibid.*
39. See *ibid.*

3.4.5.    VULNERABILITY OF PIPELINE IN REGARD TO MARKET FAILURE

Pipelines can sometimes cause environmental and ecological damage especially if they are situated through forests, wetlands or mountainous regions. Moreover, any leak in the pipeline might cause environmental damage which could be harmful to those living beside the pipeline. There is also the question of security of supply as any disruption in the supply might cause problems for the consumers. This is especially significant for gas pipelines as the chances of getting gas from other suppliers at short notice are quite slim. Once there is a market failure the government might intervene although it has to make the decision as to whether public or private control would be in the best interest of the pipeline and its stakeholders.


3.5.    THE LEGAL ASPECTS OF CROSS-BORDER PIPELINES

The legal aspect of cross-border pipelines is extremely important in the operation of a pipeline. Pipelines do not have an overarching legal framework and, as a result, each pipeline is built on a legal framework agreed between the parties. A stable and flexible legal framework is a prerequisite for the building of the pipeline as without it investors will not have the confidence to invest in the project. Most of the countries through which pipelines pass or are situated in have a weak legal framework which complicates matters for Western firms willing to invest in those regions. There are also political and legal risks which investors have to be aware of before embarking on such a project.

There are four types of legal frameworks needed for the successful operation of a pipeline. These are the agreements between the countries involved in the pipeline, agreements between the companies and the country involved in the pipeline, contracts between the different companies within the pipeline and the agreement between the pipeline company and the commercial contractors involved.[40]

The IGA signed between the different countries is 'a written agreement between two or more host countries in relation to a multi-jurisdiction project, pursuant to which the countries mutually confirm their support for the project and pledge to honour the respective HGA signed by them'.[41] Before the start of any project, an IGA is signed for the project to go through. After that, the stakeholders sign HGAs. A HGA is 'a written agreement between the government of the nation within whose boundaries some or the entire project will be constructed and operated (a host country), and the project sponsors or project company'.[42]

The IGA plays an important role in the cross-border pipeline project. The agreement brings all the countries that are involved in the project together

---

40.  See S. Vinogradov, *Cross-Border Oil & Gas Pipelines: International and Regulatory Regimes* (Dundee: CEPMLP, University of Dundee, 2001).
41.  See *ibid.*
42.  See *ibid.*

and without it there would not be any uniformity in the legal regime of the cross-border pipeline project. The government, through this agreement, helps to promote and protect the foreign direct investment in the country and promises to shield the investors and the interests of other countries involved in the project with utmost sincerity and integrity. The important features of IGAs are as follows:

1. *'Protection of investments in each host country, including provisions concerning expropriation and nationalization*

2. *Commitment of each host country to the implementation of the project*

3. *Commitment of each host country to take those steps necessary to satisfy its obligation to ratify the treaty, make enabling laws and take other steps necessary in accordance with their laws to make their promises legally binding under international and its domestic laws*

4. *Respective commitments of the host countries to guarantee performance by their state entities and agencies*

5. *Commitments to freedom of transit and the free movement of project personnel and goods associated with project activities*

6. *Government role in providing for the safety and security of the project and the personnel engaged in project activities*

7. *Application of environmental, health and safety standards which promote integrated pipeline operations in all host jurisdictions'.*[43]

The main purpose of the HGA, however, is to give confidence to the investors regarding the business climate of the country and also to assure them that their investments would be safe even if there are any political or other social problems in the country. This legal regime enables the stakeholders to be a part of the project because it gives them the uniformity they require to participate. Some of the important features of HGA are as follows:

1. *'Defining the tax regime applicable to the project within each transit state, with the project sponsors trying to avoid double taxation*

2. *Providing for the grant of rights to land (or the grant of means to acquire the necessary land rights) and commitments respecting the timing of acquisition, the right of former owners/users to use the surface once the pipeline is installed*

3. *Specifying the commonly agreed set of environmental, health, safety, human rights and other standards that will apply to the facilities while under construction, during operation, for all subsequent repairs, replacements, expansion and or extensions and for abandonment*

---

43. See *ibid.*

4. *Agreeing the necessary monetary and financial rights, including banking rights, currency restrictions and repatriation rights and rights of free movement of personnel, materials, supplies and technology related to the project*

5. *Defining the scope of local regulation of the pipelines to the elements of local service, and confirming the right of free transit as to volumes transiting across the host country'.*[44]

## 3.6. THE GEO-POLITICAL ASPECTS OF CROSS-BORDER PIPELINES

The geo-political aspect of cross-border pipelines is also an important dimension. The growing need for energy to increase economic growth and the question of energy security has caused rivalry among various nations to have a strong supply of hydro-carbon resources. Producing and importing countries, together with the transit countries, are all in competition to maximize their benefits.[45] Due to the increasing demand for energy, producing countries are more interested in making a profit, while the importing countries are interested in gaining a stake in that energy at an affordable price. Furthermore, the emergence of new states has complicated matters because these states are rich in hydro-carbon resources but reliant on transit countries to transport their commodities because they are landlocked.

Control over a transit route has become an important geo-political issue. Some countries, due to their geographical location, want to have greater access to these resources and at the same time want to be a key player in the pipeline chain.[46] Geographical rivalry becomes more complex if both countries are producing hydro-carbon resources and if one of them also becomes a transit country. This conflict of interest results in disputes between the parties. Some of the countries also suffer from political and social problems and use the pipelines as a strategic issue to bargain for something else. Disputes over transit tariff, the threat of terrorism and changes in the interests of the various stakeholders in the pipeline due to regional and international rivalry all play a part in a pipeline being vulnerable.

The case studies in the following chapters show that pipelines like BTC and CPC suffer from geo-political problems because government intervenes due to geo-political interests. The BTC pipeline is a political pipeline as it was built to bypass Russian hegemony in the Caspian region. In the CPC pipeline, there are geo-political tensions between the different actors in the pipeline regime, and each of the actors, is more concerned with fulfilling their own interests.

---

44. See *ibid.*
45. See Stevens, *supra* n. 29.
46. See *ibid.*

3.7.     THE NATURE OF CROSS-BORDER PIPELINES

Cross-border pipelines involve the participation of two sovereign countries and require contracts and legal frameworks to be drawn between the two countries in order for a cross-border pipeline to be built. One of the main differences between a cross-border pipeline and an internal pipeline is that each country has its own legal and regulatory requirements. Since cross-border pipelines do not have any unifying legal mechanism each pipeline project has its own legal framework drawn up following consultation between the countries involved. In fact, taking on board the different legal and regulatory aspects of the countries increases the transaction and operating cost of the pipeline.[47]

The interests of the countries involved in the pipeline project would also differ resulting in each country pushing for greater control over the pipeline project. One of the traits of cross-border pipelines is conflict of interests between the countries. If the countries are either exporters or importers then there would be greater conflict of interest as there would be increased competition between the two to reap the benefits of the pipeline. The difference in jurisdictions would dictate the efficiency of the pipeline because some countries have a weak legal framework and might not even be a part of international treaties like the GATT or the ECT which might make investors nervous about the project due to the various vulnerabilities of pipelines.

3.8.     THE ISSUE OF TRANSIT

The role of the transit country in any cross-border pipeline project is immense. This is especially true in cases where the energy producing country or the importing country is landlocked. A transit country does not have a role in the cross-border pipeline project other than allowing the pipeline to pass through the country. A transit country would only lose their rent in the event of any dispute. Within the pipeline chain, therefore, they have the least to lose from any conflict.[48]

A transit country gets a transit fee for allowing the pipeline to pass through their country. There is no systematic way of calculating this fee and it is totally dependent upon the bargaining power of the actors involved. There have been instances when a transit country has demanded an increase in their transit fee which is sometimes outside the purview of the negotiated fee.[49] A transit country could also ask for greater economic rent if they see the producing country is making substantial profit.[50] Sometimes a transit

---

47. See *ibid.*
48. See ESMAP, *supra* n. 1.
49. An example of this is Ukraine.
50. An example of this is Belarus and Ukraine, as they asked for greater transit tariff to pay for the gas they imported from Russia. Russia was using these countries to supply gas to Europe, where they make a lot of profit.

country is also paid in the form of oil and gas and in that case they forgo their transit tariff.[51]

There are four types of pipeline transit system. They are as follows:

1. *'A pipeline crossing sovereign territory and carrying transit gas without any connection to the gas supply system of the transit country*[52]

2. *A transit pipeline owned by a separate entity, predominantly used for gas transit but also used to supply gas of the same origin to the transit country*[53]

3. *A transit pipeline system integrated into the domestic supply system and owned and operated by the main national transmission operator, where the transit gas flow can still be traced*[54]

4. *Systems where transit volumes commingle within a highly meshed national grid'.*[55]

3.9.  IMPORTANT INDICATORS FOR BUILDING A PIPELINE

There are some important indicators which need to be taken into account before a pipeline is built. Based upon the assessments carried out by the various stakeholders it is decided whether it is feasible to build a pipeline. These factors are: resources in the ground, the need for transportation, economic viability, an entity operating the pipeline, government authorizations for the pipeline crossing another country and financing the project.[56] In the case of gas pipelines, some other factors also have to be taken into account like the supplier and purchaser of gas, price and the market for gas.

It is also important to look at the geo-political implications of building a pipeline as without political and regulatory guarantees, it would be difficult to operate the pipeline. Investors would also be looking at these factors together with the geo-political situation in the region before going ahead with the project. Due to the nature of cross-border pipelines, most pipelines are a target for terrorist activities and these have to be taken into account before a decision is reached.

---

51. An example of this is Benin and Togo in the WAGP.
52. See A. Konoplyanik, 'A Common Russia–EU Energy Space: The New EU Russia Partnership Agreement, Acquis Communautaire and the Energy Charter', JERL 27 (2009): 258–291.
53. See *ibid.*
54. See *ibid.*
55. See *ibid.*
56. See Stevens, *supra* n. 29.

## 3.10. THE RELATIONSHIP OF STATE AND STATE COMPANIES IN THE PIPELINE

The role of state companies is important in the field of oil and gas pipelines. In most instances, for example, the BTC, Maghreb–Europe, Shah-Deniz or the CPC, state companies take part or are members of the pipeline regime. The state companies in reality are like any other international oil and gas companies who are part of the pipeline project but sometimes their role is to protect the interest of the country they are representing. This is especially the case if the pipeline is running through the state company's country of origin.

Some state companies or national oil and gas companies work like any international oil and gas company as they are driven by their business interests and profit margin.[57] However, some governments totally control their national oil and gas companies to ensure that these companies fulfil the interest of the country rather than their business interests.[58] However, for the purpose of this book, a state and a state company will be considered as one entity[59] when analysing cross-border pipeline issues or analysing the behaviour of members in the cross-border pipeline regime.

## 3.11. CONCLUSION

The nature of cross-border pipelines is quite complex and it becomes more challenging as the specifics for gas and oil pipelines are quite different. There are some fundamental similarities between the two as there is a need for economic viability, a legal framework and geo-political cooperation among the interested parties for the successful implementation of building a pipeline. This chapter discusses some of the technical aspects of building a pipeline and the factors that are taken into account by the actors involved before embarking on a project.

The economic, legal and geo-political aspects are discussed to show the relevance of all these factors in building a pipeline. Economic considerations are important for the successful implementation and operation of a pipeline and is a prerequisite for any pipeline being built. The legal and regulatory framework is also important because the actors involved in the project want a stable environment where the pipeline can operate without any disruption. The geo-political factor was highlighted as without political will the pipeline might never see the light of day or, even if it is built, it might not function properly. It should also be noted that although the legal, geo-political and economic aspects are crucial for any pipeline,

---

57. An example of this is Petronas of Malaysia.
58. A good example of this is Sonatrach of Algeria.
59. This could be debatable as some commentators believe that a state and a state company are two different entities and national oil companies are not directly under government control. They are independent and run according to their own business agendas. However, this debate is not within the scope of this book. Moreover, there could also be a different consideration for a state company that is listed but the controlling stake is with the government.

they are also part of the problem as governments may try to intervene due to these three factors. The role of transit countries in a pipeline are also discussed to show their importance, as without them it might not be possible to build a pipeline. This is because of the geographical terrain of the country or the region through which the pipeline passes.

This chapter tries to portray the different features of cross-border pipelines and the various factors needed and those to be taken into account by the actors before and after building the pipeline. It has also tried to analyse the role of different factors in shaping the decisions to build pipelines. This was done purely to give a general idea of the pipeline and how it functions. The following chapters will further illustrate some of the difficulties faced by these pipelines and the different actors who are involved in the pipeline and their role in the operation of the pipeline regime.

# Chapter 4
# Strong Regimes

## 4.1.    INTRODUCTION

The main purpose of this case study chapter is to analyse the Interconnector and the FSU Pipelines in order to understand the different aspects of cross-border pipelines and then to find out the deficiencies which cause them problems from a regime perspective:

> A strong regime follows all the regime rules and principles and it has all the ingredients based upon which it can be classified as a strong regime. This includes having principles and decision making powers and also instruments through which the regime can enforce the various rules and regulations set by it and agreed between the various members of the regime.[1]

These two pipelines in the strong regime category will help us to understand how they function in their current structure and how they are reacting to the various issues affecting them and whether the legitimate expectations of the stakeholders are respected in the pipeline regime. The behaviour of the actors in the regime is also taken into consideration. As a result, an entire pipeline chain and all its different aspects are considered as a regime.

---

1.   This is considered as the definition of a strong regime for the purpose of this book.

Each case analysis is divided into three parts. The first section provides the general background of the pipeline discussing various aspects of the pipeline, the cost of building it and the different actors involved in the pipeline chain. The second section discusses the important aspects of those pipelines that affect its smooth operation. These aspects include economic, legal and geo-political as well as the interests of the parties involved in the pipeline chain. The third section uses the criteria developed in the analytical framework chapter to analyse the lessons learnt from the previous section. The four criteria[2] that would be used in order to analyse the different aspects of these pipelines are:

(i) the nature and characteristics of the regime;
(ii) the issues affecting the cross-border pipeline;
(iii) the common interests of the parties; and
(iv) the enforcement and compliance of the various cross-border pipeline agreements.

## 4.2. THE INTERCONNECTOR PIPELINE

### 4.2.1. THE BACKGROUND OF THE PROJECT

The Interconnector pipeline first came into operation in 1998 and it supplies gas from Bacton UK to Zeebrugge in Belgium. The 235 km pipeline is bi-directional and has the capacity to transport 20 billion cubic metres (BCM) per annum in UK export mode and 8.5 BCM in UK import mode.[3] The export mode of the pipeline is one third of the UK gas market and twice the Belgian gas market.[4] After the initial construction of the pipeline there were further enhancements to increase the import capacity of the UK side of the Interconnector in 2005.[5] The capacity was increased to 25 BCM.[6] A new company called Interconnector was created to finance, design, build and operate the pipeline (Figure 4.1).[7]

---

2. Chapter 2 also provides an extensive discussion regarding the four benchmarks chosen to evaluate the different cross-border pipeline regimes.
3. See J. Alcock, 'Developing European Gas Markets: Strategic Importance of the Interconnector', AIC Conference, 3–4 Apr. 1995.
4. See the Interconnector website at <www.interconnector.com>.
5. See *ibid.*
6. See *ibid.*
7. See *ibid.*

*Figure 4.1   The Interconnector Pipeline*[8]

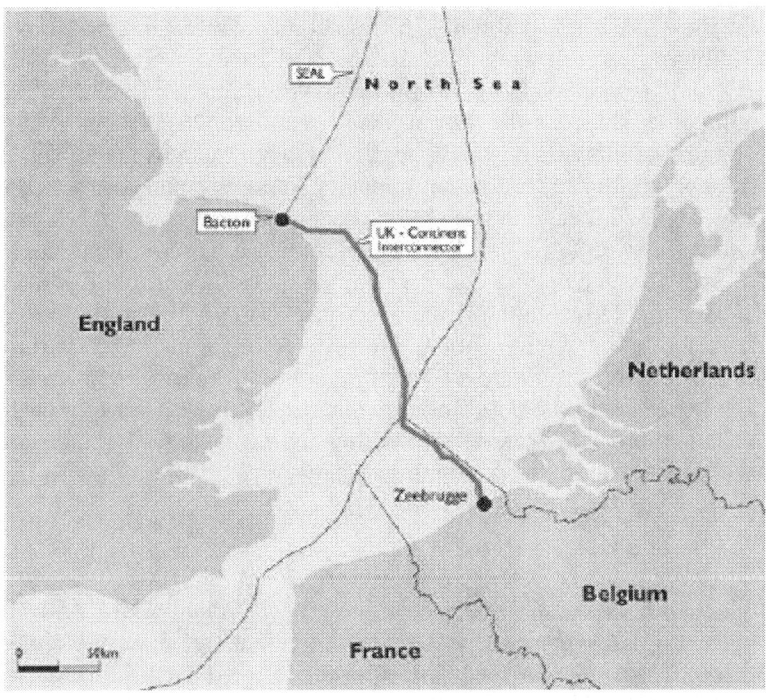

*Source*: Can be accessed via Interconnector website at <www.Interconnector.com>.

The original plan of the Interconnector pipeline was to export gas from the UK. There were compression facilities installed in the Bacton terminal to raise the pressure of gas from the UK grid for transportation under the sea to Zeebrugge.[9] The gas can also be delivered directly from the Shearwater and Elgin fields in the North Sea.[10] The function of the terminal in Zeebrugge is to control the pressure and temperature of the gas arriving from the UK and pass it on to the Belgian grid system.[11]

4.2.2.       THE RELEVANT PARTIES TO THE PROJECT

The major stakeholders of the Interconnector pipeline can be divided into equity shareholders in Interconnector (UK) Limited, shippers who own the capacity rights of the line, government authorities and landfall partners. The two landfall partners in the Interconnector pipeline are British Gas and Distrigaz.[12] Both these landfall

---

8.  The purpose of the pipeline map above is to show the pipeline's geographical location and its importance in terms of supplying gas to Belgium and the UK.
9.  See R. Cornish, *Linking the European Gas Pipeline* (World Gas Yearbook, 1998).
10.  See *ibid*.
11.  See *ibid*.
12.  See the Interconnector website at <www.interconnector.com>.

partners developed the idea of the Interconnector pipeline and both are transporters and shareholders of the project. The Canadian group La Caisse de depot et placement du Quebec has a 23.5% stake in the project while Distrigaz has 11.41%. Other shareholders include Gazprom 10%, CDP Investissements 10%, Conoco Phillips 10%, Fluxys 15%, ENI 5% and E.ON Ruhrgas 15.09%.[13]

The number of shippers for the project is well over twenty and they are more diverse than the shareholders of the company.[14] One of the reasons for this is that the shippers have a higher liquidity of capacity holding than the shareholders.[15] The current shippers other than the shareholders of the project are: Total Gas and Power Limited, ZMB, STATOIL (UK) Limited, RWE Trading GmbH, OAO Gazprom, GDF Suez, Essent Energy, EDF Trading Limited, Centrica, BG International Limited, BP Gas marketing Limited and Electrabel NV/SA.[16] The shippers also have the right to sublet their capacity right and to provide this transportation right to third parties. This in turn might create new shippers who are not directly related to the pipeline. The governments of both Belgium and the UK have a very limited function, other than their initial involvement in starting the project, as they are not directly linked to the various operating and management issues of the pipeline.[17]

4.2.3.     THE COST OF THE PROJECT

The cost of the Interconnector pipeline was about GBP 450 million.[18] The shareholders of the project went for finance leasing, debt and shareholders' equity and loan from the European Investment Bank (EIB).[19] In the end, all the loans and equity were deposited in two banks to get collateral for finance leasing from Abbey National Bank in the UK.

The shareholders of the project also had shareholders' agreements which detailed some of the criteria for securing loans or managing the finances for the project.[20] Some of these are:[21]

- There had to be several guarantees.
- There cannot be any cross-defaults.
- There should not be assignment of assets or revenue streams.
- The use of assets should be safeguarded.
- There should be a maximum equity to the loan ratio of 10%.

---

13. See *ibid.*
14. It is important to know about the shippers because they play a crucial role in the Interconnector. They are responsible for the supply of the gas and their role is to ensure an uninterrupted supply of gas through the pipeline without any disruption.
15. See the Interconnector website at <www.interconnector.com>.
16. See *ibid.*
17. See *ibid.*
18. See *ibid.*
19. See *ibid.*
20. The purpose of the bullet points below is to highlight the stringent loan finance criteria the investors in the interconnector had agreed to enter into.
21. See Cornish, *supra* n. 9.
22. The purpose of Figure 4.2 is to highlight the complex financing process of the pipeline.

*Figure 4.2    The Complex Financing of the Interconnector Pipeline*[22]

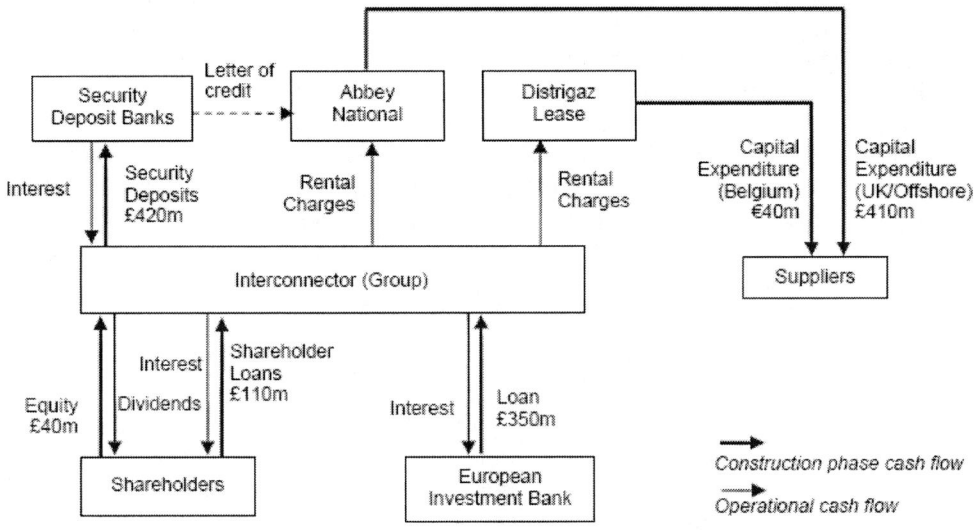

*Source*: Can be accessed via Interconnector website at <www.Interconnector.com>.

### 4.2.4.    OTHER ASPECTS OF THE PIPELINE

The role of shippers is extremely important for the Interconnector pipeline. Initially, the shareholders of the project had their own reasons for investing in the project and did not pay too much attention to capacity.[23] This resulted in the shareholders selling some of their capacity to third parties because of the separation between shareholding and capacity holding.[24] Most of the shippers need to use the line for accessing the wholesale markets, to access supplies or to take advantage of certain market situations when the price varies between markets.[25]

The governments of Belgium and the UK had to sign a treaty paving the way for the building of the Interconnector pipeline.[26] The IGA dealt with the rules of operation and taxation rules. A legal framework also had to be created for the smooth functioning of the pipeline. There were, in addition, business rules set up to

---

23.  The reason they did not pay too much attention to capacity at the beginning was because they did not know the actual demand for the gas in both the countries and did not want to invest too much on it.
24.  See A. Mulcare, 'The Impact of the UK–Belgium Interconnector', can be accessed via <www.interconnector.com/PDF/The_Impact_of_the_Interconnector.pdf>.
25.  See *ibid.*
26.  The Agreement between the Government of United Kingdom and the Government of the Kingdom of Belgium relating to the transmission of natural gas through a pipeline, between the United Kingdom and the Kingdom of Belgium, Brussels, 10 Dec. 1997.

deal with the changing structure of the Interconnector. The rules divide the pipeline capacity between the capacity holders and treat each independent quota independently and separately.[27] The business rules are contained in the Standard Transportation Agreement (STA) between Interconnector UK Limited and the shippers. Each shipper has the right to veto any changes in the STA.[28]

The business rules of the pipeline are implemented by the management system ISIS, which also acts as a communication hub between the shippers and Interconnector UK Limited.[29] The large number of shippers, three connection points, numerous traders and all their daily activities are processed by this database.

## 4.3. THE IMPORTANT ASPECTS OF THE PIPELINE

### 4.3.1. Economic Aspects

The economic aspects of the Interconnector pipeline are immense as they helped the energy needs of both the UK and Belgium. The pipeline brought about significant structural changes in the European gas market.[30] The bi-directional pipeline helped the UK both to export and import gas when required. The Interconnector also helped in the development of two wholesale trading gas hubs in Western Europe: Zeebrugge in Belgium and National Balancing Point (NBP) in the UK.[31] However, the UK gas market is open to greater competition and, due to greater liberalization of its gas market and companies, there are problems between the UK and Belgium as the latter has the Continental European Model where there is less competition and greater monopoly from state owned gas enterprises.[32] The implication is that there is greater competition in the UK[33] resulting in the consumers seeing no reduction in their energy bills, as envisaged at the beginning of the project.

The capacity of the Interconnector pipeline is limited and there are sometimes unexpected technical disruptions in the pipeline flow.[34] In addition, there is an indirect oil price linkage in the Belgian gas prices which also has an affect on the overall gas price in the UK, which links its price to the NBP rather than oil.[35] Therefore, a high oil price would result in UK consumers paying more for the gas

---

27. See S. Vinogradov, 'Cross-Border Oil and Gas Pipelines: International Legal and Regulatory Regimes', AIPN, 2001.
28. See *ibid.*
29. See Mulcare, *supra* n. 24.
30. See S. Thomas, 'The European Union Gas and Electricity Directives', September 2005 at <www.psiru.org>.
31. See *ibid.*
32. The 'legal aspect' section in this chapter will deal with the relationship between EU law and the Interconnector.
33. This is because more companies in the UK are privatized as government wants greater competition, which would drive down price rather than have a monopoly which would do the opposite.
34. See Thomas, *supra* n. 30.
35. See *ibid.*

as the high oil price is fed through the pipeline into the UK from Belgium.[36] As a result, the arbitrage[37] between the UK NBP prices and the oil price linked to the continental model followed by Belgium causes problems for the stakeholders involved in the project.[38]

There have also been unplanned outages and liquid contamination in the pipeline which is outside the control of the pipeline operator but caused disruption of supply between the two countries.[39] Although there are regular maintenance operations taking place in the pipeline, there have been quite a few breakdowns over the last couple of years.[40] Limited competition in other European markets and the inflexibility of supply causes great problems for the stakeholders involved in the Interconnector pipeline because it lowers their profits as well as the financial and strategic viability of the pipeline.[41]

### 4.3.2.  THE INTERESTS OF THE COUNTRIES

The UK's main interest in the Interconnector pipeline was to ensure security of supply and at the same time earn money by exporting some of the excess gas from the Continental Shelf.[42] Due to the dwindling reserves of gas in the North Sea and the greater need for energy security, the pipeline has helped to diversify the country's importation of gas for its own consumption.[43] The UK also wanted to spread its competition ethos to the other markets of Europe where there is very little competition in the gas market and where the governments play a direct part in the gas market of those countries.[44] They were also interested in lowering the price of gas in the home market and, according to the UK government, a pipeline venture of this magnitude would give reprieve to the UK consumers.[45]

Belgium, however, was interested in becoming the hub of activity for gas going through it to Continental Europe. The country's proximity to other major European countries, who are major gas consumers, made this an important

---

36. This is a transit versus commodity debate, which is highlighted in order to understand the overall situation in the pipeline.
37. See Thomas, *supra* n. 30.
38. The EU law dimension touched on in this paragraph will be discussed in detail in the 'legal aspects' section in this chapter.
39. See M. Futyan, *The Interconnector Pipeline: A Key Link to Europe's Gas Network* (Oxford Institute of Energy Studies, 2006).
40. See *ibid.*
41. See M. Monti, 'The Single Energy Market: The Relationship between Competition Policy and Regulation'. Speech/02/101 of March 2002.
42. See M. Albers, 'Energy Liberalization and EC Competition Law', *Fordham International Law Journal* (2002): 909–945.
43. See *ibid.*
44. See *ibid.*
45. See P. Cameron, *Competition in Energy Markets: Law and Regulation in the European Union* (Oxford: Oxford University Press, 2007).

opportunity for them to participate in.[46] Participation in the Interconnector pipeline also helped them towards their goal of energy security and allowed them to develop their gas infrastructure to come up to par with the other major European countries.[47]

### 4.3.3. THE LEGAL ASPECT

In the 1990s, due to increased focus on energy, strong foundations were laid for the future of European energy law. The three pillars of EU energy policy have been competitiveness, security of supply and environmental protection.[48] The EC recognized that there were problems in the legal framework that was currently in place because the polices advocated by them were not extensive and were partially outdated.[49] They also recognized that legal problems arose when they were trying to develop various community actions because no framework for dialogue on energy policy existed outside consultative committees. As a result, towards the end of 1990s the EC went towards strengthening community law and policy through collaboration with the energy industry.[50]

The unratified constitutional Treaty for Europe[51] signed in Rome on 29 October 2004, but not approved due to referendums in France and Netherlands, has a special section on energy policy. Article III-256 highlights the community's energy policy objectives and their powers.[52] Article III-256 states that the EU energy policy 'shall not affect a Member State's right to determine the conditions for exploiting its energy resources, its choice between different energy sources and the general structure of its energy supply . . . '.[53] Other important relevant sections are Article I-14, Article 234 and declaration twenty-two annexed to the Final Act, stating the special status of energy and its importance between the community and its members.[54]

However, the non-ratification of the 2004 Rome Treaty resulted in the signing of the Lisbon Treaty on 13 December 2007.[55] The Treaty entered into force on

---

46. See Futyan, *supra* n. 39.
47. See *ibid.*
48. See O. Adu, 'Competition or Energy Security in the EU Internal Gas Market: An Assessment of European Commission Decisions on Long-Term Gas Contracts', OGEL, 9, no. 1, 2011.
49. See M. Roggenkamp, et al., *Energy Law in Europe: National, EU and Internal Regulation*, 2nd edn (Oxford: Oxford University Press, 2007).
50. They also collaborated with other technical groups with expertise in energy in order to improve and raise the technical expertise of the EU. The creation of the Florence Forum and Madrid forum in 1998 and 1999 for electricity and gas was a part of that effort.
51. See The Draft Treaty establishing a constitution for Europe was adopted in 2003 and underwent several revisions. It could be found at <www.euabc.com>.
52. See The Draft Treaty of 2004, could be found at <www.euabc.com>.
53. See *ibid.*
54. See *ibid.*
55. See the Lisbon Treaty, 2007 at <http://europa.eu/lisbon_treaty/index_en.htm>.

1 December 2009.[56] The Treaty of Lisbon amends the previous EU and EC treaties but does not replace them. For the first time, the Lisbon Treaty also included a specific chapter on energy. Article 194(1) on the functioning of the European Union (TFEU) sets out the four major aims of the energy policy: (i) to ensure the functioning of the energy market; (ii) to ensure the security of supply of the union; (iii) to promote energy efficiency and energy saving and develop new and renewable forms of energy; and (iv) to promote the interconnection of energy networks.[57]

The new provision of the Lisbon Treaty confirms the competence to adopt preventive measures to avoid any security threats and will provide the backbone for more preventive measures in the future.[58] However, the solidarity aspect of this provision is weak. A good example of this is regulation 994/2010/EU on the security of gas supply adopted towards the end of 2010.[59] The purpose of this regulation was to avoid future gas disputes like the Russia–Ukraine dispute, where solidarity between the countries had to be improved.[60] Although the purpose of the regulation was to promote harmonized and consistent implementation of the measures for increased security of gas supply, according to experts 'it achieves little regarding solidarity amongst the Member States beyond what could already be done on a voluntary, bilateral basis'.[61]

Article 194(2) and (3) of the treaty gives the Member States the right to decide the conditions for exploiting their energy resources, choices amongst the different energy sources and the general structure of their energy supply.[62] However, this is a legal weakness from the Union perspective as it allows individual member countries to conduct their bilateral relations with non-EU countries as they see fit, although these dealings between countries are subject to TFEU cooperation and competition rules.[63] As a result, an individual member country might be more willing to protect their own interest than the interest of the Union as a whole. In fact, the Lisbon Treaty has formalized EU energy policy between EU institutions and individual member countries by 'carefully crafting compromise between national sovereignty over national resources and energy taxation issues, and a shared competence for the rest'.[64]

The treaty also went further as Article 122(1) mentions that 'without prejudice to any other procedure provided for in the Treaties, the Council, on a proposal from the Commission, may decide, in a spirit of solidarity between the Member States,

---

56. See *ibid.*
57. See *ibid.*
58. See D. Dinan, 'Institutions and Governance: A New Treaty, a Newly Elected Parliament and a New Commission', *Journal of Common Market Studies Annual Review* 48 (2010): 95–118.
59. See *ibid.* and Regulation 994/2010/EU at <www.ec.europa.eu>.
60. See S. Andoura et al., 'Towards a European Energy Community: A Policy Proposal', Notre Europe Studies and Research 76, Notre Europe, Paris, 2010.
61. See *ibid.*
62. See the Lisbon Treaty, 2007 at <http://europa.eu/lisbon_treaty/index_en.htm>.
63. See Andoura et al., *supra* n. 60.
64. See *ibid.*

upon measures appropriate to the economic situation, in particular if severe difficulties arise in the supply of certain products, notably in the area of energy'.[65] Both
Articles 122(1) and 194(1) try to promote a harmonized common energy policy.
This energy policy has the potential to change who is in or out of the regime,
however, under its current status, Article 122(1) does not compel that.

In order to establish an internal gas market, the EU has passed three sets of
directives. The main aims of these directives are to: (i) create a single European
energy market; (ii) increase competition; (iii) increase efficiency; and (iv) ensure
security of supply.[66] The first Directive (also known as the First Energy Package)
in 1998[67] tried gradually to open up the market from 20% in the year 2000 to 33%
in the year 2008, to achieve limited unbundling and a choice between regulated and
negotiated third party access.[68]

The Second directive[69] (also known as the Second Energy Package) repealed
the first gas directive and the gas transit directive of 1998. The 2003 directive
aimed at greater harmonization of national laws as it did not provide Member
States with fundamental choices of implementation.[70] The directive also called
for a system of regulated Third Party Access and establishes a sector specific
regulator, who is involved in setting the tariffs.[71] Another element of the directive
has been the requirement for legal unbundling.

The 2003 directive has not led to any changes in the upstream pipelines. As the
first directive, it allowed the consumers to enter into negotiations for gas supply
from all suppliers, including offshore producers.[72] However, the regulatory aspects
of the pipelines are different, as they are not governed by the downstream gas laws
but by the upstream gas and petroleum laws. As a result, these pipelines are not
operated by the national gas companies.[73] For example, the pipelines in the
Norwegian, UK and Dutch continental shelves have been constructed by different
oil and gas companies and access to these pipelines is therefore always based upon
negotiations between the producer and the pipeline company or operator.[74] This is
in line with the directive of 2003.[75]

The Third directive (known as the Third Energy Package) came out in 2009.[76]
The main provisions of the 2009 Directive were: (i) the new unbundling regime in
ownership unbundling, independent system operator and independent transmission
operator; (ii) improving the function of the internal electricity and gas market;

---

65. See the Lisbon Treaty, 2007 at <http://europa.eu/lisbon_treaty/index_en.htm>.
66. See M. Brazai, '3rd Energy Package of the EU and Its Practical Implications', 2009 at <www.
    kpmgsk.Icc.ch>.
67. See Directive 98/30/EC, can be found at <www.ec.europa.eu>.
68. See *ibid*.
69. See Directive 2003/55/EC, can be found at <www.ec.europa.eu>.
70. See *ibid*.
71. See *ibid*.
72. See *ibid*.
73. See Thomas, *supra* n. 30.
74. See *ibid*.
75. See Directive 2009/73/EC, can be found at <www.ec.europa.eu>.
76. See *ibid*.

(iii) establishment of the agency for the cooperation of energy regulators (ACER); (iv) enhanced powers and independence of national regulators; (v) efficient cooperation between transmission and system operators; and (vi) measures to reinforce security of supply.[77]

All three directives have been complex and have had many requirements which Member States had to follow.[78] However, the main objective of all these EC directives was to transform the gas industries from a monopoly to one operated under competitive principles by making both the wholesale and retail markets competitive.[79] The Interconnector pipeline was also no different as the UK government wanted to promote competition and was one of the first to liberalize the gas market.

Despite the liberalization of the UK gas market, prices fell until 2000 but started rising sharply after 2000.[80] Rising prices, coupled with damaging flow reversal in the prevailing price signal in 2001, led to concerns that there must be price manipulation from the Belgian side of the Interconnector due to their unliberalized market and restrictive practices.[81] Consequently, the European Commission carried out an enquiry into this matter in 2001. The commission investigated capacity exchanges and flow direction changes during that period and used the data to see whether the shippers in the Interconnector pipeline colluded to influence the flow direction of the Interconnector and whether Distrigaz had taken advantage of it position as trader and transporter from the Belgian side.[82]

The commission came to the conclusion that 'it found no evidence of cartel-like behaviour between the companies that ship gas on the Interconnector, rather that the increase in UK gas prices was due to the differences in market opening between the two markets concerned'.[83] This showed that despite liberalization of the UK gas market there were problems and, despite the building of the Interconnector pipeline, the prices for consumers did not come down. The commission also made the observation that the business rules employed by the pipelines were too rigid and restrictive for short term capacity transfers and changes in flow direction.[84]

The Belgian–UK Interconnector case was also another example of the commission becoming involved. This concerned the joint-infrastructure construction

---

77. See Directive 2009/73/EC, can be found at <www.ec.europa.eu>.
78. See Adu, *supra* n. 48.
79. See *ibid.* Also read Arts 81 and 82 of the EC deals with the rules on competition. Can be found at <www.ec.europa.eu>.
80. See Adu, *supra* n. 48.
81. See DTI Consultation URN 01/1099: Concerns about gas prices and possible improvements to market efficiency, November 2001. Can be found at <www.dti.gov.uk/energy/domestic_markets/gas_market/gascondoc.pdf>.
82. See European Commission Enquiry into Anti-competitive Use of Interconnector, March 2002. Can be found at <europa.eu.int/rapid/reference=IP/02/401>.
83. See European Commission Enquiry into Anti-competitive Use of Interconnector, March 2002. Can be found at <europa.eu.int/rapid/reference=IP/02/401>.
84. See European Commission Enquiry into Anti-competitive Use of Interconnector, March 2002. Can be found at <europa.eu.int/rapid/reference=IP/02/401>.

by the companies involved in the Interconnector pipeline.[85] There was an agreement between nine companies for the construction and operation of a UK–Belgium sub-sea gas interconnection. The commission concluded that 'the project was pro-competitive but took the view that Article 81(1)[86] applied because certain provisions allow a joint venture company to market transport capacity, thereby leading to joint selling by the joint venture partners'.[87] In the end, it was considered that joint marketing for a limited period of time was an acceptable advantage to the investors.[88] This kind of decision by the commission shows that it would take a positive view of agreements which help open up the gas market, although on a few aspects it does restrict competition.

The treaty signed between the UK and Belgium governments paved the way for the building of the Interconnector pipeline. This treaty had a common feature with other North Sea pipeline agreements in that the jurisdiction was divided at the delimitation of each state's Continental Shelf.[89] The Treaty included provisions for the inspection of the pipeline, safety standards and approval for the setting up of an independent operator for each of the pipeline sections.[90] There was agreement regarding the setting up of an Interconnector Commission, where the representatives of the two governments would be present.[91] The main role of the Interconnector commission is to facilitate and solve any cross-border issues between the two countries. The UK is represented by the department of trade and industry while Belgium is represented by their Ministry of Economic Affairs.[92]

There are also other regulatory bodies involved in the Interconnector pipeline that are responsible for following the daily activities of the pipeline and the various producers and shippers of the pipeline. They include the European Commission, the Interconnector Commission, Ofgem, the Department of Trade and Industry, the Gas and Electricity Markets Authority, the Office of Fair Trading and other relevant bodies. There are problems, however, with regard to the shippers not delivering the contractual supply of gas at certain times. Moreover, the Flemish regional authority in Belgium which recently got devolved at that time and where the pipeline makes landfall, was not happy with some of the tax provisions in the

---

85. See Case COMP/E-4/38.075, IP02/401 of 13 Mar. 2002.
86. See Art. 81 of the EC treaty which prohibits all horizontal and vertical agreements between undertakings and concerned practices which may affect trade between EU Member States and which has the effect of prevention, restriction or distortion of competition within the common market. The prohibition applies only if all the conditions of Art. 81(1) are met. For further understanding please read Art. 81(1), which can be found at <www.ec.europa.eu>.
87. See Case COMP/E-4/38.075, IP02/401 of 13 Mar. 2002.
88. See *ibid.*
89. See The Agreement between the Government of the United Kingdom and the Government of the Kingdom of Belgium relating to the transmission of natural gas through a pipeline, between the United Kingdom and the Kingdom of Belgium, Brussels, 10 Dec. 1997.
90. See *ibid.*
91. *Ibid.*
92. See Interconnector website at <www.interconnector.com>.

treaty nor the fact that it would be controlled by the federal government, which caused delay in the ratification of the various legal frameworks.[93]

### 4.3.4.  THE GEO-POLITICS OF THE PIPELINE

Before the building of the pipeline, the UK was the only country in Western Europe whose gas structure was not integrated with the rest of Europe. One of the reasons for this was that the market structure and liberalization of the UK gas industry do not sit well with the other Western European countries, who are more protectionist.[94] Although the European Commission gas directive asks for greater liberalization and competition in the gas industry of each country, this directive is not always implemented by the various governments.[95]

However, the UK does follow it and by participating in the Interconnector pipeline the country becomes closer to the integrated gas market of Europe. This is quite important for the UK because other countries like France, Germany and Holland are already diversifying their sources of energy supplies. As their overall gas reserves have been declining over the years, the UK improved their security of supply by building the Interconnector pipeline.[96] Belgium also benefits from joining this partnership, as it allows them to enter into the integrated gas structure of Europe and act as a hub for the major gas importers.[97] It also allows them to compete with other European nations for their own security of supply.

### 4.3.5.  THE CHOICE OF LOCATION FOR THE PROJECT

The choice of Zeebrugge as the landfall partner for the Interconnector pipeline is not ideal because of the long route of the pipeline. The UK government was at first interested in having the landfall point in France, Holland or in the North of Germany. However, there were problems with regard to shareholding and market competition in these countries as they were already major players in the area and the governments also did not want their national monopolies to face stiff competition from outside.[98]

---

93. See Futyan, *supra* n. 39.
94. See B. Barton et al., *Energy Security: Managing Risk in a Dynamic Legal and Regulatory Environment* (Oxford: Oxford University Press, 2004).
95. The legal aspect section of this chapter provides more details about the EC directives. In this case, since the EC gives a different time frame to implement the directives, some of the countries do not implement it in time resulting in them being fined by the EC, for example, France and the Netherlands. Also read P. Cameron, *supra* n. 45.
96. See Futyan, *supra* n. 39.
97. See *ibid.*
98. See P. Cameron, 'The Consumer and the Internal Market in Energy: Who Benefits?', ELR 31 (2006).

The Zeebrugge terminal had a few advantages which made their case stronger. There was a requirement for a well-developed onshore and offshore infrastructure with sufficient capacity in the adjacent gas transportation system for the Interconnector.[99] There was also the need for a developed trading hub and a market close to the other markets of Europe.[100] The Zeebrugge terminal fulfilled all these criteria which made it an attractive destination for UK gas. Moreover, the eagerness of the Belgian government to follow the lead of the UK also played a part in the choice of Zeebrugge as the partner for the Interconnector pipeline.[101]

## 4.4.     THE APPLICATION OF THE CRITERIA FOR THE CROSS-BORDER PIPELINE REGIME

### 4.4.1.     THE NATURE AND CHARACTERISTICS OF THE REGIME

The two main players in the Interconnector regime are the UK and Belgium as the pipeline gas flows between these two countries and the governments of both these countries are also involved in the pipeline. There are other influential players and these include the company operating the pipeline, Interconnector UK Limited, together with the companies who have shares in the pipeline as well as the shippers involved in the supply of gas through the pipelines.[102] In fact, from the regime perspective, all these actors have to play their role in order to make the pipeline regime successful but the involvement of the two governments and Interconnector UK Limited is crucial for the smooth operation of the pipeline. The reason is that they were the pioneers who formed the regime and the agreements signed between them provide the ground work based upon which the regime has been formed.

The agreement, signed in 1997 by these two countries, also provided the basis for the setting up of various regulatory bodies who would monitor the activities of the actors involved in the pipeline chain.[103] The pipeline is unique in that as it is a bi-directional pipeline with the ability to import and export gas depending upon the need of the parties. There are various shippers in the pipeline chain and some of them are not shareholders in Interconnector UK Limited. Interconnector UK Limited is responsible for the operation and maintenance of the pipeline and is also responsible for the day-to-day decision-making with regard to the pipeline chain.[104]

The agreement between the two sides also provided for the setting up of an Interconnector Commission following the implementation of the clauses of the

---

99.   See *ibid.*
100.   See Futyan, *supra* n. 39.
101.   See *ibid.*
102.   See Mulcare, *supra* n. 24.
103.   The Agreement between the Government of the United Kingdom and the Government of the Kingdom of Belgium relating to the transmission of natural gas through a pipeline, between the United Kingdom and the Kingdom of Belgium, Brussels, 10 Dec. 1997, in file with author.
104.   See Mulcare, *supra* n. 24.

agreement.[105] The commission would be made up of officials from both countries. There was also an agreement with regard to having an independent operator and that both the governments had to approve its appointment.[106] The purpose of an independent operator was to improve the level of transparency in the operation of the pipeline and also to run the pipeline in an impartial way without the interference of the parties involved in the pipeline.[107]

Interconnector UK Limited operates the pipeline in line with the principles and rules and also takes certain decisions regarding the pipeline. For example, one principle includes the responsibility for ensuring that the pipeline runs smoothly and achieves the various objectives set by the shareholders.[108] The Interconnector regime also makes the rules in line with the agreements based upon which the shippers have to carry out their various obligations.[109] The Interconnector Commission also looks after the activities of Interconnector UK Limited, acting as a watchdog to ensure that the pipeline is running according to the agreement signed by the parties.[110]

The Interconnector regime is a strong regime because it has bodies within the regime which are capable of overseeing whether the actors are abiding by the various rules and regulations agreed between them.[111] This also helps ensure that the legitimate expectations of the stakeholders involved within the pipeline are respected. All the actors who are part of the regime are clear about their roles in the regime and are aware of their obligations. Both governments and the owners and shippers of the pipeline regime ensure that the pipeline achieves its objective which are the uninterrupted supply of gas between the two countries and to protect the interests of the stakeholders involved in the regime. However, one drawback of the regime is the presence of too many enforcement agencies which, in turn, causes confusion among the actors within the regime. There are quite a few regimes within the regime and there is no central regime guarding the various activities of the actors involved in the pipeline chain.

Regulation in respect of the interconnector was important because it allowed both the Belgian and the UK governments a framework through which they could protect their national interest. Furthermore, the independence of the regulator from the government also provides a separation from political interest, which is important in the case of cross-border pipelines.[112] The change of EU directive in 2003

---

105. See Vinogradov, *supra* n. 27.
106. See Futyan, *supra* n. 39.
107. See *ibid.*
108. See *ibid.*
109. The Agreement between the Government of the United Kingdom and the Government of the Kingdom of Belgium relating to the transmission of natural gas through a pipeline, between the United Kingdom and the Kingdom of Belgium, Brussels, 10 Dec. 1997.
110. See Futyan, *supra* n. 39.
111. This is the ingredient for a strong regime, if we go by the definition of the strong regime provided at the beginning of this chapter.
112. See Thomas, *supra* n. 30.

resulted in the requirement for a system of third party access to natural gas inter-connectors with the exception of new projects.[113] The UK government went further by implementing a licensing regime for existing and new natural gas interconnectors through the Energy Act 2004.[114]

Interconnector UK Limited was not eligible for exemption from the new licensing regime of the government. The criteria for exemption included project completion after August 2003 and that the level of risk attached was such that the project might not otherwise proceed.[115] This affected the Interconnector, as they were not able to finish the project by August 2003 and it not only affected the Belgian side of the business but also the capacity holders of the pipeline.[116] Interconnector UK Limited raised the issue with DTI/Ofgem and mentioned that the 'Interconnector being an international business, there was a potential for a conflict of regulatory obligations to the two responsible regulatory bodies and that the new policy of the regulators created an uneven playing field'.[117] All these points make the entire regime complex and difficult for the actors involved.

This point could be further strengthened by the fact that recently the European Commission's third package or the 2009 directive[118] has made specific recognition of the fact that they want greater cooperation between the different regulatory agencies in order to harmonize the whole process and reduce the conflict of interest between various regulators and their regulations.[119] Articles 39, 40, 41 and 42 of the 2009 directive show the Commission's intention of creating an ACER.[120]

The Interconnector pipeline regime has certain neo-liberal tendencies in that the parties are willing to cooperate with each other and share information based upon which the pipeline is run smoothly. Interconnector UK Limited is responsible for the operation of the pipeline, although the shippers, the landfall partners and both the governments also play a crucial role.[121] The shippers' role in the pipeline is crucial and they tend to cooperate with each other and also with the company in order to protect their own interests.[122] As a result, all the actors are willing to make relative gains from their participation, which has a resemblance to the neo-liberal school of thought.

---

113. See *ibid.*
114. See Energy Act 2004, Part 3, Ch. 2: Interconnections for Electricity and Gas at <www.opsi. gov.uk/acts/acts2004/20040020.htm>.
115. See *ibid.*
116. See Response to consultation on Interconnector licenses, 2004 at <www.interconnector.com/ mediacentre/presentations.htm>.
117. See *ibid.*
118. See Directive 2009/73/EC, can be found at <www.ec.europa.eu>.
119. See Brazai, *supra* n. 66.
120. See Directive 2009/73/EC, can be found at <www.ec.europa.eu>.
121. See Mulcare, *supra* n. 24.
122. See *ibid.*

4.4.2.     THE ISSUES AFFECTING THE CROSS-BORDER PIPELINE

The Interconnector has some technical and maintenance problems which affect its smooth operation at certain times. There was a capacity constraint between June and September 2003 as a price differential of between 2p and 10p/therm arose due to operational constraints.[123] During that summer gas flow from the UK was sufficiently high but the capacity to transport that gas in response to market signals was insufficient, this caused a capacity constraint to take place.[124] It has also been pointed out by experts that only 90% of the pipeline capacity is available for market users willing to use the line to respond to market signals.[125]

There have also been unplanned outages in the pipeline and their impact has been felt by the players involved in the market, who do not have sufficient time to make any other alternative arrangements to purchase or sell gas. There were major liquid contamination incidents during the summer of 2002 and 2003 which caused the shippers to flow gas in the opposite direction to the price signal in order to help with the clean up of the pipeline.[126] The incident had the following ramifications:

> in that i) the pipeline was shut and there was price divergence, ii) this caused the NBP price to increase in anticipation of the reinstated flows, however the plan fell apart once the restart was aborted and once it was discovered that liquid had entered the offshore line, a pigging[127] operation was carried out, iii) this caused the shippers to flow gas against the price signal resulting in the price collapse in the UK to 2 pence per therm, iv) price converged and then diverged again due to second bout of contamination and v) the cleaning continued until it was the due date for maintenance and shut down.[128]

The above incidents caused great hardship for the shippers and the relevant players involved in the pipeline chain because they did not have sufficient time to protect their interest.[129] If it had been a planned outage, there would have been sufficient time to make alternative arrangements. There was liquid contamination in the pipeline chain in 2002, which also caused the closure of the pipeline.[130] This might have been caused by neighbouring gas facilities in the Bacton area. Again in 2003, water entered the pipeline during a maintenance operation, which caused significant loss for the shippers.[131] This is because the liquid contamination forced a cleaning operation to be carried out and, as a result, gas was

---

123. See A. Derek & Derek Bunn, '*Two Markets and a Weak Link*', presentation at the 3rd International Conference on Applied Infrastructure Research, Berlin, 9 Oct. 2004.
124. See *ibid.*
125. See *ibid.*
126. See Futyan, *supra* n. 39.
127. Pigging is a term signifying any independent, self-contained device, tool or vehicle that moves through the interior of the pipeline for the purposes of inspecting, dimensioning or cleaning.
128. See Futyan, *supra* n. 39.
129. See *ibid.*
130. See *ibid.*
131. See *ibid.*

piped from Zeebrugge to Bacton. This was contrary to the previous flow direction and also contrary to the price signal.[132] This caused significant losses for the Interconnector UK shippers, as buyers in Belgium became worried and the UK an anxious seller. This imbalance resulted in penalties for shippers from both sides of the pipeline.[133] However, it is also important to note that the above incidents cannot be termed as a breach of legitimate expectation of the stakeholders involved in the pipeline as the incidents were unforeseen and could not have been dealt with through the agreements signed between the parties involved in the pipeline.

There are also problems to be faced by the consumers in these countries. Due to greater liberalization and competition in the UK, consumers sometimes have to pay a higher price for the gas they are getting through the UK Interconnector pipeline.[134] High oil prices also cause gas prices to rise. This is due to the fact that Continental gas prices are linked to the price of oil which is not the case in the UK.[135] During the winter, the UK imports gas through the Interconnector, so the Continental Gas which is linked to the oil price directly affects UK consumers.[136] The discrepancy within the UK model and the Continental model has caused problems for consumers and has not been economically beneficial to them.[137] There are also certain technical disruptions in the supply of gas which cause further problems.[138]

It can also be said that there are too many regulatory bodies following the Interconnector pipeline which causes problems for the stakeholders involved in the project, as each authority has a different criterion to measure the activities of the stakeholders.[139] This causes confusion among the parties involved in the project. This problem together with the problems discussed above show that the regime is not able to deal with these issues.[140]

The actions of all the parties involved in the pipeline chain is neo-liberal in nature as the parties are willing to cooperate with each other to implement their various interests and also to ensure the smooth operation of the pipeline. The fact that they are willing to share information and also share the benefits, and go for relative rather than absolute gain, boosts their neo-liberal credentials.

---

132. See *ibid.*
133. See Thomas, *supra* n. 30.
134. See *ibid.*
135. See *ibid.*
136. See Global Insight, 'Ensuring Effective and Efficient Forward Gas Markets', 2005, can be found at <www.webarchive.nationalarchives.gov.uk/>.
137. See *ibid.*
138. See *ibid.*, and also see Cameron, *supra* n. 45.
139. The nature and characteristics of the regime section (the last four paragraphs) gives details about this assertion.
140. These factors could be linked to the original problem that this book is trying to answer which is government intervention due to geo-political, legal and economic reasons. Although there is no direct government intervention in this case there is a need for another regulatory mechanisms or an agency which can oversee the regulation of the Interconnector pipeline, as each government in this pipeline has their own regulatory authority and tries to interfere by imposing their own criteria, which lowers the performance of the pipeline and also causes disruption.

The implication of this is that parties within the regime would receive the benefits of joining the regime which in turn would make the regime stronger as they would be willing to abide by the regime's rules and regulations.

4.4.3.     THE COMMON INTERESTS OF THE PARTIES

The interests of both the UK and Belgium are similar in nature with only slight differences. The UK wanted to be a part of the integrated gas grid of Europe for security of their supply and also to compete with other energy hungry nations like France, Germany and Holland.[141] By participating in this pipeline chain they are also in competition with other countries in the fight for new energy suppliers. The dwindling gas reserves in the North Sea have made the UK look for other sources of supply.[142] The country also wanted to spread its competition ethos to other parts of Europe because this would open up other protectionist markets in Europe which, in turn, would benefit the other players in the market and would be in line with the EU gas directive.[143]

Belgium wanted to be a part of the pipeline chain due to its ambition to be a transit hub in Europe and also to develop its gas structure.[144] By participating in the pipeline the country was able to turn Zeebrugge into a major wholesale gas trade hub, which in turn would improve its energy security and increase its standing among the countries in Continental Europe.[145] The evidence for this is the fact that other landfall sites such as France, Germany and Holland were also chosen but they gave a lukewarm response because the Interconnector would increase competition for them in their own domestic markets which Belgium wanted to take advantage of in order to be the gas hub of Western Europe.[146] The other companies involved in the Interconnector pipeline also benefit from the project, as they are reaping the rewards from their investments. Although there were certain reservations about the effectiveness of the pipeline at the beginning, all such cynicism has disappeared as the Interconnector regime is making all the stakeholders involved in the regime satisfied with the returns they are receiving.[147]

The actions of all the parties involved in the Interconnector pipeline are neo-liberal in nature as both governments, the shippers, landfall partners and other actors involved in the pipeline are making a concerted effort to make it a success and reap the benefits of being a part of the pipeline. All the actors are also aware of their various obligations in the pipeline as they are willing to forgo certain benefits

---

141.  See Futyan, *supra* n. 39.
142.  See Cameron, *supra* n. 45.
143.  The legal aspects section of this chapter (s. 4.3.3) discusses the directives in detail.
144.  See Committee for Gas and Electricity and Gas Regulation Report, 2006 at <www.creg.be>.
145.  This was also discussed in the 'interest of the countries section' in s. 4.3.2. See Committee for Gas and Electricity and Gas Regulation Report, 2006 at <www.creg.be>.
146.  See Committee for Gas and Electricity and Gas Regulation Report, 2006 at <www.creg.be>.
147.  See the interconnector website at <www.interconnector.com>.

for the overall improvement in the functioning of the pipeline which further under-scores their neo-liberal attitude.

4.4.4.        THE ENFORCEMENT AND COMPLIANCE OF THE CROSS-BORDER
             PIPELINE AGREEMENTS

The treaty between the UK and Belgium in relation to the Interconnector pipeline[148] made provisions for the setting up of regulatory authorities that can monitor the activities of the parties involved in the pipeline chain. Some of the other regulatory authorities are the European Commission, Ofgem, the Gas and Electricity Consumer Council, the Office of Fair Trading, the Competition Direc-torate and so on.[149] All these regulatory bodies act as regulators for the Intercon-nector. The Interconnector Commission was set up by the Interconnector treaty between the UK and Belgium, while the Office of Fair Trading, the Electricity and Gas Council and the DTI are UK regulatory bodies.[150]

The Interconnector pipeline regime has a number of regulatory regimes within the regime[151] that are responsible for the enforcement of and compliance with the rules and regulations of the agreement signed by the parties. These also regulate on behalf of the European Commission that has its own competition directives which all EU members are obligated to follow. Together these regimes have caused a lack of coordination and since there are so many regulators it has sometimes resulted in the lack of enforcement of certain clauses due to these regulatory regimes not being sure about their jurisdiction.[152] This is an example of a breach of legitimate expectation, as the stake-holders are not aware of the individual roles of all these regulatory bodies that have different regulatory objectives causing them difficulties in abiding by their obligations.

The activities of the regulatory regime responsible for the enforcement and compliance of the various rules and regulations have been neo-realistic in nature as all of these regimes have used their superior position to their own benefit without cooperating with the actors they are regulating. This has resulted in a lack of coordination among the regulators and caused ineffectiveness in the compliance process which in turn might weaken the entire Interconnector regime.[153] Certain neo-liberal approaches have also been applied as Interconnector UK Limited,

---

148. See The Agreement between the Government of the United Kingdom and the Government of the Kingdom of Belgium relating to the transmission of natural gas through a pipeline, between the United Kingdom and the Kingdom of Belgium, Brussels, 10 Dec. 1997, in file with author.
149. See J. Vasconcelos, 'Towards the Internal Energy Market: How to Bridge a Regulatory Gas and Build a Regulatory Framework', *European Review of Energy Markets* (2005): 81–103.
150. The EU Law dimension and its regulatory aspects are discussed in the legal aspects of the pipeline section of this chapter (s. 4.3.3), while the EC's regulatory aspects are covered under the nature and characteristics of the regime (s. 4.4.1).
151. By this statement I mean all the regulatory bodies mentioned in the last paragraph.
152. See Vasconcelos, *supra* n. 149. Also see s. 4.3.1 of this chapter (the last four paragraphs).
153. In fact, this has also led the EC to ask for greater harmonization between the regulators and in their third directive in 2009, proposed the setting up of an agency for the cooperation of all the regulators in EU.

which operates the pipeline, has tried to cooperate with the various actors involved in the pipeline chain irrespective of their gains, which in turn has resulted in greater benefits for all the partners involved in the pipeline regime as they were more concerned about the financial viability of the pipeline as a whole rather than the personal benefit to each player.

## 4.5.    PIPELINES OF THE FSU

### 4.5.1.    THE BACKGROUND OF THE PROJECT

The FSU had a huge transportation infrastructure for transporting the energy needs of the various parts of the union and also to its allies in Eastern Europe. The pipeline infrastructure of the FSU extended from one part of the union to the other and some of it was so extensive and interconnected that it covered almost half the globe.[154] Most FSU pipelines were built to serve internal demand and the demand of the Pro-Soviet Allies in Eastern Europe.[155] The first Soviet Crude Oil project started in 1956 with the building of the marine crude oil export terminal at Tsemesskaya Bay, near Novorossiysk.[156] It took almost ten years to build the entire terminal. The Black Sea Pipeline Association was formed in 1967 to operate this export terminal and other regional pipelines.[157]

### 4.5.2.    THE RELEVANT PARTIES OF THE PROJECT

In 1959, the Council for Mutual Economic Cooperation (COMECON), decided to build a trunk oil pipeline to deliver oil from the Soviet Union to Poland, Czechoslovakia (now the Czech and Slovak Republics), the German Democratic Republic, Latvia and Lithuania. The pipeline became known as the Druzbha Pipeline.[158]

The 2,500 mile Druzba pipeline was one of the largest pipelines in the FSU and is currently the largest in Russia with a 1.2–1.4 million bbl/d capacity.[159] Currently, construction is under way to increase capacity in the section between Belarus and Poland. It starts at Almetyevsk in Tatarstan, in south-eastern Russia, where it collects oil from western Siberia, the Urals and the Caspian Sea.[160] It then goes through Mozyr in Belarus from where there are two branches going north and south. The northern branch goes to Germany and Poland through Belarus. This

---

154.   See ESMAP, 'Cross-Border Oil and Gas Pipelines: Problems and Prospects', ESMAP Technical Paper 035, UNDP/World Bank/ESMAP, 2003.
155.   See *ibid.*
156.   See *ibid.*
157.   See *ibid.*
158.   See *ibid.*
159.   See *ibid.*
160.   See *ibid.*

branch is also connected by the Plock–Gdansk pipeline to the Naftport terminal in Gdansk, which is used for oil re-exports.[161] In Germany, the Druzbha pipeline is connected to the MVL pipeline. The southern branch goes to Ukraine, Slovakia, the Czech Republic and Hungary, also through Belarus.[162]

The Druzbha pipeline covers 2,910 km in Belarus (Figure 4.3); in Ukraine it covers 1,490 km; in Poland it is 670 km long; in Hungary it covers around 130 km, 332 km in Lithuania, 420 km in Latvia and 400 km in Slovakia and the Czech Republic together.[163] The pipe diameter varies from about 17 inches to 40 inches and also uses twenty pumping stations.[164]

*Figure 4.3   Druzbha and Adria Oil Pipelines*[165]

*Source*: <www.caspiandevelopmentandexport.com>.

### 4.5.3.    THE COST OF THE PROJECT

The pipeline was built with the help of all the countries involved, with each country being responsible for providing the service and construction necessary.

---

161. See *ibid.*
162. See G. Chufrin, 'Russia's Caspian Energy Policy and Its Impact on the US–Russian Relationship' study conducted by the James A. Baker III Institute for Public Policy Rice University, 2004. Can be found at <www.rice.edu/energy/publications/docs/PEC_chufrin_10_20041.pdf>.
163. See *ibid.*
164. See B.A. Gelb, 'Russia's Oil and Gas Challenges', CRS report for Congress, 2006. Can be found at <http://fpc.state.gov/documents/organization/58988.pdf>.
165. The purpose of the diagram at this point is to highlight the extensiveness of the pipeline across the FSU and its impact on the country and the Eastern European countries.

The pipeline started delivering oil to Czechoslovakia in 1962, and in 1963 to Hungary, Poland and the German Democratic Republic.[166]

### 4.5.4.    OTHER ASPECTS OF THE PIPELINES

During the Soviet era, the Oil and Gas Ministry used to look after the pipelines in different regions. After the 1970s, the authorities formed the Main Industry Enterprise for Oil Transportation and Distribution (Glavtransneft, GTN).[167] The GTN trunk pipeline system (see Table 4.1) consisted of all the seventeen pipeline associations of the Soviet Union, In fact, all the pipeline associations except for those in Georgia and Turkmenistan were under the interconnected system.[168]

*Table 4.1    Trunk Pipelines in the Soviet Republics*[169]

**Trunk Pipelines in the Soviet Union Republics Operated by Glavtransneft**

| | Storage | | Length of pipelines ('000km) | Pump stations |
|---|---|---|---|---|
| *Republic* | *Number of tanks* | *Capacity ('000m$^3$)* | | |
| *RSFSR* | 981 | 13,871 | 49.0 | 442 |
| *Ukraine* | 69 | 714 | 3.5 | 31 |
| *Kazakhstan* | 114 | 1,049 | 4.9 | 46 |
| *Byelorussia* | 39 | 795 | 2.8 | 21 |
| *Latvia* | — | — | 0.4 | 3 |
| *Lithuania* | — | — | 0.3 | 3 |
| *Azerbaijan* | 27 | 204 | 0.7 | 5 |
| *Turkmenistan* | 10 | 50 | 0.5 | 5 |
| *Georgia* | 10 | 40 | 0.5 | 4 |
| *Kirgizia* | — | — | 0.4 | — |
| *Uzbekistan* | 6 | 12 | 0.9 | 8 |
| *TOTAL* | 1,256 | 16,735 | 63.9 | 570 |

*Source*: ESMAP, 'Cross-Border Oil and Gas Pipelines: Problems and Prospects', ESMAP Technical Paper 035, UNDP/World Bank/ESMAP, 2003.

The Glavtransneft crude pipeline system was extensive. The main purpose of the system was to connect the three Russian regions of Western Siberia, the Urals

---

166.  See ESMAP, *supra* n. 155.
167.  See Chufrin, *supra* n. 163.
168.  See *ibid.*
169.  This table gives a clearer picture of the route of the pipeline and the importance of each of the Soviet Republics based on the length of the pipeline passing each republic.

and Northern Russia with Kazakhstan, together with the various Soviet refining centres and the COMECON states where the crude was exported.[170] It also provided access to Western markets through its ports in Novorossiysk, Tuapse, Odessa and Ventspils.[171] The majority of the pipeline system was in the Russian Federation (74.9%), the remainder of the pipelines amounted to 10.67% in Kazakhstan, 5.24% in Ukraine and 4.51% in Belarus.[172]

The integrated pipeline system in Russia was supposed to transport around 12 million barrels of oil a day.[173] The entire system connected all the major producing regions with all the refining centres and export terminals.[174] The GTV system had approximately 63,900 km of pipeline, 570 pumping stations and a storage capacity of about 16,735 BCM.[175]

Following the breakdown of the Soviet Union, Transneft was created through two governmental acts and the Transneft product (the refined product pipeline system) was also reconstituted.[176] The Russian government claimed jurisdiction for all the refined product pipelines irrespective of their borders. The newly independent states now became the owner of pipelines passing through their territory and those pipelines became independent carriers. Transneft became responsible for operating the twelve other Russian regional pipeline enterprises after the breakdown of the Soviet Union.[177]

During the Soviet era, most deliveries to the COMECON countries were based upon IGAs signed between the governments of those countries and the Soviet authorities. The countries of the Eastern Bloc signed the agreements under multilateral interchange programmes for commodities and manufactured goods for a period of five years.[178] In the agreement signed between the respective governments, the price of oil was set in 'rubles' and was then adjusted with the international market price.[179] The agreements also allowed exporting on a barter basis and in most cases the state paid for the shipping costs.[180]

Another company, Gazprom, was also influential in both former and post-Soviet Union times. Total gas production in Russia in 2007–2008 was 23.1 trillion cubic feet, of which 85% was produced by Gazprom and the company also

---

170. See Gelb, *supra* n. 165.
171. See *ibid.*
172. See ESMAP, *supra* n. 155.
173. See M.S. Crandall, *Energy, Economics, and Politics in the Caspian Region: Dreams and Realities* (Westport: Praeger Security International, 2006).
174. See *ibid.*
175. See Gelb, *supra* n. 165.
176. See M. Ogutcu, 'Kazakhstan's Expanding Cross-Border Gas Links: Implications for Europe, Russia, China and Other CIS Countries', *CEPMLP Internet Journal* vol. 17, Art. 8.
177. See ESMAP, *supra* n. 155.
178. See *ibid.*
179. See T. Sinuraya, 'Possible International Forums for the Resolution of Legal Conflicts over Pipeline Transit in the Former Soviet Union', *Leiden Journal of International Law* 14 (2001): 445–454.
180. See *ibid.*

controls 16% of the world's gas reserves.[181] Like Transneft, Gazprom was under the Ministry of Oil and Gas. After the breakdown of the Soviet Union (Figure 4.4), Gazprom in Russia became a state company and later a joint stock company and was later privatized, with the government having 40% of the share.[182]

*Figure 4.4    Gas Pipelines of the Former Soviet Union*[183]

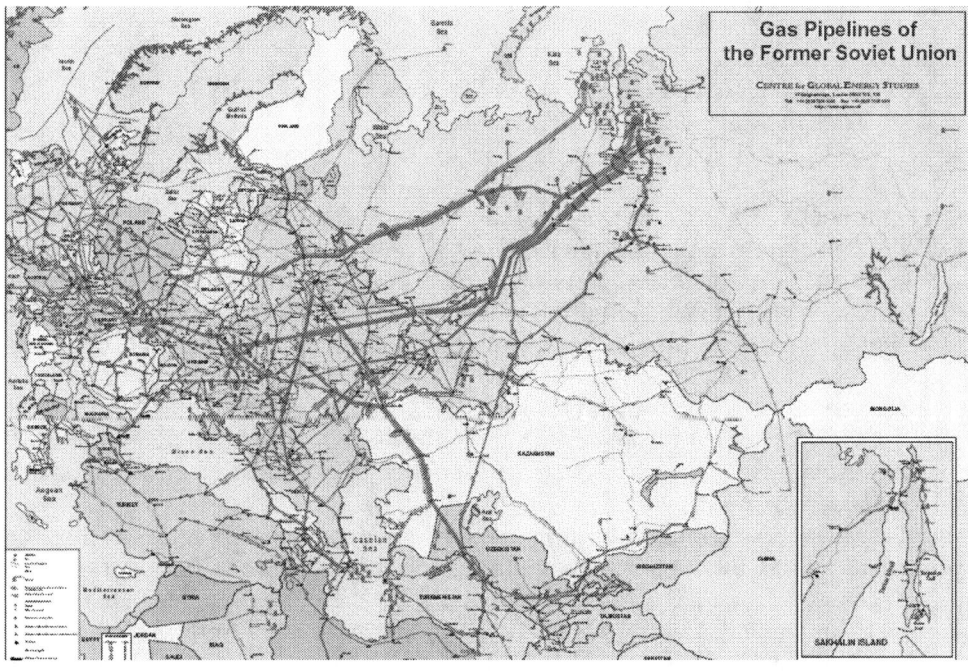

*Source*: <www.caspiandevelopmentandexport.com>.

Gazprom has the world's longest pipeline network, around 150,000 km.[184] It is also the sole supplier of gas to Bosnia and Herzegovina, Estonia, Finland, the Republic of Macedonia, Latvia, Lithuania, Moldova and Slovakia. It also provides 97% of Bulgaria's gas, 89% of Hungary's, 86% of Poland's, 75% of the Czech Republic's, 67% of Turkey's, 65% of Austria's, 40% of Romania's, 36% of Germany's, 27% of Italy's and 25% of France's gas supplies.[185]

The breakdown of the Soviet Union resulted in the old Glavtransneft regime breaking down, resulting in the old regional associations being a new regime on

---

181. See 'Caspian Development and Export, Economic, Social and Environmental Overview of the Southern Caspian Oil and Gas Projects', Briefing Paper, February 2003.
182. See *ibid.*
183. The above network shows the extensiveness of the Soviet gas pipeline network.
184. See Caspian Development, *supra* n. 182.
185. See *ibid.*

their own in their respective new republics. However, these new pipeline association regimes were still considered part of the old Glavtransneft regime because the pipeline system in the Soviet Union was so interconnected that without the cooperation of all the old pipeline associations, the pipelines in the new republics would not be able to operate properly. Furthermore, most of these new pipeline association regimes in the new republics were landlocked, resulting in them being dependent on the old Glavtransneft regime.[186]

## 4.6.        THE IMPORTANT ASPECTS OF THE PIPELINE

### 4.6.1.        ECONOMIC ASPECTS

During Soviet times most of the pipelines were used to deliver oil and gas to the COMECON countries and to other regions within the Soviet Union. Gas and oil were also delivered to other parts of Europe through these pipelines. After the breakdown of the Soviet Union, however, the COMECON countries could not afford to sustain their previous level of importation from Russia and they also wanted to diversify their sources of energy.[187] The level of oil exported to these countries and the overall demand for Russian oil declined as a result.[188] There was also a decline in demand from the former regions within the Soviet Union including Ukraine and Belarus as they were less inclined to pay the high tariff demanded by Russia for their exports.[189]

There was also competition from the newly independent countries as they too wanted to export their oil and gas through Russia.[190] Russia had to face stiff challenges with respect to price and demand from these newly independent states in the Caspian and Central Asia.[191] Tight government control over energy resources[192] and a lack of investment in the pipeline infrastructure has also caused problems for Russia.[193]

### 4.6.2.        THE INTERESTS OF VARIOUS PARTIES

The pipelines built during Soviet times allowed the country to transfer gas from different regions and deliver it to the COMECON countries, and it was also used to

---

186.  See Chufrin, *supra* n. 163.
187.  See ESMAP, *supra* n. 155.
188.  See *ibid.*
189.  See *ibid.*
190.  See Chufrin, *supra* n. 163.
191.  See *ibid.*
192.  This involves the new republics like Belarus, Ukraine, Turkmenistan and Kazakhstan, who have tight control over their natural resources.
193.  See Chufrin, *supra* n. 163.

meet domestic needs.[194] After the breakdown of the Soviet Union, the newly independent republics like Kazakhstan, Azerbaijan, Uzbekistan and Turkmenistan wanted to utilize the energy resources in their own countries to earn vital foreign exchange.[195] Due to these countries being landlocked, they were totally dependent on Russia to transfer their oil and gas to their various destinations. Russia, however, charged high transit fares for transferring these resources and to some extent bought the gas at a cheaper rate and sold it outside at a higher price.[196] The outcome is that the interests of these newly independent states and Russia are not always aligned and this can result in conflict.[197]

Although the arrival of the new players in the form of new countries and pipeline associations might have lowered the strength of the regime in terms of enforcement of various rules and regulations, due to the new and differing interests of various actors, overall, the twelve Russian pipeline associations with the five new independent associations follow the same regime rules and regulations but with different targets and objectives.[198] Any disagreement with regard to their various objectives is dealt with through regulatory aspects of the regime and any decision taken by the regulatory body of the regime is to be agreed by all members of the regime.[199] This is a far cry from the original position when a set target had to be followed by all the pipeline associations.

Western countries are also interested in the Caspian and central Asian regions and are interested in building a pipeline bypassing Russia. The BTC pipeline has been built precisely for that purpose.[200] The newly independent countries want to rely less on Russia; according to their calculations their true independence can only be achieved once they are self-reliant through exporting their energy resources without any hindrances or intimidation.[201]

4.6.3.    THE LEGAL ASPECTS OF THE PIPELINE

The Soviet legal system was not based on any form of regulation but on Communist ideology.[202] The policy of the Communist Party was implemented through the passing of various legislations. However, this changed during the latter part of the twentieth century as there were changes in the Communist Party. The soviet legal system placed the state's interest over individual interest, which resulted in

---

194. See *ibid.*
195. See A. Belyi, 'New Dimensions of Energy Security of the Enlarging EU and Their Impact on Relations with Russia', *Journal of European Studies* 25 (2003): 351–369.
196. See *ibid.*
197. See *ibid.*
198. See ESMAP, *supra* n. 155.
199. See *ibid.*
200. See Gelb, *supra* n. 165.
201. See *ibid.*
202. See E.L. Johnson, *Introduction to the Soviet Legal System*, London, 1969, 3.

people having limited or no property rights.[203] The judicial system was also weak as it was there simply to carry out the various policies of the Communist Party.[204]

Even after the break-up of the Soviet Union the judicial system has not changed although there are various laws and regulations which protect investors investing in the country. The law on Foreign Investment in the Russian Federation was passed in 1999.[205] It provides the statutory basis for the treatment of foreign investors. It states that: 'foreign investors and investments shall be treated no less favourably than domestic investors and investments, subject to certain exceptions. Such exceptions may be introduced to protect the Russian constitutional system, the morality, health and rights of third persons or in order to ensure state security and/or defence'.[206] The other laws and regulations which are important to investors are the Civil Code of the Russian Federation, the Tax Code of the Russian Federation and the Custom Code of the Russian Federation.[207] The legitimate expectations of the stakeholders involved in the pipeline regime have not changed as the pipeline association in the new regimes have the same objective of ensuring that the pipeline runs smoothly and without any disruption. The stakeholders involved in the pipeline were also the same as before.[208]

However, the situation in the post-Soviet era can be summarized and characterized through the following, 'legislation is still very much seen as a government directive rather than a system of rights and obligations which are a relatively immune form of instantaneous government intervention... since the socialist state and people subject thereunder did not have or know the rule of law as it normally operates in civil society, the importance of creating a system, institutions and culture encapsulating the rules of law was not understood'.[209] The absence of a well-developed system has resulted in instability in the system, especially in pipeline regulation.[210] This can be seen in the statute concerning the supply of production and technical commodities where there is no regulation and the relationship between the supplier and the producer was defined by the parties themselves.[211]

However, despite the above deficiencies, the Russian legal system has moved on from the Soviet legal system in the sense that there is now a greater urgency to cement the rule of law in respect of foreign investment in the country, including

---

203. See *ibid.*
204. See G. Smith, *Reforming the Russian Legal System* (Cambridge: Cambridge University Press, 1996).
205. See ESMAP, *supra* n. 155.
206. See The Legislative Act on Foreign Investment in Russian Federation, 1999.
207. See Smith, *supra* n. 205.
208. See ESMAP, *supra* n. 155.
209. See T.W. Walde & C.V. Hirschhausen, 'Regulatory Reform in the Energy Industry of Post-Soviet Countries', CEPMLP (1998): 6–7.
210. See A. Ledeneva, How Russia Really Works: The Informal Practices That Shaped Post-Soviet Politics and Business Cornell University Press, 2006.
211. See *ibid.* For details also see 'The legal regulation of pipeline transport in the USSR', Moscow, Pravovedenie, No. 2, 1962, 134–138.

investments in pipeline infrastructure.[212] The legitimate expectations of the stakeholders involved in the pipeline have remained the same despite the changes in legal system and the breakdown of the country.[213] The change that has happened is in the implementation of the rules and regulations, whereas in the past the legitimate expectations were protected through the passing of directives, they are now protected through various legislations like the tax code, civil code and the Custom Code of the Russian Federation as well as through other legislations in the newly established republics.[214]

Previously, most of the exports to COMECON countries were completed under IGAs and other bilateral agreements as there was a common understanding between the Soviet Union and its allies.[215] Currently, delimitation of borders with new states, resource jurisdiction in the Caspian State, transit and lack of proper oversight has caused friction among the various stakeholders involved in supplying oil and gas through Russia and with Russia.[216] A lack of stable legal framework within the country has also driven investors away from the country thus affecting the proper maintenance of ageing pipeline systems delivering oil to other countries.[217]

## 4.6.4 THE GEO-POLITICS OF THE PIPELINE

Pipelines during Soviet times were built keeping in mind the demand from its Eastern European allies and domestic populations within the different regions of the country. After the breakdown of the Soviet Union the entire geo-political gamut changed between the former republics of the Soviet Union and the Russian Federation.[218] Russia considers the former republics, or the CIS countries, as its own and wants to ensure all the energy resources present in these new republics have some sort of Russian influence in them.[219] Due to some of the new countries being pro-Western and the general population in those countries wanting to break away from Russian influence, this has caused geo-political and regional friction between Russia and its old Soviet regions.[220] A good example of this would be Ukraine, which is pro-Western and wanted to have greater control over the transit pipeline going through its country.[221] As a result, it wanted a greater tariff for the

---

212. See Ledeneva, *supra* n. 211.
213. See Smith, *supra* n. 205.
214. See Ledeneva, *supra* n. 211.
215. See *ibid.*
216. See K. Smith, 'Russian Energy Pressure Fails to Unite Europe', CSIS 13, no. 1, 2007.
217. See Belyi, *supra* n. 196.
218. See A. Belyi, 'Institutional Weakness of Intra-FSU Gas Trade', OGEL, 2006.
219. See *ibid.*
220. See I.A. Siddiky, 'The Caspian Energy Scenario and its Pipelines: Amalgamation of Interests?', IELR 2 (2009).
221. See J. Stern, 'The Russian–Ukraine Gas Dispute of January 2009', Oxford Energy Studies, 2009.

gas going through its pipeline, causing conflict with Russia resulting in both gas disruption and diplomatic problems in the form of the latter accusing the former of stealing gas from the pipeline.[222]

Russia is also a transit country for some of the CIS countries and some of these countries are not pleased with Russia's role, as it charges high transit fees for gas and oil.[223] The newly independent states are also aware of Russian hegemony in the region and are hesitant of conducting business with Western countries and companies, although it is the best option available to them.[224] Russia's use of its pipelines and energy strength as a 'political weapon' has also caused scepticism among the European countries dependent upon Russia for its gas.[225] Western countries are interested in bypassing Russia to get their supply of energy. In fact, some of the new pipelines built in the Caspian region are a testament to this fact.[226] One example of this is the BTC pipeline which involves Azerbaijan, Georgia and Turkey. It was built by the Western countries in order to bypass Russia and reduce its overall transportation dominance in the region.[227]

### 4.6.5.      TRANSIT ROUTE

The FSU pipelines were built to supply oil and gas to the different regions of the Soviet Union and to Eastern European countries. Following the breakdown of the Soviet Union, Russia has to rely on its former republics to supply oil and gas to Europe.[228] Ukraine and Belarus play a big part in this regard.[229] Russia is also a transit country for Kazakhstan's oil and gas. This unique position makes the country extremely important. There have been problems with Ukraine with regard to supplying gas to Europe due to a contractual dispute between the two countries while Kazakhstan is also not too happy with the exorbitant transit fees demanded by Russia.[230]

---

222. See *ibid.*
223. See Siddiky, *supra* n. 221.
224. See Belyi, *supra* n. 219.
225. See M. Walker, '*Russia v. Europe*: The Energy Wars', *World Policy Journal* 1 (2007).
226. This is again a transit versus commodity debate, which is highlighted in order to understand the overall situation in the pipeline.
227. See Walker, *supra* n. 226.
228. See *ibid.*
229. See Belyi, *supra* n. 219.
230. See *ibid.*

4.7.     THE APPLICATION OF THE CRITERIA TO THE
         CROSS-BORDER PIPELINE REGIME

4.7.1.   THE NATURE AND CHARACTERISTICS OF THE REGIME

The main player in the FSU pipeline was Glavtransneft, which controlled all seventeen pipeline associations in the FSU. It set the rules and regulations based upon which all the other associations followed. The Glavtransneft regime set the targets and objectives to which the others had to adhere in order to be a part of the regime. Although the associations involved in the regime were also important actors, they had a minor role to play other than abiding by the targets set by the regime because of the nature of the pipeline regime which, in this case, gave very little freedom of activity for these players. The Glavtransneft regime's main goal was to ensure the constant flow of energy through the pipelines and therefore the individual interests of the associations were less important to the regime as a whole.

Before the breakdown of the Soviet Union there was a single law based upon which the pipeline network used to work.[231] After the break up of the country, each country had their own new set of laws[232] and since the pipeline passed through different jurisdictions there had to be bilateral agreements signed between Russia and the newly independent countries for the smooth functioning of the pipeline.[233] There was, therefore, a lack of proper legal frameworks based upon which all the parties could carry out their obligations and these new agreements gave them a certain respite from those legal and regulatory problems.[234] The implication of this is government intervention due to legal or economic reasons, which puts the pipeline regime and its regulatory mechanisms under threat and undermines the regime framework present in the pipelines.[235]

There are regime norms present in the pipeline structure of the FSU. The entire pipeline chain was under the Oil and Gas Ministry at first and then under Glavtransneft. Under Glavtransneft, all seventeen pipeline associations carried out their different obligations. There were certain rules and decision-making procedures through which all seventeen pipeline associations under Glavtransneft had to function. For example, Glavtransneft had to implement the Soviet Union's plan of distributing its crude. As a result, it had to ensure that all cross-border exports to

---

231. The regulation under which the pipeline networks used to function was 'The Legal Regulation of Pipeline Transport in the USSR', Moscow, Pravovedenie, No. 2, 1962, 134–138.
232. For example, Kazakhstan had its own 'Subsoil Law and Petroleum Law', Ukraine has the 'legislative acts of Ukraine on Pipeline Transport' passed in 1998 through a presidential decree, 'Law of the Republic of Belarus on Pipeline transport 2002'. For further reading also see Crandall, *supra* n. 174.
233. Russia has signed Bilateral Agreements with Kazakhstan, Azerbaijan and Ukraine.
234. Russia has signed Bilateral Agreements with Kazakhstan, Azerbaijan and Ukraine.
235. The problem of government intervention in a pipeline regime is highlighted as it is the problem that this book is trying to answer.

other Eastern European countries were carried out without any disruptions.[236] Since the entire pipeline was integrated, Glavtransneft central command used to divide the amount of crude each pipeline association had to pump in order to export it to the other countries.[237] As a result, the functioning of all the regional associations was controlled and monitored by a single command to ensure that all the associations met their quota of supplying crude. Furthermore, since Glavtransneft was a single integrated system, it had considerable flexibility and reliability in ensuring that even if one of the associations failed to meet their quota of supply, the others could make up for it.[238] This aspect is reminiscent of a regime where all the actors abide by the various rules and regulations of a regime and tries to maximize the benefit for all the actors within the regime.

The FSU pipeline regime was strong because the Glavtransneft regime had rules and principles based upon which the regime was run and which all the actors followed. The strength of the pipeline regime resulted in very little disruption in the pipeline chain and the interests of pipeline capacity and demand for resources were more important than the individual interests of the actors in the regime.[239] An example of this would be Glavtransneft central command ensuring that their overall objective was to implement the plans of the Soviet Union, and all the associations in different regions had to ensure that they fulfilled the crude export requirements of Glavtransneft even if it meant that their individual regions might not get their adequate quota.[240] As a result, any shortfall in the association's individual region was covered by other associations who had a surplus supply of crude.[241] This was ideal, in a regime sense, as Glavtransneft was the sole authority regulating, providing and enforcing the various rules and regulations set by them and they ensured everyone followed them. This also enabled the regime to respect the legitimate expectations of the stakeholders involved in the pipeline regime which involved the pipeline associations being able to cater for the needs of their individual regions.[242]

The FSU pipeline regime is unique because the breakdown of the Soviet Union caused economic, legal and infrastructural problems for all the pipeline associations that were part of the regime.[243] As all the associations were part of one regime, they now find themselves in a different situation, with new found independence, while at the same time still having to be part of the old regime because of the nature of the pipelines built during Soviet times and also because of the costs and time involved if new pipelines were to be built.[244]

---

236. See ESMAP, *supra* n. 155.
237. See *ibid.*
238. See *ibid.*
239. See Crandall, *supra* n. 174.
240. See ESMAP, *supra* n. 155.
241. See *ibid.*
242. See Crandall, *supra* n. 174.
243. See *ibid.*
244. See *ibid.*

Being part of the old regime still has its benefits but with new rules and regulations.[245]

There is a mixture of both neo-liberalism and neo-realism in the FSU pipeline structure. The neo-realist ideals stem from the fact that Glavtransneft was a monopoly and the only regime guarding the different pipeline associations. All the pipeline associations were under its control and had to abide by its directives.[246] This resulted in Glavtransneft using its power and superior position over others in order to make the other subordinates achieve the various targets it set.[247] However, all the associations cooperated with each other and there was cooperation within the different pipeline associations, which showed the neo-liberal side of things. A good example of this would be the other associations trying to help each other out when there was a shortfall in crude for their particular region because of the need to meet the export target set by the Soviet authorities.[248] As a whole, the entire regime tried to work in a cooperative setting for the successful operation of the different pipeline networks in the FSU and help protect the legitimate expectations of the stakeholders involved in the pipeline.

4.7.2.     THE ISSUES AFFECTING THE CROSS-BORDER PIPELINE

The Soviet pipeline infrastructure was extremely extensive and was built to supply hydro-carbon resources to the different parts of the country as well as to some of the Eastern European countries. However, after the breakdown of the Soviet Union things were different because some of the former regions now became independent countries. The lack of infrastructure within these old pipelines together with a fall in demand and investments in these pipelines are some of the reasons the pipelines of the FSU are now suffering and there is sometimes disruption in supply.[249] Throughout the 1990s there had been no investment in the oil fields which resulted in the decline of production of crude oil and this caused some of these extensive oil pipelines to sit idle and rust.[250] The decline in production in the mid and late 1990s also affected the supply of oil to the Eastern European countries, and these countries diversified their energy imports.[251] The lack of demand together with the fall in oil production and lack of maintenance of the oil pipeline infrastructure had a negative impact on the pipelines causing supply disruption.[252]

The FSU pipelines were also built without considering the need to have the pipeline network built around the country. The result is that these pipelines now

---

245.  See D.A. Loeber et al., *Ruling Communist Parties and Their Status under Law* (Dordrecht: Martinus Nijhoff, 1986).
246.  See ESMAP, *supra* n. 155.
247.  See *ibid.*
248.  See *ibid.*
249.  See Chufrin, *supra* n. 163.
250.  See ESMAP, *supra* n. 155.
251.  See *ibid.*
252.  See *ibid.*

remain idle because some of them are situated in newly independent states who are not interested in continuing to use these pipeline networks.[253] One of the reasons they are not willing to use these pipelines is because they are situated in areas which are far away from the centre of production making it expensive and difficult to divert them towards another region. Good examples of this are Ukraine and Kazakhstan.[254]

Other issues affecting the pipelines of the FSU are the transit disputes Russia is having with the newly independent states. In 2003 and 2004, Russia had a transit dispute with Belarus, resulting in the disruption of the supply of gas to Europe and to Belarus.[255] There was a dispute between the two countries because Russia alleged that Belarus was stealing gas meant for European consumers from the pipeline while Belarus alleged that Russia was paying too little for transit.[256] Belarus also alleged that it was not receiving gas from Russia on the preferential terms agreed between the two countries.[257] This dispute resulted in the disruption of supply, with Russia cutting off supplies to Belarus which in turn affected its European consumers.[258]

However, both countries sorted out their differences through intense negotiation but this dispute showed the animosity between Russia and its neighbours (the former regions) and this does not bode well for the future of the pipeline passing through Belarus and other transit pipelines carrying Russian gas.[259] This dispute can be termed as a breach of legitimate expectation of the stakeholders involved in the pipeline as Belarus claimed that their legitimate expectation was not respected by Russia, while Russia responded by cutting gas supplies, which was also a breach of legitimate expectation for the EU consumers as they expected Russia to respect their contractual obligations.[260]

In 2006–2007 and in 2009, Russia also had disputes with Ukraine, another transit country Russia depends on for supplying gas to Europe.[261] Ukraine was accused of stealing gas from the pipeline and also not paying for the gas that it was importing.[262] This resulted in Russia stopping gas supplies to Ukraine, who in turn started taking gas from the pipelines meant for Europe.[263] Once Russia stopped supplying gas through those pipelines as well, all of its European consumers suffered for three weeks, resulting in the European Union and other international oil

---

253. See Chufrin, *supra* n. 163.
254. See Crandall, *supra* n. 174.
255. See J.C. Webb, 'Russia–Belarus Oil Trade Dispute Underscores Need for Long Term Crude Transportation Alternatives', CERA Report, 2007, can be accessed via <www.cera.com>.
256. See *ibid.*
257. See *ibid.*
258. See *ibid.*
259. See *ibid.*
260. See Crandall, *supra* n. 174.
261. See J.P. Stern, *The Russian–Ukrainian Gas Crisis of 2006* (Oxford Energy Studies, 2006), can be accessed via <www.oxfordenergy.org>. Further Reading; see Stern, *supra* n. 222; see S. Pirani, *Ukraine's Gas Sector* (Oxford: Oxford Energy Studies, 2007).
262. See Pirani, *ibid.*
263. See *ibid.*

and gas companies trying to negotiate with the two countries.[264] The problem again surfaced in 2009 when Ukraine failed to pay for the gas it imported from Russia, and Russia again stopped their supplies.[265] The main problem is that Ukraine wants to pay Russia at a subsidized rate whereas Russia is asking Ukraine for the same rate it charges its European consumers. The regular disruption of pipeline supplies due to conflict between the two parties seriously jeopardizes the security of supply of countries reliant on Russian gas and is a serious cause for concern for some importers.[266]

The geo-political and economic problems in this case show the reason why there have been frequent disagreements between the government of Russia, Ukraine and Belarus.[267] All three governments want to protect their own interests. The interference of the Russian government in the conflict with the Ukrainian government, and the latter's threat of using its transit position, shows the reason why, despite being in a strong regime category,[268] there is a need for a new regulatory mechanism or an agency which could deal with these sorts of issues.[269]

The Russian attitude towards the newly independent countries with respect to the pipelines passing through them is that of a neo-realist, as they want to use their superior military strength and geographical location to influence the outcome in their favour.[270] The country is using its power to achieve absolute gain from these smaller states and, as a result, has resorted to neo-realist ideals to attain its objectives. However, it also shows a certain neo-liberal attitude in the form of cooperation with other countries that are willing to help them achieve their objective without giving in to the other countries' demands.

### 4.7.3. THE COMMON INTERESTS OF THE PARTIES

The role of the FSU pipelines changed after the breakdown of the Soviet Union.[271] The interests of the parties have also changed. During Soviet times, the Druzbha

---

264. See Stern, *supra* n. 262.
265. See Stern, *supra* n. 222.
266. See *ibid.*
267. In April 2010, both Russia and Ukraine signed an agreement in which Russia agreed to lower the price of gas by 30% in exchange for Ukraine extending Russia's lease of a major naval base in the Black Sea port of Sevastopol for another twenty-five years with an additional five-year renewal option. This is another example of both countries' governments using their strategic geo-political position to settle their differences instead of relying on earlier agreements signed between the parties with regard to the transit of Russian gas to Europe through Ukraine.
268. The definition of a strong regime is provided at the beginning of this chapter.
269. These problems have a strong link with the problems that this book is trying to answer and the question about government or members of a particular regime interfering for their own benefits. Ch. 1 of the book discusses the problems this book is trying to answer and the issues discussed in this case study further show the reason for the requirement of an agency or another regulatory mechanism which can deal with geo-political and economic interests.
270. See Pirani, *supra* n. 262.
271. This means, with the breakdown of the Soviet Union, the pipeline is used more in commercial terms rather than ideological terms. The interests of new countries like Kazakhstan, Azerbaijan, Belarus, Ukraine and Turkmenistan have changed as they want to be self-sufficient on

and other pipelines were a sign of friendship and cooperation between the countries involved in the pipeline chain.[272] Currently, however, the interests of the parties have changed dramatically. The newly independent states are interested in gaining more benefits from the huge amount of hydro-carbon resources in their countries and consequently want to use these pipeline infrastructures.[273] Russia, however, wants to maintain its dominance in the region by using its influence to try to ensure the pipeline routes pass through its country and also to lower Western influence in the region.

Both Gazprom and Transneft, the Russian oil and gas giants, are using the country's huge gas and oil wealth and advantageous pipeline network to coax the other countries of the region to follow their lead.[274] One of the reasons for this is to make the newly independent states less competitive in the international market which in turn will make Russian exports cheaper and more accessible.[275] Russia acts as a transit country and also as an importing country due to its location and huge pipeline network, as a result, the other countries have very little option other than cooperating with it and its' national oil and gas companies.

Most of the Caspian countries are landlocked and therefore dependence on Russia increases greatly due to this problem. Russia also has to depend on other transit countries to export its gas and oil to Europe and to the other regions of the world. The interest is mutual and there has to be cooperation between the two in order to achieve smooth operation of the pipeline. Western countries would prefer pipelines bypassing Russia in order to lower its influence in the region.[276] The BTC pipeline is a good example of that.

The transit route through which the pipeline passes was also chosen during Soviet times when all these new countries where under the Soviet Union. New transport routes have not always favoured Russia as some of these countries are eager to charge high tariffs for letting the pipeline pass through their country.[277] However, most of the countries cooperate with Russia for the transportation of resources through their territory. Russia also lets some of these countries use its territory to export resources to other parts of the world.

The interests of the countries are interlinked and thus the attitude of Russia and the newly independent states are neo-liberal in nature. The reason for this is that both parties are willing to cooperate because of their common interest and are willing to undertake certain sacrifices for their ultimate benefit. However, the

---

their own terms, and the pipeline is therefore used to transport Russian crude and gas, or as transportation for other states. The Eastern European countries that also previously used to get their hydro-carbon resources at a subsidized rate or even through barter now have to reassess their situation due to the new economic situation in the region. In other words, the pipelines of the FSU represent a new convergence of interests of different players.

272. See Pirani, *supra* n. 262.
273. See Stern, *supra* n. 222.
274. See *ibid.*
275. See *ibid.*
276. See *ibid.*
277. See Webb, *supra* n. 256.

overall tendency of Russia and its two oil giants, Gazprom and Transneft, is that of a hegemony as they are willing to use their power, if needed, to achieve their ultimate objective.[278] In this sense, they are more neo-realist in nature as they use their power to achieve absolute gain rather than cooperate with the other parties.

This dual policy of neo-realism and neo-liberalism in certain situations has served Russia well at times as it was able to dictate terms like a neo-realist and achieve its ultimate objective of greater influence in the Caspian region pipeline network and other networks. In general, the common interest of all the parties involved in the pipeline chain is to maximize each other's benefit in the best possible way despite geo-political tensions, the reason being all the parties require each other's help and cooperation and that calls for a neo-liberal attitude from them.

4.7.4.     THE ENFORCEMENT AND COMPLIANCE OF THE CROSS-BORDER
           PIPELINE AGREEMENTS

During Soviet times enforcement and compliance within the various pipeline networks were undertaken by Glavtransneft. This is now done by Transneft and Gazprom for the respective oil and gas pipelines.[279] Both entities acts like a regime to ensure that the various actors associated with the pipeline chain carry out their obligations properly and enforce the different clauses of the agreements.[280] The same cannot be said of the pipelines under the jurisdictions of the newly independent countries, as Russia does not have any hold over their old pipeline network in these countries.[281] They have to rely on bilateral agreements signed with these countries to ensure that the clauses of the agreements are enforced adequately.

There have been problems with the enforcement of the clauses of the agreement because of the lack of an impartial regulatory body or a separate entity that

---

278.  See *ibid.*
279.  See Stern, *supra* n. 222.
280.  This involves the economic aspects of the pipeline including the tariff structure and the amount of oil and gas that should be passed through the pipeline. However, the interests of the parties within the regime varies following the breakdown of the Soviet Union. Due to differing commercial interests and a weak legal structure, government intervenes in order to protect its' interest, bypassing the enforcement mechanism available for the pipeline.
281.  Although the pipeline associations under the new regime are independent they are still considered to be under the old regime due to the infrastructural aspects of the pipeline. The rules and regulations of the regime have changed as they have their own interest now but, overall, since these new pipeline associations and countries are still dependent on the old Soviet pipelines and have to cooperate with both Transneft and Gazprom, they are still considered one regime with new rules and regulations and different enforcement mechanisms.

can check whether the various parties have enforced or complied with the clauses of the agreement.[282] The lack of trust between Russia and the newly independent states has resulted in conflict regarding the enforcement of the cross-border agreements as each side blames the other for lack of enforcement. There is no independent authority or regime which can verify the claims of the parties involved in the pipeline chain. For example, the conflicts Russia had with Ukraine and Belarus is a good example of this, as all three parties blamed each other for the disruption in the pipeline.[283]

Although during Soviet times the legitimate expectations of the stakeholders involved in the pipeline were protected by Glavtransneft, these are now protected by the regulatory bodies within the Transneft and Gazprom structures.[284] Furthermore, Russian legislation in the form of the Foreign Investment Act 1999 protects the legitimate expectations of stakeholders involved in the pipeline within the country.[285] However, the legitimate expectations of the stakeholders have not changed with the break-up of the Soviet Union, despite their new countries being established because the pipelines in Russia, together with all the new republics, are interlinked. As a result, the objective is to ensure that the pipelines are run without any disruption while the old pipeline associations together with the old ones in the new republics enforce the various rules and regulations individually respecting the legitimate expectations of the stakeholders in the pipeline.[286]

The actions of the parties involved in the pipeline chain have neo-realist tendencies. Russia wants to use its hegemonic power to ensure that that the other party is enforcing the clauses of the agreement. While the other country also wants to use its position to achieve its goal without implementing or enforcing the agreement. This results in conflict and blame games which disrupt the flow of oil and gas to different regions of the world. Due to a lack of cooperation and coordination, and the absence of a central regime to look after the different operations of the pipeline, there have been disruptions in supply which have caused problems for importing countries.[287]

---

282. This means that the newly independent countries want their own independence with regard to the enforcement issue. Although they are still part of the regime, unlike the old regime they will not simply carry out the different targets and regulations handed down to them by the new Transneft and Gazprom regime. As a result, there has to be a consensus in the way the enforcement of the various rules and regulations takes place in these countries which could be beneficial for all the parties in the regime, as all the parties require each other's cooperation for the pipeline to operate without any disruption.
283. See Stern, *supra* n. 222.
284. See Ledeneva, *supra* n. 211.
285. See *ibid.*
286. See *ibid.*
287. See Webb, *supra* n. 256.

4.8.        CONCLUSION

The Interconnector pipeline between the UK and Belgium is the first of its kind as it is a bi-directional pipeline, which allows the parties to export and import depending upon their needs. The pipeline regime is based upon the agreements signed between the two parties and it also involves other agreements and contracts signed between the various shippers involved in the pipeline.[288] The Interconnector regime is quite stable and organized as the pipeline is treated as one entity and there are different agencies within the broad regime following the different aspects of the pipelines. However, there are too many regulatory authorities involved which might dilute the work and activities of the main pipeline regime and this can cause a lack of coordination among the stakeholders involved in the pipeline chain causing disruption in the supply of gas.[289]

The pipelines of the FSU were also based upon agreements signed between the different partners involved in the project. After the breakdown of the Soviet Union, Russia had to sign individual agreements with the newly independent countries and also other Eastern European countries.[290] However, the Glavtransneft regime still looks after the oil pipelines within Russia while Gazprom looks after the gas pipelines. These two regimes are also in charge of pipelines used by other countries to export oil and gas to other destinations through Russia. Furthermore, they are still in charge of the vast pipeline network in Russia and have ensured that the pipeline regime is run smoothly.

The Interconnector pipeline has a mixture of strong government and private participation in the operation of the pipeline while the FSU pipeline has strong government control over the Glavtransneft regime. As a result, both were able to ensure that the actors involved were aware of their obligations towards the regime and had to abide by their norms.

The common theme among these two pipelines in strong regimes has been the less frequent disruption of supply, which still caused concerns among the importing countries and exporting countries, in this case the UK, Belgium and Russia. Although the factors affecting these pipelines were different, with Russia facing transit problems while the UK faced increasing prices for its customers and a lack of supply security, both pipeline regimes had strong regimes to deal with the issues affecting these pipelines. The regime ensured that the actors abided by their obligations and although they could not deal with all the problems, as expected by the

---

288.   Agreements have been signed between the UK Government and the Belgian Government and also between the shippers involved in the pipeline with Interconnector UK Limited, the company which is responsible for the operation of the pipeline.

289.   This is due to the fact that the actors within the regime would have to abide by different criteria set by different regulatory bodies causing confusion, which in turn would cause problems as it would be difficult for them to follow the guidelines of so many agencies.

290.   Russia had to sign individual agreements with the newly independent states including Bilateral Investment Treaties (BITs) with these new countries and other transit agreements to allow their oil and gas to pass through these countries. Some of these agreements also involved the importing countries of Eastern Europe, like Hungary, Slovakia and so on.

regime members, they provided a framework which gave stability to the stakeholders involved in the pipeline chain and also to countries depending upon the pipeline network.

The implication of this is that some players in the regime gain more than the others resulting in the stronger parties within a regime having an advantageous position.[291] It also shows that in a regime some issues will be dealt with better than others, as is the case with these two pipeline regimes. For example, in the Interconnector pipeline there has been disruption despite having strong regulatory oversight as there have been too many regulatory bodies following it. This is good in the sense that the parties will be more careful to abide by their obligations. The FSU system, however, was more centralized and could respond to any disruption decisively due to a single regulatory body. However, a single regulatory body like the FSU could also face problems as it has to investigate different pipeline chains which at times can be overwhelming, resulting in a lack of coordination.[292]

The interests of other parties in the stronger regimes are also quite similar. The Interconnector pipeline was built to serve the energy needs of both the UK and Belgium, while the FSU pipeline was built to cater for the needs of the entire Soviet Union and its Eastern European allies. There were both political and economic dimensions involved in the building of these pipelines. The implication is greater cooperation among the parties and it shows that the actors are willing to cooperate with each other to reach their common goals.

There are both similarities and dissimilarities between the pipelines within this strong regime category. The Interconnector pipeline is based upon a solid legal framework agreed between the UK and Belgium governments. There is an intergovernmental commission made up of officials from both countries and they look after the various aspects of the pipelines, to ensure that the different clauses of the agreement are followed properly and adequately.[293] There are other independent regulatory authorities that have powers to look after the various aspects of the pipeline and can enforce the rules and regulations to ensure that the actors are abiding by their obligations.[294]

The FSU pipelines are under the regimes of either Transneft or Gazprom. The oil pipelines are under the control of Transneft while the gas pipelines are looked after by Gazprom. As a result, the regulatory nature of the pipeline regime is quite strong and efficient as all the pipeline associations are under the Transneft regime.[295] They are also able to monitor the activities of the actors involved in the

---

291. See Ch. 2 of this book for a detailed analysis on regime and the advantages actors wished to gain from joining a regime.
292. See Ch. 4 for further discussion and the regulatory capabilities of these two pipelines.
293. This is open to interpretation because according to some experts the actors are not fulfilling their obligations, while others disagree.
294. For a discussion on this topic please refer to the previous chapter and also the first part of this chapter. See Anthony Mulcare's presentation for further details about this topic <www.interconnector.com/PDF/The_Impact_of_the_Interconnector.pdf>.
295. The FSU pipeline is a unique regime because after the breakdown of the Soviet Union the newly independent countries had their own pipeline associations; as a result, they had their

pipeline network and are able to enforce the various rules and regulations set by them. This shows that both the pipelines in the regime have strong regulatory aspects but at the same time the type of regulation is different because in the case of the FSU there is a single regulatory body whereas in the Interconnector there are many. This, however, does not have any impact on the workings of the actors within the pipelines, although too many regulatory bodies within a single regime might cause a lack of coordination.

The nature of the parties involved in both the Interconnector and the FSU pipeline regimes has a mixture of both neo-liberal and neo-realist tendencies. Despite the two pipelines being classified as having strong regimes there are certain actors within these two pipeline regimes who are more interested in personal gain than the gains of all the other actors involved in the regime. In the FSU pipeline, the government wants to use its superior position to coax neighbouring countries to deliver their oil and gas to Europe. This can be shown through the Ukrainian and Belarus conflicts with the Russian government.[296] However, the Russian government also wants to cooperate with them in order to ensure safe transit of their own resources. In the Interconnector pipeline, there are similar trends with both the regulators and the government working together in order to ensure that the consumers receive an uninterrupted supply of hydro-carbon resources, which is a neo-liberal trait.[297]

Both the pipeline regimes discussed here have been classified as a strong regime because of their regime strength and the strong enforceable capabilities within their respective regimes, enabling them to resolve any issues which might affect the regime in general.[298] For example, the Interconnector pipeline has regulatory authorities like the DTI/Ofgem, the Interconnector Commission and the EC ensuring that they abide by the rules and regulations set by these authorities. The EC focuses on whether it abides by the various competition laws ethos set by it which all member countries have to follow, while the DTI/Ofgem ensures whether the pipeline follows the rules of the license provided to them under the Energy Act of 2004.[299] The FSU pipelines also followed the

---

own interests. However, they still had to cooperate with the old regime framework due to infrastructural and geo-political reasons and that is why they are still considered to be a part of the old regime despite being independent. However, the rules, regulations and decision-making procedures of the regime had to change because of the change in circumstances.

296. See the FSU pipeline section discussed previously in this chapter for further discussion in this area.

297. Neo-liberals advocate for greater cooperation and sharing of information of all the actors involved in the regime. This, according to them, will bring benefits for all the parties involved in the regime. For further discussion in this area, see Ch. 2 in the regime theory section.

298. A strong regime is defined at the beginning of this chapter and these two pipelines have been categorized under it due to the attributes of a strong regime mentioned in the definition and the similarities found in these two pipelines. The 'nature and characteristics of the regime' criteria discussed previously for both the pipelines also highlights the reason these pipelines are considered as a strong regime.

299. The role of the EC, DTI/Ofgem and the European law dimension has been discussed previously in this chapter. Please see the 'legal aspect' and 'the nature and characteristics of the regime' sections for further details.

instructions given by Glavtransneft who tried to implement the Soviet plan. As a consequence, Glavtransneft gave quotas to each of the seventeen pipeline associations in order to meet the Soviet export quota.[300] The functioning of these Soviet pipeline associations were strongly monitored by Glavtransneft through constant supervision.[301]

These two pipelines, however, provide an important lesson with regard to the way a strong regime should function and the behaviour of the actors who are involved in these sorts of regimes. The lesson that can be learnt from strong regimes is that despite having strong enforcement capabilities through their regulatory bodies they still have problems[302] which cannot be solved by their strong regulatory authority. There could also be an argument that both these pipelines are examples where the governance level was totally different and this might have had an impact on them being in a strong regime, meaning the actors involved in the Interconnector had democratic and capitalist principles while FSU pipelines were run under communist and socialist ideals. However, a lesson that could be learnt is that despite originating from two different political ideals both these pipeline regimes had strong regulatory features although with different enforcement techniques.[303] It is also important to note that the purpose of the case studies have been to showcase the regime qualities rather than the political dimensions of the governments of these countries.

The transit problems faced by the FSU pipeline and the regulatory problems faced by the Interconnector have similarities with the problem that this book is trying to answer.[304] The governments tend to interfere due to geopolitical, legal and economic reasons and this is responsible for the disruption of supply in the pipeline chain. In the case of the FSU, the case study has shown that both the Ukrainian and Belarus governments had problems with their Russian counterpart which caused disruption in the supply chain.[305] In the case of the Interconnector pipeline, the problem lies with too many government

---

300. The role of Glavtransneft has been discussed in detail in the 'nature and characteristics of the regime' section.
301. See ESMAP, *supra* n. 155.
302. The problems here refer to the issues that affect the pipelines' ability to continue functioning without any disruption. The 'issues affecting the pipelines' criteria in the case study cover this aspect of the discussion.
303. This means that the Interconnector had government agencies like the Interconnector Commission, DTI/Ofgem together with independent regulatory authorities controlled by the EC, which is out of government interference. The FSU was, however, solely run by a government regulatory authority, the Glavtransneft.
304. This problem is discussed in detail in Ch. 1 of the book. The problem lies with government interference in a regime due to geo-political, legal and economic reasons and how it affects the behaviour of the other parties in the regime and its ramifications.
305. This aspect of the problem is discussed in the 'issues affecting the pipelines' section in the FSU pipeline case study. The geo-political problem resulted in the breach of the deal agreed between the parties.

agencies having their own management and operation criteria, which causes disruption.[306]

These two case studies provide an insight into what a strong regime looks like, its capabilities, functions and the behaviour of the actors involved in this sort of regime.[307] This model could be followed to build a new regime in the form of a pipeline agency, if necessary. The case studies have also shown that, despite being a strong regime, they are not equipped to solve some of the issues discussed above[308] and require another form of regulatory mechanism in order to deal with those problems.[309] The pipelines in the strong regime are not perfect but despite that, the legitimate expectations of the stakeholders are met. However, they also provide examples of how a strong regime would function, which could be something that a pipeline agency can learn from and emulate.

---

306. This is also discussed in detail in the Interconnector case study, especially when the four criteria are used to analyse the behaviour of the parties involved in the project and the problems involved.
307. Regime theory is used to analyse this. The analysis is done through using the four criteria discussed in detail in s. 2 and applied in the case studies.
308. Issues here refer to the problems that are faced by the pipelines. The problem that these pipelines are facing is covered in the 'issues affecting the pipelines' criteria of the case study. The beginning of the paragraph also offers a hint of the problem that is faced by the pipelines despite being in a strong regime.
309. The problem in this aspect hints at the requirement for something new being needed to be done in the form of an agency or mechanism. This relates to the main problem that the book is trying to answer, which is mentioned in Ch. 1 of this book.

Chapter 5

# Moderately Strong Regimes

5.1.             INTRODUCTION

This chapter looks into the BTC and WAGP pipelines. Both these pipelines are considered to have a moderately strong regime. *A moderately strong regime also has all the regime rules and principles and ensures that the members follow them. However, its enforcement mechanism is not as active despite having the mechanism within the regime. The slightly weak enforcement mechanism results in parties not abiding by their various obligations which weakens the regime.*[1]

The purpose of this chapter is to analyse the different aspects of these two pipelines and to see the trends in their disputes within a moderately strong regime. Another purpose of these two case studies is to see whether there are any differences between pipelines in a strong regime and a moderately strong regime.

As in the previous chapter, each case analysis is divided into three parts; the first section provides the general background to the pipeline, discussing the various aspects of it, the cost of building it and the different stakeholders involved in the pipeline chain. The second section discusses the important aspects of those pipelines that affect its smooth operation. These aspects include economic, legal and geo-political issues as well as the interests of the parties involved in the pipeline chain. The third section uses the criteria developed in the analytical framework chapter to analyse the lessons learnt from the previous section. The four criteria[2] that would be used in order to analyse the different aspects of these pipelines are:

(i) The nature and characteristics of the regime.
(ii) The issues affecting the cross-border pipeline.

---

1. This is considered as the definition of a moderately strong regime for the purpose of this book.
2. Chapter 2 also provides an extensive discussion regarding the four benchmarks chosen to evaluate the different cross-border pipeline regimes.

(iii) The common interests of the parties.
(iv) The enforcement and compliance of the various cross-border pipeline agreements.

## 5.2.    THE BTC PIPELINE

### 5.2.1.    THE BACKGROUND OF THE PROJECT

The BTC pipeline is one of the major pipelines in the Caspian region. It runs from Azerbaijan through Georgia to the Ceyhan Terminal in Turkey where the oil is transported to Europe and other parts of the world.[3] The other two pipelines in the area are the Western Route Export pipelines (WREP) and the Baku–Tbilisi–Ezurum (BTE) gas pipeline (Figure 5.1).[4] One of the main reasons for building the BTC pipeline was the necessity to increase the flow of oil and gas in the region as the other two pipelines had insufficient capacity to accommodate for increasing needs.[5]

*Figure 5.1    The BTC, Shah-Deniz, NREP and WREP Pipelines*[6]

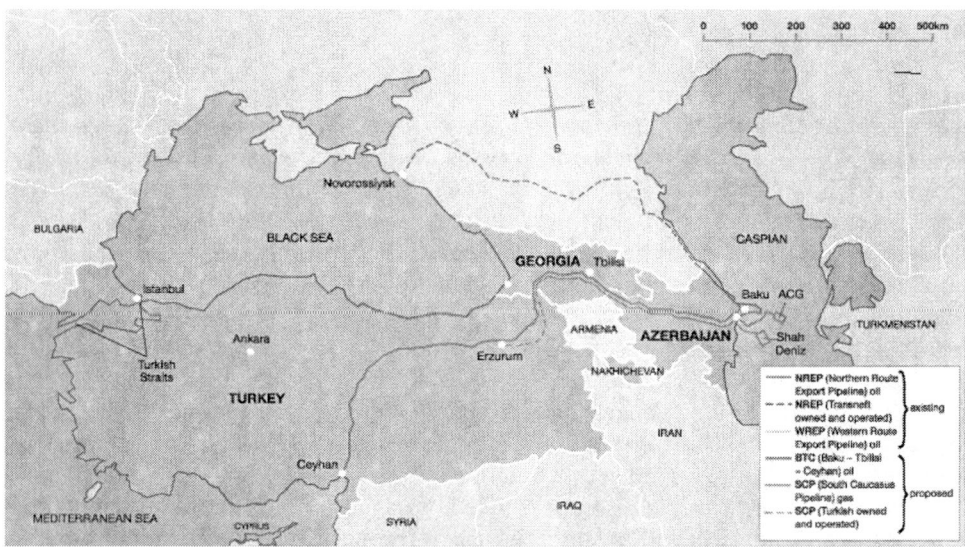

*Source*: <www.caspiandevelopmentandexport.com>.

The pipeline currently transports around 1 Mb/d or 50 Mt/y of the Caspian oil.[7] It is 1,760 km long and originates from Sangachal (Baku) in Azerbaijan, runs through

---

3. See the BTC Pipeline website at <www.caspiandevelopmentandexport.com>.
4. See *ibid.*
5. See *ibid.*
6. The diagram provides an extensive view of the BTC pipeline in order to understand the geo-political and transit issues of the pipelines.
7. See the BTC Pipeline website at <www.caspiandevelopmentandexport.com>.

Tbilisi in Georgia and terminates at a 2.5 km terminal in Ceyhan, Turkey.[8] The oil is then loaded from Ceyhan for the international market. The terminal has seven storage tanks, each with a capacity of 950,000 barrels and is capable of loading two 300,000 dead weight tonne (DWT) very large crude carriers (VLCC) simultaneously, each at the rate of 60,000 barrels per hour (Tb/h).[9] The 1 m deep pipeline has eight pumping stations along the route to increase oil pressure.[10]

5.2.2.    THE RELEVANT PARTIES OF THE PROJECT

The BTC Company is made up of 11 national and international petroleum companies with BP (30%) as the major shareholder and operator of the pipeline.[11] Other shareholders include SOCAR (25%), Unocal (8.9%), Statoil (8.71%), Tpao (6.53%), Eni (5%), Total (5%), Itochu (3.4%), Inpex (2.5%), Conoco Phillips (2.5%) and Amerada Hess (2.36%).[12] The BTC pipeline carries oil from the Azeri–Chirag–Guneshli oil fields and transports around one million barrels per day, although its capacity is likely to increase in the near future (Figure 5.2).[13]

*Figure 5.2    The Major Shareholders of the BTC Pipeline Project*[14]

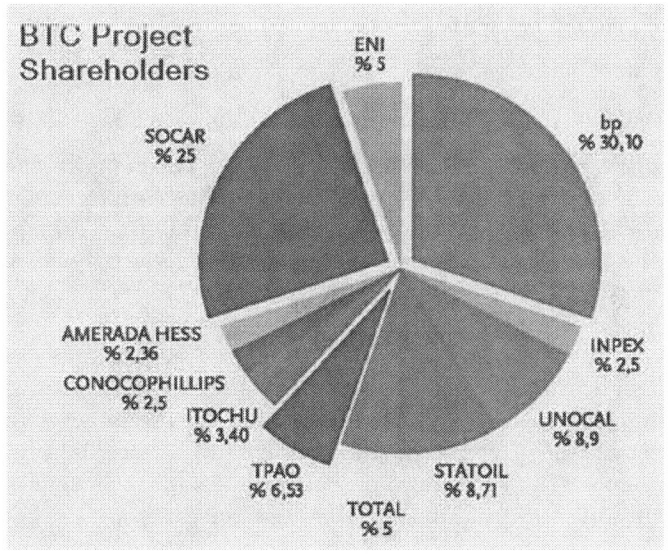

Source: <www.caspiandevelopmentandexport.com>.

8.  See *ibid.*
9.  See *ibid.*
10. See *ibid.*
11. See J. Roberts, 'The Turkish Gate: Energy Transit and Security Issues', *Turkish Policy Quarterly* 3, no. 4 (2004).
12. See *ibid.*
13. See *ibid.*
14. This figure shows all the major stakeholders involved in the pipeline. It also shows the number of International Oil Companies involved in the pipeline.

5.2.3.     THE COST OF THE PROJECT

The pipeline cost around USD 3.6 billion to build with interest and loans.[15] The cost of building the pipeline itself was USD 2.9 billion.[16] The International Finance Corporation together with the European Bank for Reconstruction and Development (EBRD) and other multinational financing agencies financed most of the USD 3.6 billion.[17] Debt comprised about 70% of the fund while the remaining 30% came from equity holders in BTC Co.[18] The breakdown of the loan is as follows:[19]

- *$1 billion provided by BTC Co. participants as senior sponsor lenders*

EBRD and IFC each provided $250 million in loans, consisting of a direct loan of $125 million each, and another $125 million each through syndication (a syndicate of 15 commercial banks led by ABN Amro, Citibank, Mizuhoand Societe Generale of just under $1 billion

$1.6 billion from export credit agencies and insurers from Japan, the US, the UK, France, Germany and Italy.

Although the project was controversial and had many political problems, the financiers kept faith with the various stakeholders involved with the project and were confident of its financial viability.

5.2.4.     OTHER ASPECTS OF THE PIPELINE

The BTC pipeline project is based upon four key agreements signed between the various parties. They are the IGA signed between the various parties involved in the project, the HGA, the Turnkey Agreement and the Turkish Government Guaranty.[20] The last two agreements were signed individually between the companies and the respective governments involved and thus would not fall within the scope of this discussion.

The IGA between the Republic of Turkey, the Republic of Azerbaijan and Georgia was signed to formalize the different responsibilities of the parties involved in the project. The agreement sets out the principles which are based upon what kind of transit would be allowed, and advocates the principle of non-discriminatory treatment, encouraging a harmonization of the legal framework and the implementation of the supranational regulatory rules.[21]

---

15. See M. Olcot, 'Pipelines and Pipe Dreams: Energy Development and Caspian Society', *Journal of International Affairs* 53 no. 1 (1999).
16. See *ibid*.
17. See *ibid*.
18. See *ibid*.
19. See *ibid*.
20. See the IGA between the Republic of Turkey, the Azerbaijan Republic and Georgia relating to the transportation of petroleum via the Baku Tbilisi Ceyhan Main Export Pipeline, 1999, can be found at <www.caspiandevelopmentandexport.com>.
21. See Roberts, *supra* n. 11.

The main purpose of signing the IGA is to provide the political, legal and economic backing required for the smooth building of cross-border pipelines.[22] The agreement strives to 'promote a legal and fiscal regime to attract investment to the BTC pipeline and establish prevailing domestic and international law through ratification and other enabling procedures'.[23] The agreement also covers matters such as the hiring of personnel, securing the facilities and other technical and environmental social concerns.[24]

The IGA also had the intention of establishing an intergovernmental commission to facilitate the implementation of various clauses of the agreement.[25] In this commission, officials from the Ministry of Energy and Natural Resources as well as officials from Foreign Affairs of the three countries would be working together for the smooth functioning of the project and the pipeline.

The purpose of the HGAs between the three countries was to determine the governments' guarantee and support regarding the project and to ensure non-discriminatory transit of energy products through their borders and beyond.[26] The HGA also held the governments responsible for the security of the pipeline, and enabled government support regarding the acquisition of land and other permits.[27] The agreement also holds the governments responsible for liabilities and compensation for failure to fulfil their obligation under the agreement.[28]

## 5.3.  THE IMPORTANT ASPECTS OF THE PIPELINE

### 5.3.1.  ECONOMIC ASPECT

Although at the beginning of the project the pipeline was not deemed to be economically feasible because of the complex route and geo-political situation in the region, it did work out successfully due to the various government guarantees and commitments towards the project.[29] The pipeline would also increase the security of supply in the region as well as other parts of the world.[30] The Turkish strait receives oil from all over the Caspian and exports it to different parts of the world, which sometimes results in tanker congestion and unwanted accidents in the area.[31]

---

22. See *ibid.*
23. See G. Bahgat, 'Pipeline Diplomacy: The Geopolitics of the Caspian Sea Region', *International Studies Perspectives* 3 (2002): 310–327.
24. See *ibid.*
25. See The Agreement between the Republic of Turkey, the Azerbaijan Republic and Georgia, 1999. Can be found at <www.caspiandevelopmentandexport.com>.
26. See the HGA between the Republic of Turkey, the Azerbaijan Republic and Georgia and the different companies relating to the transportation of petroleum via the Baku Tbilisi Ceyhan Main Export Pipeline, 1999. This can be found at <www.caspiandevelopmentandexport.com>.
27. See *ibid.*
28. See *ibid.*
29. See Bahgat, *supra* n. 23.
30. See *ibid.*
31. See Roberts, *supra* n. 11.

Often tankers are held up for weeks due to inclement weather and traffic, resulting in the disruption of supply.[32] The BTC pipeline avoids this entire problem and enhances the security of supply of oil[33] in the international market.[34]

The BTC pipeline has also increased competition for pipeline access in the area (e.g., the Northern Route Export Pipeline (NREP), Baku–Novorossiysk and Baku–Supsa pipeline). This will result in lower access fees and greater competition which in turn might reduce the delivery cost of oil in the international market making it beneficial for the consumers.[35] Pipeline owners also have to pay attention to increased exploration activities and enhanced oil recovery (EOR) to increase reserves and maintain the current full capacity operation of the pipeline.[36]

### 5.3.2.   THE INTERESTS OF THE THREE COUNTRIES

The three countries through which the pipeline passes also benefit immensely from the project as it serves their individual interests. There was an initial investment of USD 20 billion towards infrastructure development and hydro-carbon resources in the area.[37] The overall economic revenue in these countries is said to have amounted to about USD 262 million.[38] The building of the pipeline resulted in the employment of 10,000 people and the spending for goods and services within Turkey, Azerbaijan and Georgia amounted to USD 4.8 billion with USD 200 million for the construction and operation phase respectively.[39] All these factors had a positive impact on the economy of these countries and resulted in greater regional cooperation and integrity on top of the benefit these countries accrued from the building of the pipeline.[40]

### 5.3.3.   THE LEGAL ASPECTS

The legal aspects of the pipeline stem from the fact that the objectives and jurisdictions of the three countries are different, resulting in greater cooperation and

---

32. See Roberts, *supra* n. 11.
33. There might be a commodity or pipe issue here, but the focus is simply on the pipe and not the commodity.
34. See A. Seck, 'Pipelines from Central Asia and the Transcaucases: A Maze of Alternatives', in *Boundaries and Energy: Problems and Prospects*, ed. Blake, G., et al. (Kluwer, 1998).
35. See F. Weir, *Oil Pipeline Sparks Controversy in Poor Georgian Village*, Alexander's Gas & Oil Connections, <www.gasandoil.com/gol/news/ntr41095.htm>.
36. See *ibid.*
37. See Z. Baran, *The Baku–Tbilisi–Ceyhan Pipeline: Implications for Turkey*, Central Asia–Caucasus Institute, Silk Road Studies Program, available on the Internet via <www.silkroadstudies.org/BTC_6.pdf>.
38. See Roberts, *supra* n. 11.
39. See Baran, *supra* n. 38.
40. See *ibid.*

harmonization between the various countries.[41] The lack of a stable legal framework and proper implementation and enforcement of the various rules and regulations of the contract caused problems for the various parties involved in the project. For example, there were cases brought against the pipeline company in relation to the human rights abuses and allegations of land acquisitions without proper compensation resulting in courts giving verdicts asking the pipeline company to pay compensation, which the company declined to.[42] This resulted in pipeline disruption which forced the government to intervene.[43]

However, despite the agreements signed between the parties,[44] the government is the party in the pipeline which has the ultimate task of enforcing the various clauses of the obligations. The other parties who have signed the agreement look up to them to ensure their rights are protected. Despite all the guarantees provided by the government, there are still chances that they might directly intervene in pipeline matters if it affects their geo-political, legal or economic interests.[45] In that scenario, there is very little the other parties could do to protect themselves from government intervention other than depending upon some other clauses in the contract or agreement or going to some other institution or body to resolve the dispute.[46] The problem is that it takes considerable time to mitigate disputes and the parties who have invested in the project might not have time on their hands as they would be losing money if they do not renegotiate with the government or other actors causing the disruption.

### 5.3.4.    THE GEO-POLITICS OF THE PIPELINE

The geo-political dimension of the BTC pipeline also adds to its importance in the region. According to some experts, without political will the BTC pipeline might not have seen the light of day.[47] The interest of the various Western nations towards the pipeline makes the situation more complex. The pipeline was built in order to avoid Russian and Iranian influence in the region and the three countries involved in the pipeline are all pro-Western.[48]

The pipeline route chosen by the various parties involved in the project and the transit problems it might create was one of the major stumbling blocks towards the

---

41. See M. Ogutcu, 'Caspian Energy and Legal Disputes: Prospects for Settlement', OGEL 1, no. 2 (2003).
42. See *ibid.*
43. See *ibid.*
44. This means the IGAs and HGAs signed between the parties.
45. The example given in the last paragraph where the government got involved shows this fact because if the government didn't get involved then the pipeline operator might have had to pay the compensation. However, that might have gone against the government's interest as the pipeline disruption hurt the government's economic interest. The investors also want to renegotiate to solve the problem.
46. See Ogutcu, *supra* n. 42.
47. See R. Kandiyoti, *Pipelines: Flowing Oil and Crude Politics*, I B Tauris and Co Ltd, 2007.
48. See *ibid.*

successful implementation of the project.[49] The Iranian option seemed economically to be the most effective route while the Russian route could also have been chosen.[50] However, the US sanctions towards Iran and increased pressure on the Russian pipeline network together with other Western interests involved with the project made the BTC pipeline the most feasible option available, although there were strong economic concerns regarding it.[51]

## 5.4. THE APPLICATION OF THE CRITERIA ON THE CROSS-BORDER PIPELINE REGIME

### 5.4.1. THE NATURE AND CHARACTERISTICS OF THE REGIME

The main players in the BTC pipeline are Azerbaijan, Turkey and Georgia as they are the exporting, importing and the transit countries. The pipeline regime is important for all the players involved as it serves their own individual interests as well as the other countries who are reliant on the gas flowing through the pipelines.[52] Although Azerbaijan is the most important country because it provides the oil, the role of the other two players cannot be underestimated as without them Azerbaijan might not have been able to use this route to export its hydro-carbon resources.[53] The roles of all three major players are important in the successful operation of this pipeline.

The BTC pipeline project is based upon four key agreements signed between the various parties. They are the IGA signed between the parties involved in the project, HGA, the Turnkey Agreement and the Turkish Government Guaranty. The IGA among the Republic of Turkey, The Republic of Azerbaijan and Georgia was signed to formalize the different responsibilities of various parties involved in the project. The agreement sets out the principles based upon which transit would be allowed, advocates the principle of non-discriminatory treatment, harmonization of the legal framework and the implementation of the supranational regulatory rules.[54] The agreements also supply the provision for the setting up an intergovernmental commission to facilitate the implementation of the various clauses of the agreement.[55] However, government still has the scope to intervene if any of its geo-political, legal and economic interests are affected by the actions of the other members of the pipeline regime.

---

49. See *ibid.*
50. See *ibid.*
51. See *ibid.*
52. See *ibid.*
53. See *ibid.*
54. See Roberts, *supra* n. 11.
55. See the Intergovernmental Agreement between the Republic of Turkey, the Azerbaijan Republic and Georgia relating to the transportation of petroleum via the Baku Tbilisi Ceyhan Main Export Pipeline, 1999, can be found at <www.caspiandevelopmentandexport.com>.

In the BTC pipeline project, the IGA and HGA agreements act as a conduit which helps to guide the actions of various parties. The IGA has clauses which act as principles and rules controlling the actions of parties involved in the project. For example, Article VIII of the IGAs says that in case of any conflict the parties would go for private international arbitration as agreed between the parties.[56] However, this allows the parties to seek arbitration if they want to in case of any conflict without being specific. A more specific rule within the agreement would be Article VI of the IGA which mentions that 'the states hereby establish a commission consisting of two representatives from each state to oversee compliance with and facilitate the implementation of the agreement'.[57] This kind of unambiguity in rule making has resemblance in the formation of a regime. The intergovernmental commission set up to overlook the project is also run under certain regime principles as its role is to implement the different clauses set out in the contract.

The BTC pipeline is a moderately strong regime, as it follows all the rules and principles which are important regime credentials. It also has the enforcement mechanism to ensure that the actors involved in the regime abide by their obligations. However, the intergovernmental commission mentioned previously, does not play an active role in solving disputes between the players in the regime and there has not been an instance with the pipeline where they have shown independence and power to solve disputes between the parties.[58] Although they form an essential part of the regime because without their presence it would be difficult for the regime to oversee the activities of its members, they have not been able to enforce and ensure that the actors complied with their various obligations. For example, the BTC pipeline owners are from nine different countries as this was done to spread risks and raise capital and as a result each individual owner had their objectives and interests.[59] BP, for instance, being the operator puts the maintenance cost within the life time of the pipeline, which was not supported by the others as they saw it as BP's own self-interest rather than the collective interest of all.[60] The intergovernmental commission as a result failed to solve the conflict of interest between the owners resulting in the head of the three governments to intervene.[61] This results in greater opportunity for the government to intervene in order to protect their own interest rather than the interest of the regime as a whole.

---

56. See *ibid.*
57. See *ibid.*
58. The reason for this statement is because over the last couple of years (between 2006–2010) the intergovernmental commission has hardly been seen to lessen disputes between the various parties and there is very little evidence of the commission trying to ensure that the various stakeholders are abiding by their obligations. Further reading: See M. Crandall, *Energy, Economics and Politics in the Caspian Region: Dreams and Realities* (Praeger International, 2006).
59. See S. Malececk, *Pipeline Tranist States: How Can the Legal Regime Meet Investor Objectives and Internal Development needs? The Case of Georgia and Caspian Exports*, 2001.
60. See Kandiyoti, *supra* n. 48.
61. See *ibid.*

The BTC pipeline regime is a mixture of both neo-realist and neo-liberal tendencies. The cooperation among various entities in the pipeline chain despite some actors gaining more than others is a sign of neo-liberalism. According to neo-liberalism, power might be necessary for the formation of a regime but as long as different members have different interests and all advocate for collaboration amongst themselves for relative rather than absolute gain, all the actors would benefit from it. In fact, one of the clauses of the IGA mentions that 'each state shall cooperate and coordinate with the others and the applicable project investors in the formulation and establishment of uniform technical, safety and environmental standards for the construction, repair and replacement according to international standards . . .'.[62] This quite clearly shows the neo-liberal ethos as discussed previously, requiring all the actors to cooperate with each other for the ultimate goal, in this case the smooth running of the pipeline for everyone's benefit.

There are also some neo-realist tendencies present in the pipeline agreements. The fact that each state takes the responsibility for allowing transit through their territory rather than relinquishing the area that the pipeline covers shows the power transit states can have in this regard. According to neo-realists, in a regime there is always a possibility of some states gaining more than the other, while the state with most power will tend to gain most from any regime framework. A powerful hegemony or a player with a great power in a regime tends to achieve more than the rest, however, they too believe in mutual interest. In this case, Georgia and Turkey are the two most important transit countries who play a very important role in the transfer of oil to other parts of the world.[63] Turkey, due to its size and military strength, has a greater influence in the pipeline chain because of its geo-strategic position.[64]

## 5.4.2.   THE ISSUES AFFECTING THE CROSS-BORDER PIPELINE

The economic aspect of the BTC pipeline is closely linked to the geo-politics of the region and it also affects the pipeline chain. Terrorist attacks on the pipeline are quite common and, in August 2008, Kurdish separatists blew up part of the pipeline passing through Kurdistan.[65] As a result, the pipeline was shut for a few days by BP and they were also forced to cancel all shipments due to the damage done to the pipeline. The Russia–Georgia conflict in 2008 also caused disruption in the supply of oil, as part of the pipeline was affected due to Russian aerial bombing.[66]

---

62. See the Intergovernmental Agreement between the Republic of Turkey, the Azerbaijan Republic and Georgia relating to the transportation of petroleum via the Baku Tbilisi Ceyhan Main Export Pipeline, 1999, can be found at <www.caspiandevelopmentandexport.com>.
63. See L. Schaefer, *The BTC Pipeline: A Beacon of Hope or Suffering for the People?* (Covalence SA, 2006).
64. See *ibid.*
65. See Stratfor (2008), can be accessed via <www.stratfor.com>.
66. See *ibid.*

This conflict halted the alternative Azerbaijan–Georgia transit routes together with the 550 mile Baku–Supsa line, as well as the maritime oil exports from the Georgian Black sea ports of Poti, Batumi and Kulevi.[67]

The BTC also has all its pumping stations above ground together with their electrical grids. Moreover, half of the BTC pipeline passes through a Kurdish area which makes it an easy target for the separatists willing to take revenge on the Turkish Government.[68] The Kurdistan Workers Party (PKK's) chief also mentioned that 'if PKK forces in Northern Iraq were attacked, his group would assault Turkish Oil targets, since they bring huge amounts of money to Turkey'.[69] This could be termed as a breach of legitimate expectation for the stakeholders involved in the pipeline, as the government could not provide the security they guaranteed during the signing of the agreement.[70]

The closure of the BTC pipeline due to these two incidents have caused Turkey to lose USD 300,000 a day in transit revenues and it also had a negative impact on its domestic supply.[71] These incidents have also caused the port to deplete its stockpiled oil.[72] Georgia also suffered through the conflict as it could not earn the transit revenue due to the conflict.[73] This conflict also caused the suspension of shipments from Batumi of about 200,000 bpd of oil and of 100,000 bpd of oil by rail from Poti.[74] It also raised concerns about Georgia's status as a safe transit country because the conflict with Russia made the importing countries worried about their energy supplies.[75] Azerbaijan also faced loss due to the closure of the pipeline.

Another important issue affecting the pipelines is that due to the geo-political problems and conflicts mentioned above, the profitability of the BTC project is now reliant on oil from Kazakhstan instead of Azerbaijan with 3 million tonnes being exported via BTC in 2008 and 7.5 million tonnes thereafter.[76] This is despite assurances from the stakeholders that Azerbaijani oil would be enough to fulfil demand over the next forty years.[77] As a result, the legitimate expectation of Turkey from this venture is under threat as Azerbaijan could not provide the

---

67. See *ibid.*
68. See *ibid.*
69. See *ibid.*
70. See the Intergovernmental Agreement between the Republic of Turkey, the Azerbaijan Republic and Georgia relating to the transportation of petroleum via the Baku Tbilisi Ceyhan Main Export Pipeline, 1999, can be found at <www.caspiandevelopmentandexport.com>.
71. See C.K. Daly, John, *Analysis: BTC Pipeline Explosion*, UPI.com, 2008. This can be accessed via <www.upi.com/Energy_Resources/2008/08/06/Analysis-BTC-pipeline-explosion/UPI-36081218062760/>.
72. See *ibid.*
73. See *ibid.*
74. See *ibid.*
75. See *ibid.*
76. See Eurasia Daily Monitor, *Turkey and the Problems with BTC*, vol 5, Issue 155, August 2008.
77. See *ibid.*

required amount of oil as originally agreed between the parties.[78] This will also cause further environmental and economic strains on the partners involved in the project.[79] These problems have encouraged the governments of these countries to interfere to protect their own economic interest causing further strain on the regulatory features of the pipeline regime.

The opening of the BTC pipeline was also mired with lawsuits from people affected by the pipeline. Lawsuits were brought to Azerbaijan and Georgian courts in 2005, were the claimants have asked for compensation.[80] The allegations resulted from land acquisitions made by the Georgian and Azerbaijan governments which affected the livelihoods of people living in the area.[81] These lawsuits made the stakeholders extremely wary because they had the potential to disrupt the flow of oil. Moreover, BP, one of the operators of the pipeline, was also accused of violations in appropriating land and for inadequate compensation to the farmers.[82] There have also been allegations of environmental damage in the area which might cause an ecological imbalance in the region.[83] These legal problems affected the pipeline as there was negative international publicity regarding the pipeline which made the importing countries and other international lenders think twice about continuing to be involved.[84] It also forced the government of these two countries to intervene in order to protect themselves in local courts and also from the other partners involved in the project.[85]

The geo-political and legal problems highlighted by this case study shows that the current regime of regulatory mechanism is not robust enough to deal with the problems faced by the actors involved in the regime.

### 5.4.3.  COMMON INTEREST OF THE PARTIES

The interests of many parties are involved in the building of the BTC pipeline. Although there are three countries involved in the pipeline chain, there are other actors who also benefit from the pipeline being built. Azerbaijan is the exporting country, Georgia the transit country and Turkey is a transit country as well as an importing country consuming some of the oil passing through its territory. As a result, all of these actors have a common interest in mind which benefits all of them to some extent.

Azerbaijan is heavily reliant on its oil exports and being landlocked made it more desperate to find new ways of transporting its oil to other parts of the world to

---

78. See Daly, *supra* n. 72.
79. See Eurasia Daily Monitor, *supra* n. 77.
80. See Schaefer, *supra* n. 64.
81. See Eurasia Daily Monitor, *supra* n. 77.
82. See Schaefer, *supra* n. 64.
83. See *ibid.*
84. See Roberts, *supra* n. 11.
85. See *ibid.*

earn much needed foreign currency.[86] Although the obvious option was to transport its oil through Russia there was always the chance of Russia not being a stable transit country and since Russia itself is also a producer, there was the possibility of Azeri oil rivalling the Russian market.[87] Therefore, choosing that route might not have been economically beneficial to the country. In addition, the pro-Western policy of the country was not liked by Russia, who sees the Caspian as its regional domain.[88] However, Azerbaijan also wanted to be less reliant on Russia and the BTC pipeline route allowed it to align itself to the West and to reap the economic benefits that came with it.

The Georgian motive for acting as a transit country was to earn the economic benefits that came with joining the pipeline and also to align itself with the West by being a safe and reliable transit country.[89] Georgia was also sceptical and worried about the role of Russia in the region and its constant attention and interest focused on Georgia. By being pro-Western, Georgia was under the impression that they would be under Western support in time of need.[90] The recent war with Russia further highlights their anxiousness in this regard and also heightened Western concerns about Georgia's stability as a transit country in supplying their energy needs.[91]

Turkey too had a strong interest in being a part of this pipeline. The country was already a NATO member and was interested in joining the EU. Turkey was also in need of energy and had the intention of being considered the energy hub of the region. It would have also helped their case for joining the EU becoming a safe and stable partner for securing the EU's energy interests in the region.[92] Economically, the country has benefited from joining the pipeline as it is earning a considerable amount of foreign currency from it.[93] The country also had a regional ambition, as it wanted to become a regional power and by being involved in the pipeline they were not only able to enhance their status as a stable Western ally but also a credible transit country.

According to the neo-liberal school of thought actors tend to join a regime when there is a common interest and all the parties tend to gain from it even if the benefits are not the same. In this case, all the actors have their own motive for joining the pipeline but some, like Georgia or even Turkey, are gaining more than Azerbaijan. Georgia, for example, is earning a substantial amount of

---

86. See M. Crandall, *Energy, Economics, & Politics in the Caspian Region: dreams and realities*, Praeger, 2006.
87. See *ibid.*
88. See *ibid.*
89. See *ibid.*
90. See P. Freedenberg, et al., 'BTC Explosion and the Russian and Georgian War: How Big a Threat to Caspian Oil Exports?', CERA (2008).
91. See *ibid.*
92. See *ibid.*
93. See *ibid.*

foreign currency without investing anything in the project.[94] This kind of attitude is, according to neo-liberals, normal as long as all the parties are happy with the contribution of others in the regime and are satisfied with their respective gains.

The neo-realists, however, consider the effect of regime only beneficial to the actor with power and who can act as a hegemony. According to them there is always a chance of some of the actors cheating on their fellow regime members. They also point out that states are more interested in relative gains rather than absolute gains because larger gains can sometimes lead to confrontation.[95] From this perspective the actors involved in the BTC pipeline are not really confrontational or worried about the gains each party is making. Although some are gaining more than another, they are not overly worried about the fact that in order to preserve their self-interest some might gain more.

Another important aspect of the pipeline is that although the BTC pipeline was not really the natural choice of architects, it was more of a political pipeline than a commercially viable one.[96] However, due to the political will of the countries involved in the project, especially the US, the project has become a success so far.[97] However, the US acted like a hegemony making sure that the pipeline was built bypassing Iran and Russia to serve their own regional interests.[98] The actions of the US are more neo-realist in nature because it used its power and influence to carry out any actions required to get their own way, in this case, the building of the pipeline.

The BTC pipeline is therefore the amalgamation of the interests of all the actors involved in the project as well as outside powers who had their own self-interest in the project. The three countries involved have a common interest to maintain the pipeline without any disruption and they are also aware of the ramifications of any disruptions caused in the pipeline which would affect their own self interests.

5.4.4.      The Enforcement and Compliance of the Cross-Border
             Pipeline Agreements

The enforcement and compliance mechanism of a pipeline is extremely important for any pipeline regime. This is because if there is any dispute between the stakeholders involved then there has to be a way to mitigate those problems. There is also a need to find out whether the various actors involved in the project are

---

94. See *ibid.*
95. Middle East Economic Survey (MEES), *US Opposed to Any Pipeline Crossing Iran*, vol. XL, no. 43, 1997. Also see Crandall, *supra* n. 87.
96. See Crandall, *supra* n. 87.
97. See *ibid.*
98. See *ibid.*

carrying out their duties according to the agreements signed between the countries involved in the pipeline network.

The creation of the intergovernmental commission to look after the implementation and supervision of the different clauses of the agreement serves the purpose of all the actors well as it is there to enforce the agreement signed by all the parties.[99] It also serves as one of the regime principles, as regimes which are effective tend to have a strong enforcement and implementation mechanism to ensure that all the parties within a regime benefit from joining it. In the case of the BTC pipelines, it seems the commission has not been effective as they did not manage to solve the problems arising due to all the stakeholders unwillingness to share the cost of the pipeline maintenance along with BP.[100] The commission also could not deal with the legal proceedings brought against the pipeline company by people affected by the pipeline, which caused disruption and was eventually solved through government intervention.[101] This could be a breach of legitimate expectation as the regulatory body could not deal with the disputes expected of them under the agreements signed by the parties.

The role of the agreements and the intergovernmental commission is more neo-liberal in nature as the parties are cooperating to achieve their common aim of solving any disputes which might take place between the actors involved in the project. This objective can only be achieved through the proper implementation and enforcement of the various clauses of the agreement and by less interference from the government.


5.5.          THE WEST AFRICAN GAS PIPELINE (WAGP)

5.5.1.        THE BACKGROUND OF THE PROJECT

The plan to build the WAGP pipeline was first conceived in 1982 at the conference of the Economic Community of West African States (ECOWAS).[102] After the feasibility study was carried out by the World Bank regarding its commercial viability in the 1990s, the governments of Nigeria, Ghana, Benin and Togo signed agreements for the pipeline to begin building work in the early part of 2005.[103] However, after repeated delays due to technical and other unforeseen problems the pipeline finally started delivering gas in December 2007 (Figure 5.3).

---

99. See *ibid.*
100. See Kandiyoti, *supra* n. 48. Also see the 'the nature and characteristics of the regime' section of this chapter for more examples of the regulatory body's failures.
101. See Kandiyoti, *supra* n. 48.
102. See G.S. Akpan et al., 'The West African Oil and Gas Pipeline Project: Problems and Prospects', OGEL 2, no. 1 (February 2004). This can be accessed via <www.gasandoil.com>.
103. See the IGAs signed between Nigeria, Ghana, Benin and Togo, 2005.

*Figure 5.3    The WAGP Route*[104]

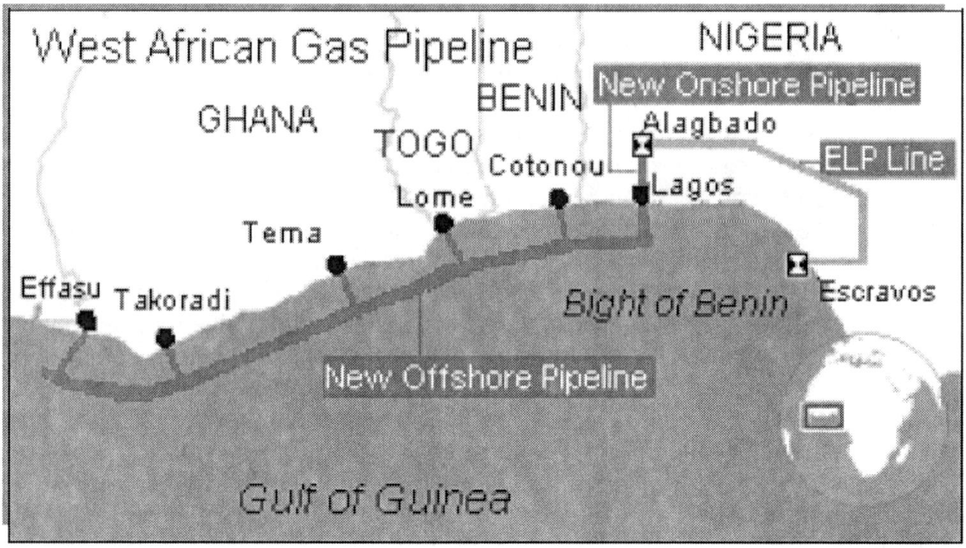

West African Gas Pipeline      NIGERIA

GHANA     BENIN   New Onshore Pipeline

TOGO   Cotonou   Alagbado

Lome    ELP Line

Tema    Lagos

Effasu Takoradi    *Bight of Benin*   Escravos

New Offshore Pipeline

*Gulf of Guinea*

*Source*: Energy Information Administration website at <www.eia.org>.

The WAGP is 680 kilometres long; it starts in Nigeria and snakes both onshore and offshore before delivering the gas to Ghana.[105] The onshore part of the pipeline starts at Alagbado, on the outskirts of Lagos, and reaches the Lagos beach, where an 18,000 horsepower onshore compression station has been installed.[106] Offshore pipelines then extend for 560 kilometres from Lagos beach to Takoradi, Ghana and continues for another 80 kilometres before reaching its final destination in Effasu, Ghana.[107] The WAGP pipeline also connects with the Escravos–Lagos pipeline which is owned by the Nigeria Gas company, which is a subsidiary of the Nigerian National Petroleum Corporation.[108]

The original plan was to transport 120 mcf/d of gas to Ghana, Benin and Togo with the option to further increase the transportation of gas depending upon demand.[109] In 2007, 150 mcf/d gas was transported with the plan to increase it to 210 mcf/d in 2014 and then 400 mcf/d by 2020.[110] However, in order to deliver

---

104. This diagram of the pipeline is provided to give a broader picture of the pipeline passing two transit countries and also its starting points. It is important to know the terrain the pipeline is passing in order to understand the geo-political and economic implications.
105. See Akpan, *supra* n. 103.
106. See *ibid.*
107. See *ibid.*
108. See *ibid.*
109. See E. Omonbude, *How Feasible is a West African Market for Natural Gas?* (Unpublished) Post Graduate Dissertation, CEPMLP, University of Dundee, 2002.
110. See *ibid.*

this increasing amount of gas, there has to be development in the power facilities of these four countries.[111]

### 5.5.2.    THE PARTIES OF THE PROJECT

The governments of the four countries involved in the project set up a public–private partnership company called the West African Gas Pipeline Limited Company (WAPCO), which was granted the right to develop, construct, own and operate the pipeline.[112] The major stakeholders of the company and participants of the project are: ChevronTexaco 36.7%, Nigerian National Petroleum Corporation 25%, Shell Petroleum Development Company 18%, Volta River Authority (VRA) 16.3 %, SoBeGaz 2% and SoToGaz 2%.[113]

### 5.5.3.    THE COST OF THE PROJECT

The total cost of the WAGP project was about USD 600 million.[114] The shareholders of the project financed on the basis of a gas purchase contract with the VRA of Ghana, who receive 90% of the gas, followed by Communaute Electrique du Benin of Benin and Togo receiving the remaining 10%.[115] The Nigerian government gave a loan of USD 40 million to the Ghanaian Government to complete their part of the pipeline project.[116]

The World Bank also assisted with USD 125 million while the International Development Association, another arm of the World Bank, guaranteed USD 50 million for twenty-two years.[117] The World Bank's MIGA provided the political risk insurance of USD 75 million.[118] The project was also financed by USID with USD 1.5 million and the Overseas Private Investment Corporation (OPIC) providing a further USD 45 million in reinsurance to one of the stakeholders involved.[119]

### 5.5.4.    OTHER ASPECTS OF THE PIPELINE

The main goal of the WAGP project was to substitute natural gas from Nigeria for alternate fuels used by the power, industrial and mining sectors in Ghana, Togo and

---

111.  See World Bank Project Appraisal Document on WAGP Report No. 30335, 2 Nov. 2004.
112.  See Omonbude, *supra* n. 110.
113.  See Akpan, *supra* n. 103.
114.  See M. Karikpo, *Negotiating Resource Sovereignty, Fueling Conflicts: The Case of West African Gas Pipeline Project*, can be accessed via <www.eraction.org/publications/presentations/negotiating_resource_sovereignty.pdf>.
115.  See *ibid.*
116.  See Friends of Earth International (FOEI), *The myths of West African Gas Pipeline*, 2006, can be accessed via <www.foei.org/en/publications/pdfs/wagp-inet.pdf/view>.
117.  See *ibid.*
118.  See *ibid.*
119.  See *ibid.*

the Benin Republic.[120] The World Bank terms this project the Regional Integration Assistance Strategy (RIAS).[121] This project would also help the West African Power Pool Project.[122] Another reason for the involvement of the World Bank is because the pipeline would increase greater regional harmony among the countries of Western Africa which in turn would improve the regional legal and fiscal aspects of these countries.[123]

The heads of government of these four countries signed a Memorandum of Understanding in 1995, establishing the legal framework based upon which the WAGP would be operated.[124] The legal aspects of the WAGP include a Joint Venture Agreement naming Chevron as the WAGP project manager, an IGA and administrative support from the ECOWAS.[125] The treaty between the four countries was signed in 2003, for a period of twenty years, and provides legal, regulatory and other important aspects of the pipeline.[126]

The agreement between the four countries also establishes the West African Gas Pipeline Authority (WAGPA), which would be considered as a separate legal entity.[127] The main function of this entity would be to monitor and regulate the various activities of WAPCO and also to ensure that the company abides by the various obligations within the agreement.[128]

It is also estimated that the pipeline project created 10,000–20,000 primary sector jobs and increased secondary jobs threefold.[129] The World Bank has estimated that Benin, Togo and Ghana can save up to USD 500 million in energy costs over a period of twenty years.[130] Furthermore, there was an investment of USD 1 billion in the region which came along with the pipeline investment that further fuelled growth in these countries.[131,132]

---

120. See Karikpo, *supra* n. 115.
121. See World Bank Project Appraisal Document on WAGP Report No. 30335, 2 Nov. 2004.
122. See Omonbude, *supra* n. 110.
123. See World Bank, *supra* n. 122.
124. See the Memorandum of Understanding signed between the Republic of Nigeria, Ghana, Benin and Togo, 1995.
125. See Akpan, *supra* n. 103.
126. See the Treaty on the WAGP Project between the Republic of Benin, Republic of Ghana, Federal Republic of Nigeria and The Togolese Republic, 2003.
127. See Akpan, *supra* n. 103.
128. See *ibid.*
129. See E. Duruigbo, 'Permanent Sovereignty and Peoples Ownership of Natural Resources', *Washington Law Review* (2006).
130. See *ibid.*
131. See Akpan, *supra* n. 103.
132. Moreover, the recent discovery of new gas in Ghana could also propel the government to interfere more as it will have more bargaining power and would want to protect its interest more if there is any disruption.

5.6.    THE IMPORTANT ASPECTS OF THE PIPELINE

5.6.1.    ECONOMIC ASPECT

One of the important aspects of the WAGP pipeline is that it would supply the entire demand for gas needed by the Volta Authority in Ghana.[133] However, there is some scepticism regarding the demand for gas in Ghana, Togo and Benin as, according to some experts, the demand and use of gas in these three countries does not warrant the need for pipeline gas to be delivered to these countries.[134] There would be a lot of unused gas in the pipeline and the pipeline would be functioning below its actual capacity resulting in lower profits for the stakeholders involved in the project.[135] The low level of energy consumption in these countries can cause problems for all the stakeholders involved in the project.[136]

Another interesting aspect is the ability of the Volta Authority to pay for the gas that is being delivered to them. The Volta Authority used to import gas from Cote d'Ivoire and the gas supply was stopped after they failed to repay their debts.[137] One of the reasons why the Volta Authority failed to repay its debt was because of the gas pricing policy in Ghana.[138] Gas prices are heavily subsidized by the government resulting in a lack of investment and profit in this sector.[139] According to some experts, a question also arises regarding the capability of Ghanaian people to pay for their pipeline gas, which will be priced higher than before, and this might result in lower gas consumption.[140] As a result if Ghana fails to pay for the gas that is being imported from Nigeria, then they will be in breach of Nigeria's legitimate expectation under the agreement signed between the parties.

The pipeline is supposed to lower the level of gas flaring in Nigeria as the associated gas released from the oil wells would be used in the WAGP pipeline.[141] However, currently, no infrastructure exists at present in the pipeline to do so and the existing Lagos–Escravos pipeline, which is part of the WAGP pipeline, is in a dilapidated condition which might disrupt the flow of gas to Ghana.[142]

5.6.2.    THE INTERESTS OF THE COUNTRIES

Ghana's interest involves securing a supply of gas for its industries and electricity companies in order to carry on its impressive economic growth.[143] Its current

---

133.    See Duruigbo, *supra* n. 130.
134.    See *ibid.*
135.    See *ibid.*
136.    See *ibid.*
137.    See Akpan, *supra* n. 103.
138.    See Duruigbo, *supra* n. 130.
139.    See *ibid.*
140.    See *ibid.*
141.    See Omonbude, *supra* n. 110.
142.    See *ibid.*
143.    See *ibid.*

reliance on oil and other fuels has made the establishment in Ghana transfer to cheaper alternatives and lower their dependency on oil.[144] The WAGP pipeline was built to satisfy the energy needs of Ghana, as they are the main buyers of this gas.[145] The pipeline gas is essential for Ghana's power sector and would greatly enhance their reputation as a stable country in West Africa.

Benin and Togo are the two transit countries in the pipeline chain and they are also to gain from allowing the pipeline to pass through their country. This is because they are to receive a certain amount of gas for their own use, which would greatly enhance their economic growth.[146] Their main interest is to benefit from the pipeline gas passing through their territory and also to have good relations with their neighbours. Nigeria would earn a substantial amount of money by exporting the gas to Ghana. It would also help the country to solve its gas flaring problem.[147] However, internal problems within the country may undermine the project, as most of the population in the country are without gas supplies.[148] The WAGP project also allows Nigeria to show its authority in the region, and in the continent as a whole, which might have a positive effect at home.[149]

### 5.6.3. THE LEGAL ASPECT

The treaty between the four countries mentions the legal and regulatory aspects of the WAGP pipeline.[150] However, divergent legal systems in all the countries at first caused a few problems for the stakeholders involved in the project. For example, Ghana and Nigeria are common law countries whereas Benin and Togo follow civil law systems.[151] Further weak legal systems and instability in some of these countries has caused distress to some of the partners involved in the project. There were problems in Nigeria regarding the right of way for pipelines and the appropriate compensation for people who allowed the pipeline to pass through their property.[152] This resulted in lawsuits against the various partners in the project causing them distress.[153]

There were also environmental concerns raised against the Nigerian government regarding the environmental safety in the Niger delta region, which has resulted in lawsuits being served against the pipeline stakeholders and the

---

144. See *ibid.*
145. See FOEI, *supra* n. 117.
146. See *ibid.*
147. See Omonbude, *supra* n. 110.
148. See *ibid.*
149. See FOEI, *supra* n. 117.
150. See the Treaty on the WAGP Project between the Republic of Benin, Republic of Ghana, Federal Republic of Nigeria and The Togolese Republic, 2003.
151. See Akpan, *supra* n. 103.
152. See *ibid.*
153. See *ibid.*

government.[154] The legal factors discussed above are the reasons why the Nigerian government intervenes to protect their own interest as it wants to lower the amount of compensation that it has to pay and also protect its credibility in any lawsuit being brought on environmental grounds.[155] As a result, instead of the regulatory body handling these legal issues, the government becomes directly involved rather than simply acting in its capacity as a member in the pipeline regime, resulting in greater government intervention which might not be supported by the other members of the pipeline regime.

5.6.4.          THE GEO-POLITICS OF THE PIPELINE

The countries involved in the project have their own interests in mind while the Western donors and multinational donor agencies also want greater harmony and regional integrity between all the West African nations.[156] Another reason they were involved in the project was to create a single integrated energy network in West Africa.[157] The WAGP was built primarily for that reason and it is said that it is more of a political pipeline than a financially viable one.[158] However, Nigeria and Ghana are two important West African countries and the Western countries are interested in seeing greater cooperation and understanding between them for regional prosperity. Nigeria would like to dominate the region politically and through the ECOWAS and WAGP project it is able to increase its influence in the region.[159]

5.6.5.          THE TRANSIT ROUTE

The transit route chosen for the WAGP pipeline is the most feasible one as without the cooperation of both Benin and Togo the WAGP pipeline could not have been implemented.[160] The WAGP pipeline is also important for both these countries as they would be able to off-take some of the gas passing through the country and they are also partners in the WAGP project. The two countries also require a substantial amount of gas to develop their power sector and this opportunity allows them to tackle some of those problems.[161] There are also plans to extend the pipeline up to Cote d'Ivoire but nothing has been decided in that regard.

---

154. See Duruigbo, *supra* n. 130.
155. See *ibid.*
156. See World Bank, *supra* n. 122.
157. See *ibid.*
158. See FOEI, *supra* n. 117.
159. See *ibid.*
160. See Duruigbo, *supra* n. 130.
161. See *ibid.*

5.7.     THE APPLICATION OF THE CRITERIA FOR THE
         CROSS-BORDER PIPELINE REGIME

5.7.1.     THE NATURE AND CHARACTERISTICS OF THE REGIME

The major players in the WAGP are Nigeria, Ghana, Benin and Togo. Nigeria is
the exporting country and Ghana is the importing country whereas Benin and
Togo are the two transit countries through which the pipeline passes. Of the four,
Nigeria is the most influential player because the gas comes from Nigeria and this
country has made substantial amounts of investment in the pipeline project.[162]
Ghana too has an interest in the pipeline as it will be receiving the gas and would
be reliant on this import. The roles of the two transit countries are also important
but they are smaller players compared to the other two, Ghana and Nigeria, who
are also regional powers who formed the regime for the successful operation of
the pipeline.[163] The other two entities, WAPCO and WAGPA, are responsible for
running and enforcing the various rules and also play an important part in the
pipeline regime.

The WAGP pipeline is based on the various IGAs and HGAs signed by the
four countries involved in the pipeline project.[164] The parties signed a memorandum of understanding in 1995 and agreements in 2001. These agreements between
the parties have also resulted in the creation of the WAGPA which is a separate
legal entity.[165] The main function of WAGPA is to look after the activities of the
WAPCO which is responsible for the operation of the pipeline and is the entity in
charge of the smooth functioning of the pipeline.[166] WAPCO is also responsible for
taking decisions regarding the pipeline and the joint venture company is made up
of all the stakeholders involved in the pipeline chain.[167]

The WAGPA and WAPCO are the two entities responsible for the smooth
running of the pipeline. There are certain regime principles and rules in these two
regimes which make them act as one entity. The main principle of WAGPA is to
ensure that the pipeline is run in accordance with the rules and regulations agreed
by all the stakeholders.[168] Some of the rules that WAGPA oversees are: monitor
the compliance by the company of its obligations under the International Project
Agreement, negotiate and agree with the company the terms of amendments to the
conditions on which Pipeline Licenses are granted and give the company notice in

---

162.  See Akpan, *supra* n. 103.
163.  See *ibid.*
164.  See the IGAs were signed between Nigeria, Ghana, Benin and Togo whereas the HGAs were
      signed between Chevron and The World Bank with the governments of Nigeria and Ghana.
      Other foreign companies involved in the project have also signed agreements with the
      Nigerian and Ghanaian Governments.
165.  See Akpan, *supra* n. 103.
166.  See *ibid.*
167.  See *ibid.*
168.  See Article IV of the WAGP Treaty, available at <www.wagp.org>.

case of failure to abide by its obligations under the agreements.[169] Although WAGPA cannot take any decision with regard to the running of the pipeline, their main objective is to oversee the activities of WAPCO. WAPCO, however, is responsible for the implementation of the rules and regulations in the day-to-day operation of the pipeline and to ensure that the pipeline achieves the objectives set by the various stakeholders who are also part of the company.[170]

The WAGP is a moderately strong regime as it has all the qualities based upon which it can be termed as a regime. However, the various organs of a regime like the WAGPA, which is entrusted with the enforcement and compliance of the regime rules, have not been able to stamp their authority as expected due to a great deal of internal and external pressure from the various stakeholders, which ultimately has a negative impact on the regime.[171] For example, there have been instances when there have been frequent disruption in the supply of gas in the pipeline and despite giving frequent notices to the pipeline company the maintenance problem which caused the disruption was not fixed till the stakeholders (governments) involved in the pipeline got involved.[172] There is also an intergovernmental commission who looks after the various aspects of the pipeline in order to ensure that the actors are abiding by their obligations. However, this commission together with WAGPA has been under constant pressure from the stakeholders involved in the pipeline, resulting in a lack of coordination in their activities.[173]

Furthermore, the WAGP regime has regimes within a regime which might sometimes cause confusion for the stakeholders involved in the pipeline chain, resulting in problems between the stakeholders involved in the pipeline. This might weaken the regime as a whole as the different authorities might not be aware of their individual tasks and goals. For example, the WAGP pipeline has WAPCO that runs the pipeline and WAGPA which monitors their actions. However, WAGPA's role is simply to monitor without having the right to take any punitive actions against any violation of the laws.[174] This weakens the regime as the actors might sometimes disregard the direction given by them, resulting in the breakdown of the regime's authority.

The activities of the actors in the WAGP pipeline regime are closer to a neoliberal ethos as all the actors are willing to cooperate for the smooth running of the pipeline. Although there are two different entities following the various activities of the pipeline, most of the actors in the pipeline regime are willing to cooperate for the benefit of other actors. Although there are some stakeholders who are more powerful than the others, all are willing to make sacrifices for the successful

---

169. See *ibid.*
170. See A. Oluwatosin, *The Future of West African Gas Pipeline Project on Gas Market Development in the West African Sub-Region*, unpublished dissertation, NHH, 2010.
171. See Akpan, *supra* n. 103.
172. See S.R.A. Macaulay, et al., 'West African Gas Pipeline Project: Associated Problems and Possible Remedies', in *Appropriate technologies for Environmental Protection in the Developing World*, ed. Yanful, E. (Springer, 2009).
173. See *ibid.*
174. See *ibid.*

operation of the pipeline as they are more inclined towards relative gain rather than seeking absolute gain over others.

5.7.2.     THE ISSUES AFFECTING THE CROSS-BORDER PIPELINE

The WAGP was supposed to have been in operation from 2005 but following repeated delays the pipeline started functioning towards the end of 2008.[175] However, even after the official start of the pipeline there have been issues with the moisture level in the gas that is being produced which again disrupted the flow of gas towards the beginning of this year.[176] In fact, the gas that is available is wetter than the gas that can be shipped through the pipelines under the contract signed by the various parties. This has caused disruption and has affected Ghana which is dependent upon the gas imported from Nigeria.[177] Ghana has had to import light crude for its Takoradi plant which could not function due to a low water level. This cost Ghana approximately USD 650–700 million in 2007 and 2008.[178] This is a breach of legitimate expectation for Ghana, as Nigeria could not supply the required amount of gas agreed between the parties, resulting in disruption in the pipeline.[179] Nigeria also did not pay any compensation for this breach of legitimate expectation.

There were also problems in the Niger Delta region at the beginning of 2009 which affected the supply of gas in the pipeline.[180] The communities living in the region have alleged that they have not been paid adequate compensation for the pipeline passing through their region and also that it caused environmental pollution which is detrimental to their health.[181] There were instances in 2007 and 2008 when a part of the pipeline was damaged by these communities cutting off supplies.[182]

Another issue affecting the pipeline has been the increased demand for gas within Nigeria and the lack of infrastructure to capture flared gas and use that gas in the pipelines.[183] Although the main aim of the pipeline was to lessen the gas flaring problem in Nigeria, the pipeline currently still lacks the capacity to do so and as a result it is one of the reasons for frequent disruption in the pipeline chain.[184] Since it began, the pipeline has been prone to disruption due to these technical problems

---

175. See ISODEC (Integrated Social Development Centre), *The West African Gas Pipeline Project: A Critical Perspective*, vol. 2, no. 1 (2003). This can be accessed via <www.isodec.org.gh>.
176. See FOEI, *supra* n. 117.
177. See *ibid.*
178. See M. Karipko, *The West African Gas Pipeline Project*, Testimony for the Public Hearing on the World Bank, 15 Oct. 2007.
179. See Macaulay, *supra* n. 173.
180. See WAGP website at <www.wagpoco.com>.
181. See Karipko, *supra* n. 179.
182. See A. Iwayemi, 'Nigeria's Dual Energy Problems: Policy Issues and Challenges', IAEE (2008).
183. See *ibid.*
184. See Omonbude, *supra* n. 110.

and also because of the poor state of the eastern and western pipeline infrastructure within Nigeria.[185]

The economic problem resulting from the infrastructure not being in place and the increased legal complications arising with compensations not being paid by the government has caused frequent disruptions in the pipeline.[186] There have also been problems of insurgency in the Niger Delta region together with pressure from multinational donors advocating the spread of benefit earned from the pipeline to the wider community.[187] The government has had to interfere regularly to ensure that there is enough gas in the pipeline to be imported and they feel that there is too much interference from the other stakeholders which might affect their own interest, which is both geo-political and economic in nature.[188] These interferences have resulted in the regulatory body being sidelined, which in turn weakens its enforcement power.

The technical, geo-political and economic problems discussed above have caused the stronger parties within the regime to interfere for their own benefit. For example, the Nigerian government has interfered when enough gas was not available to be exported, while the government of Ghana, instead of bringing the issue of gas disruption to the notice of the regulators, directly negotiated with the Nigerian government.[189] The reason the government of Ghana decided to negotiate directly with the other governments rather than rely on the mechanism available in the pipeline regime is because they thought the process or the disruption could be shortened if the other governments quickly intervened rather than waiting for the pipeline mechanism to take action.[190] This has caused among the other members of the regime, in this case the two transit states and other multinational stakeholders, a conflict of interest, which disrupts the functioning of the pipeline.[191]

The attitude of the actors involved in the WAGP pipeline is mainly neo-liberal in nature because all the actors are cooperating to turn the pipeline into a successful venture as all their interests are involved in it. They are also willing to sacrifice

---

185. The pipeline infrastructure between the eastern and western part of Nigeria is not well developed and in certain parts requires maintenance. This has caused regular disruption of supply which in turn has caused electricity blackouts and other problems. The same pipeline structure is being used or connected to the WAGP pipeline which, according to some experts, might cause problems and even disruption. For further reading, see I. Banego, *The Development of Downstream Gas Market in Nigeria*, CEPMLP, University of Dundee, Unpublished dissertation, 2005. Also See A. Akpan, *What is the Potential for Developing the Domestic Gas Markets in Nigeria*, CEPMLP, University of Dundee, Unpublished Dissertation, 2006.
186. See I. Banego, *The Development of Downstream Gas Market in Nigeria*, CEPMLP, University of Dundee, Unpublished dissertation, 2005.
187. See *ibid*.
188. See *ibid*.
189. See Oluwatosin, *supra* n. 171.
190. See *ibid*.
191. This has a link with the problem that this book is trying to answer with regard to the interference of the parties within a regime due to geo-political, legal and economic aspects which might cause a breach of a pipeline deal and the reasons these actors behave in the way they do in order to protect their own interest.

certain of their benefits for the greater success of the pipeline and to them relative gain is more important than absolute gain. All these traits point towards a neo-liberal attitude as all the parties in the pipeline regime are cooperating with each other for the smooth running of the pipeline and to protect their own interests.

### 5.7.3. THE COMMON INTEREST OF THE PARTIES

The common interest of all the parties involved in the WAGP is to benefit from the pipeline. Nigeria, being the strongest country in West Africa and in the pipeline chain, wants to show its leadership in the region and also wants to use the pipeline for economic and political gains.[192] The pipeline would not only lead to an overall improvement in the pipeline infrastructure in the country but would also lessen the gas flaring problem which cause damage to the local environment.[193] The country is also eager to participate because of Western interest in the region and because of the World Bank's involvement in the area. All these factors together with the increasing revenue that the pipeline is going to generate would be beneficial for the country.[194]

Ghana, however, is in urgent need of gas to service its increasing energy requirements and to fuel its economic growth.[195] The country would benefit from the gas coming through the pipelines as it would be used to supply power to households and also for other economic needs. The country also wanted to join because of its standing in the area and to keep pace with Nigerian leadership in the region.[196] Benin and Togo also benefit from the pipeline passing through the country as their demand for gas has increased over the years.[197] Although their demand is not that high they earn their tariff in the form of royalty gas which in turn would help them economically.[198] Furthermore, being part of the pipeline also increases their stature in the region.

The Western companies who are involved in the pipeline chain also benefit from this venture. They are not only receiving a good return on their investment but are also able to use this participation to further increase their hold on the region.[199] The involvement of the World Bank and other multinational corporations has also increased the profile of the WAGP, as the pipeline is part of the World Bank's Regional Integrity Strategy.[200] The participation of international oil companies with Western affiliations has also caused Western countries to keep an eye on

---

192. See Iwayemi, *supra* n. 183.
193. See *ibid.*
194. See *ibid.*
195. See FOEI, *supra* n. 117.
196. See *ibid.*
197. See *ibid.*
198. See Omonbude, *supra* n. 110.
199. See *ibid.*
200. See The World Bank Information Centre News: <www.bicusa.org/en/Project.Concerns.39.aspx>.

the project for their own security of supply and to protect the interest of their oil companies.[201]

The attitude of the parties involved in the pipeline chain is a mixture of both neo-realism and neo-liberalism. The Western donors and the World Bank have acted in a neo-realist fashion as they sometimes use their superior power to force some of the actors to carry out certain tasks which might not have been beneficial to them. For example, the cost of the project spiralled to USD 1.4 billion which according to some economists is not financially viable.[202] However, despite the reservations, these countries had their aid tied with the completion of this project.[203] The actions of Nigeria are also that of a neo-realist because of their dominant position in the pipeline chain and their objective of absolute over relative gains. The other actors, in certain circumstances, had to accept their demands. However, even Nigeria and the other actors involved in the pipeline chain have cooperated in most matters for the smooth running of the pipeline. This cooperation has links to a neo-liberal ethos, as parties were willing to reach out to each other and were also willing to sacrifice their individual interest for the operation of the WAGP regime.

5.7.4.     THE ENFORCEMENT AND COMPLIANCE OF CROSS-BORDER PIPELINE AGREEMENTS

The IGAs and HGAs signed between the various parties provide the legal framework based upon which the WAGP functions. The divergent legal systems in all these countries made it a necessity to have a single legal and regulatory framework based upon which the pipeline can function.[204]

Although there is an enforcing agency monitoring the various activities of the actors involved in the pipeline chain, WAPCO have not been able to enforce various clauses of the agreement as they do not have enough compliance power.[205] Most of the disputes that take place between the countries have been solved through negotiation at government level without going through the proper channels or authorities, due to the nature of the problem and low confidence on WAPCO by the stakeholders.[206] The WAGPA regime has been able to monitor various actions but without being able to take any concrete measures against actors who breaks various clauses of the agreements. A good example of this is when during a supply disruption, WAGPA could not take any action despite giving

---

201.   See *The Critical Reassessment of the West African Gas Pipeline*, 25 Degrees in Africa, vol. 3, no. 3, 2008 at <http://25degrees.net/index.php>.
202.   See R. Goodland, 'Oil and Gas Pipelines: Social and Environmental Impact Assessment', *International Association of Impact Assessment* (2005).
203.   See *ibid.*
204.   See Akpan, *supra* n. 103.
205.   See *ibid.*
206.   See Macaulay, *supra* n. 173.

notices to the pipeline company, and the matter was solved through government intervention.[207]

The nature of the actors in the WAPCO and the WAGPA regime has been a mixture of both neo-liberalist and neo-realist. Although all the parties have cooperated with each other towards the setting up of this authority to make the pipeline function smoothly, there has not been enough cooperation between the parties in order for it to work properly. There are some neo-liberal traits in that the actors are willing to work together for the common benefit rather than being concerned only with absolute gain. An example would be both the Nigerian and Ghanaian governments trying to cooperate at the time of disruption in the pipeline.[208] The neo-realist actors within the pipeline regime have tried to bend the rules in order to maximize their own benefit and also because of their superior power in the pipeline regime. The example of this would be Western stakeholders influencing the respective governments involved in the pipeline to go ahead with the project despite spiralling costs and their aid being tied up to the completion of the project.[209] In general, these actors have been cooperative in the WAGP pipeline as without cooperating with each other the pipeline regime would not be able to function smoothly which in return might jeopardize all the actors' interests.

5.8.      CONCLUSION

The BTC pipeline regime is based upon the various IGAs and HGAs signed between Azerbaijan, and the Turkish and Georgian governments.[210] The case study showed that the pipeline is run according to the various rules and regulations agreed between the parties, and the intergovernmental commission which was formed of representatives from each country also keeps a watchful eye over the entire pipeline chain.

The WAGP pipeline regime is, however, made up of the countries involved in the pipeline chain together with other private partners who have also financed the pipeline project.[211] The legal framework agreed between all the parties have allowed the pipeline regime to monitor the various activities of the actors involved and also ensures that they abide by the rules and regulations needed for the smooth functioning of the pipeline. There is also WAGPA, which oversees the activities of the parties in the pipeline chain and acts as a regulatory authority. However,

---

207.  See *ibid.*
208.  See *ibid.*
209.  See Goodland, *supra* n. 203.
210.  The IGAs are signed between the three governments of Azerbaijan, Turkey and Georgia, while private companies like BP signed HGAs with Azerbaijan to develop the field and also build the pipeline.
211.  There are four countries involved in the chain, including Nigeria, Ghana, Benin and Togo together with other private partners like Shell, the World Bank and the IFC. The IGAs are between the four countries while the HGAs are between Shell, AGIP, Total, the Nigerian government and the other governments through which the pipeline passes.

there are quite a few regimes within the broad WAGP regime, which sometimes take decisions without coordination between different members, causing problems for the stakeholders involved.[212]

The BTC and WAGP regime are moderately strong regimes because they have the capability within their regime framework to ensure that their members follow the rules and principles set by their regime. The intergovernmental commission in both these pipeline regimes also ensures that the regime rules are followed and acts as an enforcement agency within the broader regime framework.[213] However, the compliance level of the members of both these regimes is not at the same level of stronger regimes due to a lack of enforcement of the various rules and regulations.[214] Another important implication of this regime is that the frequency and opportunities to intervene by government are higher than those in the strong regime despite the existence of enforcement agencies. This can be seen by the number of times stronger members intervened for their own benefit.[215]

For example, the BTC pipeline, despite having certain regime principles present in the pipeline chain, does not have a centralized body or an independent regulatory authority entrusted to look over the activities of all these actors.[216] The success of the pipeline and its regime depends upon the goodwill and cooperation of all the actors involved in the pipeline chain.[217] The WAGP pipeline, however, has regimes within a regime which makes it weak in terms of ensuring that the parties carry out their obligations in accordance with the agreements signed by them. The regulatory authority in the pipeline regime has acted in response to actions taken by the parties involved in the pipeline due to government interference in the regime and to their strength in the regime framework.[218] This lessens the

---

212. The other regimes include the intergovernmental commission and the WAGP authority and also WAGPCO which has responsibility for the pipeline operation. All these three try to enforce the rules and regulations of the regime causing a lack of coordination among the different members of the regime.

213. This means that the intergovernmental commission set up in the regime ensures that all the parties abide by their obligations and the rules are complied with. There is a regulatory mechanism which oversees the activities of actors in the pipeline regime and they act according to the obligations the actors have signed up for. See Ch. 5 on moderately strong regimes for further discussion and how the actors in these two pipeline regimes work.

214. The two case studies in this chapter have shown that. For further clarification in this area read the 'nature and characteristics of the regime' and 'the issues affecting the pipelines' sections of the case studies.

215. The 'issues affecting the pipelines' part of the analysis of both the pipelines shows the times government intervened for their own benefit. This is also discussed in the geo-political, legal and economic aspects of the pipelines parts before the four criteria are used for analysis.

216. See the previous sections of this chapter for further clarification in this area.

217. The BTC pipeline actors tend to cooperate and negotiate between each other if there is any conflict of interest rather than the regulatory body playing its part. This is because the regulatory body is not independent or centralized as found in the Interconnector pipeline. The previous sections of this chapter have examples which show this fact.

218. The intergovernmental commission and the regime members sometimes interfere with the work of the WAGPA as a result, they are not sure about their enforcement jurisdiction. The strongest member of the regime: Nigeria, sometimes influences the regime authorities.

regulatory powers and compliance with the regulatory regimes as they would loose their credibility among the other members of the pipeline regime.

The WAGP and the BTC pipeline regimes, however, face some common problems in economic and geo-political areas, however, the nature of those problems are different. There is a similarity in that both pipelines are situated in a volatile region and the players involved in the regime have to deal with many external problems including terrorism and threat from other hegemonies in the region. There are also problems within the regime, as some of the actors within the regime use their regime strength to fulfil their own interest rather than that of the regime.[219] Both these pipelines fall under the moderately strong regime category due to the stronger members of the regime being able to use their influence, which sometimes undermines the enforcement capability of the regime itself as agreed between the various actors.

These two moderately strong regimes do differ in the rate of disruption that takes place in the pipeline chain. The BTC pipeline has a slightly better record than the WAGP pipeline because its pipeline was finished on time and the level of disruption is lower than the WAGP pipeline.[220] Another important difference is that one supplies oil while the other supplies gas. Accordingly, the level of security of supply differs between the two pipelines although both of the pipelines have a similar regime structure.[221] The implication of this is that although both pipelines are in the same regime category and have a similar regulatory structure there can be differences in the way the pipeline is run and operated. This can be due to the fact that the pipelines are in a different region and have to deal with factors like geo-politics and the behaviour of the actors involved in the regime and these plays a part in the way the pipeline operates.

The enforcement mechanism also differs between the two pipelines. The players behind the BTC pipeline are different from those in WAGP. While many Western countries and oil companies have a stake in the pipeline to ensure that the pipeline is out of Russian hegemony and to provide an alternative transport route for energy rich but landlocked countries, the pipeline became commercially viable because of the involvement of so many governments and their political commitment and interests in it.[222] This results in the actors being aware of all

---

Also See Friends of Earth International (FOEI), *The myths of West African Gas Pipeline*, 2006. This can be accessed via <www.foei.org/en/publications/pdfs/wagp-inet.pdf/view>.

219. A particular country within the regime, in this case Nigeria, tries to influence others to follow its lead and interests rather than the interests of the regime or other members. They can do this due to their strength within the regime and in the region.

220. This statement is based on the fact that the WAGP pipeline is still incurring problems with the pipeline and there are frequent disruptions. Moreover, the pipeline has taken more time to be built resulting in it being over budget. The BTC pipeline was finished on time and the pipeline has fewer technical faults.

221. Due to a lower rate of disruption BTC performs better, giving the importers greater security of supply.

222. The evidence for this statement is based on the fact that the financiers of the BTC pipeline were not willing to build the pipeline at the beginning because of the increased cost of the project and uncertainties of the actors involved in the project. However, after negotiation between the

the rules and regulations required for the pipeline to function and the level of interference that is possible from the members within the regime.

The WAGP pipeline involves four countries as well as a number of multinational donors because the main reason for building it was to make the pipeline system in the region more integrated.[223] Due to the involvement of so many Western donors, the pipeline regime and its regulatory mechanisms are balanced out between these donors and the governments involved in the pipeline.[224] The governments involved in the pipeline regime know the level of interference that is expected from them due to their regime membership and there is a structure in the way the regulatory mechanism functions within the pipeline.

Despite the pipeline regime being different, both the BTC and WAGP have regulatory features but lack independence, like the Interconnector pipeline,[225] to take action against the actors when they breach their obligations. This is also a reason for the pipeline regime to be termed a moderately strong regime.

The activities of the players in both pipeline projects are a mixture of a neo-liberal ethos and a neo-realist ethos. In the WAGP pipeline, the governments of Nigeria and Ghana, together with the other multinational players involved in the project, are dominant because of their financial strength and resource ownership and this ensures that most of the gains from the pipeline project serve their own interest.[226] This behaviour is more akin to the neo-realist school of thought as neo-realists are more interested in their own gains rather than the gains of others in a regime.[227] There is also cooperation between all the players and this includes the transit country as without their help the project might not have gone ahead. This aspect is more neo-liberal in nature.[228] In the case of the BTC pipeline, most of the actors tend to cooperate with each other to ensure that the gains are shared among all the actors involved in the project which in turn ensures that all the parties have some form of relative gain from joining the regime.[229]

The lessons learnt from these two pipeline regimes is that despite the two pipelines having a moderately strong enforcement capacity there are still

---

US and other Western allies and the BTC actors, the financiers decided to go ahead with the project as they were given the guarantee they were looking for. See Ch. 5 of the book for detailed analysis in this regard.

223. See Karipko, *supra* n. 179.
224. See *ibid.*
225. The previous chapter has an in-depth discussion about the Interconnector pipeline.
226. Neo-realist and neo-liberals are two schools within the regime theory. There is more discussion about this area in Ch. 2 of the book.
227. According to neo-realist the reason of joining any form of regime is to further one's own interest and gain and this could be done through their hegemonic power. There is more discussion about this in Ch. 2 of the book.
228. Neo-liberals call for greater cooperation among all the regime members. See Ch. 2 for further analysis.
229. According to neo-liberals relative gain for members of a regime is more important than absolute gains. See Ch. 2 for further analysis in this area.

problems[230] which these regimes are not able to act upon. In the case of the WAGP pipeline, the governments tend to interfere regularly for economic reasons, bypassing the role of the regulators involved in the pipeline.[231] While in the BTC pipeline there are geo-political and economic ramifications which sometimes result in the disruption of the supply.[232]

These aspects of the pipelines in this regime category can be linked to the problem this book is trying to answer and the reasons for government intervention due to geo-political, legal and economic aspects.[233] The behaviour of the actors in this regime category is similar to those of stronger regimes but, unlike the pipelines in the stronger regimes, the two pipelines in this category have weaker enforcement mechanisms[234] which make the job of the regulatory body in these pipelines more difficult when dealing with geo-political, legal and economic problems.[235] The WAGP pipeline highlighted government interference due to lack of gas in the pipeline and other economic issues affecting the partners in the pipelines while in the BTC pipeline there also was interference from the government due to economic aspects.[236]

The breach of legitimate expectation in the form of Turkish government not being able to provide the security agreed between the stakeholders in the BTC pipeline agreement and Nigeria failing to abide by their contractual obligations of supplying gas to Ghana in the WAGP are problems disrupting the flow of resources in the pipeline. As a result, although the legitimate expectation of the stakeholders are not respected in the way agreed between the parties, the governments who are also stakeholders in the pipeline, try to resolve the breach through diplomacy or other negotiation means available outside the purview of the agreement signed. This in turn shows the need for another mechanism or a new regime to deal with the problems faced by these regimes.[237]

---

230. The problems that the pipelines are facing can be found in the previous sections of the two case studies. The 'issues affecting the pipelines' discusses the problems faced by the pipelines.
231. One of the criteria 'the issues affecting the pipelines' try to analyse these problems in the case studies.
232. These problems are highlighted throughout the four criteria that were used to analyse the case study. See the section on 'issues affecting the pipelines' for further clarification in this area.
233. See Ch. 1 of the book which talks about the problem this book is trying to answer.
234. The definition of a moderately strong regime is provided at the beginning of the chapter and the reason for these pipelines being slightly weaker is also given throughout the conclusion section of this chapter. The reason they are moderately strong is because of their enforcement capacity compared to the strong regimes.
235. These problems link in with the original problems that this book is trying to answer. See Ch. 1 detailing the problem this book is trying to answer and Ch. 2 for further analysis in this area.
236. These aspects of the pipeline are covered in the 'issues affecting the pipelines' section of the case study. The whole case study in general discussed various aspects of the pipelines including legal, economic and geo-political issues.
237. A new regime here means an agency or another form of mechanism which is needed to deal with the problems that mechanisms in moderately strong regimes are unable to resolve.

Chapter 6

# The Weak Regimes

## 6.1. INTRODUCTION

The purpose of this case study chapter will be to analyse the Shah-Deniz, CPC and Maghreb–Europe Pipeline. All three pipelines are in the weak regime category. *A weak regime is where all the regime rules and principles are present but its members do not abide by their obligations and also do not follow the guidelines set by the regime. There is also no enforcement mechanism present to ensure that the actors are abiding by the rules and regulations of the regime.*[1] This chapter will not only include a discussion with regard to the different trends in these pipelines and the various problems faced by each of them but will also try to understand the differences and behaviour of the actors in this regime.

This chapter, as in previous chapters, has been divided into three sections. In each case analysis, the first section provides the general background of the pipeline discussing various aspects of the pipeline, the cost of building it and the different actors involved in the pipeline chain. The second section discusses the important aspects of those pipelines that affect its smooth operation. These include economic, legal, geo-political aspects as well as the interests of the parties involved in the pipeline chain. The third section uses the criteria developed in the analytical framework chapter to analyse the lessons learnt from the previous section. The four criteria[2] that would be used in order to analyse the different aspects of these pipelines are:

   (i) the nature and characteristics of the regime;
   (ii) the issues affecting the cross-border pipeline;

---

1. This is considered as the definition of a weak regime for the purpose of this book.
2. Chapter 2 also provides an extensive discussion regarding the four benchmarks chosen to evaluate the different cross-border pipeline regimes.

(iii)  the common interests of the parties; and

(iv)  the enforcement and compliance of the various cross-border pipeline agreements.


6.2.        SHAH-DENIZ GAS FIELD/SCP

6.2.1.      THE BACKGROUND OF THE PROJECT

The Shah-Deniz gas field is the largest natural gas field located in Azerbaijan. It is in the Southern Caspian Sea off the coast of Azerbaijan. The gas field is under 600 metres of water and is 100 km south east of Baku.[3] It was discovered in 1999 and is estimated to have 400 billion cubic metres of gas reserves.[4] The first Shah-Deniz well initially produced 3.4 million cubic metres of gas and 1,300 tons of gas condensate per day, which soon grew to 5.6 billion cubic metres and 2,500 tons per day (Figure 6.1).[5] Three new wells raised the output to 6 to 7 billion cubic metres from 2007.[6]

*Figure 6.1    The Shah-Deniz Pipeline*[7]

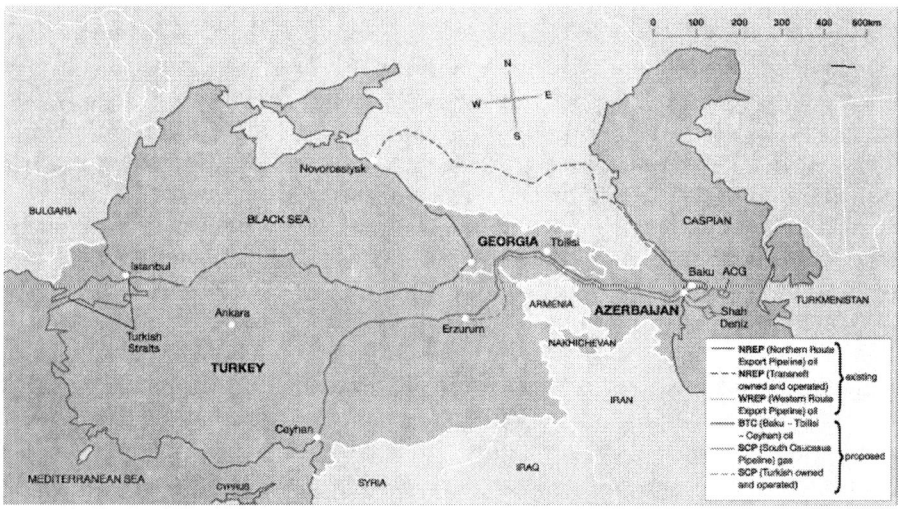

*Source*: <www.caspiandevelopmentandexport.com>.

---

3.  See the Company website at <www.caspiandevelopmentandexort.com>.
4.  See Alexander's Gas and Oil connections, *Shah Deniz Gas Pipeline expected to Cost $1bn*, News and trends, vol. 6, no. 14, in <www.gasnadoil.com/goc/news/ntc13120.htm>.
5.  See the Company website at <www.caspiandevelopmentandexport.com>.
6.  See *ibid.*
7.  The diagram gives an extensive picture of the pipeline and the countries it is passing. The purpose is to show the different countries surrounding the pipeline and the geo-political and economic implications of it.

The pipeline transferring gas from the Shah-Deniz gas field to Turkey through Georgia is known as the South Caspian Pipeline (SCP). The SCP became operational in 2006 and runs parallel to the BTC pipeline. A fixed production platform near the gas field has also been installed which is linked by sub-sea pipelines to the onshore terminal. The SCP is 690 kilometres long, and was expected to be capable of carrying up to 7 billion cubic metres of gas every year from 2006.[8] However, there were problems with the pipeline in the first part of 2007 causing it to close down for six months resulting in supply disruption.[9] The pipeline again became operational towards the end of July 2007.

### 6.2.2.    THE RELEVANT PARTIES OF THE PROJECT

The pipeline is owned and managed by the State Oil Company of the Republic of Azerbaijan, Turkish Petroleum Overseas Limited and six other national and international oil companies including BP, SOCAR, ELF, Lukoil and Statoil.[10] Among them BP has a share of 25.5%, Statoil 25.5%, SOCAR 10%, Total S.A. 10%, LukAgip (a joint company of Eni and Lukoil) 10%, Oil Engineering and Construction 10% and the Turkish Petroleum Overseas Company Limited 9%.[11]

### 6.2.3.    THE COST OF THE PROJECT

The cost of the project is estimated to have been around USD 2.7 billion, while the total investment in the project, including the construction and development of the gas field, was around USD 3.2 billion with interests.[12] The pipeline cost around USD 1 billion to build as it required substantial engineering work. EBRD provided a loan of about USD 250 million to SOCAR for the project, while the State Company fulfilled the remaining USD 70 million on its own.[13]

In this project, Georgia, the transit country, has not contributed towards the implementation of the pipeline. However, it has negotiated an off-take agreement without playing any part in the ownership, construction or operation of the pipeline. Georgia would get 5% of the gas as its transit fee, with an option to buy a further 0.5 bcm per annum.[14] Both Turkey and Azerbaijan directly contributed

---

8.  See the Company website at <www.caspiandevelopmentandexport.com>.
9.  See *ibid.*
10. See *ibid.*
11. See *ibid.*
12. See Alexander's Gas and Oil connections, *Shah Deniz Gas Pipeline expected to Cost $1bn*, News and trends, vol. 6, no. 14, in <www.gasnadoil.com/goc/news/ntc13120.htm>.
13. See *ibid.*
14. See F. Weir, *Oil Pipeline Sparks Controversy in Poor Georgian Village*, in Alexander's Gas and Oil connections, <www.gasandoil.com/gol/news/ntr41095.htm>.

towards the building of the pipeline and they have stakes in the project.[15] They are also involved in the operation of the pipeline.

6.2.4.       OTHER ASPECTS OF THE PIPELINE

The project is owned and managed by the State Oil Company of Azerbaijan, Turkish Petroleum Overseas Limited and other national and international companies according to the Production Sharing Agreements (PSA) signed by the three countries.[16] The legal aspects of the project are covered by the production sharing agreements between different parties, the 2001 IGA between Azerbaijan and Turkey and Azerbaijan and Georgia and an agreement between SOCAR and BOTAS.[17] There were also HGAs between the international companies involved in the project and the governments of Azerbaijan and Turkey, and the owners' agreement.[18] The Turkish side of the pipeline would be owned by the Turkish government and not by any other partners within the project.[19]

6.3.       THE IMPORTANT ASPECTS OF THE PIPELINE

6.3.1.       ECONOMIC ASPECT

The economic aspect of the pipeline is immense for all parties involved in the project. Georgia is receiving 5% of the gas transported through the pipeline as a transit fee and they would also be able to sell this gas for USD 100 per thousand cubic metres to others while this can rise a further 2% in the next few years.[20] As a result, Georgia is benefiting economically from allowing the gas to pass through its country and is also able to use the gas for their domestic needs or sell it abroad to earn extra currency when necessary.

---

15. See *ibid.*
16. See the IGA between the Republic of Turkey and the Azerbaijan Republic Concerning the Delivery of Azerbaijan Natural Gas to the Republic of Turkey available at <http://subsites.bp.com/caspian/SHA/Eng/inter-gov/Azerbaijan%20Turkey%20Inter-governmental%20Agreement.pdf>.
17. See J. Roberts, 'The Turkish Gate: Energy Transit and Security Issues', *Turkish Policy Quarterly* 3, no. 4 (2004).
18. See the HGA between Azerbaijan and BP and other companies involved in the project at <www.caspiandevelopmentandexport.com>.
19. See the IGA between the Republic of Turkey and the Azerbaijan Republic Concerning the Delivery of Azerbaijan Natural Gas to the Republic of Turkey available at <http://subsites.bp.com/caspian/SHA/Eng/inter-gov/Azerbaijan%20Turkey%20Inter-governmental%20Agreement.pdf>.
20. See Roberts, *supra* n. 17.

Turkey is also a beneficiary as the pipeline was built to take Azeri gas to Turkey through Georgia.[21] Turkey has a huge demand for natural gas and its willingness and ability to pay for the gas makes it an ideal importing country for Azerbaijan, which also needs a secure buyer for their gas.[22] The Turkish domestic demand has allowed Azerbaijan to export huge quantities of gas to Turkey through Georgia, which also requires gas for its domestic needs.

### 6.3.2.    THE INTERESTS OF THE COUNTRIES

All three countries involved in the pipeline have their own interest at heart. Azerbaijan wants a market which has a high demand for its gas and can also be relied on for future export.[23] Turkey requires a secured supply of gas and an able ally willing to cooperate and offer the country a good and acceptable rate for imported gas.[24] Georgia, being a transit country, is also in a good position as it is earning a substantial amount of foreign currency and is also able to use the gas for its domestic needs.[25] The main incentive for all the three countries is to protect their interest and maximize their benefit by joining the regime.

Western countries are also pleased with the arrangement because it allows them to participate in this venture and the pipeline bypasses both Russia and Iran who are against Western investment and influence in pipelines in the region.[26] Furthermore, this route is considered as an energy corridor which could also be used for future energy supplies to other Western countries.[27]

### 6.3.3.    THE LEGAL ASPECT

The project is based upon the IGAs between the Turkish, Azeri and Georgian governments and the HGAs between international companies and the governments.[28] For example, in one of the agreements signed between the Azerbaijan and Turkish governments, Turkey has promised to buy certain amounts of gas from Azerbaijan for a certain period of time; there was also a penalty clause if it failed to abide by this

---

21. See M. Crandall, *Energy, Economics, & Politics in the Caspian Region: Dreams and Realities* (Praeger, 2006).
22. The focus is on the pipeline rather than gas, as without sufficient Azeri gas the pipeline would not have been built.
23. See Crandall, *supra* n. 21.
24. See *ibid.*
25. See *ibid.*
26. See Roberts, *supra* n. 17.
27. See *ibid.*
28. See the IGA between the Republic of Turkey and the Azerbaijan Republic Concerning the Delivery of Azerbaijan Natural Gas to the Republic of Turkey and HGAs between them and the international oil companies, available at <http://subsites.bp.com/caspian/SHA/Eng/inter-gov/Azerbaijan%20Turkey%20Inter-governmental%20Agreement.pdf>.

obligation.[29] However, there have been quite a few instances when the Turkish government failed to abide by this obligation resulting in problems between the two governments. For example, this is when the Turkish government intervened to ensure that they were not penalized for not being able to pay for the gas imported into the country.[30] After renegotiation with the Azerbaijan government they sorted out a deal which allowed them to pay later.[31] These kinds of interferences, despite there being clear indications of the penalty if one of the parties fails to abide by their obligations,[32] lowers the regulatory capabilities of the pipeline regime and makes them look weak and powerless and gives scope to a government or any other members to intervene for their own interest.

The SCP pipeline also passes through private lands which some of the governments have not acquired properly from their citizens resulting in a long and protracted legal battle between that government and the private citizens, which sometimes causes problems for the operators of the pipeline.[33] There were also environmental concerns expressed during the building of the pipeline resulting in legal battles between the owners of the pipeline and some environmental groups causing further legal problems for the stakeholders involved.[34]

6.3.4.     THE GEO-POLITICS OF THE PIPELINE

The SCP pipeline is known as the second corridor after the BTC pipeline. The main purpose of the pipeline was to lessen the pipeline monopolies of Russia and Iran and to diminish their influence in the region.[35] By depending less on Russian gas, Georgia could fully enjoy its independent status as a country and could also avoid the exorbitant price that Gazprom would have charged for importing gas.[36] Azerbaijan has also benefited from this venture as it was looking for a market to sell its gas at the right price and also to distance itself from Russian influence.[37] There was always the possibility that Russia would not have paid the right price for the gas and as Azerbaijan had to depend on Russia to transport their gas elsewhere they might not have been able to have the export country of their choice.[38]

---

29. See *ibid.*
30. See T. Krysiek, et al., *Cracks In The Bridge: The Uncertaintaies of Turkish Gas Transit*, CERA Report, 2008.
31. See *ibid.*
32. See the IGA between the Republic of Turkey and the Azerbaijan Republic Concerning the Delivery of Azerbaijan Natural Gas to the Republic of Turkey available at <http://subsites.bp.com/caspian/SHA/Eng/inter-gov/Azerbaijan%20Turkey%20Inter-governmental%20Agreement.pdf>.
33. See V. Socor, *Shah-Deniz Gas Buttressing Georgia, Azerbaijan Economically and Politically*, The Jamestown Foundation, 2007. This can be accessed at <www.jamestown.org/single/?no_cache=1&tx_ttnews%5Btt_news%5D=32396>.
34. See *ibid.*
35. See Crandall, *supra* n. 21.
36. See Krysiek, *supra* n. 30.
37. See *ibid.*
38. See *ibid.*

Turkey's benefit was two-fold as it not only bought gas from Azerbaijan but was also fortunate to get a secured supplier for its domestic needs.[39] It also increased Turkey's standing in the international arena as a credible ally of the West in the region and could act as a transit hub for delivering gas to Europe and to other parts of the world.[40]

The main aspect of the pipeline is that it transfers gas from one point to the other, which makes it different from an oil pipeline.[41] This is because gas sales are tied to specific markets and have to be complemented by a gas sale and purchasing agreement unlike oil, where the market is normally open.[42] From this perspective, the SCP fits the demand perfectly, as it can transport Shah-Deniz gas to the nearest market, in this case Turkey.

There were other routes which were contemplated through Russia, Iran and Armenia but due to the political problems in those countries and lack of support from Western countries and other multinational donors, the current route was chosen as it satisfied all the parties involved in the project.[43]

## 6.4. THE APPLICATION OF THE CRITERIA ON THE CROSS-BORDER PIPELINE REGIME

### 6.4.1. THE NATURE AND CHARACTERISTICS OF THE REGIME

The main players in the Shah-Deniz/SCP pipeline are Azerbaijan, Turkey and Georgia. Azerbaijan is the exporting country whereas Turkey is the importing country while Georgia provides the transit facilities for the pipeline. All three actors are extremely important for the pipeline as without their cooperation the pipeline operation would be disrupted. The interests of the three countries are interlinked as all of them have something to gain from joining this pipeline regime.

The Shah-Deniz gas field or the South Caucasus Pipeline (SCP) is founded upon the IGAs and HGAs signed between the various countries and companies involved in the pipeline project.[44] The IGAs between Turkey, Georgia and Azerbaijan and the HGAs between these governments and the companies involved in the project provide the legal and regulatory framework through which the pipeline is operated. There is also an additional take or pay agreement between Turkey

---

39. See S. Ibrahim, 'The EU Russian Gas Interdependence and Turkey', *Insight Turkey* 9, no. 4 (December, 2007).
40. See *ibid.*
41. See *ibid.*
42. See *ibid.*
43. See *ibid.*
44. See the IGA is between Turkey, Azerbaijan and Georgia. The HGAs are between Azerbaijan and BP and the other foreign companies involved in the project.

and Azerbaijan, which obligates Turkey to take a certain amount of gas at a certain price through the pipeline.[45]

There are regime principles and rules present in the pipeline. The agreements signed between the parties involve certain rules and principles by which they have to conduct themselves.[46] For example, in the Shah-Deniz IGA, Article VII(4) states that 'if there is any disruption in the supply of gas in the pipeline, a state will take all lawful and reasonable endeavours, taking into account all democratic, economic and commercial principles to stop the disruption'.[47] This is an example of a principle where as a typical rule would be Article VIII(3) which says that 'this agreement shall terminate upon the termination or expiration of all project agreements . . .'.[48] These regime-like qualities allow them to behave in a way which makes all the stakeholders abide by their various obligations. The framework provides the regime platform needed for the smooth functioning of all the activities of the parties involved in the project.

The Shah-Deniz/SCP pipeline regime has the regime principles and rules which give it a regime framework. However, the enforcement mechanism of those rules and regulations is weak[49] and there is no mechanism present within the regime with regard to whether the actors are following the rules set by the regime. For example, despite Turkey faltering on its payments to Azerbaijan, it still demanded gas and the regulatory body could not enforce it to pay in order to fulfil its contractual obligations.[50] There were disruptions in the pipeline as there was disagreement between the two countries, and they later had to bargain for another means of payment at a later date while Azerbaijan continued to supply gas without being paid.[51] This was a breach of Azerbaijan's legitimate expectation of being paid for the gas exported to Turkey. The lack of an enforcement mechanism and also of a regulatory body to look after the different actors in the pipeline makes the entire regime weak because actors tend to carry out things which serve their own interest rather than the regime as a whole. Turkey has considerable power within the regime compared to the other two players, and this results in a lack of balance within the regime which is not favourable to the other players.[52] Due to the weak enforcement

---

45. See the take or pay agreement between the Republic of Turkey and Azerbaijan. This can be found at <www.caspiandevelopment andexport.com>.
46. See the IGA is between Turkey, Azerbaijan and Georgia. The HGAs are between Azerbaijan and BP and the other foreign companies involved in the project.
47. See Shah-Deniz IGA between Azerbaijan and Georgia relating to the transportation and sale of Natural Gas In and Beyond the Territories of Georgia and Azerbaijan Republic through the Shah-Deniz Pipeline.
48. See *ibid.*
49. There will be further discussion in s. 6.4.4 and the conclusion part of this chapter and also in Ch. 7 as to why the pipeline regime is considered weak but one of the reasons is the high level and greater frequency of government intervention in the pipeline whenever the interest of the actors are affected.
50. See Krysiek, *supra* n. 30.
51. See *ibid.*
52. See Socor, *supra* n. 33.

mechanism, which is the main component of a regime, the Shah-Deniz/SCP pipeline regime has a weak structure.

There is a mixture of both neo-realism and neo-liberalism present in the actions of all the actors involved in this pipeline regime. Cooperation amongst all three countries in order to make the pipeline a successful venture is a sign of neo-liberalism, which advocates for greater cooperation among the actors of a regime. In this case Azerbaijan, Georgia and Turkey had to cooperate with each other despite being aware that the gains of all three countries differ depending on their own particular participation in the project.[53] For example, Azerbaijan had to supply gas without getting paid for a long period of time, while Turkey enjoyed their gas supplies and Georgia also got their transit fees.[54] Although it would have been more profitable for Azerbaijan to sell the gas to Europe or to some other region, they decided to sell the gas to Turkey because of the lack of a transportation route and to avoid Russian hegemony in the area.[55] These compromises are neo-liberal signs showing that the parties are willing to make relative instead of absolute gains by cooperating with the other members of the regime.

Turkey and Georgia are the two most important partners in the pipeline chain. The role of Turkey is to some extent that of a neo-realist because of its military strength and importance as both a transit and importing country. According to neo-realists, in a regime there is always a possibility of some actors gaining more than the other. For example, Turkey receives a preferential rate for the gas that is being imported to the country.[56] Georgia also needs Azeri gas because it wants to lower its dependence on Russian gas coming into the country.[57] These two actors are gaining more because of their geographical location and increased domestic need for gas. This results in them having an upper hand and acting like a hegemony in the pipeline chain because Azerbaijan needs the Turkish market in order to diversify its export market and requires Georgia's transit facilities to transport the gas.[58]

6.4.2.     THE ISSUES AFFECTING THE CROSS-BORDER PIPELINE

The SCP pipeline came into operation in 2007 after a year's delay and the pipeline supplied gas to Turkey via Georgia from Azerbaijan. The take or pay contract between Azerbaijan and Turkey was signed in March 2001 and the gas was supposed to have been delivered to Turkey by 2004.[59] However, the deal was renegotiated in 2003, with exports starting in 2006 at 71 Bcf per year, increasing to 222 Bcf per year in 2009.[60] Part of this gas was also supposed to be taken by Georgia as

---

53.  See *ibid.*
54.  See Krysiek, *supra* n. 30.
55.  See Socor, *supra* n. 33.
56.  See Krysiek, *supra* n. 30.
57.  See *ibid.*
58.  See Socor, *supra* n. 33.
59.  See *ibid.*
60.  See *ibid.*

a transit tariff. In 2007, Turkey failed to abide by certain provisions of the take or pay contract as it failed to pay for the specific amount of gas it imported from Azerbaijan.[61] This failure to pay did not cause any disruption in the supply of gas to Turkey as there was a penalty provision which allowed Azerbaijan to seek compensation.[62] In this instance, the failure to pay was solved through negotiation between the two governments as both parties needed each other and had a mutual interest at stake. This failure by Turkey to pay for the gas was a long-term concern that many observers had pointed out beforehand.[63] This action by Turkey is a breach of Azerbaijan's legitimate expectation to be paid for the gas.[64]

Another issue affecting the pipeline was the failure of the Georgian and Azeri governments to pay compensation for the pipeline passing through private property. During the building of the pipeline between 2004 and 2006, there were a number of lawsuits brought against the international consortiums involved in the pipeline and the respective governments which further delayed the start of the pipeline.[65] After the opening of the pipeline there were still lawsuits being brought by the affected parties which resulted in the courts asking the stakeholders involved in the pipeline to pay a substantial amount of compensation to the affected parties.[66] This caused considerable anxiety and bad publicity for the stakeholders and also had the potential to cause supply disruption.

Intervention by the two governments, which resulted in a negotiation between the two parties, is the reason that the regulatory mechanism available in the regime could not act.[67] In this case, the pipeline regime lacked a regulatory mechanism which could deal with the breach of the take or pay deal agreed between the two parties.[68] The strength of the government also matters as the Turkish government was in a better bargaining position due to its strength and its importance for the pipeline to function.[69] This allows them to interfere in the pipeline operations freely or whenever their interests are affected.

The tendencies of the various actors are a mixture of both neo-realism and neo-liberalism. The SCP pipeline acts as a second corridor through which Caspian resources can be transported to other parts of the world.[70] This is due to the

---

61. See V. Socor, 'Azerbaijan-Georgia Corridor: Growing Transit Volumes Bolster Security', *Eurasia Daily Monitor* 5, no. 221 (November 2008). This can be accessed via <www.jamestown.org/single/?no_cache=1&tx_ttnews%5Btt_news%5D=34135>.
62. See *ibid*.
63. See Krysiek, *supra* n. 30.
64. See *ibid*.
65. See Socor, *supra* n. 61.
66. See G.M. Winrow, *Turkey as an Energy Transit State*, Black Sea: Energy and Environment Conference, Marine Law and Policy Research Centre, 2003.
67. See *ibid*.
68. This shows a clear link between the problems faced by actors in this case study and the problem that this book is trying to solve, which is parties within the regime interfering due to economic, geo-political and legal reasons resulting in a breach of the original deal agreed between the parties. See Chs 1 and 2 of the book for a detailed analysis in this area.
69. See Krysiek, *supra* n. 30.
70. See Crandall, *supra* n. 21.

neo-realist tendencies of Russia, which is a hegemony in the region. To counter this neo-realist threat from Russia and also to gain economic independence, Azerbaijan wanted to diversify its export base and also to choose countries favourable for their gas export.[71] Turkey, the importing country, is a Western ally and a very important player in the region. Due to its military strength, it also receives certain preferential treatment which makes its actions neo-realist in nature. The cooperation of Georgia and Turkey together with Azerbaijan's policy of export diversification in order to avoid Russia has resulted in a partnership among these three countries which is neo-liberal in nature. All the countries involved in the pipeline chain are willing to cooperate for their own interest and also for the interest of others.

6.4.3.     THE COMMON INTEREST OF THE PARTIES

All the parties involved in the pipeline chain have different interests at heart. Azerbaijan required a market to sell its gas and also to diversify its export market to protect its economic interests.[72] Georgia, being a transit country, also benefits from being a part of the pipeline. The country is in need of gas for its domestic electricity and also for its economic growth and this opportunity allows them to solve their energy problems.[73] They also wanted to rely less on Russian gas because of the high price charged by Gazprom.[74] Turkey, however, also required a secure and stable supplier for its gas imports. All three countries had their own interests before the building of this pipeline.[75]

The three countries involved in the pipeline chain also had to consider the geopolitical ramifications involved in the building of the pipeline. Azerbaijan wanted to free itself of Russian control over its natural resources and also wanted to avoid an Iranian transportation route.[76] One reason for avoiding Iran was because of the country's huge gas and oil deposits. Both Iran and Russia's gas deposits dwarfs that of Azerbaijan and to be economically competitive Azerbaijan had to find a way to deliver its gas to a market with high demand and less competition in order to earn profits.[77] Turkey and Georgia are both pro-Western in their policies and this venture suited them well because they required gas for their own domestic use and also wanted to show their credibility and geographical importance to their Western allies.[78]

---

71. See *ibid.*
72. See *ibid.*
73. See Socor, *supra* n. 61.
74. See *ibid.*
75. See E. Hassan & Y. Yusuf, 'Whither Turkey's Energy Policy', *Insight Turkey* 9, no. 4 (December 2007).
76. See *ibid.*
77. See *ibid.*
78. See *ibid.*

The transit route chosen was also important for Azerbaijan, as it wanted to avoid the influence of both Russia and Iran.[79] This route gave them access to other markets which would be financially viable to them and they can also reach markets beyond the Caspian by extending the current route if they can find a market in need of their gas.[80] Geo-politically, the Georgian route is favoured by the Western countries because of its avoidance of both Russia and Iran and this also helps Azerbaijan economically by providing them with greater financial assistance.[81]

The actions of all the parties involved in the pipeline chain are neo-liberal in nature because of the common interest of all the parties involved in the pipeline was to be a part of the pipeline regime in order to protect their own interests. According to the neo-liberal ethos, actors tend to join a regime where there is common interest and all the parties tend to gain from it even if the benefits are not the same. In this case, all parties gain although some gain more than others. Turkey and Georgia gaining more than Azerbaijan although their level of benefit is not too high compared to Azerbaijan. Although the role of Turkey is to some extent that of a neo-realist because of its superior strength among the three countries and also because of its geo-strategic position, it hardly acts like a hegemonic power despite failing to abide by some of its obligations. The parties in the pipeline chain are not confrontational and are willing to cooperate with each other for the successful operation of the pipeline, due to their common interests and also of the interests of the other Western countries who are represented in the pipeline chain through their International Oil Companies.[82]

6.4.4.     THE ENFORCEMENT AND COMPLIANCE OF THE CROSS-BORDER
           PIPELINE AGREEMENTS

The enforcement and compliance mechanism for the various rules and regulations of the pipeline is guided by the IGA and HGA signed between the various actors of the pipeline.[83] The Turkish side of the pipeline is controlled by the Turkish government and is outside the jurisdiction of others. As a result, the enforcement and compliance is carried out by each government rather than a single entity despite there being provisions about a regulatory commission[84] The take or pay provision signed between Turkey and Azerbaijan is also another factor which plays a very important role in the pipeline chain.[85]

---

79. See Crandall, *supra* n. 21.
80. See Erkaya & Yusuf, *supra* n. 75.
81. See Krysiek, *supra* n. 30.
82. Here the interest refers to the interest of the government.
83. See the IGA between the Republic of Turkey and the Azerbaijan Republic Concerning the Delivery of Azerbaijan Natural Gas to the Republic of Turkey available at <http://subsites.bp.com/caspian/SHA/Eng/inter-gov/Azerbaijan%20Turkey%20Inter-governmental%20Agreement.pdf>.
84. See Krysiek, *supra* n. 30.
85. See the take or pay agreement between the Republic of Turkey and Azerbaijan. Can be accessed at <www.caspiandevelopmentandexport.com>.

There have been instances when Turkey failed to abide by their take or pay obligation resulting in monetary loss to Azerbaijan.[86] The penalty clause allowed Azerbaijan to charge them extra but on very few occasions have they been able to enforce it.[87] Environmental regulations agreed between the parties also cause problems as there are no set standards present based upon which it can be monitored.[88] As a result, enforcement of the various clauses is not as effective and sometimes disputes between the various parties are solved amicably rather than resorting to other measures available in the contract.[89] One of the reasons for doing so is to maintain a stable relationship between all the partners even if it results in loss for some of the actors involved in the project.

There is a mixture of both neo-liberalism and neo-realism in the enforcement mechanism. All the parties are trying to cooperate with each other to maximize their benefits, which show a neo-liberal ethos. However, the fact that at certain times one of the parties gets away with not carrying out their obligations due to their hegemonic power shows the neo-realist side of things. Turkey, due to its importance in the pipeline chain, can sometimes act in a way which is contrary to the spirit of cooperation and can make the pipeline regime look weak due to a lack of enforcement of their contractual obligations.

## 6.5.  THE CASPIAN PIPELINE CONSORTIUM (CPC)

### 6.5.1.  THE BACKGROUND OF THE PROJECT

The CPC (Figure 6.2) is a shipper-owned oil pipeline extending from an existing oil pipeline to produce a new cross-border crude oil pipeline between the Tengiz oil field of Kazakhstan to a marine terminal in Novorossiysk on Russia's Black Sea coast.[90] The pipeline is 1,510 kilometres long and has a diameter of 1,067 millimetres between Kropotkin and the marine terminal and 1,016 millimetres for the rest of the pipeline.[91] The marine terminal in Russia has single point moorings and is built to handle tankers up to 300,000 dead weight tonnes.[92] The Marine pipeline also has three 1,067 millimetres submarine pipelines, with the throughput capacity of 12.7 thousand cubic metres per hour.[93]

---

86.  See Krysiek, *supra* n. 30.
87.  See Erkaya & Yusuf, *supra* n. 75.
88.  See *ibid.*
89.  The 'nature and characteristics of the regime' and 'the issues affecting the pipelines' section further elaborates in this area.
90.  See ESMAP, *Cross-Border Oil and Gas Pipelines: Problems and Prospects*, ESMAP Technical Paper 035, UNDP/World Bank/ESMAP, 2003.
91.  See *ibid.*
92.  See the CPC company website at <www.cpc.ru>.
93.  See *ibid.*

*Figure 6.2    The Caspian Pipeline Consortium Route*[94]

*Source*: <www.cpc.ru/portal/alias!press/lang!enus/tabID!3357/DesktopDefault.aspx>.

The CPC currently has the capacity to transport 30 million metric tonnes of crude per year, although the capacity is expected to rise to 67 million metric tonnes after the expansion of the pipeline.[95] The pipeline is a joint venture between the government of Russia, Oman and Kazakhstan and international oil companies. There was, in fact, public–private cooperation towards the successful implementation of the project.

6.5.2.    THE RELEVANT PARTIES OF THE PROJECT

The original plan to build the CPC pipeline was conceived by John Deuss in 1992 but the plan failed to gather any pace due to lack of funds in the three participating countries namely Russia, Kazakhstan and Oman. However, in 1996, the three participating countries decided to involve international oil companies to finance the pipeline. This caused them to sell of the 50% equity in the pipeline. Russia had 24%, Kazakhstan had 19% and Oman had a 7% stake in the pipeline.[96] The private companies respectively had the following shares: Chevron Caspian Pipeline Consortium Co (15%), LukArco B.V. (12.5%), Rosneft-Shell Caspian Ventures Ltd (7.5%), Agip International (2%), British Gas Overseas Holding Ltd

---

94. The diagram shows the geographical terrain of the pipeline. The pipeline map shows the extensiveness of the pipeline.
95. See the CPC company website at <www.cpc.ru>.
96. See *ibid*.

(2%), Kazakhstan Pipeline Ventures LLC (1.75%) and Oryx Caspian Pipeline LLC (1.75%).[97]

The public–private cooperation in the pipeline management and structure made the entire pipeline consortium unique and complicated and this also affected the enforcement of the various rules and regulations of the pipeline.[98] It also showed the delicate balance between suppliers and operators, the former owning the oil and delivering it while the latter receiving transit fees and allowing their infrastructure to be used.

### 6.5.3.    THE COST OF THE PROJECT

The cost of building the CPC was approximately USD 2.65 billion and this covered installation of the new pipeline as well as renovation of the existing infrastructure.[99] The money was also spent in upgrading the existing facilities including the pump stations, valve stations, cathodic protection, a supervisory control and data acquisition system (SCADA) for monitoring the pipeline, storage links and volume metering.[100]

The private companies involved in the project financed the entire project while the Russian Federation contributed unused pipelines worth USD 293 million.[101] The Consortium also had to pay compensation for using the land within the Russian Federation.[102] The Consortium was also split between two joint stock companies, CPC-R (Russian section) and CPC-K (Kazakhstan section) with each country having their own management in the running of the pipeline together with the consortium management.[103]

### 6.5.4.    OTHER ASPECTS OF THE PIPELINE

The CPC oil pipeline is the only pipeline passing through Russia which is not owned by the state monopoly Transneft.[104] The consortium is a joint venture company with a management structure which is quite complex. For example,

---

97. See *ibid.*
98. The reason it affects enforcement is because each pipeline member has different interests to fulfil resulting in difficulty to ensure that the members are abiding by the rules and regulations of the pipeline regime. This is especially the case if the regulatory authority is weak or absent in a pipeline.
99. See the CPC company website at <www.cpc.ru>.
100. See *ibid.*
101. See *ibid.*
102. See *ibid.*
103. See S.N. Heslin, *Key Constraints to Caspian Pipeline Development: Status., Significance and Outlook* in the working paper series titled Unlocking the Assets: Energy and the Future of Central Asia and the Caucasus, in The James Baker III Institute for Public Policy, Rice University, April 1998.
104. See *ibid.*

there is no board of directors and the pipeline is run by the management team and their deputies while the Russian and Kazak sides of the pipeline have their own management team.[105] A lot of coordination is required for the effective running of the pipeline.[106] Most of the decisions are taken at the shareholders' meetings and all the decisions regarding the pipeline have to be reached through consensus as there is no majority voting available.[107]

The Russian, Omanese and Kazak government also had to enter into agreement for the smooth functioning of the pipeline project.[108] The Russian Federation agreed to enter into agreements and treaties and the government also passed a decree affirming the agreements signed by the Russian government.[109] The agreements also mentioned that the relevant authorities within the Russian Federation have to abide by all the rules and regulations of the agreements and that the President would exempt the companies participating in the project from currency conversion requirements.[110]

The Kazak government also signed similar agreements and treaties with the respective companies involved in the project and the government also passed decrees ensuring the agreements are complied with properly.[111] Some of the other obligations that the Russian, Oman and Kazakhstan governments had to ensure are as follows:[112]

- *To guarantee the stability of the legal and economic terms including rights of way, taxation, tariffs and environmental provisions*
- *To facilitate the use of their infrastructural facilities*
- *To cooperate with the private companies in order to get funds from other sources should the need arise*
- *To confirm the exemption from all sorts of taxation*
- *To confirm that the project would not be subject to pipeline transportation or port fees*
- *To agree to take all legal measures to maintain and restore economic parameters of the project*
- *To permit the currency transaction to US Dollars*[113]

---

105. See A. Dellecker, *Caspian Pipeline Consortium, Bellweather of Russia's Investment Climate*, in IFRI website at <www.ifri.org/files/Russie/ifri_RNV_Dellecker_CPC_ENG_juin2008. pdf>, 2008.
106. This means that the CPC is run based upon consensus and the opinion of all the stakeholders have to be taken in to account before any final decision is reached.
107. See Dellecker, *supra* n. 105.
108. See the Pipeline Consortium Agreement between the Government of the Republic of Kazakhstan, the Government of the Sultanate of Oman and the Government of the Russian Federation, 1992.
109. See ESMAP, *supra* n. 90.
110. See the Pipeline Consortium Agreement between the Government of the Republic of Kazakhstan, the Government of the Sultanate of Oman and the Government of the Russian Federation, 1992.
111. See *ibid.*
112. See *ibid.*
113. See *ibid.*

6.7.  THE APPLICATION OF THE CRITERIA ON THE
CROSS-BORDER PIPELINE REGIME

6.7.1.  THE NATURE AND CHARACTERISTICS OF THE REGIME

The main players of the pipeline regime are Russia and Kazakhstan together with the other private companies involved.[146] The pipeline regime is made up of public and private partnership and the number of important players in the regime is large. Russia, being the transit country, is one of the major players due to their increased share, together with Kazakhstan, the exporting country. The various shippers involved in the pipeline also play a crucial role as without their investment the pipeline regime would not have been operating successfully.[147] The private partner' interests and the interests of the transit and exporting countries are similar as all the players want to extract the maximum benefit from the pipeline regime.[148]

The CPC pipeline is a complex pipeline in terms of structure as there are many parties involved in the project. It is a shipper-owned pipeline and the public–private partnership has to be balanced in order for the smooth running of this joint venture. The shareholders have substantial input in the running of the pipeline and the joint venture is made up of all the stakeholders involved in the pipeline chain.[149] The Consortium is also broken down into two other joint stock companies, CPC-R looking after the Russian side of the pipeline and CPC-K following the Kazakhstan side.[150] There were also IGAs and HGAs signed by the various parties involved in the pipeline chain which provided the legal and regulatory framework required for the smooth operation of the pipeline.[151]

Agreements were signed between the Russian and Kazakhstan governments for the smooth transportation of the oil through Russia.[152] The HGAs signed by Russian and Kazakhstan governments with the international oil companies advocated for a stable legal and economic framework for the private investors, tax exemption and greater cooperation of all the government agencies in the country.[153] There were also BITs signed between Russia and Kazakhstan to provide the much needed framework for the other partners to join the project. One of

---

146. See ESMAP, *supra* n. 90.
147. See Dellecker, *supra* n. 105.
148. See *ibid.*
149. See *ibid.*
150. See *ibid.*
151. The IGAs are signed between Russia, Oman and Kazakhstan, where as the HGAs are signed between the international companies investing in the pipeline and the respective governments, in this case between the companies and the Russian and Kazak governments respectively.
152. See Pipeline Consortium Agreement between the Government of the Republic of Kazakhstan, the Government of the Sultanate of Oman and the Government of the Russian Federation, 1992.
153. See the HGA Agreement Between Russia and Kazakstan with Chevron, British Gas Overseas Holding Ltd.

the reasons for this was the lack of a proper legal and regulatory framework in both the countries which resulted in problems for the investors in the region.[154]

The management structure has certain rules and principles and decision-making procedures which have all the ingredients necessary to be classed as a regime. The IGAs and the HGAs signed between the various parties provide the framework by which all the parties are aware of their various roles and obligations.[155] The BITs also provide the framework through which the stakeholders are aware of the legal and regulatory requirements.[156] As a result, the management structure of the CPC pipeline had input of all the shareholders of the project and they tried to enforce the various rules and regulations agreed between the parties. The decision-making procedure was decided upon collectively at shareholders' meetings where various issues of the pipeline operation are discussed.[157] However, the two other companies set up, CPC-R and CPC-K, are responsible for the pipelines in Russia and Kazakhstan while CPC management runs the rest of the pipelines.[158] These two companies act like two different regimes within the bigger regime.

The CPC pipeline regime is weak despite the regime having regime rules present. The reason for this is that the actors involved in the regime do not follow all the regime rules and principles properly. This is because the pipeline is made up of three governments and ten companies representing seven countries, there are two further companies CPC-R and CPC-K within the CPC which are independent, the management is made up of the representatives of the shareholders while the pipeline was built with assets given by the governments and financed by the private shareholders.[159] All these factors make the entire pipeline chain complex and there is no central authority following the entire pipeline chain.[160] Since most decisions are taken through consensus, the decision-making procedure is dependent upon the shareholders' interest rather than the interest of the regime.[161] The stakeholders with greater power can also veto any decision which harms the effectiveness of the regime.[162] As a result there is no chain of command due to their being smaller

---

154. See ESMAP, *supra* n. 90.
155. The IGAs are signed between Russia and Kazakhstan, where as the HGAs are signed between the international companies investing in the pipeline and the respective governments, in this case between the companies and the Russian and Kazak governments respectively.
156. The BIT is signed between Russia and the government from which the oil company has originated. This involves the US and Russia BIT, the US Kazakhstan BIT and also between the governments of other countries. The purpose of the BITs is to provide some kind of guarantee from the government side from expropriation or other eventualities which might harm the companies' business interests.
157. See ESMAP, *supra* n. 90.
158. See Dellecker, *supra* n. 105.
159. See *ibid.*
160. It is important to have a central authority or an enforcement mechanism within a pipeline regime in order to ensure that all the actors are abiding by their obligations. See Dellecker, *supra* n. 105.
161. See Dellecker, *supra* n. 105.
162. See *ibid.*

independent regimes within the bigger regime, resulting in a lack of coordination and order in the implementation of the various rules and principles of the regime framework.[163]

There are both neo-liberalistic and neo-realist ideals in the CPC pipeline regime. The shareholders act in a collective way and cooperate with each other in order for the smooth functioning of the pipeline. Most of the decision-making procedure in the pipeline operations is reached through consensus and the stakeholders are also willing to sacrifice certain benefits for the greater interest of the pipeline regime.[164] These are all neo-liberal ethos, as the neo-liberals advocate for greater cooperation between all the stakeholders involved in the regime and according to them relative gains should be more important than absolute gains for the actors. However, there are powerful and hegemonic actors within the pipeline regime trying to influence the decision-making procedure and they also try to use their superior position within the pipeline chain to implement their objectives. For example, the CPC pipeline could not be expanded for years due to differences between Russia and the other stakeholders.[165] These neo-realistic tendencies can result in the actor with the most power getting away with actions furthering their own ulterior motives.

6.7.2.      THE ISSUES AFFECTING THE CROSS-BORDER PIPELINE

The CPC pipeline started operation in 2001. It became quite successful as shippers wanted to be a part of the pipeline and it was functioning above the 27mt/y capacity by 2004.[166] As a result of this success there was a need for expansion of the pipeline to fulfil the demands of the importers and the shippers.[167] This prompted CPC management to plan for an expansion of the pipeline to make it financially viable for all the stakeholders involved. A preliminary expansion plan was presented to the shareholders in 2003 and all the parties involved agreed with the plan as it allowed them to make more profit and also make the pipeline successful.[168] However, the problem was the basis upon which the expansion could take place. The CPC management system was run by consensus, which means anyone not agreeing with the plan has the right to block it.[169] Satisfying and meeting everyone's needs became a problem. The block in this case was Russia.

---

163.  See ESMAP, *supra* n. 90.
164.  See PFC Memo, *supra* n. 133.
165.  See *ibid.*
166.  See ESMAP, *supra* n. 90.
167.  See *ibid.*
168.  See *ibid.*
169.  See Dellecker, *supra* n. 105.

The former Director General of the consortium stated that 'what the other partners saw as business imperative to survive, Russia saw as an opportunity to increase its clout'.[170]

Russia had a list of demands based upon which it would decide whether to agree to the CPC expansion. These demands were: *'(i) change in the tariff review mechanism, so that tariff can be increased accordingly (ii) a dismissal of CPC claims to account for the rehabilitation of transferred assets in its balance sheet (iii) the lowering of the interest rates for the loans provided to the consortium by the operating companies and iv) the introduction of send or pay clauses'.*[171] Russia also wanted to get rid of the management secondees and wanted to create a board of directors according to the proportion of the stakes held by each party.[172] Russia was the only roadblock towards expansion as the others felt favourably towards the idea.[173] Although the agreements allow a stakeholder to block in case of any disagreement, this is a breach of legitimate expectation of the other stakeholders involved in the pipeline, as all the stakeholders agreed to undertake any measures which will benefit them and allows them to maximize their profit.[174]

The new demands by Russia in order to allow expansion of the pipeline were not accepted by all the shareholders as meeting these demands would fundamentally change the structure of the contract originally agreed and signed between the parties.[175] The change in the tariff structure would allow some actors to earn more than others, the send or pay clause would change the contractual framework of the quota system, while the setting up of a new board of directors would also create a change in the management structure which would not be supported by the other stakeholders.[176] All these factors caused a stalemate and are causing the pipeline a loss of USD 60 million every month.[177] However, the other actors in the consortium are also aware of the implication if they fail to reach a consensus over the issue. According to one expert 'the partners involved in the pipeline chain might be forced to invest elsewhere if the CPC expansion stalemate is not solved soon'.[178]

In 2006, one of the Russian demands was met by the consortium with the appointment of a new Director General from Russia, Vladimir Razdukov.[179] After

---

170. See *ibid.*
171. See *ibid.*
172. See V. Socor, 'Transneft Squeezing Western Oil Majors in Caspian Consortium', *Eurasian Daily Monitor* (July 2007).
173. See *ibid.*
174. See Dellecker, *supra* n. 105.
175. See Socor, *supra* n. 172.
176. See *ibid.*
177. See Dellecker, *supra* n. 105. (According to the former director general, by single-handedly holding this project up, Russia is set to lose USD 173 million a year in transit fees, together with other revenues the pipeline generates).
178. See R. Hickox, 'The Caspian Pipeline Consortium Project', *Pipeline and Gas Journal* (February 2007). This can be accessed via <www.undergroundinfo.com>.
179. See *ibid.*

his appointment, Transneft called for several extraordinary general meetings to change the management structure of the CPC and has also advocated to get rid of the consensus-based system.[180] In July 2007, they tried to pass this motion but it failed in the vote.[181] All these factors are indirectly affecting the operation of the CPC pipeline as the chances of disruption are pretty high.

Another issue which also affected the pipeline was when the Russian Federal Tax service claimed back taxes in 2006 for a sum of 2.1 billion rubles for 1999–2002 and 4.7 billion rubles for 2002–2003.[182] This attitude of the Russian government is completely contrary to the original agreement signed between the CPC stakeholders and the Russian government, where they clearly agreed to provide tax free access to all the parties involved in the consortium.[183] Accordingly, these tactics by Russia are contrary to the original contract and have caused friction between the different stakeholders involved in the pipeline which might ultimately have an effect on the supply of resources through the pipeline.[184]

The problems highlighted above show the geo-political and economic interests at stake which have prompted one of the stronger members within the regime to interfere, resulting in the delay of the pipeline expansion.[185] Other members of the regime were also put under intense pressure when the Russian government claimed back taxes from them.[186] This shows a lack of any form of regulatory mechanism within the regime itself which could have dealt with this kind of situation. The regime members were also not in a position to ask for any assistance due to this lack of regulation or enforcement of the various rules and regulations and also because of a lack of any independent regulatory mechanism within the regime.[187]

There is a mixture of both neo-liberal and neo-realist ideals among the parties involved in the pipeline. Russia acts like a hegemony and wants to influence the decision-making procedure of the shareholders. It also wants to lessen Western influence in the region.[188] These neo-realist ideals allow Russia to implement their

---

180. See Dellecker, *supra* n. 105.
181. See J. Webb, et al., *From East Siberia to Pacific: Putin's Oil Pipeline Project of the Century,* CERA private Report, March 2008. This can be accessed via <www.cera.com>.
182. See Socor, *supra* n. 172.
183. See Webb, *supra* n. 181. Also read the HGA Agreement Between Russia and Kazakstan with Chevron, British Gas Overseas Holding Ltd.
184. See Webb, *supra* n. 181.
185. See *ibid.*
186. See *ibid.* Also read the HGA Agreement between Russia and Kazakstan with Chevron, British Gas Overseas Holding Ltd.
187. Economic and geo-political problems due to the interference of a strong party within the regime have a clear link with the problem the book is trying to solve. It also highlights the behaviour of the parties within a regime and the tactics used by them to safeguard their interest above others of the regime.
188. See Webb, *supra* n. 181.

objectives as they are after absolute gain and their geographical location and military strength within the pipeline chain and in the region allows them to do so. However, most of the other shareholders are willing to cooperate with each other and believe the consensus system is ideal for the smooth functioning of the pipeline. The Western oil companies and Kazakhstan lean more towards cooperation and relative gains for all the partners in the project, as this would maximize their benefits as well as the benefits of all the stakeholders.[189] They are striving to keep a balance between the geo-politics in the region and their own interests in the pipeline.

6.7.3.     THE COMMON INTEREST OF THE PARTIES

The interests of all the parties involved in the CPC pipeline are different as each stakeholder is trying to protect their own interests. Russia has earned extra revenue through transit tariffs.[190] It was also able to get its dilapidated pipelines upgraded to increase capacity and this will help them with their own exports to other countries should they wish to use it.[191] Geopolitically, they have also gained because they will be able to keep a closer eye on Caspian resources going to other parts of the world and may try to influence the various decision-making processes of the CPC through their role as a transit country and as a regional hegemony.[192] Kazakhstan, however, was able to diversify its export route and also find another market for their resources. By using Russia as a transit country they are also able to maintain a good relationship with Russia, as they are dependent on their transit facilities.[193]

The international oil companies involved in the project are also benefiting from participating in the project as they are getting a steady return on their investment. Their interest is to ensure a balance between the governments and themselves in order to maintain the smooth functioning of the pipeline.[194] The Western countries are also keen to see them succeed as they want some sort of Western influence on Caspian hydro-carbon resources.[195] As a result, there is a divergence of interest among all the stakeholders in the pipeline. The only common interest holding them together is their intention of maximizing their profit by being a part of the pipeline.

---

189. See *ibid.*
190. See *ibid.*
191. See Ogutcu, *supra* n. 138.
192. See *ibid.*
193. See *ibid.*
194. See *ibid.*
195. See Webb, *supra* n. 181.

The actions of all the parties involved in the pipeline chain are neo-liberal in nature due to their interests being interlinked. The common interest of all the parties involved in the pipeline chain was to maximize benefits and to ensure that everyone makes a gain out of the venture. Although the actions of Russia can be compared to that of a neo-realist due to its hegemonic power and its aims to get its own objectives implemented, even they are willing to cooperate for the greater good of all the stakeholders involved. The expansion of the pipeline to increase its overall capacity and the joint decision-making process towards the operation of the pipeline shows the cooperative nature of the stakeholders involved in the pipeline. Although the interests of the parties can be different, due to their divergent objectives, the stakeholders in the CPC pipeline want to ensure the smooth operation of the pipeline because of the huge amount of investments made by all the parties and the revenue it generates for the shareholders.[196]

6.7.4.     THE ENFORCEMENT AND COMPLIANCE OF THE CROSS-BORDER
           PIPELINE AGREEMENTS

The IGAs and HGAs signed between the stakeholders in the pipeline clearly state the enforcement and compliance mechanism within the various clauses of the agreement. In fact, due to the weak legal and regulatory framework of the countries through which the pipeline passes, these agreements were essential for the smooth running of the pipeline.[197] It also made the parties aware of the different rules and regulations they are obliged to follow. However, despite the signing of the agreement there have been instances when these rules and regulations were not enforced or followed. For example, the tax exemption of the international oil companies was suddenly changed due to a change in policy of the Russian government.[198] The Russian government also found technical faults when they were directed by the other stakeholders to abide by the agreements signed by their respective governments.[199]

The creation of two other joint stock companies, CPC-K and CPC-R, has also made matters difficult as there is no single monitoring authority following the actions of the parties involved in the project. Accordingly, each entity acts on its own or does not leave its area of jurisdiction, resulting in a lack of coordination

---

196.  See Ogutcu, *supra* n. 138.
197.  The IGAs are signed between Russia and Kazakhstan, where as the HGAs are signed between the international companies investing in the pipeline and the respective governments, in this case between the companies and the Russian and Kazak governments respectively. Also read the Agreement on Common Conditions for Transit through the Territory of the Custom Union Member-Countries, between Belarus, Kazakhstan, Kyrgyz Republic and the Russian Federation, 1998.
198.  See Webb, *supra* n. 181.
199.  See *ibid.*

in the implementation and enforcement of the various clauses of the cross-border pipeline agreements.[200] For example, Article 3 of the transit agreement mentions that 'the parties shall commit themselves to taking necessary measures, including joint measures, to ensure that none of the parties is faced with a threat of disconnection from the sources of gas supply and that the interest of natural gas supplier States and transit States are not infringed upon'.[201] However, Russia threatened to disrupt the flow of the pipeline and also decided against pipeline expansion which lowered the supply of gas in the pipeline which is clearly against Article 3 of the agreement.[202]

The action of the parties involved in the pipeline have certain neo-liberal and neo-realist traits. Russia being the strongest player in the pipeline chain, is aware of its hegemonic power and acts like a neo-realist to further its absolute gain. This means the other actors are not able to enforce the rules and regulations of the contract resulting in a lack of enforcement and compliance in the CPC pipeline regime.[203] Some of the other parties involved in the chain have neo-liberal tendencies, as they are willing to cooperate with each other in order to enforce the clauses of the agreement for the benefit of all the actors within the pipeline chain. In general, it is difficult to enforce the various rules and regulations of the agreement because of the many sub-regimes within a regime causing a lack of coordination and impartiality in the enforcement process.[204]

## 6.8.        THE MAGHREB–EUROPE PIPELINE (MEP)

### 6.8.1.        THE BACKGROUND OF THE PROJECT

The Maghreb–Europe gas pipeline is one of two pipelines supplying gas to Europe from Algeria. The Maghreb–Europe pipeline is also known as Pedro Duran Farrel Pipeline (Figure 6.3). The pipeline is 1,620 kilometres long and brings gas from the Hass R'mel Field in Algeria through Morocco and Cordoba in Andalusia, Spain, where it is connected to the Spanish and Portuguese gas grids.[205] The pipeline has the capacity of supplying 8.6 billion cubic metres of natural gas and there are plans to increase its capacity to 18.5 billion cubic metres by adding more compressors in the route.[206]

---

200. See Socor, *supra* n. 172.
201. See the Agreement on Common Conditions for Transit through the Territory of the Custom Union Member-Countries, between Belarus, Kazakhstan, Kyrgyz Republic and the Russian Federation, 1998.
202. See *ibid.*
203. See Socor, *supra* n. 172.
204. See *ibid.*
205. See A. Aissaoui, *Algeria: the Political Economy of Oil and Gas* (Oxford: Oxford University Press, 2001).
206. See *ibid.*

*Figure 6.3    Algerian Oil and Gas Supply Pipelines to Europe*[207]

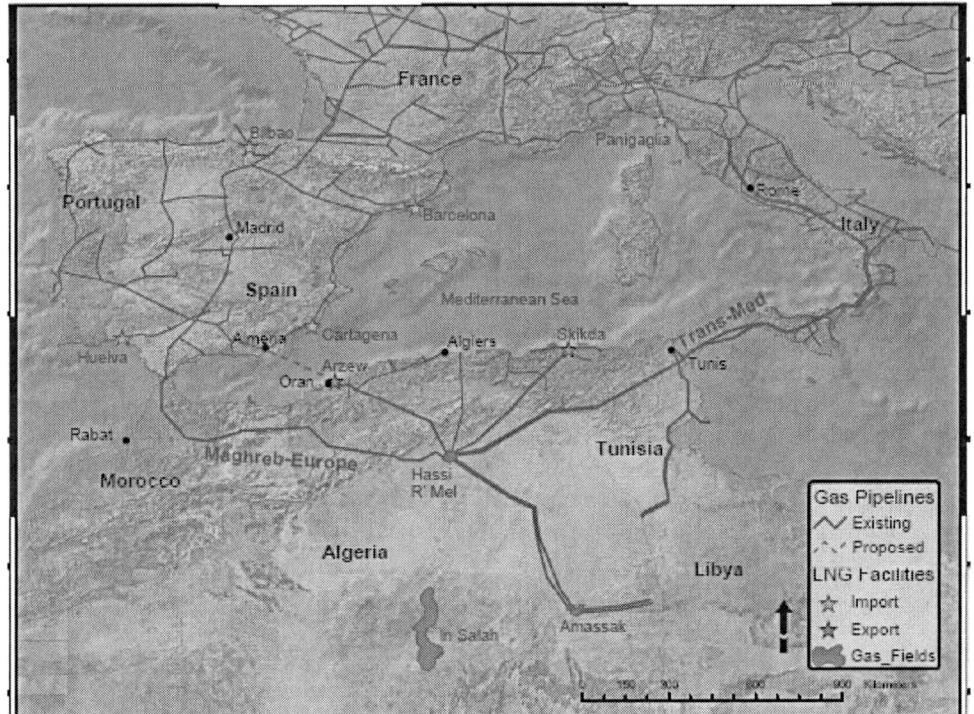

*Source*: Victor, D.G., et al., *Natural Gas and Geopolitics: From 1970–2040*, Cambridge University Press, 2006.

The MEP has five sections. The pipeline's Algerian, Moroccan and Spanish sections are 48 inches in diameter, the link to Portugal is 7–8 inches in diameter while the underwater section has two 22 inch lines.[208] The Algerian section of the pipeline is 530 kilometres long and runs from the Hassi R'mel field in Algeria to the Moroccan border and is owned and operated by the Algerian state company Sonatrach.[209] The 540 kilometres long Moroccan section of the pipeline is owned and operated by the Moroccan state company Metragaz, which is a joint venture company owned by Sagne of Spain (a subsidiary of Gas Natural of Spain), Transgas of Portugal and SNPP of Morocco.[210] The offshore section of the pipeline passing through the Strait of Gibraltar is 45 kilometres and is owned by Engas of

---

207. The purpose of this pipeline diagram is to show the extensiveness of the pipeline and the geographical terrain it crosses and its geo-political implications.
208. See Aissaoui, *supra* n. 205.
209. See *ibid.*
210. See *ibid.*

Spain, Transgas and the Moroccan state.[211] The Spanish section of the pipeline is 275 kilometres long and the Portuguese section is 500 kilometres long, while a further 270 kilometres goes through the autonomous region of Extremadura in Spain.[212]

6.8.2.        THE RELEVANT PARTIES OF THE PROJECT

The main partners of the MEP project are Sonatrach of Algeria, Engas of Spain and Transgas of Portugal (Figure 6.4).[213] The Moroccan state company Metragaz is also involved but only in transit terms. In 1992, Sonatrach and Engas signed a natural gas agreement for the delivery of 6 billion cubic metres of gas through to 2020.[214] In 1994, Sonatrach also signed another gas sales agreement with the Portuguese state company Transgas for a delivery of 2.5 billion cubic metres of Algerian Gas through to 2022.[215] The transit country, Morocco, would receive 7% of the gas passing through the pipeline as royalty gas or, in other words, tariff for letting gas pass through their territory.

The 1992 Agreement between the Moroccan government, Engas and SNPP (SNPP holds legal title to the gas pipeline in Morocco) allowed Engas to build, use and operate the pipeline within the corporate structure allowed in the agreement.[216]

6.8.3.        THE COST OF THE PROJECT

The cost of building the entire pipeline was USD 2.2 billion.[217] Each owner of the pipeline paid 15% of the section cost as the payment structure depended upon the stake held by each partner in the project.[218] The remaining 85% was financed by multilateral agencies, credit agencies and commercial banks.[219] The European Investment Bank (EIB) also provided a significant amount of funds and helped to gather finances from other sources.[220]

The Moroccan section of the pipeline was financed by Engas (9%) and the Spanish government (91%) and in 1992 a new company was created called Sagane SA, which in turn created EMPL in 1994.[221] Transgas of Portugal acquired a 27% stake in the company, while the construction and operation of the pipeline was

---

211.  See D.G. Victor et al., *Natural Gas and Geopolitics: From 1970–2040* (Cambridge: Cambridge University Press, 2006).
212.  See *ibid.*
213.  See *ibid.*
214.  See *ibid.*
215.  See ESMAP, *supra* n. 90.
216.  See *ibid.*
217.  See Victor, *supra* n. 211.
218.  See *ibid.*
219.  See ESMAP, *supra* n. 90.
220.  See *ibid.*
221.  See *ibid.*

*Figure 6.4   The Main Sections and Investment of the
Stakeholders in the MEP Project*[222]

| | Kilometres | Diameter | Property | Investment Million US$ |
|---|---|---|---|---|
| Algeria | 520 | 48" | Sonatrach | 675 |
| Morocco | 540 | 48" | Morrocan State | 760 |
| Off-shore | 45 | 2X22" | Enagas/Transgas/ Moroccan State | 146 |
| Andalucia | 275 | 48" | Enagas/Transgas | 277 |
| Extremadura | 270 | 32"/28" | Enagas/Transgas | 167 |
| Portugal | 500 | 28" | Transgas/Enagas | 275 |

*Source*: P. Moraled, 2002.

undertaken by Metragaz of Morocco, which is jointly owned by EMPL and SNPP.[223]

6.8.4.      OTHER ASPECTS OF THE PIPELINE

The 1992 contract between Sonatrach and Engas obligated Sonatrach to provide delivery of Algerian gas to Spain. Delivery started in 1996 and by 1997 the delivery reached about 3.2 billion cubic metres of gas.[224] However, the quantity reached a plateau level of 6 billion cubic metres by 2000 and this is supposed to continue till 2020.[225] Gas delivery to Portugal is supposed to reach a plateau level of 2.5 billion cubic metres following initial delivery from 1996.[226]

---

222. The purpose of this table is to provide an idea about the level of investment by each party involved in the pipeline and the length of the pipeline passing each country.
223. See Victor, *supra* n. 211.
224. See *ibid.*
225. See ESMAP, *supra* n. 90.
226. See *ibid.*

The principal contractual parties in the MEP are Sonatrach, Engas and Transgas.[227] There is a price review clause in the contract between the three parties which mitigates any risks that might be undertaken by the parties.[228] The principle function of this clause is to adjust the commercial balance of the contract by the agreement of the parties.[229] However, in case of any disagreement, there is a provision for third party involvement in the contract and the provision for arbitration.[230]

Another interesting feature of the pipeline is that any reduction in production would be shared by all the parties involved in the project. Any disruption in the gas delivery from Algeria would result in Morocco losing their transit revenues, Algeria losing out on their gas sales and Spain and Portugal losing out on their gas supplies, resulting in the customers in those countries being deprived of gas supplies and the two gas companies in Spain and Portugal losing out on their revenues.[231]

Sonatrach would also be able to enforce their claim on payments for the gas in convertible currency at internationally competitive prices.[232] The currency convertible risk in Algeria is minimal because most of the gas sales agreement only allows payments to be made in US dollars.[233] Spain and Portugal also allow domestic prices to follow international prices for energy resulting in greater flexibility in payments and currency convertibility.[234]

## 6.9.    THE IMPORTANT ASPECTS OF THE PIPELINE

### 6.9.1.    ECONOMIC ASPECT

Algeria's Sonatrach is totally dependent upon the demand of gas from Spanish and Portuguese markets.[235] The gas supply in these countries would increase depending upon the demand for gas in their domestic markets.[236] The Spanish government introduced a new National Energy Plan which advocates the conversion of 7,300

---

227.  See the agreement between Sonatrach, Engas and Transgas and also the HGA between Spain and Sonatrach. Can be accessed via <www.sonatrach-dz.com>.
228.  See *ibid.*
229.  See *ibid.*
230.  See *ibid.*
231.  See Aissaoui, *supra* n. 205.
232.  See ESMAP, *supra* n. 90.
233.  See *ibid.*
234.  See J. Stern, *International Gas Trade in Europe: The Policies of Exporting and Importing Countries* (Aldershot: Gower, 1986).
235.  See *ibid.*
236.  See *ibid.*

MW of existing power generation into gas.[237] This would increase gas consumption. In Portugal, the government has built new gas infrastructures and gas powered power plants which would increase gas consumption.[238]

The collapse of demand for gas in any of these markets would protect Sonatrach to some extent because of the minimum payment provision in the contract, which would insulate the risks involved.[239] The capacity of the MEP pipeline could also be increased if the demand for gas rises in these countries.[240] For example, the contract price for gas is linked to the prices of displaced fuels, as a result, any fluctuations in the changing oil prices would be borne by the seller, in this case Sonatrach.[241]

### 6.9.2.    THE INTEREST OF THE COUNTRIES

The main interest of Spain and Portugal is to get a secure and reliable source of energy for their domestic energy needs and Algeria provides them with that option.[242] However, they are a bit sceptical of relying on Algeria for all their supplies because of the domestic problems in the country which might jeopardize the supply of gas to these countries.[243] Algeria, however, is keen to increase its export of gas to Europe and to the other regions of the world. The country is totally reliant on gas and oil export as it is one of its main export earnings and therefore relies on demand for gas and oil from different regions.[244]

The role of Morocco in the MEP project is also crucial because without its cooperation the project might not have seen the light of day. Although Morocco is earning tariffs in the form of gas by allowing the pipeline to pass through the country, it does not have good relations with its North African neighbour, Algeria.[245] The MEP pipeline allows Morocco to show its influence in the region and also enhance its reputation as an important strategic country in the Maghreb region.[246]

---

237. See P. Moraleda, *How the Major Barriers to Cross-Border Gas Trade were Overcome in the Case of Maghreb Pipeline*, IEA Cross-Border Gas Conference, Paris, March 26, Paris International Energy Agency, 2002.
238. See Stern, *supra* n. 234.
239. See the Agreement between Sonatrach, Engas and Transgas and also the HGA between Spain and Sonatrach. Can be accessed via <www.sonatrach-dz.com>.
240. See ESMAP, *supra* n. 90.
241. See *ibid.*
242. See *ibid.*
243. See Moraleda, *supra* n. 237.
244. See *ibid.*
245. See *ibid.*
246. See *ibid.*

6.9.3.          THE LEGAL ASPECT

The gas sales agreement signed between Sonatrach, Engas and Transgas is quite flexible and allows all the parties to manoeuvre if there is any difficulty in implementing the contract.[247] For example, there is a provision for arbitration which allows the parties to ask for third party help if there are any disputes.[248] There are also some regulatory risks involved as Spain and Portugal have to abide by the EU gas directive of 1998, which calls for greater competition and choice for suppliers.[249] Sonatrach might therefore have to face greater competition from other suppliers in Spain and Portugal which might lower the demand for their gas, forcing both Spain and Portugal to accommodate other additional suppliers.[250] Although both Spain and Portugal have to buy a minimum amount of gas under the agreement, Sonatrach would lose out on substantial revenues if that was to happen.[251] This has resulted in government intervention from both Algeria and Spain as they had to renegotiate their contractual obligations in order for Spain to avoid any penalty.[252] This direct intervention by these governments lessened the role of the regulator of the pipeline and made the regime weak.

Another contractual risk may also arise due to the change in the nature of the partners involved in the project through privatization.[253] In that case, the new partner has to abide by all the rules and regulations of the previous partner, which in some cases might be a problem if the new partner has a different vision for the project, or if they decide to avert the various risks involved. However, governments still tend to intervene in the pipeline. For example, the Spanish government had to intervene when one of the companies came under new ownership.[254] It had to intercede to ensure that the new company abided by all the obligations of the previous companies which it had declined to do at the beginning.[255] This kind of intervention makes the role of the regulator weak, as it is the role of the regulator to ensure that the stakeholders involved in the pipeline carries out their obligations rather than government getting involved.

---

247. See the Gas Sale Agreement between Engas, Sontrach and Transgas, available at <www.sonatrach-dz.com/NEW/>.
248. See the IGA between the Kingdom of Spain, People's Democratic Republic of Algeria and the Kingdom of Morocco concerning the supply of gas from Algeria to Spain through Morocco, 1992.
249. See Directive 98/30/EC, can be found at <www.ec.europa.eu>.
250. See Victor, *supra* n. 211.
251. See *ibid.*
252. See ESMAP, *supra* n. 90.
253. See *ibid.*
254. See Victor, *supra* n. 211.
255. See *ibid.*

*Figure 6.5   The Contractual Structure of the MEP Pipeline*[256]

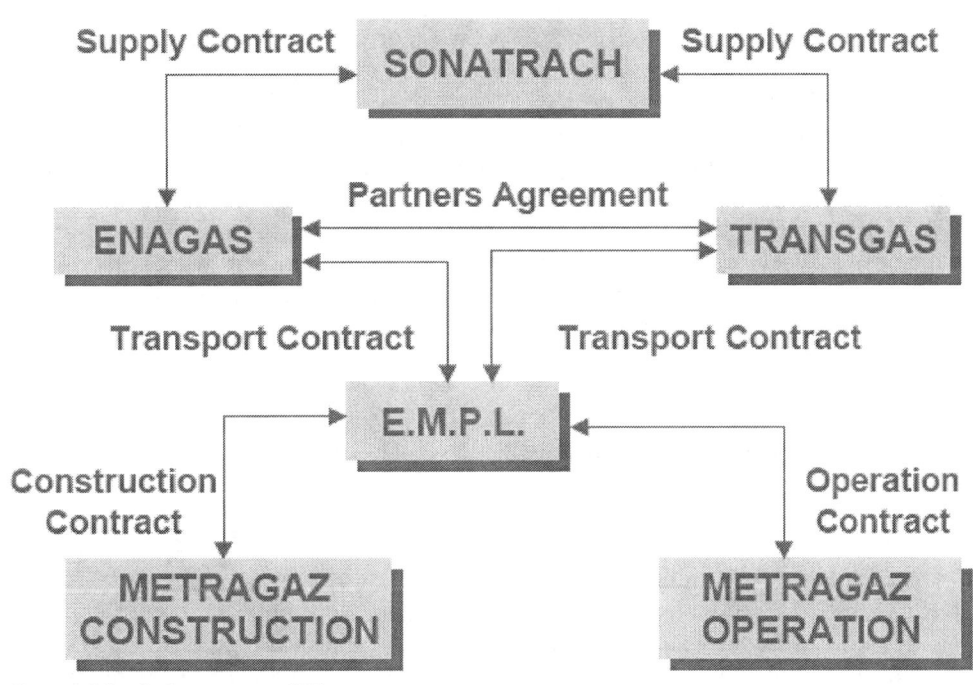

*Source*: Moraleda, *supra* n. 237.

6.9.4.        THE GEO-POLITICS OF THE PIPELINE

The main purpose of the MEP pipeline is to deliver gas to Spain from Algeria (Figure 6.5). Although Algeria wanted to avoid the pipeline going through Morocco because of their strained diplomatic relations with that country, Spain was willing to take the risk of the pipeline going through Morocco.[257] There were problems with the route when the pipeline was first envisaged during the 1970s and 1980s, and due to financial and geo-political relations between the two countries, the project was not implemented.[258] However, Spain's greater need for energy coupled with Algeria's need to export its resources resulted in Spain courting the Moroccan government.[259] Morocco set aside its differences with Algeria in agreeing to let the country be used as a transit route.

---

256. The purpose of this diagram is to highlight the complex contractual structure between the different stakeholders involved in the pipeline.
257. See Victor, *supra* n. 211.
258. See *ibid.*
259. See Aissaoui, *supra* n. 205.

Portugal, which also receives gas from Algeria through Spain, is another beneficiary of this pipeline.[260] This was only possible due to better relations with Spain, as the two countries had been bitter enemies in the past.[261] These two Iberian countries have set their geo-political ambitions and rivalries aside to cooperate in this pipeline project.[262]

The transit route chosen by the various stakeholders is beneficial for all the parties involved in the project. Morocco borders Algeria and the cost of the pipeline would be significantly lower going through the country rather than on the sea bed.[263] The LNG option was also expensive.[264] The pipeline route was chosen to solve both financial and geological problems.[265] Although there were reservations about Morocco as a transit country due to its hostile relationship with Algeria, both countries have so far avoided any disputes.

## 6.10. THE APPLICATION OF THE CRITERIA ON THE CROSS-BORDER PIPELINE REGIME

### 6.10.1. THE NATURE AND CHARACTERISTICS OF THE REGIME

The main players within the Maghreb–Europe pipeline regime are Algeria, Spain, Portugal and Morocco. Algeria is the exporting country supplying gas to Spain and Portugal via Morocco. The roles of Algeria and Spain in the pipeline regime are quite important because they initiated the regime framework from the beginning and also provided the groundwork of the pipeline to be built. Although Morocco plays an important role as a transit country, Spain and Algeria are dominant actors within the regime because of their interests in the pipeline. Spain is dependent upon the gas from Algeria for its domestic needs whereas Algeria requires Spain for its gas exports.[266] Morocco provides the transit although it has little to gain other than transit tariffs.

There are various IGAs and HGAs between the parties involved in the pipeline in order to effect its smooth functioning.[267] These agreements provide the legal and regulatory framework based upon which the cross-border pipeline is operated.[268] There is also a take or pay agreement signed between Sonatrach of Algeria, Transgas of Portugal and Engas of Spain based upon which Spain and Portugal have to

---

260. See *ibid.*
261. See *ibid.*
262. See *ibid.*
263. See Moraleda, *supra* n. 237.
264. See *ibid.*
265. See *ibid.*
266. See ESMAP, *supra* n. 90.
267. See the IGA between the Kingdom of Spain, People's Democratic Republic of Algeria and the Kingdom of Morocco concerning the supply of gas from Algeria to Spain through Morocco
268. See *ibid.*

take a certain amount of gas every year for an agreed fee.[269] This agreement mitigates the price risk Algeria might face if the demand for gas decreases in these countries and the parties decide not to continue with the import.[270] Despite that, Algeria had to renegotiate with Spain when Spain could not take the required amount of gas and should have been penalized.[271] The Spanish government had to intervene before both parties renegotiated.

The pipeline regime has various rules and regulations which gives it a regime structure. EMPL is the company that has implemented the project and has the right to use the pipeline for twenty-five years.[272] All shareholders involved in the pipeline chain have shares in the company. The company carries out the various functions independently, takes decisions and maintains rules based upon their requirements.[273] The agreements signed by the various parties have also provided guidelines regarding the various obligations of the parties and their roles within the pipeline regime.[274]

The Maghreb–Europe pipeline regime is weak, because the enforcement mechanism of the regime is non-existent as the actors within the regime carry out their various obligations depending on their own personal interest.[275] As a result, the regime does not provide the platform based upon which all the actors within the pipeline regime can gain from being a part of the regime. This makes the regime weak because there is very little a regime can do to find out whether the actors are complying with their obligations. For example, the regulatory authority did not fine the Spanish company despite failing to take the required amount of gas that they were supposed to take under the contract.[276] This caused financial loss and uncertainty for Sonatrach of Algeria.[277,278] This is also a breach of legitimate expectation for Algeria as they expected to supply a certain amount of gas to Spain over a period of time as agreed between the parties in the agreement. However, through negotiation with the Spanish government they are not being able to go back to the original position of the contract which would have enabled them to earn more revenue than now.[279]

The attitude of the parties involved in the pipeline chain are neo-liberal in nature as all the parties cooperate with each other for the successful operation of the pipeline. Although there are certain parties who gain more than others, most of the

---

269. See the Gas Sale Agreement between Engas, Sontrach and Transgas, available at <www.sonatrach-dz.com/NEW/>.
270. See Aissaoui, *supra* n. 205.
271. See *ibid.*
272. See ESMAP, *supra* n. 90.
273. See *ibid.*
274. See the Gas Sale Agreement between Engas, Sontrach and Transgas, available at <www.sonatrach-dz.com/NEW/>.
275. See Victor, *supra* n. 211.
276. See *ibid.*
277. See *ibid.*
278. See Aissaoui, *supra* n. 205.
279. See Victor, *supra* n. 211.

parties have set aside their rivalry in the region and worked for the benefit of all the actors involved in the pipeline regime.[280] All these factors have similarities to a neo-liberal ethos, which advocates for greater cooperation amongst all the actors in a regime because the common good should be the main aim of all actors within a regime and that relative gain should be pursued rather than absolute gain to ensure the success of the regime.

### 6.10.2.    THE ISSUES AFFECTING THE CROSS-BORDER PIPELINE

The Maghreb–Europe pipeline began operation in the mid 1990s supplying gas to Spain and Portugal via Morocco.[281] One of the factors affecting the pipeline has been terrorist activities in Algeria and instability in the country which caused disruption towards the end of the 1990s.[282] The political problems within the country ultimately did not have too much of an impact but the terrorist activities caused security of supply concerns to Spain and Portugal.[283] There have been minimal interruptions in the pipeline since the end of 1990s, which has given some respite to Algeria.[284] The frosty relationship between Algeria and Morocco however has not helped matters, as both countries have held each other responsible for instigating internal problems within their respective countries.[285] However, most of their stand-offs during the 1990s were dealt with through intense negotiation by Spain and Portugal.[286]

The EU competition directive of 1998 also had a negative impact on the pipeline chain, as it opened the markets of both Spain and Portugal to outside competition.[287] The first Directive (also known as First energy Package) in 1998 tried to gradually open up the European market from 20% in the year 2000 to 33% in the year 2008, to achieve limited unbundling and a choice between regulated and negotiated third party access.[288] The 1998 directive was EU's first step towards liberalizing the various energy markets of Europe in order to create single EU market for Energy.[289] This was detrimental for Algeria as they faced

---

280. In this case, Spain and Portugal gained most followed by Algeria and then Morocco. The reason they gained more is because they got a secure supply of gas and also got away without paying the penalty they were supposed to and can be considered to have gained more than Algeria who lost out financially.
281. See ESMAP, *supra* n. 90.
282. See A. Babajide, *How Do Developing Countries React to the Economic Problems that Come with Resource Abundance: The Case Study of Nigeria and Algeria*, CEPMLP, University of Dundee, unpublished dissertation, 2006.
283. See *ibid.*
284. See *ibid.*
285. See *ibid.*
286. See Aissaoui, *supra* n. 205.
287. See Directive 98/30/EC, can be found at <www.ec.europa.eu>.
288. See *ibid.*
289. See *ibid.* For a further understanding about the EU dimension and its competition law ethos, go to Ch. 4, s. 4.4.1, for a detailed discussion about EU law and its impact on pipelines and competition.

competition from outside which in turn reduced their exports to these countries. This decline continued over the years as Spanish and Portuguese demands from the year 2000 onwards did not increase the way it was expected to by Algeria and these two countries.[290] This has created an additional burden for Algeria because they had intended to increase the capacity of the pipeline to increase their export revenues and make the pipeline chain financially viable.[291]

Another factor affecting the pipelines has been the lack of infrastructure in these countries. Spain and Portugal still have not built up sufficient gas grids within their countries resulting in lower demand for the pipeline gas in the face of competition from other suppliers.[292] The Spanish government, during the early part of 2001, vowed to solve this problem by increasing government participation in infrastructural projects but this still has not increased the capacity as expected.[293] This factor has created an additional burden on the pipeline gas flowing into the country.

The economic problems highlighted by the case study shows the interference by the three big members of the regime to help and negotiate the capacity problems affecting the pipelines.[294] There were also other issues like Spain not taking the required amount of gas obligated under the contract and not paying any compensation.[295] This is a breach of legitimate expectation for Algeria as they will now be worse-off because of the changed circumstances and also because of losing out on the compensation they were supposed to have received under the agreement.[296]The lack of a regulatory mechanism to deal with economic issues affecting the stakeholders involved in the pipeline shows the need for an agency or a mechanism which can help alleviate the problems faced by regime members.[297]

The attitude of the parties involved in the pipeline chain are a mixture of both neo-liberal and neo-realist ideals. Although Algeria and Morocco do not have the best of relations they have decided to cooperate with each other irrespective of the amount of gain each party is going to make from the venture. This neo-liberal thinking has made the pipeline work efficiently and without any dispute. Spain, however, due to its superior position and strength has used its power to convince Morocco to act appropriately towards the pipeline chain.[298] This neo-realist attitude was needed for the smooth operation of the pipeline and to improve security of supply, which was their biggest gain from the pipeline regime.

---

290.  See Victor, *supra* n. 211.
291.  See Babajide, *supra* n. 282.
292.  See Victor, *supra* n. 211.
293.  See Babajide, *supra* n. 282.
294.  See Victor, *supra* n. 211.
295.  See *ibid.*
296.  See *ibid.*
297.  This shows the link between the economic problems faced by the actors in the pipeline and the problem that this book is trying to solve. Interference by the governments of Algeria, Spain and Portugal has resulted in negotiations which in turn have resulted in a breach of the contract originally agreed between all the parties in the regime.
298.  See Aissaoui, *supra* n. 205.

6.10.3.        THE COMMON INTEREST OF THE PARTIES

All the parties involved in the pipeline chain had their own interests. However, the common interest of all the parties in the venture was to participate in the project so that they could reap their respective benefits. Algeria needed a market to which it could export its gas and it was also aiming to diversify its export market. It has been supplying gas to Italy through the Transmed pipeline but wanted another market in order to earn greater revenue.[299] Although it supplied LNG gas to Spain, this was a costly venture.[300] Both parties were looking for a cheaper option, as the price for gas was falling during that time.[301] A pipeline through Morocco was the best option available under the circumstances.

Spain and Portugal also wanted to avail themselves of this opportunity as they required gas because of their increasing domestic demand.[302] The two countries were sceptical at the beginning because the pipeline had to go through Morocco and, due to Morocco's poor relationship with Algeria, the entire venture became difficult to implement.[303] Further terrorist activities in Algeria during that time also caused a considerable amount of doubt in their minds as security deteriorated over time.[304] However, the countries were able to convince Morocco of the benefits of joining the pipeline network and the tariff they would be able to earn.[305] Morocco, however, wanted to be a part of the project because of its standing in the region and also because of the royalty it would be earning without investing very much.[306] So they also had an interest in being involved in the pipeline chain.

The transit route chosen was also the most feasible one, as any other route bypassing Morocco would have cost more, resulting in greater financial pressure for all the stakeholders involved in the project.[307] Since the pipeline was supposed to carry gas to Europe, Morocco was the ideal location and its eagerness to join the pipeline chain for its own benefit has also been an important factor in choosing this route. Spain also had better bilateral relationships with Morocco which ultimately helped in the negotiation process.[308]

The attitude of all the parties involved in the pipeline chain has been neo-liberal in nature due to the cooperation extended by all the stakeholders for the smooth operation of the pipeline. Although there were signs of neo-realistic behaviour by Spain, due to the nature of the pipeline and their interest being at stake, the

---

299. See Victor, *supra* n. 211.
300. See *ibid.*
301. See *ibid.*
302. See ESMAP, *supra* n. 90.
303. See *ibid.*
304. See *ibid.*
305. See Victor, *supra* n. 211.
306. See *ibid.*
307. See Babajide, *supra* n. 282.
308. See *ibid.*

overall cooperation of the actors involved made the pipeline operation easier. Since the common interest of all the parties is to ensure the proper functioning of the pipeline because of the various interests involved, the neo-liberal tendency of relative gain rather than absolute gain has been ideal for all parties involved.

6.10.4.     THE ENFORCEMENT AND COMPLIANCE OF THE CROSS-BORDER PIPELINE AGREEMENTS

The IGAs and the HGAs signed between the parties in the pipeline chain provide the basic framework based upon which all the parties are aware of their obligations.[309] The EMPL is responsible for the day-to-day operation of the pipeline and all the actors involved in the pipeline have shares in the company based upon their investments.[310] However, they are not the only regime running the pipeline as the Moroccan government is responsible for the pipelines in its territory.[311] This dual enforcement mechanism can sometimes cause problems as there is a lack of coordination and clarity among the regulators.[312]

The enforcement and compliance mechanisms of the agreements are weak and there is also no independent regulatory body within the pipeline regime to enforce the rules and regulations of the regime.[313] Further the failure of the regulatory body to penalize Spain for not abiding by its obligations and also Portugal not having required infrastructure to import gas and the regulatory body not being able to deal with those problems themselves showed its weaknesses.[314] Further the Moroccan side of the pipeline is under the control of the Moroccan government and due to a lack of coordination and the importance of being a transit country gives it an extra edge over the others.[315] As a result, it can afford to act like a neo-realist, showing its power in the pipeline chain and ensuring that it makes absolute gains from the pipeline venture. The other parties tend to be more cooperative due to their huge investments in the pipeline.[316] They prefer to have a neo-liberal attitude for the successful operation of the pipeline and relative gain is more important to them than absolute gain for the benefit of the other players in the pipeline regime.

---

309. See the IGA between the Kingdom of Spain, People's Democratic Republic of Algeria and the Kingdom of Morocco concerning the supply of gas from Algeria to Spain through Morocco.
310. See Aissaoui, *supra* n. 205.
311. See *ibid.*
312. See *ibid.*
313. See the IGA between the Kingdom of Spain, People's Democratic Republic of Algeria and the Kingdom of Morocco concerning the supply of gas from Algeria to Spain through Morocco. Also see The Gas Sale Agreement between Engas, Sontrach and Transgas, available at <www.sonatrach-dz.com/NEW/>.
314. See Victor, *supra* n. 211.
315. See *ibid.*
316. See *ibid.*

## 6.11. CONCLUSION

It is important to note that not all the problems within a pipeline regime cause disruption in the pipeline. However, the breach of a legitimate expectation of the stakeholders involved in the pipeline can cause disruption in the pipeline. As a result in a weak regime, due to a weak enforcement or regulatory mechanism within the pipeline, government intervenes frequently resulting in the breach of stakeholder's legitimate expectations.[317]

The legitimate expectation of the stakeholders in the Shah-Deniz pipeline was breached when Turkey failed to pay for the gas it imported from Azerbaijan as agreed between the parties. The country also did not pay the penalty it was supposed to pay under the contract and Turkey decided to bargain and negotiate with Azerbaijan regarding it.[318] In the CPC pipeline, the shareholders legitimate expectation was breached when Russia withheld the consortium expanding the pipeline as agreed between the parties under the agreement signed between them.[319] Russia used its position in the pipeline as a leverage to ensure its demands were first met before agreeing to the expansion scheme.[320] In the case of Maghreb–Europe Pipeline Algeria's legitimate expectation was breached when Spain decided against importing the amount of gas it originally intended, resulting in Algeria suffering financial loss as Spain also did not pay any penalty or compensation for it as agreed before.[321]

The reason a stakeholder's legitimate expectation is not protected is because the government tends to intervene in the pipeline due to geo-political, legal and economic reasons. In the case of Shah-Deniz, the Turkish government wanted to protect its economic interest, while in the CPC pipeline and Maghreb–Europe Pipeline, the governments intervened to protect their geo-political and economic interests.[322]

Although there could be an argument that the agreements signed between the stakeholders allows the parties to negotiate resulting in the legitimate expectation not being breached, the problem is even if one of the parties within the agreement wants to enforce the clauses of the agreement they are not being able to do so before trying to negotiate the terms of breach rather the parties in cross-border pipeline

---

317. In other words, the government gets involved rather than use the legal process available within the agreement.
318. See 'the issues affecting the pipelines' section of the Shah-Deniz pipeline case study for further details in the area.
319. See 'the issues affecting the pipelines' section of the CPC pipeline case study for further details in the area.
320. Since consensus is needed between the stakeholders for anything to go ahead in the CPC pipeline, Russia disagreed with the idea of expansion and wanted greater stake within the pipeline in order to agree on the expansion of the pipeline. Read the 'issues affecting the pipelines' section of the CPC pipeline for greater understanding of the issue.
321. See 'the issues affecting the pipelines' section of the Maghreb–Europe pipeline case study for further details in the area.
322. See 'the issues affecting the pipelines' section of both the CPC and the Maghreb–Europe Pipeline for details in the area.

tend to negotiate outside the realms of the agreement. For example, in the case of Shah-Deniz pipeline, Turkey decided to negotiate even before contemplating to pay the penalty accrued to Azerbaijan or in the case of CPC pipeline Russia used its transit position in the pipeline to bargain for more power in the pipeline regime, which is outside the scope of the agreement signed by the parties.[323] As a result the strength of the agency or the unifying mechanism would be to bind everyone to act within the realms of the agreements signed and not outside it.[324]

Although the CPC, Shah-Deniz and Maghreb pipeline have certain regime rules and principles their members tend to act in ways which serve their own interest more than the interest of the regime as a whole.[325] The CPC pipeline regime is quite difficult to manage because of the interests of the various actors and the complex framework based upon which it is run. The management structure has certain rules and regulations and the input of all the shareholders involved in the pipeline regime is also taken into account.[326] The shareholders can also veto any new rules which they are against.[327] There is no separate body within the regime to monitor the activities of the actors involved in the pipeline chain, as the enforcers are also the decision makers.[328] Each party then carries out its own obligations which are to its own benefit but to some extent to the pipeline chain's benefit too.

The Shah-Deniz and the Maghreb–Europe pipelines, however, both have a pipeline regime which does not have any specific regulatory features or authority needed to oversee the activities of the actors, although the participating countries try to cooperate and share information with regard to the pipeline.[329] There is a chance then of each party guarding its own interest rather than acting for the benefit of the pipeline as a whole, as it is a separate entity. The stakeholders involved in the pipeline chain are also the decision and rule makers, and this makes for a lack of transparency with regard to the activities of different players in the pipeline chain.[330] The pipelines are also broken down into separate entities at times due to the sovereignty issue of the transit country in the pipeline chain, which breaks up the chain of command needed for a stable regime.[331]

---

323. See the HGA Agreement Between Russia and Kazakhstan with Chevron, British Gas Overseas Holding Ltd and the IGA between the Republic of Turkey and the Azerbaijan Republic Concerning the Delivery of Azerbaijan Natural Gas to the Republic of Turkey.
324. This means that the parties have to abide by the rules and regulations of the agreements signed by them and the mechanisms or the pipeline agency would use its regulatory powers to ensure that the agreements entered into between the parties are complied with. Ch. 8 will discuss the proposed IPA.
325. Chapter 8 of this book will discuss the reasons for joining a regime and how the interests of all the regime members are more important than a single regime member.
326. See Dellecker, *supra* n. 105.
327. See *ibid.*
328. See *ibid.*
329. See *ibid.*
330. The discussion in the previous two case studies of this chapter has highlighted this fact. Read the four criteria used to analyse the pipelines for greater details.
331. The examples provided in the 'nature and characteristics of the regime' and the 'issues affecting the pipelines section' of these two pipelines further reiterates this point.

The three pipeline regimes mentioned above can all be considered weak regimes due to their lack of enforcement capabilities and also because of the members not abiding by the various rules and regulations of the regime. The implication of all this is increased conflict and problems arising between the different actors involved in the pipeline chain which ultimately cause disruption in the pipeline. It also shows that due to the lack of a strong independent or autonomous regulatory body, the parties within a pipeline regime cannot cooperate with each other and solve their problems amicably before they get out of hand. A strong regulatory body within the regime framework could have overseen the activities and ensured the parties abided by their obligations which in turn would have avoided conflict.

There are neo-liberal and neo-realist tendencies present among the parties involved in the pipeline project. The actors in the pipelines of CPC, Shah-Deniz and Maghreb–Europe sometimes use their hegemonic power to ensure that they get maximum benefit from joining the pipeline regime. Due to their increased strength over the other actors in the pipeline they gain more at the expense of the other actors. In the CPC pipeline, Russia being the dominant party tries to get the maximum out of the regime by blocking the expansion of the pipeline because it does not suit its interest.[332] However, all the parties involved in the pipeline regime also cooperate to gain any form of benefit they can. This aspect of cooperation is neo-liberal in nature as without the cooperation of the actors the pipeline regime would not work properly.[333]

The lesson learnt from weak regimes is that the enforcement mechanism compared to the strong regimes and moderately strong regimes is either extremely weak or non-existent.[334] Due to weak regulatory aspects for these pipelines, the various rules and regulations of the pipeline regime is not being enforced properly which in turn causes some members to gain in absolute terms[335] over others. The problems highlighted in the weak regime also have economic, legal and geo-political aspects and government interference is also prevalent.

One significant lesson that can be taken from the case studies is the nature and level of government interference or interference from other partners. In the case of strong and moderately strong regimes any form of interference by the parties in the regime or the government is subtle[336] and although there might be disruptions in

---

332. The case study in the previous section gives a detailed analysis of this aspect.
333. These forms of behaviour by the actors involved in the regime are neo-liberal in nature, as the neo-liberals call for greater cooperation between the actors. Ch. 2 of this book gives a detailed analysis of this school of regime theory.
334. The definition of a weak regime is provided at the beginning of this chapter. Also read the 'enforcement and compliance of the cross-border pipeline agreements' section of the case studies for further details in this area.
335. 'Absolute terms' is used by neo-realists who join the regime for maximum benefits without thinking about the benefit of others. Ch. 2 of this book gives a detailed analysis in this area.
336. Subtle here means that government interferes in pipelines through the regulatory body in the form of trying to control the regulatory body within the pipeline regime and they do not directly contradict their policies. In weak pipeline regimes, government or the stronger members in the regime try arbitrarily to pass their agenda onto the other partners directly as there is a lack of regulatory mechanisms in the weak pipeline regimes.

the pipeline chain the regulatory bodies within those regimes try to counter those interferences or the members within the regime through respective regulatory bodies try to keep those interferences to a minimum.

In the case of weak regimes, the level of interference from the strong parties within the regime is extremely high to the extent that the other weak parties in the regime do not have any mechanism to stop the aggression of the strong parties in the regime. The lack of regulatory features or bodies in these pipelines is taken advantage of by the stronger members of the regime and the economic, geo-political and legal problems are dealt with arbitrarily by the stronger parties themselves without any participation from the weaker members. This makes the regime weak and makes the life of the other members within the regime very difficult because they have very little to gain as they do not have any protection from the regime itself. The CPC pipelines are an example where the stronger party holds the other parties hostage due to its own interest. In the case of Shah-Deniz, Turkey, being a strong country, gets away with not fulfilling its contractual obligations as the Azeri's need their support to make the pipeline work. All are examples of this kind of behaviour.[337]

The lack of a regulatory mechanism within the weak regime has caused the members within the regime to suffer from economic, geo-political and legal problems as the regime is not adequate to deal with those problems.[338] The stronger parties can use the weak regime for their benefit and it is easier for them to breach any contractual obligation compared to the strong and moderately strong regimes because the regulatory and enforcement features present are weak and non-existent. However, the main difference between the two regimes is that one is due to a lack of regulatory mechanism, the level of disruption in the pipeline chain is more and the benefits of being a party to the regime is less.[339] This is especially problematic for the long-term investors and contractors who are part of the project and now see that their investment will not bring them the required benefits.[340]

The problems faced in the weaker regimes require another form of mechanism to deal with the problems highlighted in the case studies.[341] This can either be a new regime in the form of an agency or a regulatory mechanism which would take into account the interests of the parties involved in the regime and provides a safety net from the intervention of powerful governments or members in the pipeline regime.

---

337. The case studies in the previous sections highlighted this fact. See the 'issues affecting the pipelines' section, which is one of the criteria used for an in-depth discussion in the area.
338. These are exactly the problems the book is trying to solve. See Ch. 1 for the 'statement of the problem' as it has a link with the problems shown in these case studies.
339. The evidence for this can be found in the CPC pipeline and the Maghreb–Europe pipeline where there have been numerous disruptions due to differences between the members of the regime and also due to various interferences from the stronger parties in the regime.
340. See Ch. 2 of the book for a detailed analysis in this area and also Ch. 1 of the book as the problems highlighted have similarities with the problem this book is trying to focus upon.
341. See the section on the 'issues affecting the pipelines' of each case study for an in-depth discussion in the area.

Chapter 7

# The Existing Regulatory and Enforcement Mechanisms

## 7.1.    INTRODUCTION

This chapter looks at the existing regulatory and enforcement mechanisms to see whether they can deal with the cross-border pipeline problems identified at the beginning of the book and further highlighted through the case studies. The ECT, the WTO Dispute Settlement Mechanism and the role of BITs are first discussed in detail to show how they work and their relevance in dealing with disputes. The ECT is the first treaty of its kind which deals with energy related aspects and is used widely. The WTO Dispute Settlement Mechanism is also used by parties in order to settle disputes although it is not energy specific and deals with trade in general. BITs also allow private companies to bring claims against the host government if they have been wronged by that government.

The purpose of discussing these three sets of mechanisms is to understand their role in cross-border pipelines and whether their model is adequate to deal with cross-border pipeline issues. However, it is highlighted in this chapter that these three mechanisms are not suitable for application in cross-border pipeline issues and neither can their model be used to form a new agency or a unifying mechanism to deal with the problems faced in cross-border pipelines as highlighted in the previous chapters.

The IAEA model is then discussed in great detail in order to understand the working of this agency in dealing with nuclear materials. The IAEA framework has been adopted in certain aspects in order to create a new framework for dealing with cross-border pipeline issues.[1] The reason is that this agency's regulatory model is

---

1.    It is important to note that the IAEA is not relevant to cross-border pipelines or any other energy related aspect other than nuclear energy but the only reason it is discussed in this chapter is

more suited to the rigours of cross-border pipelines along with other factors which are discussed in detail in this chapter.

## 7.2.        THE ENERGY CHARTER TREATY

### 7.2.1.        THE BACKGROUND AND GOAL OF THE ENERGY CHARTER TREATY

The idea for the ECT was first conceived during the 1990s by the former Dutch Prime Minister, Ruud Lubbers, who thought that the breakdown of the Soviet Union would cause many problems for Eastern European countries because of their dependence on the Soviet Union. To save these countries from economic and political turmoil, the idea was devised in order for them to be a part of the greater European family. At a ministerial meeting in the Hague in 1991, forty-nine countries signed the European Energy Charter, which led to the signing of the ECT in 1994.[2]

One of the objectives of the ECT was to help the economies of the Eastern European countries and by signing the ECT most of their economies were supposed to receive a boost. It was also meant to help the newly independent countries of the Caspian region who needed some kind of legal and investment framework for big multinationals investing in the region. Some of the other important aspects of the ECT were to promote energy related investment and trade, to alleviate any transportation and political risks involved and also to protect the investment of the multinationals investing in the region.[3]

### 7.2.2.        THE IMPORTANT FEATURES OF THE ECT

The main features of the ECT are related to investment protection, trade and transit. The ECT considers these three areas as the most important goals of the EU for the future and wants to ensure that the newly independent counties of the Caspian region and the Eastern European countries take advantage of liberal EU ideas. The ECT, by focusing on these three areas, would facilitate these states towards reaching the goal of economic and political stability.

The investment protection regime of the ECT helps investors to invest in all the countries of the signatory states and protects their investment from expropriation and legal and political problems. It gives the stability needed by big companies to make long-term investments in these countries. The ECT subjects all its

---

because of its regulatory feature which could be helpful and beneficial in dealing with cross-border pipeline disputes and in the making of the agency, which could follow some of its stringent enforcement mechanisms. See s. 1.7 and n. 62 in Ch. 1 of this book for further clarification and the reason for choosing IAEA.

2. See *The Energy Charter Treaty: the Reader's Guide*, at <www.encharter.org>.
3. See T.W. Walde, *The Energy Charter Treaty: An East-West Gateway for Investment and Trade* (Kluwer Law International, 1996).

signatory states to the provisions of GATT, which advocates for free trade all over the world.[4]

Transit is also another important issue that is covered under the ECT. One of the main objectives and goals of the ECT was the transportation of energy products without any hindrances or discrimination. This is extremely important because a large number of countries are either landlocked or have to depend upon other countries for their secured supply of energy, so strong and fair transit facilities would help mitigate some of the problems that countries might face. Article 7 of the ECT deals with the energy transit issue and defines the concept of energy transit in Article 7(10) along the following lines: '(i) the carriage through the area of a contracting party, or to or from port facilities in its area for loading or unloading, of energy materials and products originating in the area of another state or (ii) the carriage through the area of a contracting party of energy materials and products originating in the area of another contracting party and destined for the area of that other contracting party . . . '.[5]

7.2.3.        THE TRANSIT OF ENERGY

The energy transit issue is an important part of the ECT because it allows countries and companies to invest in this field and also to get their required supply of energy. The interests of all the parties are dealt with under Article 7 of the ECT which deals with transit. The transit issue is extremely complex because a substantial amount of capital and technological investment goes on in this area and most of these investments are long term in nature. There are many different parties involved and it is quite difficult to fulfil the demands of everyone. As one of the experts pointed out *'carriage of energy materials, petroleum and especially gas, requires costly investments, sometimes as costly as or costlier than the investments needed for production. This requires a stable legal framework because it is a long term approach and this is precisely what the ECT seeks to achieve by providing a sectoral international legal regime for energy'.*[6]

Article 7 of the ECT deals with access to transit, non-discrimination and condition of transit. Some of the important features of Article 7 of the ECT on transit are: Article 7(1) which mentions that: The contracting parties shall take measures to facilitate the transit of energy materials, non-discrimination of passage with no distinction allowed as to origin and absence of unreasonable delays.[7] Article 7(2) highlights the modernization of infrastructure.[8]

---

4.  See W. Shan, 'Towards a Common European Community Policy on Investment Issues', *Journal of World Investment* 2 (2001).
5.  See the Energy Charter Treaty at <www.energychartertreaty.org>.
6.  See *ibid.*
7.  See *ibid.*
8.  See *ibid.*

The interests of the exporting, importing and transit countries vary greatly. The exporting country's interest is to transfer its energy with little cost and it will choose the transportation route which will lower cost and increase profit. The exporting country wants to export its resources as soon as possible especially if the country is heavily reliant on its energy exports. The importing country wants to get energy at an affordable price and wants a stable and secure source of supply. The transit country, however, has an important part although their role is limited to the supply of energy through their territory. They would earn a substantial amount of revenue for permitting the energy resources to pass through their country and might also get hydro-carbon resources at a preferential rate. However, due to geo-political problems, and sometimes if the transit country is also the exporting or importing country, this might then cause problems because its interests are diversified and it would not be willing to jeopardize its various interests.[9]

### 7.2.4.     THE ECT AND TRANSIT DISPUTES

One of the major roles of the ECT is resolving transit disputes. The settlement of disputes is undertaken under Articles 7(6)(7), 26 and 27.[10] Article 7(6) mentions the non-interruption of transit in case of any dispute.[11] Article 7(6) is an important part of the ECT. The article highlights the fact that even if there is any form of dispute between the parties they cannot disrupt the flow of any resources due to their conflict until and unless the dispute is settled. This is important in the sense that in most disputes supply is disrupted; this article would stop countries taking advantage of this situation.

Article 7(7) of the ECT highlights the various mechanisms available to parties to resolve their disputes. Article 7(7) mentions that 'it shall apply to a dispute over any matter arising from an existing transit'.[12] If there is dispute between the parties, they first inform the secretary general of the Charter Conference Secretariat about the dispute. The secretariat then takes into account whether the parties have fulfilled all their obligations and whether they have taken advantage of all the mechanisms available to them. Once they are satisfied that all the mechanisms have been exhausted by the parties they then give time to the parties in the conflict to prepare for the procedure. During this time all the signatory countries are also informed about this conflict. After consultation with all the parties involved, the secretary general then appoints a conciliator within thirty days and the main role of

---

9. Chapters 4, 5 and 6 discuss these problems in detail e.g., some of the pipelines such as BTC, WAGP and FSU. They are good examples of pipelines where geo-politics play an important role.
10. See The Energy Charter Treaty at <www.energychartertreaty.org>.
11. See J. Dore & R. De Bauw, *The Energy Charter Treaty – Origins, Aims and Prospects* (London: Royal Institute of International Affairs, 1995).
12. See the Energy Charter Treaty at <www.energychartertreaty.org>.

the conciliator would be to resolve the differences between the two sides and help them reach an agreement.[13]

However, if the conciliator fails to help the conflicting parties reach an agreement within ninety days of his appointment, he can pass an interim order regarding the tariffs and other matters that the parties have conflict with under Article 7(7)(c) and both the parties are bound to follow that decision for a year. If the parties agree and reach an agreement before the decision of the conciliator then they are bound by that agreement and the conciliator does not have to adjudicate on the matter. The ECT also has a conciliation mechanism intended to help disputing parties before the parties go before their national courts for relief.

After the expiry of one year, if the parties still cannot reach an agreement, they can then go to arbitration under Articles 26 and 27 of the ECT. According to Article 26, 'disputes arising from any sort of investment can be addressed under this article'.[14] Transit in this case is considered as an investment under Article 1(6) of the ECT.[15] However, if there is any dispute regarding the interpretation of the treaty, Article 27 deals with those problems.[16]

### 7.2.5. THE DRAFT ENERGY CHARTER PROTOCOL ON TRANSIT

Negotiations on the draft protocol of the ECT on transit started in 2000 and until now the parties have not fully agreed on the various terms and conditions of the protocol.[17] There is emphasis on the definition of available capacity and to establish the principles governing transit tariffs.[18] It is widely acknowledged that a successful implementation of the transit protocol would lower the risks involved in transit, improve the financing of the projects related to transit, improve the competitiveness of supplies and provide greater energy security.[19] At the Energy Charter Conference in 2002, all fifty-one members agreed on the initial draft of the protocol but there are still countries that have problems with it and have not signed.[20] Some of the features of the new Protocol are as follows:

1. the obligation to observe transit agreements[21]

2. the prohibition of unauthorised taking of energy materials and products in transit[22]

---

13. See *ibid.*
14. See K.P. Waern, 'Transit Provisions of the Energy Charter Treaty and the Energy Charter Protocol on Transit', JENRL, 20 (2002): 172–183.
15. See *ibid.*
16. See the Energy Charter Treaty at <www.energychartertreaty.org>.
17. See A. Konoplyanik, 'Gas Transit in Eurasia: Transit Issues between Russia and the European Union and the Role of Energy Charter', JENRL (2009): 445–486.
18. See *ibid.*
19. See *ibid.*
20. See the Energy Charter Treaty Protocol at <www.energychartertreaty.org>.
21. See *ibid.*
22. See *ibid.*

3. the definition of available capacity in energy transport facilities[23]

4. negotiated third party access to available capacity[24]

5. the duty to facilitate construction, expansion or operation of energy transport facilities used for transit[25]

6. coordination in the event of accidental interruption, reduction or stoppage of transit[26]

7. the requirement of the transit tariff to be non-discriminatory, objective, reasonable and transparent, not affected by market distortions and cost based.

7.2.6.     THE EFFECTIVENESS OF THE ECT IN RESOLVING
            TRANSIT DISPUTES

One of the weaknesses of the ECT transit provision is the definition of transit provided under Article 7(10) of the ECT. The definition provided in the treaty has many similarities with the definition provided in other international agreements but its main difference is that even non-signatory states that are part of the transit process but not the treaty itself can fall under this definition. Moreover, one of the parties involved in the transaction has to be a member of the ECT other than the transit state.[27] This causes problems because this means that the party that is not part of the treaty cannot avail themselves of the same dispute settlement facilities if there is any form of dispute between them, although the other two parties can.[28]

Article 7 also does not provide any guideline during the contractual agreement between the parties.[29] This involves the ownership of pipelines, environmental aspects, the legal regime that should be followed, tariffs and so on.[30] Due to the lack of a general framework in resolving disputes under this section, the above factors have to be negotiated by the parties without any guidance in reaching an agreement.

---

23. See *ibid.*
24. See *ibid.*
25. See *ibid.*
26. See *ibid.*
27. See the Energy Charter Protocol on Energy efficiency and Related Environmental Aspects, 17 Dec. 1994, 33 *International Legal Materials* 445–454, 1995. Reprinted in T.W. Walde (ed.), *The Energy Charter Treaty – An East–West Gateway for Investment and Trade* (London: Kluwer Law International, 1996): 660–670.
28. See A.A. Fatouros, 'Energy Transit and Investment in the Energy Charter Treaty', *Greek Journal of International Law* 2 (1996) 185–221.
29. See Waern, *supra* n. 14.
30. See *ibid.*

The interests of the parties also differ and most of the transit agreements that take place depend upon the bilateral or multilateral negotiations between the parties involved in the project. The ECT objective of no discrimination does not always feature in those negotiations as the parties are more inclined to uphold their profitable position.[31] As a result, the parties are more willing to put their own interest ahead of the provision of Article 7, which advocates for non-discrimination.[32] In addition, the ECT provisions are ill equipped to deal with the many other problems that a transit country might face. There may be an instance when the transit country is also a producing country and in that case if it allows the transit it would be in direct competition with its own supplies which would lower its export revenue. In these instances it would be difficult to uphold the EC ethos of non-discrimination because it would jeopardize their position. In another scenario, the transit country could also be an importing country and in that case it would always be tempted to siphon off certain supplies if there was any conflict with the exporting country. These factors show some of the inadequacies and contradictions of the ECT transit provision.

According to Article 7(1) of the treaty 'the contracting parties shall facilitate the transit of energy'.[33] This is quite ambiguous as it could mean anything and different states might have a different definition of facilitation. There may be an instance when the state might have facilitated to the best of it abilities without jeopardizing their interests, but which might not be enough for the transit to take place, causing the exporting country disruption in its supply. However, the GATT provision of transit which the ECT closely follows is more direct and less ambiguous. The ECT is much more lenient in this respect as there can always be an argument regarding whether the transit country really facilitates towards the transit of hydro-carbon resources.

Another weak feature of the ECT is Article 7(6), as it does not have adequate power to stop the disruption of supply. Sometimes there can be a dispute between the exporting and transit countries and because of this conflict the importing country might not get its required supply of energy if the transit country has siphoned off their supply. In this scenario, although it is the transit country which is at fault, the exporting country would be in violation of Article 7(6) as it did not carry out its respective obligation towards the importing country. The importing country cannot hold the exporting country accountable for this disruption although the exporting country would be fined for not fulfilling its obligation.[34]

Article 7(6) of the ECT is also not effective in reducing the interruption of supply. Although the article advocates that there should not be any interruption or

---

31. See T.W. Walde & K.M. Christie (eds), *Energy Charter Treaty: Selected Topics*, University of Dundee, and Centre for Energy Petroleum Mineral Law and Policy, 1995.
32. See *ibid.*
33. See the Energy Charter Treaty at <www.energychartertreaty.org>.
34. See M.M. Roggenkamp, 'Transit of Network bound Energy: The European Experience', in *The Energy Charter Treaty – An East West Gateway for Investment and Trade*, ed. T.W. Walde (London: Kluwer Law International, 1996), 495–515.

disruption of supply during a conflict between parties it leaves room for ambiguity as it mentions that interruption can take place if it is specified in the contract.[35] This can be used by parties during a conflict as the interruption mentioned in the contract might be different from the real cause of interruption of supply.[36] The dispute settlement mechanism under Article 7(7) is also quite complex and time consuming as the parties have to exhaust all avenues before they can use the mechanism. In addition, the decision given by the panel is not final and can be appealed further, which causes more delays.[37] The conciliation mechanism used under the treaty simply allows the parties to negotiate further and tends not to solve disputes. This process can be used by parties to kill time while the supply is being disrupted which makes the entire situation difficult for the parties involved.

The ECT makes provisions for transit which are not as effective as they could be and there is a lot of ambiguity regarding these provisions. Some countries have also not enacted these provisions within their domestic legislations which further complicates matters because there would then be a contradiction between the domestic law and the ECT.[38] The ECT provisions also need to be more robust in order to meet the challenges the exporters, importers and transit countries face.

## 7.2.7.    WHY NOT ECT?

The ECT's main role since its inception is to secure Western investment in Eastern Europe and the newly independent states in the Caspian. The treaty provided Western companies and their governments with the required legal framework to ensure a return on their investment. It particularly helped in the field of energy, as these countries were rich in hydro-carbon resources and the western European countries needed a secured supply.

Things have changed over time, as these new countries now have a more stable legal and regulatory framework and require a more precise and less ambiguous framework than the ECT for their export trade. The ECT, other than the new transit protocols, has not evolved with the changing times and this has diminished its importance. One point of major contention is whether GATT Article V on freedom of transit applies to network infrastructure like pipelines and if it does which one is the more appropriate rule to follow, Article V of GATT or Article 7 of the ECT in terms of freedom of transit.[39] This has caused problems among the many actors involved in the energy trade as there is a lack of clarity on the term freedom of

---

35. See R.S. Axelrod, 'The European Energy Charter. Reality or illusion?', *Energy Policy* 6 (1996): 497 –505.
36. However, the Russia–Ukraine contract did not have any such clause to allow interruption and the parties were expected to carry out their obligations while their disputes were dealt with in any tribunal they preferred. See the PCAs signed between Russia and the EU and Ukraine and the EU.
37. See *Gas transit tariffs in Selected ECT Countries*, Energy Charter Secretariat, January, 2006.
38. See Waern, *supra* n. 14.
39. See the Energy Charter Treaty at <www.energychartertreaty.org>.

transit. According to some it needs a legal definition.[40] According to other experts the term needs to take into account the 'realities of energy transport infrastructure and the interests of shippers, owners of the transport facilities, investors and the producer, importer and transit states'.[41]

Another cause of the ineffectiveness of the treaty is that it is only geared up to deal with the security of supply concerns and investment issues of the European states. It does not appeal to countries outside the EU or the Caspian which is a major cause of concern.[42] Because of this it lacks the global dimension which is required in the energy field to secure its credibility. Some of the exporting countries are also sceptical about the ECT because they see the treaty as being geared up for consuming states rather than exporting states. For example, Russia is of this opinion.[43]

Furthermore, the ratification of the transit protocol by most of the signatory states also does not look secured because of the controversial nature of the 'right of first refusal term'.[44] According to this term if, for example, the supply contract runs for ten years but the transit contract for five years then it is normal for the party using it to renew it or the transit country to offer the exporting or importing country the right to renew the term as before.[45] However, this term is not accepted by the European Community because it contradicts their competition law ethos, which further causes problems for countries that have been depending upon this clause. Because of this, some of the countries are not willing to ratify the protocol which further weakens the transit aspects of the ECT.

Another problem of the ECT has been its failure to attract developing oil producing countries to join the treaty.[46] Countries like Libya, Algeria, Iran, Kuwait, Nigeria, Saudi Arabia, the UAE and Venezuela have not found the urge or the need to join the treaty.[47] According to one commentator 'when comprising those who have signed and ratified with those who have neither signed nor ratified, it is hard to escape the inference that the ECT is regarded favourably by

---

40. See *Gas transit tariffs in Selected ECT Countries*, Energy Charter Secretariat, January, 2006.
41. See *ibid*.
42. Although there are countries like Pakistan, Nigeria and China who have observer status in the ECT, this does not prove that they are going to follow or sign the ECT. Their observer status shows their interest in the treaty but just by being an observer in the treaty does not obligate them to follow any of the treaty obligations. As a result, their observer status cannot be interpreted as their intention to sign the treaty or the ECT being popular but simply their interest in being part of the whole process.
43. See A. Konoplyannik, 'Russia: don't oppose the Energy Charter, help to adapt it', *Petroleum Economist* (2009). Also see D. Azaria, 'Energy Transit under the Energy Charter Treaty and the General Agreement on Tariffs and Trade', *Journal of Energy and Natural Resources Law* 27, no. 4 (2009).
44. See D. Azaria, 'Energy Transit under the Energy Charter Treaty and the General Agreement on Tariffs and Trade', *Journal of Energy and Natural Resources Law* 27, no. 4 (2009).
45. See *ibid*.
46. See A. Konolpayanik, 'Energy Security: the role of Business, Governments, International Organizations and International Framework', IELTR 6 (2007).
47. See *ibid*.

countries which are primarily consumers, but that most producers (with the exceptions of the United Kingdom, the Netherlands and Kazakhstan) have serious reservations about it'.[48]

The recent act by Russia to withdraw from the ECT is a further blow to the treaty. Russia signed the ECT in 1994 and since then they have not ratified the treaty. However, Article 45 of the treaty mentions that 'provisional application of the treaty by all signatory states between December 1994 and its entry into force in April 1998, unless a Member State expressly declared that it was unable to apply the ECT provisionally'.[49] Russia never made such a declaration after signing the treaty and thus were obligated by the treaty to this provisional application, as the provisional application of the treaty was restricted to those states that still did not ratify the treaty.[50] However, Russia maintained the position that since they did not ratify the treaty, the provisional application clause is not applicable to them although this is contrary to Article 45 of the Treaty.[51]

One of the reasons for Russia's withdrawal is because of its allegation that the ECT has a bias towards investors.[52] Furthermore, the 'treaty focuses mainly on the protection of investment but not on the obligations of investors and the process of investment itself'.[53] As a result, a resource rich country like Russia would like to have greater control over their resources and is not willing to share the sovereignty of their natural resources with other investors.[54]

The early warning mechanism of the ECT has also not worked during transit disputes. The objective of the early warning mechanism was to 'set out practical measures aimed at preventing, and rapidly reacting to an emergency situation to be undertaken by the EU–Russia Energy Dialogue Coordinators and the structure reporting to the Coordinators'.[55] However, this mechanism did not come into play during the 2009 dispute between Russia and Ukraine and neither party

---

48. See A. Popov et al., 'Russia and the Energy Charter Treaty: Common Interests or Irreconcilable Differences', IELTR 7 (2006): 189.
49. See *ibid.*
50. See *ibid.*
51. In a recent arbitration decision between the Russian Federation versus Yukos, the tribunal came to the view that 'the whole of the ECT applied provisionally in the Russian Federation until such provisional application was terminated, in accordance with the notification that the Russian Federation made on 20th August 2009' The tribunal also mentioned that Part V of the ECT allows investors the right to arbitrate for twenty years from the time of termination of the treaty, which means that claims can be brought against Russia till 2029. However, the Russian government rejected this verdict. See *Yukos Universal Ltd v. Russian Federation*, PCA Case Nos AA 226.
52. See Popov, *supra* n. 48.
53. See T. Walde & S. Dow, 'Treaties and Regulatory Risk in Infrastructure Investment – The effectiveness of International Law Disciplines versus Sanctions by Global Markets in Reducing the Political and Regulatory Risk for Private Infrastructure Investment', *Journal of World Trade* 34 (2000).
54. See *ibid.*
55. See K. Hober, 'Russia's Energy Policy and Dispute Settlement: An Overview', in *European Energy Law Report VII*, ed. Roggenkamp, M., et al. (Intersentia, 2010).

made use of the dispute resolution mechanism available to them by their signing of the ECT.[56] This further shows the weakness of the ECT in resolving disputes.

The ECT also does not address the problem of government intervention due to geo-political, legal and economic reasons in the pipeline regime. The case studies in the previous chapter have shown that governments have intervened for these reasons in a pipeline regime resulting in them not standing by their original position in the pipeline. The ECT supports or gives credibility to government intervention as it is designed for them to intervene in the case of these problems. Instead of giving support to the other parties in the pipeline regime it indirectly supports government intervention which fails to protect the other actors in the regime.[57]

For example, in the CPC pipeline, Ukraine being a signatory country of the ECT could have asked this body to mediate between them and Russia during the pipeline dispute. However, none of the parties decided to do so which is further proof that the parties are not optimistic about getting their disputes solved through the ECT. According to experts, the arbitration procedure of the ECT 'may do little to help solve the operational problems often linked to transit disputes. It is not speedy enough to be used in case of urgent transit disputes . . . '.[58]

In the case of cross-border pipelines, there is a requirement for a more pro-active institution or a framework which cannot only regulate the activities of the actors involved in the pipeline but also be a regime where the rules and regulations agreed between the parties are enforced. The cross-border pipeline regime also needs to be impartial and has to consider and take into account the various concerns of its members and to act accordingly without bowing to the pressure of the various actors.

There is also a need to deal with conflicts quickly so that there is minimal disruption to the flow of hydro-carbon resources. The regime also needs to ensure that all the actors abide by their obligations and the regime regulations. The ECT also lacks the power to deal with government intervention in the pipeline due to geo-political, legal and economic reasons, which is one of the main reasons for pipeline disruption. The reason for this is that it is looked upon as a treaty support-ing the governments as it derives its power from them and there is this pessimism that they might not be able to deal with a strong government intervening in a pipeline for its own interests.

---

56. See *ibid.*
57. The reason for implying this is that the whole reason the ECT was signed was to protect the investment of the companies and governments investing in Eastern Europe. As a result, the government can use the argument that they are interfering to protect their interest as advocated and intended by the treaty.
58. See V. Rakhmanin, *Transportation and Transit of Energy and Multilateral Trade Rules: WTO and Energy Charter* in Global Challenges at the intersection of Energy, Trade and Environment, Centre for Trade and Economic Integration (CETI) (2010), 123–131.

7.2.8.        THE ECT AS A REGIME

The main principle of the ECT regime was to promote the investment of Western oil and gas companies in the former Soviet republics.[59] The main rules of the ECT were contained within the treaty, for example, Article 7 in respect of transit of energy and Article 7(7) which sets the mechanisms available for settling disputes.[60] As a result, the ECT can be considered as a regime which has both neo-liberal and neo-realist ethos.

The treaty depends upon the cooperation of all the signatory states and its main aim is to help investors to invest in countries without a stable legal framework.[61] It also provides mechanisms which help the investors settle their disputes against states and also provides a transit framework for countries exporting their energy resources. Therefore, from this perspective, it could be considered as a neo-liberal regime trying to ensure that the benefits of all the signatory countries and the companies are protected and there is a gain for all the parties involved in the regime.

The ECT also has enforcement mechanisms for ensuring that all the signatory countries abide by their rules and regulations. It sometimes enforces its rules like a hegemony and takes the side of the investors against the states that also want to have sovereignty over its natural resources.[62] For example, Article 10 of the treaty demands the creation of a stable, favourable, equitable and transparent condition for investors.[63] In *TOPCO and Nykomb Synergetics Technology v. Latvia case*, the arbitration tribunal came down on the side of the investors against the state even though the states made decisions which served their own national interest.[64] This shows the treaty's neo-realist side as it intends to promote the interests of the investors in a strong manner.

The ECT regime can be classified as a moderately strong regime.[65] Although it has a strong enforcement arm ensuring that all the signatories abide by their rules and regulations, it has failed to deal with disputes relating to transit of energy.[66] Russia's decision to opt out of the ECT and also ECT's delay in dealing with the *Ukraine v. Russia gas dispute* cast doubts on its ability to resolve disputes and enforce its rules and regulations. Neither Russia nor Ukraine availed themselves of the ECT's dispute settlement mechanisms during the dispute.[67] Furthermore, the lack of participation by other oil producing countries in the ECT and their decision

---

59. See Konolpayanik, *supra* n. 46.
60. See the Energy Charter Treaty at <www.enchartertreaty.org>.
61. See Konolpayanik, *supra* n. 46.
62. See *ibid.*
63. See the Energy Charter Treaty at <www.energychartertreaty.org>.
64. See *Nykomb Synergetics Technology Holding AB V Latvia, Stockholm Rules Award*, 16 Dec. 2003, Stockholm International Arbitration Review, 2005.
65. It is classified as a moderately strong regime from the enforcement aspect.
66. See J. Westerhof, 'The Transit Conflict between Russia and Ukraine from a Legal Perspective', in *European Energy Law Report VII*, ed. Roggenkamp, M., et al. (Intersentia, 2010).
67. See *ibid.*

not to join formally also shows its handicap.[68] However, the ECT as a regime has been robust in dealing with disputes related to investment and has been able to ensure that the investors feel safe investing their money in the states that are signatories to the treaty. The Latvia and Yukos cases are two examples of the ECT dealing with investment disputes decisively and which served its regime purpose.[69]

## 7.3. THE WTO DISPUTE SETTLEMENT MECHANISM[70]

### 7.3.1. THE BACKGROUND TO THE WTO DSM

The current WTO DSM originated from the previous GATT dispute settlement system formulated in 1947.[71] The previous system was known for its inefficiency and lack of transparency while adjudicating claims.[72] In fact, the number of claims brought before it was minimal. Very few developing countries (DCs) brought claims before the panel. One of the problems with the previous system was the positive consensus rule. The idea was to ensure that there was absolute consensus from all the parties regarding the panel being set and there also had to be total consensus while adopting the panel report. This helped the developed countries to stall the entire process which went against the interests of the DCs bringing the claim. There was also more emphasis on solving the claim between parties on a bilateral level than actually following the procedures laid down in the GATT dispute settlement system.

However, the current DSM is totally different from the previous system which was totally dysfunctional. The current WTO DSM is more accessible and more countries are willing to take advantage of it. In fact, the number of developing countries taking advantage of it has increased, making the system more credible. There have been a few changes in the current system which has made the DSM more popular.

---

68. This means that although there are some countries that are within the treaty as monitors, they have not fully committed to the ECT by signing the treaty. As a result, their monitor status cannot be interpreted as them being in the ECT framework.
69. See Hober, *supra* n. 55.
70. The reason for looking at the WTO Dispute Settlement Mechanism (DSM) is to see whether it could deal with the cross-border pipeline disputes described in Ch. 1 of the book and shown in the case studies in Chs 4, 5 and 6. The WTO DSM is adept at dealing with various trade disputes all over the world and although it does not specialize in energy related disputes, it is an option that is open to its members that are also energy exporters, importers or transit countries. The WTO DSM would also help in the understanding of whether it has any regulatory and enforcement capabilities that could be used in cross-border pipelines or are relevant to it.
71. See WTO Dispute settlement procedure, WTO, Switzerland.
72. See G. de Burca & J. Scott, 'Neutrality or Discrimination? The WTO, the EU and External Trade', in *The EU and the WTO: Legal and Constitutional Aspects* (Oxford: Hart Publishing, 2001).

The negative consensus rule has also been adopted in the new system which made the whole process quicker and more effective. The negative consensus rule means that all the parties have to disagree if they do not want the panel report to be adopted or when choosing panel members.


### 7.3.2.    THE LEGAL FRAMEWORK

The WTO DSM has a legalistic approach which makes it more popular among the members. The entire judicialization of the process has helped them to resolve trade disputes more efficiently. The settlement of disputes, which is currently known as a Dispute Settlement Understanding (DSU), is the agreement governing the entire system. This system is based on the Uruguay Round negotiations. The agreement came into effect in January 2001.

The settling of disputes is the responsibility of the Dispute Settlement Body (DSB), which consists of all the WTO General Council members.[73] The first stage of the procedure is to go for consultation or mediation between the parties in dispute.[74] The member who feels that his rights are being violated has to write a letter asking for consultation and the other party has to respond within ten days; the entire process has to start within thirty days.[75]

If the consultation fails, the DSB will then set up a panel of leading experts to tackle the matter. However, this panel is set with the consultation of all parties involved in the claim. The panel also has the right to hear other parties (third parties) if they feel the need to know more about the claim. Article 13 of the DSU mentions that 'the panel shall have the right to seek information and technical advice from any individual or body, which it deems appropriate'.[76]

After hearing all the parties, the panel submits a report to the parties and the DSB and if it is not rejected by all the members it is adopted. If the parties are not satisfied with the panel report they can appeal the panel's ruling to the seven member Appellate Body (AB). However, the AB will only provide legal interpretation of the reasons given by the panel and there would not be any re-examination of evidence.[77] The AB decision is final if it is not rejected by all the parties involved in the dispute.

After the ruling, the party who has been found to be in violation of the agreement has to submit a report to the panel detailing how they intend to implement and comply with the recommendations made. The country then has to fulfil all its obligations, however, if it fails, then it has to negotiate for the amount of compensation it has to pay. Furthermore, if the parties fail to reach an agreement

---

73. See *ibid.*
74. See *ibid.*
75. See *ibid.*
76. See WTO Dispute Settlement Procedure, WTO, Switzerland.
77. See World Trade Organization: *The WTO Dispute Settlement Procedures – A Collection of the Legal Texts* (Geneva: WTO Geneva, 1995).

regarding compensation, the AB has to step in and the party who suffered can ask for their permission to retaliate. However, the retaliation has to be proportionate to the original trade barrier imposed.

### 7.3.3.    THE TUG OF WAR BETWEEN DEVELOPED COUNTRIES

Most of the claims brought before the panel were from developed countries. The US, Canada, the EU and Japan were the most frequent users of the system. For example, the EU brought claims against the US over the issue of a ban on the import of hormone treatment and meat products and Canada brought claims against the US for its anti-dumping measures. However, one interesting feature in these trade disputes between developed nations has been the constant bickering about each individual country's national laws being contrary to the rules of the WTO. The DSB has since scrutinized the various legislation and laws passed in these countries. Before the setting up of the WTO DSM this was not possible.

Most of the developing countries have been at loggerheads over anti-dumping provisions, countervailing duties, the trade restriction on beef and bananas and so on. However, most of the developed countries have accepted the authority of the WTO DSM and are comfortable with bringing claims into the forum, although sometimes the WTO DSM has to struggle to cope with the demand of these nations. In general, however, the overall importance of the system has increased among these nations.

### 7.3.4.    THE IMPLEMENTATION RECORDS OF DEVELOPED COUNTRIES

The implementation records of most of the Developed Countries are fairly good. The US implemented 12 of the 23 cases brought against it,[78] Canada implemented 4 of the panel's reports out of 6,[79] the EU implemented 3 out of the 6 reports within a reasonable time, while the other 3 have stalled,[80] and Japan has implemented 3 of the adverse panel reports out of 5.[81]

Some of the Developed Countries have also failed to implement certain panel reports. The reports for the banana and beef cases have still not been implemented by the US and the EU. This does not set a good precedent for the other countries, especially the DCs. It simply shows that the Developed Countries choose the cases or scenarios where they do implement the panel recommendations. In general, most of the panel reports have been implemented without delay.

---

78. See *ibid.*
79. See B.L. Das, *The WTO Agreements: Deficiencies, Imbalances and Required Changes* (Malaysia: Third World Network, 1998).
80. See 'The WTO Dispute Settlement System', *Journal of International Economic Law*, 200, 15.
81. See *ibid.*

7.3.5.    THE WTO AND THE DEVELOPING COUNTRIES

The WTO DSM is no doubt more popular than the previous GATT DSM among the developing countries. The reasons for this are manifold. The number of developing countries now participating in the DSM has increased quite dramatically and this is extremely important for the WTO DSM because it not only enhances its credibility as a body but also allows the smooth and quick resolution of trade disputes between nations.[82]

The WTO DSM has in fact made considerable improvements over the previous GATT DSM. The new DSM has introduced a judicial aspect in the settling of disputes which was missing previously.[83] There is the Dispute Settlement Body and the Appellate Body, two organs of the DSM, which have made the system more consistent and predictable.[84] As a result, developing countries are more comfortable bringing claims to the WTO DSM. Additionally, the shift in the DSM from unilateralism to multilateralism has made the new system more popular.

The negative consensus rule also helps the developing countries. The reason is that the previous body was structured around the positive consensus rule meaning that there had to be consensus at every stage of the proceeding.[85] However, with the negative consensus rule the opposite is the case, with a consensus being needed to halt the proceedings at any stage. This was important because it allowed the DSB to settle claims quickly and efficiently, where as before the whole process of settling the claims could be stalled by developed nations if they wanted to delay the process for their benefit. The negative consensus rule has made the proceedings more automatic.

7.3.6.    CRITIQUE OF THE PRESENT STRUCTURE

Although the new WTO DSM increased the amount of claims brought by DCs, it still has quite a few drawbacks. One factor is the high cost involved in bringing the claim. Most of the developing nations cannot afford to bring claims to the DSM because they do not have the relevant resources available. In fact, before bringing a claim, instead of worrying about the merits of the claim, they are more worried about the amount of money it is going to cost them than the end result. Sometimes, even if the claim is justified, they are not able to bring it because of fund constraints. Moreover, most claims in the WTO DSM run for about two to three years which adds to the burden.

---

82. See G. Goh, 'The World Trade Organization, Kyoto and Energy Tax Adjustments at the Border', JWT 38 (2004).
83. See C. Van Grasstek, *Why Demands on Acceding Countries Increase Over Time: A Three-dimensional Analysis of Multilateral Trade Diplomacy' in WTO Accessions and Development Policies*, UNCTAD, United Nations, 2001.
84. See *ibid.*
85. See *ibid.*

Another problem is a lack of information and legal experts. Most DCs do not have people who are experts in WTO DSM procedures. While the developed nations have a whole machinery in place working solely in this line of work, the DCs have to search around to find if there is anyone available who could help them. The legal assistance provided by the secretariat is not sufficient as there are only two experts. Although they could hire private lawyers, as is presently allowed, the problem lies with the fact that private help is also quite expensive. As a result, they have to think twice before bringing the claim.

Another problem is the lack of information regarding the various articles of the DSM. The DCs in most cases cannot make use of some of the special considerations given to DCs in general because they are not aware of their presence. Some of the articles in the DSM could be said to be hortatory in nature.[86] This is because some of the articles regarding special treatment of DCs are ambiguous in nature and in reality cannot be implemented or taken advantage of. One such Article is 3.12 of the DSU which mentions the fact that 'Recommendations and rulings of the DSB cannot add or diminish the rights and obligations provided in the covered agreement'.[87] This is contradictory in nature and in reality questions the legal power of the DSB, when its actual job is to resolve trade disputes between countries by providing solutions which can have real impact. This ambiguous clause to some extent puts a dent in that impact.

Even after the panel report or other recommendations by the AB go in favour of the DC, there is a problem with the implementation of the decision. In most cases, the party who is found to be in violation of the agreement has either to pay compensation or withdraw the various barriers it put in place in the first instance. However, in most cases the Developed Countries simply withdraw the barrier which is of no use to the DCs because by then two or three years have already elapsed and the barrier has already served the interest of the violating nation. The DC cannot get back the profit it has lost over those two or three years, which means the end product for the DC is zero, apart from the fact that the barrier has been removed.

Although the affected country is sometimes given the choice of being awarded compensation, they cannot for the most part enforce it. This is especially the case if the claim is between a DC and a developed nation. If the DC goes for retaliation it would not do them any good because their economy is much smaller than that of the developed country and it would do them more harm than good if they opted for retaliation. Accordingly, the level of implementation is quite poor and the DSM fails to provide them with any kind of guarantee.

There are also some problems with the special considerations accorded to the DCs. The articles that allow the DCs to make use of those special considerations are not clearly drafted making them imprecise and lacking direction. By relying on

---

86. See A.H. Qureshi, *The WTO: Implementing International Trade Norms*, Melland Schills Studies in International Law, Manchester University Press, Manchester and New York, 1996.
87. See WTO Secretariat, *Guide to Dispute Settlement* (The Hague: Kluwer Law International, 2002).

those articles DCs have on occasion got nowhere and in most cases they have lost out on a technicality. For example, Article 24(2) which claims to give special rights to the least developed countries actually does not give any special rights, the same right is provided to all other member countries.[88]

The assistance provided by the secretariat to the DCs is not sufficient, as mentioned before. However, there is also the problem that legal assistance can only be taken up once the claim has been brought. In addition, the legal experts providing the DCs with their opinions cannot provide adequate and effective advice. This is because they have to act in a neutral manner at all times; there have been instances when they have given advice to two opposing parties within the same claim. Therefore, they cannot give expert opinions on the legal arguments and can only provide help with the procedure, which does not help the DCs at all.

The amicus curiae brief is also another point of contention. Most of the developed and developing countries are against this sort of brief being provided to the Advisory Body. This not only has a negative impact on the countries contending the claims but also brings in uncalled for opinions and arguments. The AB claims that it gives an added insight into the problem while it also has the discretion to take other matters into account while deciding the claim. The fact is that this causes more problems for DCs since more time is spent on the claim and there is a chance that the AB might change its mind if they take an outside brief into account, although in reality they are not supposed to do so.

In addition, by giving third parties the right to bring in claims in the DSM this is beneficial for the DCs. The problem is that it also allows the developed countries to be part of the claim even though they do not need to be. The Banana III case[89] is the perfect example of this. The case was between the EC and the other banana producers of Latin America. The US, although not a banana producer, brought the claims along with the other Latin American countries because the EC actions caused problems for two of their firms. This sort of participation by developed countries, who are willing to get some sort of benefit from the claims of other DCs, wastes the time of the DSM and slows the entire process down, as the Dispute Settlement Body could finish the claim more quickly if these third parties did not participate.

7.3.7.     How Effective is the WTO DSM?

There can be little argument regarding the effectiveness of the present WTO DSM. The number of cases has increased threefold in the last six years.[90] The number of developing countries bringing a claim to the WTO DSM has also increased

---

88. See World Trade Organization, *supra* n. 77.
89. See Appellate Body Report, European Communities – Regime for the importation, sale and Distribution of Bananas (EC-'Bananas III'), WT/DS27/AB/R, adopted 25 Sep. 1997, DSR 1997: II, 591.
90. See J. Lacarte-Munro & P. Gappah, 'Developing Countries and the WTO Legal and Dispute Settlement System: A View from the Bench', *Journal of International Economic Law* (2000): 395–401.

dramatically, which is a positive sign. All these factors prove that the system is operating well and is slowly gaining the trust of the DCs.

The action by Venezuela against the US regarding increased VAT on gasoline imported from Venezuela, the shrimp case involving Pakistan, Thailand, India and others against the US and the textile case of India against the US all highlight the fact that developing countries have started to take advantage of this system.[91] However, it is important to keep in mind that the overall picture is still in favour of the developed countries. The EU, US and Canada still make up more than half the cases that the WTO DSM body has to deal with.[92]

It is important to note that the success and failure of the WTO DSM or even its effectiveness cannot be judged by the amount of cases it has to deal with or the amount brought before it to be resolved. More important is whether it helps resolve trade disputes between countries. Are DCs being helped by their decisions? Are the least developed countries getting adequate support? Is the enforcement mechanism or the compensation provided truly helping?

Therein lies the problem, because the answers to most of the questions posed above would be in the negative. The rate of implementation of AB reports is not that successful in the case of DCs. Even if a report is favourable towards a DC, it takes a long time for the implementation of that award to reach the developed country. Although there are stringent time limits within which all measures have to be implemented, it is rarely achieved. After the removal of one barrier another subtle barrier is put up by the developed countries which make the whole AB report and the compensation negotiated quite meaningless.

DCs do not have the administrative and human resource capability to undertake the entire burden of making the claim to the WTO DSM. Due to a lack of understanding of the WTO DSM articles and the fact that they cannot afford to train people who could be experts in the future, DCs are lagging behind and are not getting proper access to the facilities provided. In order for the DSM to function effectively, it is important that DCs have their own experts, who can provide them with proper interpretations of the rules and procedures. In the short term, however, it might not be feasible for them to train the required number of people because it requires time and money.

It is also important to take into account that, in order to carry out the decision of the panel report or final decision of the AB, DCs do not have the proper administration in place to handle those measures. Most DCs have a great deal of bureaucracy and red tape and they are not in a position to deal with the measures proposed by the WTO DSM effectively and quickly, which is the main slogan of the DSM.

Although the new WTO DSM has earned the respect of the DCs and is trying its best to resolve trade disputes amicably and quickly, there are problems which need urgent attention. In general, however, it has been quite successful in keeping

91. See T.L. Brewer & S. Young, 'International Trade WTO Disputes and Developing Countries', *Journal of World Trade* 33, no. 5 (1999): 169–182.
92. See W. Davey, 'The WTO Dispute Settlement System', *Journal of International Economic Law* (2000): 15.

the balance right between the developed nations and the DCs in resolving trade disputes.


### 7.3.8.   THE POLITICAL ASPECT

Although it is claimed that the WTO DSM is free of international politics and is a completely fair body whose only aim is to resolve disputes between nations, there have been allegations of developed country bias. In fact, most of the DCs feel that, in most cases, the panel or AB tend to favour the rich and powerful nations of the WTO.[93]

The panel body which issues the report and the AB which has the final say, is made up of members from the developed countries. If there is a claim between a developed country and a DC, there has to be one panel member from a DC, although this hardly helps because that panel member's view can easily be overridden by the other panel members.[94] Since these permanent panel members mostly represent either the EU or the US, their impartiality is sometimes questionable especially when they have worked for their respective governments and are also panel members when claims are brought against their own governments. This is clearly in violation of Article 8.3 of the DSU.[95]

Another interesting feature is that most panel reports do not reveal any dissenting opinions, which closes the door for any kind of future argument. Even if the panel members of the DCs went against the panel members from the developed countries, this would not be revealed. According to Article 17.3 of the DSU, the opinions expressed in the AB by members should be anonymous.[96]

The doctrine of Judicial Economy is also an interesting idea. By applying this principle, the panel or AB does not have to answer all the questions put before them.[97] They could easily discard any politically sensitive issues or in fact any other sensitive issues about which the parties have asked questions. In taking this stance, the panel means to ensure that they do not offend the political sensibilities of the parties. The Indian shirts and blouses case against the US,[98] the EC beef hormones and US import measures[99] are perfect examples of these.

The AB of the DSM does have substantial discretion in how it handles cases. The reason it takes third party views and amicus curiae briefs into account is

---

93. See R.B. Ginsburg, 'Remarks on Writing Separately', *Washington Law Review* 65, no. 133 (1990): 48.
94. See *ibid.*
95. See WTO Dispute Settlement Procedure, WTO, Switzerland.
96. See WTO Secretariat, *supra* n. 87.
97. See M. Footer, 'Developing Country Practice in the Matter of WTO Dispute Settlement', *Journal of World Trade* (2001): 55–98.
98. See Appellate Body Report, USA – measure affecting shirts and blouses from India, WT/DS33/AB/R and Corr.1, adopted 23 May 1997, DSR 1997: I,323.
99. See Appellate Body Report, EC Measures concerning Meat and Meat Products (Hormones) (EC-Hormones'), WT/DS26/AB/R, WT/DS48, adopted 13 Feb. 1998, DSR 1998: I 135.

because it wants to hear the views of other governments. This in turn allows it to act diplomatically rather than being completely fair and in the process invoke the wrath of the developed countries. Furthermore, the fact that US congress twice tried to establish a commission of federal judges to review the decisions of the WTO[100] also shows the political pressure that is applied.

Moreover, it is important to remember that most of the cases brought to the WTO DSM are by the US, EU and Canada. As a result, the AB of the DSM feels that if too many decisions go against the major countries bringing a claim there is a possibility that these nations, who were an integral part of the setting up of the WTO DSM, might withdraw, which in turn would cause the organization to lose credibility. Although the panel and the AB do not blindly support the claims brought by these countries, they are diplomatic in their approach and listen intently to their views before reaching a final decision.[101]

Another political aspect commonly faced by the DCs is that of retaliation. Most times a DC cannot retaliate against a developed country because it is not economically as powerful. Even if the DC considers retaliation it might not be able to do so because of the political pressure it would face from the donor agencies.[102] The developed countries would use the IMF and World Bank to put more stringent measures and conditions in place which would make it impossible for DCs to opt for any sort of retaliation. Going against the donor agencies would cause the DCs to lose their aid packages. In addition, most DC economies are totally dependent upon the developed countries.

### 7.3.9.       THE WTO AND THE ENERGY SECTOR

Although the GATT and WTO principles are geared towards international trade, they can have implications for energy trade. Article 1 of GATT deals with most-favoured nation treatment (MFN). The MFN means that 'WTO members are obliged to extend any advantage, favour or privilege or immunity granted to any product originating in or destined for any country to like product originating in or destined for the territories of all other WTO members'.[103] The MFN clause ensures that there is no unfair advantage enjoyed by one country over the other. This relates to custom duties, charges that are imposed on international export or import of international transfer payments and so on.[104] In the case of energy, if a WTO member imposes any border tax, regulations or any internal measure on an energy product from a particular country, they have to provide similar conditions or measures for energy products coming from other countries.

---

100. See R. Bhala, 'The Myth about Stare Decisis and International Trade Law', *American University International Law Review* 14, no. 845 (1999a).
101. See *ibid.*
102. See *ibid.*
103. See Y. Selivanova, *The WTO and Energy: WTO Rules and Agreements of Relevance to the Energy Sector*, Energy Charter Secretariat, ICTSD, Issue Paper No. 1, August 2007.
104. See *ibid.*

Article III of GATT deals with the national treatment of goods coming into the country. Article III provides that 'with respect to internal taxation and domestic laws, regulations and requirements, imported products shall be accorded treatment no less favourable than that accorded to domestic products'.[105] The national treatment clause is different from the MFN clause in that the clause takes effect once the goods enter the domestic market. MFN applies to both export and import of goods whereas national treatment applies only for non-discrimination of imports and does not deal with exports.[106] In the case of energy trade, the imported energy products have to be dealt with in the same way as domestic products and there cannot be any extra charges or custom duties imposed which might provide domestic goods with an unfair advantage. However, this relates only to 'like' products meaning that the government cannot impose taxes or charges on imported products which are similar to domestic energy products produced at home. This means that the government can impose taxes and charges on imported products which are not 'like' the domestic products.[107]

Quantitative restriction is another aspect of the WTO rules which can have an impact on energy trade. Article XI which deals with quantitative restrictions mentions that 'protection should be carried out through tariffs and not through measures directly affecting the volumes'.[108] This protection of export or import is also relevant to energy trade. This is because this requirement would lower the amount of import or export that can be carried out by any country. For example, if the imported goods are cheaper than the domestic goods, then such a restriction would not allow them to compete effectively in the domestic market. Similarly, exports also might not be competitive due to higher prices. An energy exporting or importing country can invoke this article if there is a serious shortfall of energy products in their county. In that case, it would allow them to fulfil their needs and the short term ban or restriction on energy export and import would help them to overcome their problem.

Market access is another aspect of WTO rules. Energy products, however, do not have problems with market access because of their nature. During the Uruguay Round of negotiations, tariffs for hydro-carbons were reduced.[109] Hydro-carbon exports have normally faced high tariffs because of the price fixed by the exporters. However, it is in the exporter's interest not to overcharge because it might make them less competitive. The importing countries are interested in receiving energy supplies at a low price. However, the export duty placed on these resources has to be made on the MFN basis.[110,111]

---

105. See the GATT Agreement at <www.wto.org>.
106. See *ibid.*
107. See Selivanova, *supra* n. 103.
108. See the GATT Agreement at <www.wto.org>.
109. See Selivanova, *supra* n. 103.
110. See J. Pauwelyn, *Trade in Energy: WTO Rules Applying under the Energy Charter Treat*, ECS, Brussels, Belgium, 2001.
111. Pipelines are specifically excluded from this.

The role of the state trading enterprises is another aspect of the WTO which has caused worry among the energy trading countries. In the energy sector, state companies play an active role in the transportation, production and management of energy resources. As a result, they are dominant in the energy field as they have a separate entity. Since these enterprises are actively involved in the export and import of energy goods, questions have been raised regarding their role under WTO rules.

According to Article XVII, 'GATT members undertake to ensure that state trading enterprises act in a manner consistent with the general principles of non-discrimination prescribed under GATT'.[112] Although this article clearly imposes obligations on the states towards their state enterprises, most of these state enterprises are involved in the transportation of energy resources and they in turn give access to third parties. A problem arises as to whether this article imposes obligations on the state run enterprises controlling the transportation infrastructure to act in a non-discriminatory manner with the other companies or their competitors.[113]

It is difficult to interpret this article in line with energy trade especially in relation to transportation infrastructure. In most countries, the energy companies are totally privatized raising the question of whether they have the same obligation as the state or state run enterprises. According to some experts, private companies might also fall under this article, as Article XVII 'applies to any enterprises that possess exclusive or special privileges granted by the state'.[114] This is quite ambiguous and lacks precision which will further increase conflicts among energy trading countries.

Transit is another issue dealt with in the WTO rules.[115] Article V mentions that 'there shall be freedom of transit through the territory of each member, via the routes most convenient for international transit, for traffic in transit to or from the territory of other members'.[116] The rules also mention that any form of transit cannot be subject to delays or any form of restrictions.[117] It also advocates for exemption of transit duties or any other charges. This means that WTO members involved in transit cannot charge custom duties or tariffs for the hydro-carbon resources passing through their country.[118]

However, they can charge for administrative, transportation and other expenses related to transit.[119] These expenses have to be in line with Article V.

---

112. See the GATT Agreement at <www.wto.org>.
113. See Pauwelyn, *supra* n. 110.
114. See the GATT Agreement at <www.wto.org>.
115. Again with exception to pipelines.
116. See the GATT Agreement at <www.wto.org>.
117. See *ibid.*
118. The reason why this is not a solution to the transit problems seen in pipelines is because Art. V does not take into account the geo-political aspects of the pipeline. This is because geo-politics is the reason transit countries wished to increase their transit fees and, despite this Article, countries still tend to do this. A good example of this is the Belarus and Ukraine case.
119. See UNCTAD, *Trade Agreements, Petroleum and Energy Policies*, UNCTAD/ITCD/TSB/9. United Nations, 2000.

This aspect of the WTO rules is not followed within the energy trade as the transit country can charge excessive fees depending upon its bargaining power. Good examples of this are Ukraine and Belarus, when they asked for an increase in the transit tariff despite there being an agreed tariff structure between the two countries and Russia.[120] Moreover, all forms of transit are based on negotiation between the actors involved in the project. There are instances where the producing country is also a transit country. Some hydro-carbon rich countries are landlocked and in those instances bilateral negotiation rather than WTO rules and regulations play an important role. The WTO DSM until now has not dealt with a single case relevant to transit problems, which further puts this body in a difficult situation.

### 7.3.10.    WHY NOT WTO DSM?

The WTO DSM may not be the appropriate body to bring energy related claims to either, because the WTO rules do not specifically deal with energy related problems although they are not excluded from its rules. Some of the WTO rules, like Article XI dealing with quantitative restrictions or Article I dealing with the most-favoured nation treatment, are relevant to energy but they are not always ideal in dealing with the energy trade. Some of the reasons for this are the uniqueness of the energy trade, resources are not always distributed evenly and consequently there are vital economic and social issues for countries dependent upon the resource, there are natural monopolies dominant in the sector and the interests of the exporting and importing countries are totally different which makes it quite challenging to reach a consensus among the different parties.[121] All these factors go against some of the key ideals of the WTO rules making it difficult for the DSM to consider the conflicts brought before it.

The WTO rules also deal with more import barriers than export barriers which are also problematic for energy exporting countries. The energy exporting countries would like to see greater access to markets and fewer hindrances to their export. This is especially the case with countries heavily reliant on their energy exports and any import barrier or higher taxes would lower their revenue, which is not ideal. Therefore, the WTO rules might not always be suitable for them. There are also many countries involved in the energy trade that are not members of the WTO because they are sceptical of the rules and regulations of the organization.[122] In fact, Non-WTO members make up 50% of world trade in energy products.[123] However, as these countries are becoming more powerful over the years it has become imperative for the WTO to try to bring these countries

---

120. See A. Belyi et al., 'A New Energy Charter: Myth or Reality?', OGEL, 2009.
121. See T. Walde & A. Gunst, *International Energy Trade and Access to Competing Networks* in *Energy and Environmental Services: Negotiating Objectives and Development Priorities,* UNCTAD, United Nations, 2003.
122. See *ibid.*
123. See *ibid.*

into their fold. Any conflict between a WTO member and a non-member cannot be brought before the WTO DSM because one of the parties is not a member of the organization.[124] This further lowers the effectiveness of the WTO DSM in energy disputes.

Transit is another issue which is extremely important in energy trade. Although the WTO rules indirectly deal with this factor, it is not ideal for the actors involved in the energy business. Article V of GATT highlights the issue of freedom of transit. The article calls for the exemption of transit duties and a uniform way of calculating costs and services. In reality, this does not happen as the transit country can bargain for a higher rent with the exporting or importing country and depending upon its bargaining power the transit tariff is agreed between the parties. If the country is landlocked, the demand by the transit country might even be greater. Accordingly, up to the present, no case regarding transit has been brought before the DSM and most of the problems regarding transit have arisen out of the WTO DSM framework.

Some of these states are not members of the WTO. The transit problems in the energy trade do not always involve these states but powerful and influential energy companies who are part of the consortium which owns the pipeline. Article V of GATT however 'does not provide any effective obligation on the members of the WTO to ensure that the companies owning the pipelines abide by the transit obligation enshrined in Article V'.[125] This further highlights the lack of relevance of the WTO DSM in dealing with energy disputes.

Although the WTO rules and its DSM are innovative and flexible in dealing with trade disputes it could also be helpful in dealing with energy related conflicts. By being a member of the WTO and bringing various claims to the DSM, energy trading countries could benefit by bringing claims relevant to discriminatory aspects of energy related environmental regulations, border tax problems, energy efficiency standards, greater inspection and regulation, greater access to markets and so on.[126] The WTO DSM provides this platform for energy trading countries. However, the problems related to restrictive practices within the energy exporting countries, the monopolistic nature of companies involved in the energy trade, their special privileges and rights and transit problems are some of the factors that make the WTO DSM less attractive for those countries relying on energy for their economic development.[127]

Most energy related agreements are bilateral or regional in nature and therefore a multilateral framework like WTO, lacking any specific provision regarding energy, might not be beneficial for the energy exporting, importing and transit countries. The energy trade is a unique and niche area which requires technical

---

124. See *ibid.*
125. See the GATT Agreement at <www.wto.org>.
126. See S. Zarilli, *International Energy Trade and Access to Competing Networks* in *Energy and Environmental Services: Negotiating Objectives and Development Priorities,* UNCTAD, United Nations, 2003.
127. See Selivanova, *supra* n. 103.

knowledge and a more customized approach.[128] The WTO DSM does not seem to provide this.

The WTO DSM also does not address the problems faced by participants involved in the pipeline regime. Although the organization has a mechanism to deal with economic disputes after they have taken place, it does not provide any kind of safety net to the other actors involved in a pipeline regime when there is intervention from government or actors in a pipeline due to economic, geo-political or legal reasons.

The DSM is more focused on trade related issues and the transit aspect of things and was not originally envisaged to deal with pipeline or energy issues. The case studies have shown that most of the problems faced by pipelines are related to any one of the three reasons[129] mentioned previously and the nature of pipeline disputes is such that it requires a quick resolution of disputes by experts who are aware of these sorts of problems. The WTO DSM does not have the expertise to deal with the problems quickly and any issue brought before it would take a long time to get settled.

For example, if the Shah-Deniz pipeline dispute, which involves legal and geo-political issues, or the WAGP dispute, which involves both economic and geo-political issues, was brought before the WTO DSM, all parties would have to spend a lot of time and money before the dispute was settled. What these pipeline regimes require is a mechanism which can enforce the various clauses of the agreement. It would ensure that the actors abide by their obligations and that any interference by members of the regime can be handled by the regulatory body of the regime whose remit involves ensuring pipeline regimes operate without any disruption and that actors abide by their original agreement.

The WTO DSM cannot provide that regulatory feature and can only become involved once the parties approach it with a problem. This might not be suitable in cross-border pipeline disputes as a more proactive and regulatory approach is needed to protect the interests of all the actors in a regime when there is intervention from other members of the regime or from an outside body due geo-political, legal or economic reasons.

The WTO DSM might not be useful for dealing with problems in cross-border pipelines for the reasons discussed above. The WTO rules and regulations and its DSM are not geared for this kind of dispute and neither does it have the required expertise in the area to deal with the various conflicts affecting cross-border pipeline projects. The economic, legal and geo-political implications are not looked into either by this body, which are all important in resolving cross-border disputes. The cross-border pipeline conflicts require enforcement of various rules and regulations between the various stakeholders involved which the WTO mechanism, together with its DSM, does not provide for.

The WTO mechanism is also not adept at dealing with government intervention due to the three reasons mentioned before and this is seen as a stumbling block

---

128. See *ibid.*
129. The three reasons involve geo-political, legal and economic aspects.

as the WTO is viewed as protecting the interest of the government. According to experts 'WTO rules provide some basic disciplines for energy transport and transit. These disciplines are incomplete and have rarely been tested in practice. Further, only government can have access to its sophisticated dispute settlement system . . . in this regard, WTO rules go less far than ECT, BITs and even some preferential trade agreements'.[130] Hence, in a pipeline dispute involving the government it might not be able to protect the interests of other pipeline regime members, especially vulnerable governments or weak members of the pipeline regime. Many countries involved in the energy trade are not comfortable with the idea of mixing energy trade with other forms of normal trade as it is a strategic resource for a lot of countries.[131] All these factors make the WTO DSM unsuitable for cross-border pipeline conflicts.

| 7.4. | THE ROLE OF BILATERAL INVESTMENT TREATIES (BITs)[132] |
|------|--------------------------------------------------------|

| 7.4.1. | THE OBJECTIVE OF BITs |
|--------|------------------------|

BITs have been signed since the 1950s and their main objective was to protect foreign investment in another country.[133] BITs can be defined as 'agreements between two states aimed at promoting investment flows between them'.[134] The main reason BITs are signed is to increase the level of foreign investment in developing countries by providing the investors with greater security over their investment through tax breaks and stopping expropriation by host governments and other facilities to repatriate the profits to the private company's home country. The host government, by providing these facilities, is protecting foreign investment beyond the requirement of international law.[135]

Some BITs also contain provisions regarding the movement of important employees from one country to the other and the transfer of technology between the two countries but does not require the private companies to adhere to any form

---

130. See M. Cossy, 'Energy Transport and Transit in the WTO', in *Global Challenges at the intersection of Energy, Trade and Environment*, Centre for Trade and Economic Integration (CETI), 113–121, 2010.
131. See *ibid.*
132. It is important to note that all the issues discussed in this section would be defined as 'legal issues' in nature as BITs only tend to deal with the legal aspects of things, whereas in cross-border pipelines there are issues other than legal ones which cause problems. As a result, the legal and economic aspects of cross-border pipelines would be considered as legal issues in this section.
133. See A. Guzman, 'Why LDCs Sign Treaties that Hurt Them: Explaining the Popularity of Bilateral Investment Treaties', *Journal of International Law* 38 (1998): 639–654.
134. See *ibid.*
135. See H.M. Driemer, *Do Bilateral Investment Treaties Attract Foreign Direct Investment? Only a Bit . . . and They Could Bite*, Policy Research Working Paper, The World Bank, 2003.

of performance requirements.[136] The treaty covers all sectors of the economy unless it is specified that one of the sectors would not come within the purview of the treaty. In most cases, the treaty would come into effect once the industry or factory has been established but there have been instances when the treaty took effect during the building stage.[137]

### 7.4.2. THE MAIN FEATURES OF A BIT

Most BITs have some important features which protect the investment of foreign companies. Some of these are as follows:

1. 'The national treatment and most-favoured nation principles, whereby the host state must apply to foreign investors a treatment no less favourable than that applied to its own nationals (national treatment) and/or to nationals of other states (most-favoured nation)[138]
2. Fair and equitable treatment, whereby the host state must treat foreign investment according to minimum standards of fairness, irrespective of the standards it applies to domestic investment under its national law[139]
3. Full protection and security, whereby the host state must take steps to protect foreign investment from damage caused by third parties[140]
4. *Provision of currency convertibility, profit repatriation and related aspects, which allow investors to repatriate returns from their activities in the host state'.*[141]

Some BITs include provisions to ensure that local businesses are also promoted through their involvement, while some have provisions which make the foreign companies employ a local workforce and follow local customs while doing business.

### 7.4.3. THE POPULARITY OF BITs

The first BIT was signed in the 1950s between Pakistan and Germany and since then the number of BITs has greatly increased, especially from the 1990s onwards.[142] Since 1959 more than 2,000 BITs have been concluded between countries and the numbers have been increasing over the years.[143] Most BITs

---

136. See *ibid.*
137. See *ibid.*
138. See L.E. Peterson, *Bilateral Investment Treaties and Development Policy Making*, International Institute for Sustainable Development, 2004.
139. See *ibid.*
140. See *ibid.*
141. See *ibid.*
142. See *ibid.*
143. See *ibid.*

are signed between developed and developing countries. However, after the break-down of the Soviet Union, there has also been a trend for BITs to be signed between two developing countries.

One of the reasons for this increasing number of BITs being signed is because of the interest of developing countries to secure foreign investment in their country. Due to weak legal frameworks and political risk in these countries, foreign inves-tors are sometimes sceptical of doing business in the developing world. By signing these BITs developing countries are trying to lure foreign investment into vital parts of their economy. However, it is not always possible to attract foreign investment just by signing BITs. Evidence for this can be seen in sub-Saharan Africa where, despite entering into various bilateral agreements, it has failed to attract investment from other countries.[144] However, countries like Cuba and Bra-zil, despite not having BITs with other countries, have secured a huge amount of investment from Western companies.[145]

### 7.4.4.    THE ARBITRATION PROCEDURE

One of the main features of a BIT is the dispute settlement procedure agreed between the parties while signing the treaty. A typical treaty allows the parties to choose one arbitrator each while a third one is chosen by agreement between the two parties.[146] The arbitrators can be chosen from practicing lawyers who are specialists in the area. The arbitration rules are based upon the Washington based dispute settlement centre known as ICSID, which is part of the World Bank. Most BITs prefer ICSID to solve their dispute. Some BITs also have other options or another set of rules such as the Stockholm Chamber of Commerce (SCC) or the United Nations Commission for International Trade Law (UNCI-TRAL).[147] However, there have been allegations that these kinds of choices allow 'rules shopping' which might lower the level of transparency and cause confusion due to different arbitration rules which might in turn cause problems during a review of any decision given by the arbitration panel.[148]

Most of the arbitration that takes place between the parties is confidential in nature and never open to public scrutiny. It is difficult therefore to find out the actual contents of arbitration and the relevant law used by the arbitrators to reach their decision. Neither will the decision of the arbitrators always be accessible because it is rarely published.

---

144. See *ibid.*
145. See *ibid.*
146. See W.D. Rogers, *Emergence of the International Centre for Settlement of Investment Dis-putes (ICSID) as the Most Significant Forum for Submission of Bilateral Investment Treaty Disputes*, presentation to Inter-American Development Bank Conference, 26–27 Oct. 2000.
147. See *ibid.*
148. See *ibid.*

The nature of arbitration from BITs has varied over the years. Previous arbitration arose due to some form of expropriation from the government or if the investor's rights had been violated in certain respects. These days, investors are resorting to arbitration due to excessive regulation by the government, privatization of certain utilities or even in sensitive areas like electricity and water services.[149] The investors have gone as far as bringing the government into arbitration in sensitive public policy cases where the former believed they had been wronged or the action of the government was in breach of the BIT.[150] In one of those cases, the host government and the investor had a dispute with regard to 'the method of measuring water consumption, the level of tariffs for customers, the timing and percentage of any increase in tariffs, the remedy for non-payment of tariffs, the right of the investor to pass through to customers certain taxes and the quality of the water delivered'.[151]

The arbitration procedure also ensures that local courts do not have the power to stop any reward given by the arbitration panel. The ICSID rules of arbitration clearly state this fact, as any arbitration reward passed by the panel under its rules cannot be scrutinized by local courts. Other arbitration rules give very limited power to the host government to approach local courts. This point is succinctly pointed out by Professor Sornarajah, who states that 'if the arbitration was legally sited in a country other than the host state, then there may be no capacity whatsoever for the host government to challenge this award in its own legal system'.[152]

### 7.4.5. THE CONCEPTS OF THE STABILIZATION CLAUSE AND EXPROPRIATION

The stabilization clause ensures that nothing in the contract changes even if there is change in legislation or a change of government or change in government policy. This gives some sort of stability to the contract, which the private companies want, to ensure the smooth functioning of the project. In addition, the companies invest billions of dollars in projects to ensure that they get a profitable return. A constant change in government policies regarding the fiscal and regulatory regime has an adverse effect on the policies of the company to get a return on those investments. A stabilization clause gives them the confidence to carry out their venture.

The traditional stabilization clause ensures that no change in domestic law and regulation would affect the contract. Stabilization clauses *specifically seek to ensure the agreement against future government action or changes in law, either*

---

149. See I. Shihata & A. Parra, 'The Experience of ICSID', *ICSID Review* 14, no. 2 (Fall, 1999): 319–336.
150. See L.E. Peterson, 'All Roads Lead Out of Rome: Divergent Paths of Dispute Settlement in Bilateral Investment Treaties', in *International Investment for Sustainable Development: Balancing Rights and Rewards*, ed. Zarsky, L. (Earthscan, 2004).
151. See Compania De Augus Del Aconquija, S.A. & Compagnie General des Eaux v. Argentine Republic, ICSID ARB/97/3, Final Award, at para. 32.
152. See M. Sornarajah, *Affidavit in Ontario Superior Court Of Justice case between The Council of Canadians, et al. and Canada*, Court file No. 01-CV-208141, at para. 13.

*legislative or regulatory'.*[153] It is, in fact, a commitment by the host state that changes in law would not affect the contract signed. Another type of stabilization clause is where the parties perform the contract in good faith. This ensures that both parties are aware of their respective position and would not do anything to jeopardize the contract.

A stabilization clause no doubt helps companies to mitigate the risks involved in the industry. It also helps to mitigate the political risks which might arise. It ensures that there is some kind of stability in the contracts and protects a company in countries with a volatile political situation or a country whose government has strong nationalistic fervour.[154]

Expropriation, however, means the regulatory taking of an industry or infrastructure by the government.[155] Further expropriation can only take place if it is for a public purpose, is done in a non-discriminatory way and compensation is paid.[156] The compensation also has to be paid in a prompt, adequate and effective manner to the sufferer.[157] A host government might threaten to expropriate the properties of the private companies if they did not accept their demand to pay more taxes or royalties or accept the government proposal to increase their stake in the project. This was a common practice in the 1960s and 1970s when many countries nationalized the properties of the oil companies.[158]

A host government might also try to cancel a contract made by the previous government in order to prove publicly that there were illegal dealings made with the private companies which went against the interest of the nation and they felt it important that the contract be rescinded. This is more of a political decision than a clearly thought out economic decision beneficial for the country. Most claims under BITs therefore take place because of expropriation by the government and all the claims in front of the arbitration tribunal involve some form of arbitration.[159]

### 7.4.6.    THE ADVANTAGES OF A BIT

BITs have increased the level of investment in developing countries which not only benefits these countries economically but also increases their credibility on the

---

153.  See C.T. Curtis, 'The Legal Security of Economic Development Agreements', 29 *Harvard International Law Journal* 29 (1988): 317, 317–318.
154.  Although there could be an argument that stabilization clauses might not be enough to stop government reneging on their contractual obligations, it still acts as a deterrent and gives confidence to investors investing in countries which are volatile. See Peterson, *supra* n. 150.
155.  See Curtis, *supra* n. 153.
156.  See *ibid.*
157.  See Driemer, *supra* n. 135.
158.  See O. Anderson, *Risk: Emphasizing Political Risk*, CEPMLP Course materials, contracts used in International Oil Industry development, slides p-18-19 CEPMLP, University of Dundee, 2004.
159.  See Driemer, *supra* n. 135.

world stage as a safe place to do business. It provides those countries which have a fragmented and weak legal structure with a framework which helps them to satisfy the needs of investors. According to the Government of India 'Bilateral Investment Treaties have found favour with developing countries like India because they do not place any restrictions on host countries in following their own foreign direct investment policies in the light of each country's unique need and circumstances'.[160]

The use of a third party to settle disputes between a host country and a private company is also another important advantage of the BIT. It allows the company to bring a claim against the government in front of an independent arbitration panel who would be able to resolve the differences and conflicts between the two sides. It also gives the investors confidence because most investors are of the opinion that they might not get justice from local courts. As a result, the institutional dispute settlement mechanisms used to solve their disputes gives them confidence regarding the legal aspects of their investment.

The use of a third party to resolve any disputes is also beneficial to developed countries because it removes the requirement for state espousal of claims.[161] The current regime under international law gives the home states jurisdiction to decide whether the state should pursue the claim or not for any breach of obligation by the home state. However, this is a problem because the home state may only pursue claims which involve a considerable number of investors or parties and this is not favourable for a single claimant or small investors. By removing the requirement for espousal, a BIT allows the investors or companies to bring in more claims, especially if their investment has been expropriated.[162]

The treaty is also helpful in countries where there is political instability and risk. Investors can rely on the treaty during political instability. There have been instances in the past when a change in government has brought about a change of policies which might affect companies negatively.[163] The treaty gave the companies some form of guarantee that their investment would not be affected and the government of the day had to abide by its obligations.

The increasing level of BITs being signed by countries and the fact that more developing countries are signing BITs between themselves in order to benefit from the advantages provided by the treaty in respect of property rights, a stable investment climate and greater investment flow shows the increasing advantages of signing a BIT. Countries like South Korea, Taiwan and some East Asian countries have benefited tremendously from investment by foreign companies as a result of signing BITs.[164]

---

160. See *Stocktaking of Indian Bilateral Agreements for the Promotion and Protection of Investment*, Communication from India to the Working Group on trade and Investment, 3 Apr. 1999, WT/WGTI/W/71.
161. See Peterson, *supra* n. 150.
162. See *ibid.*
163. See *ibid.*
164. See Driemer, *supra* n. 135.

7.4.7.    THE DISADVANTAGES OF A BIT

One of the main disadvantages of a BIT is that the language of the treaty is not precise, it is ambiguous and open-ended, which causes problems when lawyers are trying to find the actual meaning of the treaty during any form of arbitration. Some lawyers involved in the whole process have pointed put that 'the terms are maddeningly imprecise as to the substantive legal standard to be applied by the tribunal'.[165] This also causes problems for governments because it narrows the scope they have to make policy decisions which can have a detrimental effect on their economy or some other strategic and important national issues. Furthermore, due to the imprecise nature of the terms in the treaty, the number of arbitrations which have simply dragged on for years has increased over time.[166]

There are other complications in the arbitration procedure. There have been instances when several arbitration cases have been lodged in parallel against a host government and each arbitration panel has reached a different decision.[167] Since arbitration panels are not obliged to follow any precedence, this offers a dangerous example where there is no consistency in the arbitration awards given by the panel. It also erodes confidence in the arbitration panel if each panel gives different verdicts in cases where the principle reason for arbitration is the same. A good example is that of the Czech Republic, where the tribunals have provided two contradictory rulings.[168] Failure to bring all these cases under one body has caused frustration and anxiety among investors and host states.[169]

Many investment treaties failed to identify their real objective and purpose during the draft process. This resulted in a treaty becoming one-dimensional and narrow.[170] Some treaties have identified the broader objectives and what is expected from all the parties involved others have not. Due to this narrow interpretation, the arbitration panel can sometimes analyse and interpret these objectives from a narrow perspective and this tends to favour the investors more than the host state.[171] There are recent cases where the arbitrators have interpreted the real objective of the BIT narrowly. In a case against Chile, the tribunal noted that it would interpret the treaty 'in the manner most conducive to fulfil the objective of the BIT to protect investments and create conditions favourable to investments'.[172] Another tribunal also observed that 'it is legitimate to resolve uncertainties in its interpretation so as to favour the protection of covered investments'.[173] These

---

165.  See Rogers, *supra* n. 146.
166.  See *ibid.*
167.  See *ibid.*
168.  See *ibid.*
169.  See J. Werner, 'Making Investment arbitration More Certain- A Modest Proposal', *Journal of World Investment* 4, no. 5 (October 2003).
170.  See *ibid.*
171.  See *ibid.*
172.  See MTD Equity Sdn.Bhd. and *MTD Chile S.A. v. Republic of Chile*, decision on Jurisdiction, at para. 104.
173.  See *SGS v. Philippines*, Decision on Jurisdiction, January 2009, 2004, at para. 116.

narrow interpretations by the panel hurt the host governments most while protecting investors.

The cost of undertaking this sort of arbitration is also extremely high which causes further problems for the host government. Companies sometimes tend to have multiple claims which not only delays the entire process but also costs more money. The average cost of hiring ICSID lawyers is close to USD 500,000.[174] The cost of hiring lawyers for other institutional arbitration is higher. For example, the Metalcald Corporation has spent USD 4 million in an arbitration case under NAFTA.[175] The Czech Republic has spent USD 10 million in defending claims brought against it.[176] Arbitration under the BIT can be disastrous for the host state, especially if the country is a developing one; the cost of arbitration can sometimes cause budget defaults in those countries.[177]

7.4.8.      WHY NOT BIT?

Bilateral Investment Treaties between two governments allow companies to claim against any injustice that might have occurred against them. There can be an argument that the private companies involved in cross-border pipeline projects might use BITs to solve their problems because they contain dispute resolution clauses, rather than go to the agency with their dispute. However, till now, no parties have used the BIT option to settle their disputes.[178]

BITs are bilateral in nature whereas the nature of cross-border pipelines is multilateral. There are many players involved in the building, operation and maintenance of cross-border pipelines and there are agreements signed between various actors to ensure that each actor fulfils its obligations. There are also bilateral agreements between parties but they are in the context of bigger multilateral agreements signed between the parties. The BITs, however, are only relevant between the host government and the private company and it involves setting up infrastructure and investment in the country.

Another problem with BITs is the lack of consistency and clarity with regard to the provision of the treaty. This uncertainty and the wide powers given to the arbitrators to interpret the treaty causes problems for the host state as most arbitration panels interpret the treaty provision within its narrow scope which tends to favour the investors.[179] Sometimes the arbitration panel can come to different

---

174. See J.C. Thomas, 'A Reply to Professor Brower', *Columbia Journal of Transnational Law* 40, no. 3 (2002).
175. See L.P. Peterson, *Croatian Firm Invokes Investment Treaty to Challenge Czech Eviction Notice*, INVEST-SD News Bulletin, 1 Oct. 2004, available at <www.iisd.org/pdf/2004/investment_investsd_oct1_2004.pdf.>.
176. See *ibid.*
177. See Thomas, *supra* n. 174.
178. See *ibid.*
179. See Rogers, *supra* n. 146.

conclusions based on the same facts.[180] All these signs might not be favourable in the case of cross-border pipelines as both the investors and the host state need each other for the successful implementation of the project.

For example, in the case of the CPC pipeline, if the private companies signed a BIT with the Russian government and brought a claim against them with regard to the pipeline through a BIT, then the stakes would be much higher for both parties.[181] The reason for this is that it involves a natural resource which the country is dependent upon and considers a strategic resource, and the company which brought the claim has also invested billions of dollars. If the arbitration panel decides the case based on its current standards it might not only escalate the conflict between the parties but might also cause geo-political tension. As a result, BITs are not equipped to deal with cross-border pipeline conflicts.

Although BITs could be helpful in defining in clear terms the role of the oil exporting and importing states, there are certain problems. They suffer from incoherence, imbalance and a lack of uniformity.[182] The reason for this is that each state comes to the negotiating of BITs with their own interest in mind and with their own model agreements and even if draft models are agreed between the parties the clauses are still not drafted in a uniform manner or interpreted consistently.[183] It is also asserted that 'BITs do endorse a one sided focus on investor protection and thereby government – only discipline'.[184] As a result, this might be a problem in cross-border pipeline disputes as there needs to be a balance between all the parties involved in a pipeline regime.

The tribunals deciding conflicts under BITs are also not consistent in their decisions which will dissuade stakeholders involved in cross-border pipelines to avail themselves of this mechanism. In *CMS v. Argentina*, the claimant alleged that the Emergency law imposed by Argentina in response to the financial breakdown significantly impaired its values in a minority Argentinean gas company thereby constituting a breach of the US–Argentina BIT.[185] Argentina argued that it had to take the decision because of the state of necessity in the country. The tribunal disagreed and asked Argentina to pay compensation.[186] However, in a very similar case two years later in *LG&E v. Argentina*, the tribunal came to the completely opposite decision based on identical facts.[187] In another case between *Continental Casualty v. Argentina*, the dispute was again about the measures taken by the

---

180. See *ibid.*
181. See Peterson, *supra* n. 150.
182. See Konolpayanik, *supra* n. 46.
183. See *ibid.*
184. See *ibid.*
185. See *CMS Gas Company Transmission Company v. Argentine Republic*, ICSID Case No. ARB/ 01/8, 2005.
186. See *ibid.*
187. See B. Maier, 'How Has International Law Dealt with the Tension between Sovereignty over Natural Resources and Investor Interests in the Energy Sector? Is there a Balance?', IELR (2010).

Argentinean government during the financial crisis of 2001.[188] In this case, the tribunal took another stance on the defence of necessity and its relationship with Article XI of the US–Argentina BIT.[189]

The economic perspective of BITs is also not favourable in the case of cross-border pipelines. For example, if we assume that the demand for natural resources is inelastic without signing any BITs, this would make the price of natural resources higher because of low protection levels. It would allow the country exporting the natural resources to earn more money. A higher level of protection through a BIT would lower the price of the natural resource and favour countries that are importing it as well as the investors. So, for example, if Algeria exports gas to Spain and Portugal via its pipelines, increased protection would suit both the Europeans buyers and the investors[190] but it would lower the profit for the Algerians. This is the case even if the level of investment is constant; there would still be repercussions for the distribution of profit.[191] In the case of cross-border pipelines, this would not be favourable at all to the energy exporting countries as it would lower their profit and cause them to earn less foreign exchange, which might affect them economically. No energy rich country would therefore be willing to put its strategic resource under the purview of the BIT, as it is not applicable in the complex world of energy trade.

The dispute settlement procedure of the BIT is also not suited to cross-border pipeline disputes. This is because the latter involves geo-political, economic and legal aspects in areas which might not be covered under the narrow scope of the BITs. Hence, the arbitration tribunal might not be able to ascertain the true nature of the conflict. The concept of expropriation also might not be relevant in the case of cross-border pipelines because it is considered as a national and strategic asset and as a result governments consider it within their domain and area of protection.[192] Although private companies might have invested in the project, any sort of conflict that arises between them and the government is extremely delicate and requires careful examination, cooperation and negotiation between the parties. Simply relying on the BIT or bringing a claim under it might not solve the problem and could further disrupt the flow of hydro-carbon resources, causing problems for the other stakeholders involved in the project.

BITs certainly provide the option for actors in a pipeline regime to protect their investment if they feel it is under threat or if there is any dispute with the government. However, they fail to address the intervention by governments or

---

188. See *LG&E v. Argentina*, ICSID Case No. ARB/02, 2006.
189. See *ibid*.
190. See Peterson, *supra* n. 150.
191. See *ibid*.
192. Although the investors investing in cross-border pipelines have certain rights, it is protected under the various host government and inter-government agreements and despite all these agreements the governments consider the pipeline as their strategic asset. As a result, any conflict that arises is solved through negotiation, cooperation and bargaining between the parties rather than relying on any form of BIT or even HGAs. The case studies in Chs 4, 5 and 6 have shown this fact. For further discussion please read these previous chapters.

other actors involved in the pipeline regime for economic, geo-political or legal reasons. The intervention by any of the stronger members of the regime results in these parties not abiding by the original position they agreed to as part of the contract. This results in negotiation which might not be ideal for the other members of the regime. BITs do help those regime members who are affected by it to apply for arbitration but this might take a long time and is not ideal in a cross-border pipeline scenario. It also does not contain the regulatory mechanisms necessary to ensure that parties abide by their obligations and nor is it able to deal with the various interventions by the members in a regime while protecting the interests of all the actors involved.

The case studies have showed that frequent intervention due to the three reasons mentioned above, by governments or other actors in a regime, have resulted in pipeline disruption. In most of the pipeline regimes such as the CPC or the BTC, BITs were signed between the respective governments but none of the members took advantage of it in times of dispute. This is because it is the governments in a pipeline regime who intervene due to geo-political and economic reasons and other governments who might be involved might also choose not to use the BIT route to solve the dispute because they are aware that they might have to take the same action as the intervening government if they were faced with a similar situation. The behaviour of governments in this regard depends on whether their own interest is at stake and on their relevant powers within that particular regime to fulfil their individual demands.

The role of BITs is more legal in nature as it is a treaty protecting the investments of countries. They do not deal with geo-political or economic issues,[193] and these are important areas which often cause cross-border pipeline disputes which feature government intervention because of those very reasons. BITs therefore might not be appropriate tools to restrict government intervention in cross-border pipeline disputes.

The role of the BIT as a regime is more neo-realist in nature. The main principle of the regime is to protect investors of countries signing the treaty, whereas the rules would be with regard to expropriation of companies assets by any government.[194] The neo-liberal side of the treaty would be two countries cooperating with each other in the signing of the treaty and provision of a framework based upon which both the countries can do business. As result the main goal is to share the benefit of this cooperation.

However, there can also be neo-realist tendencies, when a country has to take decisions resulting in the taking over of companies due to national security or other economic, political or social factors. In those situations, the investors could take the country to arbitration or courts and the tribunal in those situations could go against the government despite the government's aim being to protect the interest

---

193. Although during negotiation of the agreements there will be consideration given to geo-political and economic interests, the bargaining power of individual countries determines whether the treaty is favourable to them or not.
194. See the Argentina–US Bilateral Treaty.

of the country. This act is thus more neo-realist in nature as the tribunal could act as a hegemony in coming to a decision which could serve the interest of the companies due to the structure of the BIT. However, the main goal of the BIT is to constrain frequent government intervention and protect the interest of the stakeholders doing business.

## 7.5.     THE INTERNATIONAL ATOMIC ENERGY AGENCY (IAEA)[195]

### 7.5.1.     THE HISTORICAL BACKGROUND OF THE IAEA

After the end of second World War in 1945, the Prime Minister of the UK, Attlee, Mackenzie King of Canada and President Truman of the US met in Washington to declare the 'Three Nation Declaration on Atomic Energy', where they decided 'to proceed with the exchange of fundamental scientific literature for peaceful ends with any nation that will fully reciprocate but only when it is possible to devise effective reciprocal and enforceable safeguards acceptable to all nations against its use for destructive purposes'.[196] The three leaders also agreed that the newly formed United Nations should also play an active role in this regard. As a consequence, in December 1945, the UK, US and Canada, together with the USSR, created the United Nations Atomic Energy Commission to carry out research and investigate the benefits and problems of atomic energy and other matters.[197] Once the commission had finished its work both the US and USSR agreed that they were more inclined to get rid of nuclear weapons altogether rather than trying to prevent their spread although beneficial nuclear activities would not be stopped.

In 1953, President Eisenhower of the US, in his speech to the United Nations General Assembly, advocated the creation of an organization which promoted the peaceful use of nuclear energy and tried to ensure that this energy is not used for military purposes. On 4 December 1954, the US President's proposals led to the creation of the IAEA.[198]

The makeup of the IAEA has changed over the years due to various disagreements between the US and the former USSR. Although the agency was supposed to have acted as a kind of clearing house for all nuclear fissile materials, the former USSR had reservations regarding this, as they did not want the agency to have so much power and leverage. The first few decades of the IAEA were relatively quiet

---

195. See n. 1 in s. 7.1 of this chapter in regard to the reason for analysing the different aspects of IAEA in respect to cross-border pipelines.
196. See D. Fischer, 'Chapter Two: The Creation of the IAEA, 1939–1953: The Dual Challenge of Nuclear Energy', in *History of the International Atomic Energy Agency: The first forty years*, Vienna: IAEA can be found in <www-pub.iaewa.org/MTCD/publications/PDF/Pub1032_web.pdf>.
197. See *ibid.*
198. See *ibid.*

until the Cuban missile crisis of 1965.[199] However, after this crisis both the US and the former USSR decided to cooperate with each other in controlling the nuclear arms race. The end of the Cold War has also led to military stocks of fissile materials coming under the surveillance of the IAEA.

### 7.5.2.    THE IAEA STATUTE

The IAEA's statute was passed at a conference on 20 September 1956.[200] The statute was ratified by twenty-six states and entered into force on 29 July 1957.[201] The statute brings into focus the three pillars of the Agency's work. They are (i) nuclear verification and security; (ii) safety; and (iii) technology transfer.[202] Some of the important features of the statute are as follows:

1. 'Examine and approve the design of nuclear plants (but solely in order to verify that they would not further any military purpose, would comply with the safety standards and would permit the application of safeguards)[203]
2. Require the keeping of operating records[204]
3. Call and receive reports regarding various nuclear facilities[205]
4. Approve the means used for reprocessing spent fuel to ensure that reprocessing did not lend itself to diversion and the complied with applicable safety standards[206]
5. Send inspectors to the recipient State or States designated by the IAEA in consultation with the States. The inspectors shall have access at all times to all places and data and to any person dealing with nuclear items required to be safeguarded. The inspectors would also account for all nuclear materials covered by the IAEA's agreement with the State and must verify accordingly.'[207]

---

199. See D. Fischer, 'Chapter One: The Creation of the IAEA, 1939–1953: Eisenhower proposes a New Agency', in *History of the International Atomic Energy Agency: The first forty years*, Vienna: IAEA can be found in <www-pub.iaewa.org/MTCD/publications/PDF/Pub1032_web.pdf>.
200. See *ibid.*
201. See *ibid.*
202. See IAEA website at <www.iaea.org>.
203. See *ibid.*
204. See D. Fischer, 'Chapter Three: The Creation of the IAEA, 1954–1956: Negotiation of the IAEA's Statute', in *History of the International Atomic Energy Agency: The first forty years*, Vienna: IAEA can be found in <www-pub.iaewa.org/MTCD/publications/PDF/Pub1032_web.pdf>.
205. See *ibid.*
206. See *ibid.*
207. See *ibid.*

7.5.3.    THE OBJECTIVES AND THE ROLE OF THE IAEA

The main objective of the IAEA is to respond to requests from member countries and assist them with their nuclear security and activities. The purpose of this is to lower the risk of any nuclear accidents or terrorism which might take place due to the lack of expert and technical assistance. This objective of the IAEA is achieved through the following mechanisms: facilitating the development of and adherence to legally binding and non-binding international instruments; developing international guidelines and recommendations which would be applicable and acceptable to the countries; providing assessment services[208] and providing and exchanging information and other services.[209]

The IAEA, being an independent international organization, reports to the UN General Assembly annually. The IAEA can also report to the UN Security Council when one of the Member States is not complying with the IAEA with regard to its security obligations or if the agency thinks that there is a threat from a country which is intending to produce nuclear weapons. As a result, the IAEA has direct access to the UN and can use it to make countries which do not abide by their obligations comply with their demands.

The IAEA has currently tried to strengthen its nuclear security programme to ensure that nuclear and other radioactive materials are safe. After the events of 11 September 2001, the agency formulated new plans to strengthen its nuclear safety regime. These include offering extensive help to Member States upon request with regard to prevention and detection of and response to nuclear terrorism and other subversive acts.[210] The Agency also intends to work on the following areas: *'(i) improving the physical protection of nuclear materials and facilities; (ii) detecting malicious activities involving nuclear and other radioactive materials; (iii) strengthening the security of radioactive materials; (iv) assessing the security/safety vulnerabilities of nuclear facilities; (v) responding to malicious acts and threats; (vi) ensuring compliance with international agreements and guidelines and (vii) share and coordinate information between the member countries'.*[211] This plan was formulated by the agency to detect any nation pursuing its nuclear weapons ambition and also to protect Member States from terrorist threat. It was also formulated to make states better prepared for terrorist attacks. The agency is helping member countries to prepare emergency measures and response arrangements.[212]

The Office of Nuclear Security was established in 2002, to help Member States and other countries deal with nuclear terrorism. The office is also

---

208.  See the IAEA website at <www.iaea.org>.
209.  See A.K. Semmel, *Future Goals and Challenges of the IAEA Nuclear Security Programme*, in the US Department of State, 2005, available at <www.state.gov/t/np/rls/rm44213.htm>.
210.  See IAEA website at <www.iaea.org>.
211.  See I. Khripunov, 'Nuclear Security: Attitude Check', *Bulletin of the Atomic Scientists* (2005): 58–64, 2005, available at <www.thebulletin.org/article.php?art_ofn=jf05khripunov>.
212.  See *ibid.*

responsible for implementing, planning and evaluating the agency's nuclear security programme. Through this office the agency has so far helped seventy-five countries to upgrade their nuclear security and has also provided them with equipment and other technical assistance. There have also been other non-member countries who have used the IAEA's guidelines while setting up their own security framework. The agency has also provided both member and non-member countries with equipment to monitor their borders.

The IAEA board also approved another nuclear security plan in 2005 which ran until 2009. The new plan had three main objectives. These are: (i) Needs Assessment, Analysis and Coordination; (ii) Prevention; and (iii) Detection.[213] Needs Assessment, Analysis and Coordination included the following:

(i) Having a comprehensive set of information which supports implementation of the nuclear security plan.[214]
(ii) Understanding nuclear security needs on a global scale to identify areas of cooperation between and among the agency and Member States.[215]
(iii) Understanding illicit global trafficking trends and patterns, including theft and other malicious acts involving radioactive material.[216]
(iv) Fully protecting sensitive nuclear security information and disclosure.[217]
(v) Fully coordinating nuclear security support programmes of Member States and international organizations with those of the Agency.[218]

The purpose of the prevention mechanism was to protect Member States and non-members states from nuclear terrorism, sabotage and other malicious acts involving radioactive materials.[219] The mechanism is also supposed to help states create national regulatory frameworks, accounting and control, transport security, and so on.[220] These prevention mechanisms include the following:

(i) To enhance adherence or political commitments by States.[221]
(ii) To achieve effective protection, control, accountancy and registry of all nuclear and other radioactive material and associated facilities, as requested, within a State.[222]

---

213. See *ibid.*
214. See the IAEA's Director General, *Nuclear Security–Measures to Protect Against Nuclear Terrorism, Progress Report and Nuclear Security Plan for 2006–2009*, Forty-ninth regular session of the General Conference, GC(49)/17, 2005.
215. See *ibid.*
216. See *ibid.*
217. See *ibid.*
218. See *ibid.*
219. See *ibid.*
220. See *ibid.*
221. See *ibid.*
222. See Khripunov, *supra* n. 211.

The third mechanism in the new plan is detection, which highlights the agency's role in helping States to combat illegal trafficking of nuclear materials and radiological devices. They also include:

(i) Enhancing the states capabilities to detect, interdict and respond to illegal acts involving nuclear and other radioactive material and associated facilities.[223]

(ii) To make internationally accepted guidance and technical information available to States that will assist them, upon request, in their efforts to detect and respond to unlawful use/possession of nuclear and other radioactive material.[224]

7.5.4.      INTERNATIONAL INSTRUMENTS USED BY THE IAEA

The IAEA is working tirelessly to ensure that the nuclear and other radioactive materials used by states are used for peaceful purposes. As a consequence, the agency has been working with both members and non-members alike to highlight the concept of nuclear security to protect the various nuclear establishments physically and also to prevent the illegal trafficking of nuclear materials. Some of the instruments that are used to ensure the safety of nuclear material are as follows:

(i) The IAEA's own Nuclear Security plans.

(ii) The UN Security Council Resolution 1373(2001), calling for all states to become parties as soon as possible to the relevant international conventions and protocols relating to terrorism and other nuclear safety measures and emphasizing the need to strengthen a global response to the challenge of the illegal movement of nuclear materials.[225]

(iii) The UN Security Council Resolution 1540.

(iv) The Convention on the Physical Protection of Nuclear Material (CPPNM), which entered into force in 1987 and its aim is to ensure the protection of nuclear material.[226]

(v) The Code of Conduct for the Safety and Security of Radioactive Sources, which is a non-binding international legal instrument that applies to civilian radioactive sources that may pose risks to individuals and the environment.[227]

(vi) The G8 Global Partnership against the spread of Weapons and Materials of Mass Destruction.

The IAEA also has it own set of agreements signed by all its members as well as some non-members. Some of these are: INFCIRC/66 which is signed by states that

---

223. See *ibid.*
224. See *ibid.*
225. See Semmel, *supra* n. 209.
226. See *ibid.*
227. See *ibid.*

signed the safeguard agreement, INFCIRC/153 which is used as a basis for states wishing to sign the Nuclear Non-proliferation Treaty (NPT), the treaty for the prohibition of Nuclear Weapons in Latin America and the Caribbean known as the Treaty of Tlateloco, the South East Asia Nuclear Weapon Free Zone Treaty known as the Treaty of Bangkok, the African Nuclear Weapon Free Zone Treaty known as the Treaty of Pelindaba, the South Pacific Nuclear Free Zone Treaty known as the Treaty of Rarotonga and the Brazilian-Argentine Agency for Accounting and Control of Nuclear Materials.[228] The IAEA, with the help of all these agreements signed by the states, tries to ensure the safety of nuclear weapons and to discourage states from attaining nuclear capabilities for military purposes.

7.5.5.     THE SAFEGUARD SYSTEM OF THE IAEA

The main purpose of the safeguard system is to ensure and assure states that the nuclear and radioactive materials used by most states are for peaceful purposes and would not be diverted for military purposes. The following procedures allow the IAEA to carry out its work: (*i*) *the agency has statutory authority to establish and administer safeguards, (ii) the rights and obligations given in the safeguard agreements and other additional protocols and finally, (iii) the technical measures undertaken and implemented in accordance with those agreements.*[229] These rights allow the agency to verify the claims of states independently and to see whether they are abiding by their various obligations. However, the nature of the agency's verification and inspection of a state's nuclear and other radioactive materials depends upon the nature of agreement signed by the state with the agency.

Article III A.5 of the IAEA statute empowers the agency to carry out its safeguard work.[230] This statute allows the agency to sign agreements with states and regional regulatory bodies in order to apply the safeguards. The agreements signed by the agency are of three types. They are comprehensive safeguard agreements, item-specific safeguard agreements and voluntary offer agreements.[231] The states signing these agreements can also sign a protocol agreement which increases it obligations.

Most states sign comprehensive safeguard agreements and these cover all the nuclear activities carried out by the state. Under this sort of agreement the state 'undertakes to accept Agency safeguards on all source or special fissionable material in all peaceful nuclear activities within the territory of the state, under its jurisdiction, or carried out under its control anywhere'.[232] The agency, however,

---

228. See the IAEA website at <www.iaea.org>.
229. See IAEA website, *Promoting Nuclear Security: What the IAEA is doing*, in the IAEA information Series 1/03/E, 2006, available at <www.iaea.org>.
230. See *ibid.*
231. See *ibid.*
232. See *ibid.*

has the responsibility to ensure that the state is carrying out its obligations. The comprehensive safeguard agreements are signed by almost all the non-nuclear weapons states as part of their obligation under the NPT treaty. Moreover, they also have to sign this with regard to any other bilateral and multilateral agreements involving nuclear materials and products. Since 1992, the agreement not only requires states to declare all of their nuclear products and materials but also obliges the agency to ensure that those declarations are correct and accounted for.

The item-specific agreements between the agency and the state involve agreements with regard to certain specific materials. These agreements are in fact the 'result of conditions agreed upon with a State supplying the items in question to another state and includes nuclear material, non-nuclear material like heavy water, zirconium tubes and so on'.[233] The agency has to ensure that these items are not used for the making of nuclear weapons or other weapons of mass destruction.[234]

The voluntary offer agreements are normally signed by nuclear armed states although according to the NPT signed by these states it does not require them to do so. However, all five nuclear armed states – the US, China, France, the UK and Russia have signed the safeguard agreement and voluntarily allowed the agency to apply its safeguards.[235] The agency uses this agreement in these states to 'test innovative safeguard methods or to give the agency experience that it might not otherwise gain in safeguarding advanced nuclear fuel cycle facilities and to fulfill expectations of non-nuclear states that some facilities in nuclear-weapon states are subject to safeguard'.[236]

7.5.6.     THE STRENGTHS OF THE IAEA

The IAEA has been able to make very important progress in the field of nuclear materials and technology. The agency has been able to increase its membership to 146 countries and most of these countries have signed the NPT treaty, which demonstrates its success as an agency. The agency has also been able to put in place reliable and effective safeguard mechanisms which ensure that nuclear and other radioactive materials are not used for military purposes but for peaceful means. The IAEA has also helped countries formulate their own nuclear regulatory framework and helped them with various technologies and the expertise needed to ensure the safety of nuclear materials.

The IAEA has improved global nuclear security through its strong verification and compliance regime. The inspectors of the agency are highly trained and are able to detect beforehand any country that might be using nuclear materials for military purposes. The success of discovering that North Korea was developing

---

233.  See *ibid.*
234.  See *ibid.*
235.  See Semmel, *supra* n. 209.
236.  See IAEA website, Nuclear security, 2006, available at <www-ns.iaea.org/security/>.

nuclear weapons lies solely with the IAEA inspectors when other intelligence agencies failed to spot the real intention of the North Koreans.[237] The agency also ensures that the countries signing up to its various agreements comply with their obligations and implement them. The IAEA also provides international service missions, training, expert advice and supplies countries with equipment whether requested by a Member or a non-Member State.[238] The IAEA also has the following strengths:

   (i) Supports and supervises the Code of Conduct.[239]
  (ii) Established a comprehensive set of nuclear security guidelines and recommendations.[240]
 (iii) Helps states improve their regulatory and technical nuclear security systems.[241]
  (iv) Coordinates their activities and efforts with other bilateral and multilateral assistance programmes.[242]
   (v) Advises Member States on the importance of being a party to international instruments relevant to combating nuclear terrorism and helps states in that regard.[243]
  (vi) Promotes the enhanced exchange of nuclear security relevant information.[244]
 (vii) Takes an active role to facilitate effective cooperation and coordination at international or regional levels.[245]
(viii) Established a road map to identify and prioritize their future activities.[246]
  (ix) Enhanced level of cooperation with states that might have nuclear terrorism threats.[247]
   (x) There is a greater cohesion and understanding among all the branches of the agency.[248]
  (xi) There is understanding and partnership with all the members and donors in order to have effective monitoring of the Nuclear Security Programme.[249]

---

237.  See the IAEA's Director General, *supra* n. 214.
238.  See Semmel, *supra* n. 209.
239.  See E. Maman, *Nuclear security and the IAEA*, The International University Vienna, 13th (February 2006): 1–26.
240.  See *ibid.*
241.  See *ibid.*
242.  See *ibid.*
243.  See *ibid.*
244.  See *ibid.*
245.  See *ibid.*
246.  See the IAEA's Director General, *supra* n. 214.
247.  See Semmel, *supra* n. 209.
248.  See *ibid.*
249.  See *ibid.*

7.5.7.       THE WEAKNESSES OF THE IAEA

There are some weaknesses in the agency. The discovery of weapons of mass destruction in Iraq in 1991 and the detection of illegal uranium for the making of nuclear weapons has shown the weaknesses of the agency. In this respect, the agency's safeguard mechanism was not as robust and thorough as it was supposed to be. The agency can only send inspectors once it suspects something or if there is some form of agreement between the agency and the respective countries. Because of this legal constraint the agency sometimes cannot carry out its intended inspections and detections. There are also a number of deficiencies in the administrative and technical arrangements of the agency.[250]

The problem with the IAEA has been the lack of enforcement of the various provisions of the NPT. Once the IAEA refers the country to the Security Council, the IAEA does not have any control over the enforcement process.[251] Moreover the Security Council can take any decision it likes without consulting the IAEA.[252] It is also difficult to define compliance under Article IV of the NPT, which advocates the use of nuclear technology for peaceful purposes.[253] The reason it is difficult to define the compliance issue is because it has been defined inconsistently in the treaty and is considered as a 'grey area'.[254] For example, Iran's action over the years has highlighted this fact. Despite clear violations of the NPT, the IAEA has simply asked Iran to suspend uranium enrichment and allow stricter inspections.[255] Since then Iran has still not allowed inspectors to inspect their nuclear facilities, neither have they complied with IAEA regulations.[256] In 2004, the IAEA condemned Iran's lack of cooperation after the country admitted to understating the amount of plutonium it had enriched.[257]

Another weakness of the NPT is Article X, which allows withdrawal from the treaty if there are extraordinary events that could harm a country's national security.[258] North Korea used this clause to get out of the treaty as it failed to cooperate with the IAEA regarding inspections at their nuclear facility.[259] This resulted in direct negotiations between North Korea and the US, which resulted in North Korea halting the production of nuclear grade materials.[260] The IAEA again failed to declare North Korea non-compliant with the treaty and did not even refer

---

250.   See Maman, *supra* n. 239.
251.   See Semmel, *supra* n. 209.
252.   See *ibid.*
253.   See The Treaty on Non-Proliferation of Nuclear Weapons, 1968.
254.   See J. Choe, 'Problems of enforcement: Iran, North Korea, and the N.P.T.', *Harvard International Review* (2006).
255.   See *ibid.*
256.   See *ibid.*
257.   See *ibid.*
258.   See The Treaty on Non-Proliferation of Nuclear Weapons, 1968.
259.   See R. Butler, 'Improving Non-Proliferation Enforcement', *The Washington Quarterly* (2003): 133–145, 2003.
260.   See *ibid.*

the case to the Security Council.[261] The IAEA could have immediately referred North Korea to the Security Council and prevented the country from leaving the treaty. However, this was not done by them.

The IAEA also has internal problems which stops it from stamping its authority. The Board of Governors within the IAEA often fail to reach consensus resulting in a divided board which stops the agency from acting firmly.[262] There is a clash of interest between China, Russia and the US resulting in the agency sending mixed signals to the violating states.[263] An example of this is North Korea and Iran where China wanted to negotiate with the individual country whereas the US wanted tougher sanctions.[264] Moreover, due to the agency's weak verification system, violating states are able to prevent IAEA inspectors from visiting the country.[265] These states are also able to exploit the agency's weakness of being unable to stop the supply of sensitive nuclear technologies and know-how to other states and actors.[266]

Another argument presented by states wishing to establish themselves as nuclear weapons powers is the issue about granting nuclear privileges to any country being inadmissible, either all the countries are entitled to it or none.[267] As a result, it becomes difficult for the IAEA to implement its rules and regulations and go ahead with stricter compliance because of its board favouring certain countries while being strict with the others.[268] A good example of this is Israel, as the country denies having any nuclear arsenal although the US helped them acquire it without the IAEA's mandate.[269] The recent US–India civil-nuclear deal has also come under criticism as it does not help stop the proliferation of nuclear weapons and makes the IAEA look weak.[270]

The failure of the IAEA to punish those who are involved in supplying sensitive nuclear equipment and materials, together with not being able to enforce its regulations on violating states, has weakened the agency.[271] The failure of the IAEA to stop India, Pakistan and even Israel acquiring nuclear weapons and

---

261. See *ibid.*
262. The IAEA board normally takes decision through consensus as they prefer all the board members to agree with the decisions or else it sends a mixed signal to the violating countries. See Choe, *supra* n. 254.
263. See Butler, *supra* n. 259.
264. See Choe, *supra* n. 254.
265. See *ibid.*
266. See *ibid.*
267. In fact, it is also argued that 'the legitimacy of IAEA measures would be enhanced by the commitment of the nuclear-weapon powers to continue to dismantle their own nuclear arsenals and to conclude a comprehensive nuclear test ban treaty' (R. Vayrynen, 'Economic Sanctions and the Enforcement of Nuclear Non-Proliferation', *African Defence Review* 19 (1994)). Also See M. Seener, 'Can the IAEA be Saved?', *Focus Quarterly* (2009).
268. See M. Seener, 'Can the IAEA be Saved?', *Focus Quarterly* (2009).
269. See *ibid.*
270. See J. Pilat et al., *The Future of the Nuclear Non-proliferation Treaty Regime*, Los Almos National Laboratory, 2009, available at <www.lanl.gov/orgs/nso/docs/fy07/LA-UR-07-1574_The_Future_of_the_NPT_Regime.pdf>.
271. See *ibid.*

also not being able to rein in North Korea, Iran and Syria are some of the failures on the agency's part.[272] Other concerns about the work of the IAEA includes growing non-compliance and limited consensus about the ways of enforcement, the issue of the NPT's relevance to activities by non-state actors and the tension between commercial interests in the civil-nuclear fuel cycle and the aims of non-proliferation.[273]

Funding is another problem for the agency as there is no steady flow of funding from its members. There is no obligation for member countries to fund the work of the agency and the states with more at stake tend to provide more funds. It becomes difficult for the agency to have any long-term targets, which can be detrimental to the long-term detection of nuclear weapons or any other nuclear materials being used for military purposes.[274] The agency has been stretched to its limit due to the renewed interest in nuclear power by many countries because of its environmental safety record. The agency has to provide an advisory service and opinion together with inspections of all these facilities, which greatly increases its workload.

The work of the nuclear security programme is not coordinated with other important nuclear donor states like the US and Russia, with the outcome being that these countries work bilaterally with other countries rather than through the agency.[275] This sometimes undermines the role of the agency. Another important weakness of the agency is the highly political nature of its work. Some Western countries are alleged to have put extra pressure on the agency to come out with reports against certain countries they are having problems with.[276] There is also a north–south divide within the agency which makes matters complicated because this has the potential to ruin the independent status of the agency which in turn might lower its credibility in the international community.[277]

7.5.8.    THE IAEA MODEL AS A FRAMEWORK FOR
          CROSS-BORDER PIPELINES

The IAEA model framework has been able to lower the number of countries wishing to use nuclear materials for making weapons. The strong verification and compliance regime makes the agency credible in the eyes of the international community. The verification and compliance regime is an important part of the agency and ensures that the states that have signed up to the agreement carry out their obligations. This model could be suited to a cross-border pipeline model

---

272. See *ibid.*
273. See Seener, *supra* n. 268.
274. See Maman, *supra* n. 239.
275. See *ibid.*
276. See Pilat, *supra* n. 270.
277. See *ibid.*

where there is a need for a similar regime to look after the activities of the various actors.

The IAEA has also been able to garner the necessary political support for it to carry out its many different activities. Without the political support of its members the agency might not have been able to work as effectively as it currently can. However, the agency has been able to maintain a fine balance between working independently and gaining political support which makes it more credible in the eyes of the international community.

The agency has also provided member and non-Member States with expert advice, technological expertise and help in the formulation of their own regulatory framework which further enhances its position among states in the nuclear community.[278] They have a strong regime chain as all the different parts of the agency coordinate with each other and there is cooperation among all the different organs which makes it more robust. This kind of framework could also be helpful in the case of cross-border pipeline regimes as there are different actors with different problems and a pipeline agency with multiple dimensions would be able to deal with cross-border pipeline problems early to minimize any disruption that might take place because of conflicts between the different actors involved.

The early detection and prevention of a problem by the agency is also another interesting concept as it uses its inspectors to verify the declarations made by the states regarding their nuclear materials and if the inspectors find any discrepancy they can then report that state to the agency. The enforcement of the agency's rules and regulations are also quite stringent which gives the agency power to ensure that the states are abiding by their obligations. The agency can report any violating state to the United Nations Security Council who can then take appropriate measures. This aspect of the IAEA increases its regime credentials as members of the regime would have an incentive not to break the regime rules and regulations. All these features make the IAEA framework more workable than the others for cross-border pipelines.

Despite all its weaknesses, the IAEA still has a strong verification and compliance mechanism which helps to deter countries from trying to acquire nuclear weapons and to abide by the NPT. Over the years the agency has been able to deter countries like Argentina, Brazil, South Africa and Libya from trying to acquire nuclear weapons.[279] This was done through early detection and the threat of economic sanctions.[280]

Although the IAEA inspections are subject to the approval of states, the fact that the agency is in search of illegal nuclear materials acts as the deterrent and

---

278. See D. Fischer, at <www-pub.iaewa.org/MTCD/publications/PDF/Pub1032_web.pdf>.
279. See Seener, *supra* n. 268.
280. In fact, the threat of economic sanctions and early detection isolated both Argentina and South Africa. Further 'diplomatically they became pariah states and the sources of foreign capital largely dried up and this persuaded the political elite of these countries to understand that internal democratic reforms and the change of tack in economic policy were needed' (R. Vayrynen, 'Economic Sanctions and the Enforcement of Nuclear Non-Proliferation', *African Defence Review* 19 (1994)).

keeps the states that would like to use nuclear materials for non-peaceful matters under check.[281] Even if a state declines to let the agency inspect their nuclear programme, it sends a clear message and indication to the world community about the states attempt to hide their illegal activities.[282] As a result, this allows the Security Council to take further action if needed.

The IAEA model, of the three mechanisms discussed previously, holds ground and is able to address the economic, geo-political and legal issues which are the main problems responsible for causing disputes in cross-border pipeline regimes. The proactive nature of the IAEA, together with its strong regulatory credentials ensuring that all signatories abide by their various obligations, is the mechanism needed in cross-border pipeline regimes. The case studies in the previous chapters have shown the requirement for a mechanism which cannot only handle a dispute once it arises but also for an agency or mechanism which can provide an impartial assessment of each pipeline regime and whether its actors are aware of their obligations.

The case studies in the previous chapters also highlighted that any dispute which arises in a pipeline regime requires experts in that field who can help the disputing parties mitigate their differences and avert any disruption to the pipeline. Economic, legal and geo-political issues require a mechanism which can identify the main points of contention between the parties in a regime and hold them accountable to their obligations so that they stand by their original position. The IAEA model provides similar services with regard to nuclear issues which help its members with any technical and legal assistance required. A similar sort of mechanism which can oversee disputes between parties and can identify problems before they result in a full blown dispute, which then results in government intervention causing problems to the other regime members, is what is required and the IAEA model leans towards that kind of mechanism.

### 7.5.9.     THE IAEA AS A REGIME

The IAEA has regime rules and principles which allow it to ensure that all its members abide by its rules and regulations. The main principle of the regime is to ensure the peaceful use of atomic energy in accordance with the Nuclear NPT.[283] There are also specific rules like Article X which allow a signatory to leave the treaty if it affects the country's national security.[284] The role of the agency is a mixture of both neo-liberal and neo-realist tendencies. It requires the cooperation of the countries and their permission to send the inspectors to check their nuclear installations, if the agency suspects them of carrying out actions contrary to their treaty obligations. The agency also depends upon the cooperation of the board of

---

281.   See Seener, *supra* n. 268.
282.   See *ibid.*
283.   See The Treaty on Non-Proliferation of Nuclear Weapons, 1968.
284.   See *ibid.*

governors of the agency in order to implement its various enforcement mechanisms and as a result requires the consensus of the board. All these aspects show its neo-liberal side.[285]

The neo-realist side of the agency stems from its verification and compliance mechanisms as this acts as an enforcer in ensuring that the signatories and non-signatories are not carrying out actions which are contrary to the NPT. The IAEA inspectors have substantial powers and any non-cooperation can lead them to report back to the agency that can then refer the country to the Security Council. As a result, the agency can act like a neo-realist if it does not get its way in terms of checks and inspection. The agency could also ask for an inspection any time it pleases especially if it suspects countries of carrying out actions which are contrary to its obligations under the treaty.

The enforcement aspect of the agency is extremely crucial and is akin to a neo-liberal ethos. In fact, 'the success of the enforcement approach would require firm commitment and coalition building by the members of the security council to use the available means of enforcement, further any economic sanctions given to states depends upon cooperation of leading states'.[286] This clearly shows the neo-liberal attitude, which advocates greater collaboration and cooperation between actors. Further, although the IAEA is not always successful in stopping states from acquiring nuclear weapons, its enforcement capabilities act as a deterrent against recalcitrant states and is an important part of a regime.[287] The threat of enforcement can deter weak proliferators from acquiring a nuclear bomb.[288]

7.6.        CONCLUSION

This chapter began with a description and analysis of the ECT, the WTO DSM and the BITs and their role in handling disputes within the energy trade. The reason for choosing the ECT, the WTO DSM and BITs was because of their previous roles in dealing with energy disputes.[289] The ECT is the only treaty of its kind to deal with the energy trade while the WTO DSM also has certain rules and regulations which deal with energy. The BIT allows private companies to bring claims against the government although its function is minimal in respect of energy and transit

---

285.  See Choe, *supra* n. 254.
286.  See R. Vayrynen, 'Economic Sanctions and the Enforcement of Nuclear Non-Proliferation', *African Defence Review* 19 (1994).
287.  See *ibid.*
288.  See *ibid.*
289.  However, it should be mentioned that, among the three, BITs have still not been used when dealing with energy disputes. It is more adept with investments in other sectors of an economy. The purpose of mentioning BITs was to highlight one of the options available to private companies if there is any breach on the part of the government. The BIT section of this chapter has clearly identified the reasons why BITs might not be applicable in any form of energy dispute especially those related to transit.

disputes. The latter is more relevant, however, to trade in general and is not energy specific.

An attempt was made to highlight their roles in cross-border pipeline issues and how they could help to deal with the various disputes taking place in this area. However, it was concluded that both of these organizations together with BITs are not suitable for dealing with cross-border pipelines issues because of their lack of enforcement capabilities, lack of expertise in the area and also because of their standing among other countries. The ECT is more of a regional treaty and does not have the global dimension required, while the WTO DSM and BITs are not geared to dealing with cross-border pipeline issues. For example, the dispute between Russia and Ukraine could have also been raised in front of an arbitration panel. It could have been done under the PCA agreements signed by both countries.[290] The dispute could also have been settled by Ukraine under the WTO dispute settlement rules.[291] Finally, the procedures available under the ECT could also have been used by Russia and Ukraine. However, none of these were used. In fact, both countries preferred to settle their differences politically, diplomatically and through negotiations than in front of arbitrators.[292] The ECT secretariat even offered to mediate between the two parties under Article 7(7) but both parties rejected the offer.[293] All these factors show the complexities that the current mechanism cannot deal with.

The role of the IAEA was then investigated to see whether its regulatory feature could be applicable to the framing of a new cross-border pipeline agency. The proactive nature of the work done by the IAEA and their stringent enforcement and compliance regime was ideal for the formation of an IPA which could play a similar role in the field of cross-border pipelines to ensure that the actors involved in the cross-border pipeline projects abide by their various obligations and are able to provide uninterrupted supply of hydro-carbon resources.

---

290. See the PCAs signed between Russia and Ukraine with the EC.
291. See Hober, *supra* n. 55.
292. See Westerhof, *supra* n. 66.
293. See *ibid.*

Chapter 8

# Towards a New Framework for Cross-Border Pipelines: The International Pipeline Agency (IPA)

8.1.    INTRODUCTION

This chapter draws from the deficiencies of the existing regulatory and enforcement mechanisms discussed in the previous chapter and also shown in the case studies, in order to set up an agency or a unifying mechanism which could deal with the various cross-border pipeline problems. The chapter starts with an analysis of the reasons why countries should join the agency and the position of the countries that opt not to join. It then goes on to highlight the various ways in which the agency or the unifying mechanism would function and this would include both its functioning process and its enforcement capabilities.

There is also a discussion about the legal basis of setting up the agency together with an in-depth discussion with regard to how this regime would look from a regime theory perspective. In conclusion, this chapter discusses the role this agency would play towards achieving its goals and how it would be different from the current regulatory and enforcement mechanisms available to deal with cross-border pipeline problems.

8.2.    THE PURPOSE OF STATES JOINING AN AUTONOMOUS
         BODY (INTERNATIONAL PIPELINE AGENCY)
         OR UNIFYING MECHANISM

It is normal for states to join organizations or international bodies to serve their own interest. Some states join for economic benefits while others join for political alliances or for geo-political and security reasons. As a result, self-interest plays a big role in any decision to join a particular organization. The states joining this proposed autonomous body would benefit because it would allow them to fulfil their economic potential and, by cooperating with other states, would allow them to strengthen their position internationally and strategically. Energy exporting, importing and transit countries through which a pipeline passes would be able to share and exchange information between themselves and would be able to use that information to make the pipeline run without any disruption, thereby increasing the security of supply for both the exporters and importers.

By joining a regime, a state would also benefit from the cooperation of other states. According to neo-liberals, cooperation among states in a regime would allow them to reap benefits and although they might not be able to achieve absolute gains, the actors would be content with relative gains.[1] The neo-realists, however, believe in absolute gains and for them joining a regime is only beneficial if their own interest is served rather than others. For a regime like this, it is normal for states to win on certain aspects and lose on others. As long as members were willing to cooperate and abide by its various obligations, an autonomous body would be able to work for the benefit of all its members and be relevant to their needs. This is closest to neo-liberal ideals.

Although there are many countries in a pipeline chain that are stronger than others there can be an argument that the stronger countries that use the pipelines or act as a transit country might not choose to join an autonomous body because they are able to fulfil their interests irrespective of whether they are part of any body or mechanism. However, this autonomous body is beneficial for all parties willing to be a part of it because it allows them to cooperate in the area of cross-border pipelines which is quite unique. It takes substantial investment, legal agreements, common interests, geo-political will, years of planning and implementation for such a project as well as the cooperation of all the actors involved to make a pipeline operational.[2] As a result, any disruption in the pipeline could hurt every party no matter how strong and influential they are.

Even if one of the parties is strong they might still like the cooperation and support of the others to make their claims credible, as no matter how big and strong a country is, it always wants some sort of cooperation and support from others. This fact makes the joining of all the parties, irrespective of their size, strength and influence, beneficial so that they can take the advantage of being a member. Such a body could work with a consensus and ensure that all members benefit from joining and this autonomous body would promote common interests at the expense of self-interest. The reputation of states that are part of a unifying mechanism or agency would also be enhanced as investors would feel more comfortable investing their

---

1. See Ch. 2 for an in-depth discussion in this area. The position of neo-realists and neo-liberals is discussed in detail.
2. See Ch. 3 to read in detail about the nature of cross-border pipelines and what is required to have one built.

money in pipelines in those countries. In times of dispute, the country could also use the regime as a platform to support their position.[3]

There is always the uncertainty of whether a state would attain its own expectations by joining an autonomous body or mechanism. The fact remains that no one can predict the level of benefits before joining an autonomous body. Once a state becomes a member, it would gain on certain aspects and might lose out on others. The fact that it is satisfied with the credibility and impartiality of the autonomous body and its various actions would keep it interested in being a part of the regime because there is always something a state can gain from being a part of such an organization.

Another advantage for states joining a new autonomous body would be the greater transparency between all the pipeline countries. This could lower the level of disputes between the various actors involved in the pipeline regime and enhance greater cooperation. States would also have to give greater accountability for the actions they take with regard to the pipeline regimes they are part of. This in turn would also address some of the problems that may arise between shareholders in the pipeline regime and would enable the autonomous body to intervene where needed.

This unifying mechanism or autonomous body would do three things which could increase a state's interest in joining such an agency: it would increase the level of compatibility of interest in the issues area of cross-border pipelines, which would help members to protect their various interests and could act as a stepping stone for constraining government intervention; it would enhance a state's willingness to compromise as it encourages countries to give into certain matters while reaping the benefits in other issue areas; and finally, it would help with the sharing of information which could help countries protect their interest and also collectively improve the benefits of all the members who are part of the pipeline agency.

It is also important to remember that even if a state does not wish to join a new pipeline agency, there is still the possibility for it to use the unifying mechanism to solve a particular dispute. For the purpose of this book, even if states do not join a new pipeline agency or the body, it does not affect the overall function of the pipeline agency as it is a unifying mechanism which could be used by a country in need of protecting its interest in a pipeline regime, or it could also be implanted in a pipeline regime where the members are not part of the pipeline agency.

8.3.     THE CONSEQUENCES OF STATES NOT
         JOINING THE AGENCY

There is a possibility of some states or members involved in a pipeline regime not wanting to join the proposed pipeline agency or the unifying mechanism as it might

---

3.   By joining an agency or mechanism, some governments that have a track record for intervention in pipelines for geo-political, legal and economic reasons could improve their image and standing among those investors and other countries who might be sceptical of their credibility and past record of intervention.

not serve their interest. This will result in some states being members of the agency and others not, resulting in credibility problems for those states wishing to be outside the agency. From the state perspective the latter will find it harder to arrange the huge investment required for a pipeline project. The governments of these states would find it difficult to attract the level of investment needed to implement the project, as most investors and states would be of the opinion that the states outside the agency network think of their own self-interest than the collective interest of all the partners of an individual pipeline regime. The states who are members of the agency would also be reluctant to collaborate with a state outside the agency as the other members of the agency might not look on it favourably.

The perspectives of investors will also be important in this regard as they would be hesitant to invest their money in pipeline projects which includes states that are not part of the agency. The investors might feel less protected as they will feel that during a time of dispute in a pipeline project their investment might get locked resulting in them suffering losses. In those kinds of scenarios, the agency could come to their aid in ensuring that all parties abide by their obligations.

The non-participating states would also find it geopolitically challenging to be a part of a pipeline regime as the states within the agency might be wary of the pipeline passing through that state as their interests would be different. This might be a particular challenge for states that are landlocked. In a scenario when a state outside the agency is an essential partner required for the pipeline to be implemented, there is then a chance that states that are members of the agency would want to include that particular non-member for their benefit. However, even in that scenario, once the non-Member State joins the pipeline regime together with the other agency members, it would still be bound by the various rules and regulations of the pipeline regime and if the pipeline regime incorporates the unifying mechanism the agency could still be involved to provide assistance during any dispute.

The states wishing to be outside the agency network would need to be in a strong bargaining position in order to get involved in any pipeline regime. Even if they are geopolitically strong they might not have sufficient finances to build the pipeline. Being a part of the agency would increase the credibility of the state and allow it to get the help and cooperation required for the successful implementation and running of the pipeline regime.

## 8.4. THE STRUCTURE OF THE AUTONOMOUS BODY OR THE IPA

### 8.4.1. MEMBERSHIP

The initial members of this autonomous body could be all the countries through which the pipeline passes and this includes the exporting, importing and transit countries. All states that are members of the United Nations can become members of this body. The body is based on the principle of 'the sovereign equality of all its members, and all members, in order to ensure to all of them the rights and benefits resulting from membership and also fulfill in good faith the obligation assumed by them in accordance with the objective of the autonomous body'.[4]

For example, Russia, Kazakhstan and Oman, which are all part of the CPC pipeline regime, could be members of this body.[5] This is because the pipeline passes through these countries and also because they are the major actors in the pipeline regime. Oman can be a member although the pipeline does not pass through the country because they are one of the stakeholders in the pipeline regime. The other private companies who are also involved in the regime[6] become indirectly part of the regime because the countries they represent can also become members of this regime and, once they are members, they have to abide by similar obligations. Any country, including the exporting, importing and transit country, can be a member of this regime.

### 8.4.2.    GENERAL CONFERENCE

A general conference consisting of all the members could meet for regular annual sessions and in such special sessions as convened by the Director General at the request of the Board of Governors or of a majority of members.[7] The general conference shall deal with things like the election of the Board of Governors, approve states for memberships, analyse the report of the board, approve the budget, approve the various rules and regulations of the body, approve any agreements between the body and the United Nations and other states or cross-border pipeline companies and approve the appointment of a Director General.[8]

### 8.4.3.    BOARD OF GOVERNORS

The Board of Governors could include members of the ten most important[9] cross-border pipeline countries and they would represent countries from all regions of the

---

4.  See IAEA Statute at <www.iaea.org>.
5.  See Chs 4, 5 and 6 of the book. The case studies show that there are different countries and stakeholders involved in a pipeline project. All these stakeholders can become members of this autonomous body. In the case of the BTC pipeline, Azerbaijan, Turkey and Georgia can become members together with the private companies involved because the private companies can be represented through their respective country of origin. The same is applicable to the other pipeline projects discussed in Chs 4, 5 and 6.
6.  See the regime definition in Ch. 2, as it also involves a private company. According to the definition all the stakeholders of the pipeline project can become members of the regime. The reasons are that most pipelines are joint ventures between governments and private companies and as a result there is a need for cooperation from both sides in order for the successful implementation of the project.
7.  See IAEA Statute at <www.iaea.org>.
8.  See *ibid.*
9.  Important countries in this sense means those countries through which a lot of pipelines travel or those countries that are major oil and gas exporters and importers and have advanced knowledge of pipeline technology together with substantial hydro-carbon resources.

world including: North America, Latin America, Western Europe, Eastern Europe, South Asia, the Caspian region, Central Asia, the Middle East, South East Asia, West Africa and North Africa. The General Conference shall elect members of the Board of Governors. Members of the Board of Governors would be in office for a period of three years.

### 8.4.4.    STAFF

The staff of the autonomous body would be led by the Director General. The Director General would be appointed by the Board of Governors with the approval of the General Conference.[10] The Director General would be responsible for the appointment, organization and functioning of the staff and be under the authority of and subject to the control of the Board of Governors.[11] The staff members of the body would include qualified technical and other personnel as may be required to fulfil the objectives and functions of the body.

### 8.4.5.    DISPUTES WITHIN THE BODY'S JURISDICTION

The autonomous body would deal with any disputes in cross-border pipelines which might be economic, legal or geo-political in nature. The members could ask for the intervention of the autonomous body if they feel that any of the parties within the pipeline chain were not abiding by their various obligations which might result in loss for that member. Some of the problems that the body could look into include any economic discrimination including the arbitrary increase of tariff without consultation,[12] hindrances within the pipeline chain which could disrupt the flow of hydro-carbon resources[13] or government decisions which could disadvantage the parties involved in the pipeline chain.[14]

The legal problems include the lack of enforcement of the various rules and regulations of the agreements signed between the parties, contradictory laws in member countries causing problems for the actors in the pipeline chain, any sudden change in government policies which could discriminate against the actors

---

10. See IAEA Statute at <www.iaea.org>.
11. See *ibid.*
12. This means that one of the parties in the pipeline regime increasing the tariff without consulting any of the other parties in the pipeline regime or not abiding by the agreements signed by the parties.
13. This involves creating a situation which would cause a disruption like sudden closure of gas or switching off gas supplies due to a dispute.
14. This means the government not abiding by the agreement signed between them and the pipeline actors, this can involve increasing taxes although this was exempted at the beginning or passing contradictory laws which might disrupt the operation of the pipeline and which was contradictory to the original agreement signed.

involved in the pipeline chain.[15] The geo-political aspects that the body would look after include whether the members involved in the pipeline chain were using politics as a weapon to coerce others partners in the pipeline chain, the use of geo-politics to discriminate against certain member countries or using politics for the gain of certain members within the pipeline chain, which could be detrimental to the other actors involved in the pipeline chain.

The case studies discussed in the previous chapters can be used as examples to show the kind of disputes that could come under this body's jurisdiction. In the CPC pipeline case, the body could look into whether the role of the Russian government in asking for back taxes is valid and whether the country could use its transit status to ask for greater leverage in the pipeline project, thereby stopping the expansion of the pipeline.[16] In the BTC pipeline case, it could look into whether Turkey is abiding by its obligations to pay for the resources it is receiving,[17] and in the WAGP and the Interconnector case, the causes of disruption in the operation of the pipeline.[18] The body could also scrutinize any legal implications affecting the pipeline, like the BTC case where Turkey, in certain instances, failed to pay for the hydro-carbon resources it received.[19] The enforcement and regulatory aspects of all the pipelines discussed in the previous chapter would also come under its jurisdiction to see whether geo-political, legal or economic factors play a part in causing some of the actors to not abide by their obligations.[20]

### 8.4.6.  How Does the Body Get Involved

If any party suffers any form of discrimination or if there is any difference of opinion between the various actors involved in the pipeline chain, then any actor within the pipeline chain could ask the body to interfere and provide an impartial assessment of the situation. This would only be possible if the pipeline agreements signed between the various actors included a clause which would allow the unifying mechanism or the autonomous body to intervene. The autonomous body could get involved in any dispute provided the party calls for its intervention and if there is no requirement for all the actors in the pipeline chain to agree on the autonomous body becoming

---

15. This means any sudden change in government policy which might hold the pipeline actors hostage, like change in tax laws or using tax and legal issues as bait to get leverage from the pipeline actors.
16. See Ch. 6 for more explanation and analysis of the various problems faced by the actors involved in the CPC pipeline.
17. See Ch. 5 to read some of the problems faced by the actors involved in the pipeline project. Some of these problems are geo-political while others are more economic in nature.
18. See Chs 4 and 6 where the cause of disruption in the Interconnector and WAGP pipelines are discussed.
19. See Ch. 5 of the book for some of the legal problems faced by actors in the BTC pipeline.
20. See the case studies in Chs 4, 5 and 6 to see the regulatory and enforcement problems faced by most of the pipelines. Some of the actors do not abide by their various obligations, which not only weakens the regime framework but also causes problems for the actors involved in the pipeline.

involved. However, a request by one of the actors would have to be seconded by another partner or actor in the pipeline regime. The autonomous body could also have certain guidelines which the member countries had to follow and the body would investigate from time to time whether these were being followed.

Once any of the parties in the pipeline regime requests the intervention of the autonomous body, that body would send its inspection staff to investigate and submit a report on the actual situation and circumstances of the problems causing disruption or problems for the partners in the pipeline regime. The inspectors shall have responsibility for examining all operations conducted by the various actors involved in the pipeline and this would cover all relevant aspects of the cross-border pipeline regime including the economic, geo-political and legal aspects. After careful evaluation of the various factors, the inspectors would submit a report to the Board of Governors of the autonomous body via the Director General and the Board would then take into consideration what the non-complying actors in the pipeline regime needed to do so that all the actors in the pipeline regime can benefit from its operation.

The Russia–Ukraine dispute is a good example where such a body could get involved.[21] If any of the parties came to the body with a complaint then the body could send inspectors to see the real cause of the problem and find the truth about the matter. In the CPC pipeline case, where there were disruptions between the various actors involved in the pipeline, the body could also have got involved.[22] Some of the actors could have brought to the agency's attention the problems they were facing and the agency could have sent inspectors and experts to investigate the matter or see whether the parties were abiding by their obligations.

The private parties involved in this case could also bring the conflict to the agency's attention as they are represented through their countries. The pipelines of the FSU also illustrate another case where the agency could investigate whether geo-political factors play a part in the frequent disruption in the pipeline or whether economic factors are responsible for the frequent disruption in the WAGP.[23]

### 8.4.7. SETTLEMENT OF DISPUTES

After the inspectors have submitted their impartial report to the Board of Directors through the Director General, the Board of Governors would make recommendations to all the members in the General Conference and after their approval could set up a dispute settlement panel if the original claimant to the pipeline dispute

---

21. See Ch. 4 for a detailed analysis on the Russia–Ukraine crisis and the cause of it. There are also discussions on the pipelines of the FSU.
22. See Ch. 6 to read more about the CPC pipeline and the problems faced by the various stakeholders involved in the project.
23. See Ch. 6 to read about the WAGP pipeline. There have been frequent disruptions in the pipeline due to lack of gas in the pipeline and also due to certain operational problems. There are also infrastructural problems involved in the pipeline as the two transit countries cannot use the gas given to them as tariff, due to the lack of proper infrastructure. There is also geo-political rivalry between the two important West African countries, Ghana and Nigeria.

wishes to pursue this course.[24] The number of arbitrators in the panel would be 3, with each party nominating one arbitrator and the 2 nominated arbitrators nominating the chairman through consensus. If one of the party declines to go for the settlement of disputes, the other party or parties can still ask the panel for a decision irrespective of the position of the discriminating party.[25] Once the panel has given its findings, depending upon the problems faced by the claimant in the pipeline regime, the decision would be binding on the other parties and the Board of Governors through the autonomous body has to enforce it.

In the case of the CPC pipeline, if the private shareholders wanted to go to the agency without Russia's approval, they could do so and the agency could get involved to verify the allegations of the actors involved in the pipeline.[26] The number of private companies would be enough for the agency to get involved even if Kazakhstan and Oman did not support their decision to go to the agency. However, their case would be stronger if Kazakhstan supported the claim due to their status as a state party.[27] In the case of the BTC pipeline, if Azerbaijan had problems with both Georgia and Turkey, they could ask the agency to settle the disputes and the agency would try to deal with the problem quickly.[28]

The geographical link between the members of the agency and the affected pipe is also important. Members from a particular region would be better equipped to understand the regional problems and if there is a dispute they would be able to help the agency with the enforcement of their obligations or with any other technical and material help.[29] However, there would be no requirement for a member

---

24. Although there could be an argument that the decision on whether to set up a dispute settlement panel can be obstructed by powerful members, the chances of this are slim because the decision depends upon a simple majority of members not by a consensus system as seen in other regimes where powerful regime members try to obstruct the activities of a regime.

25. Although there can be an argument here that if one of the parties does not want to be a party to the arbitration process it should not have to pay any attention to the findings of the panel, there will be a provision (unifying mechanism provision) which would be put in the pipeline agreements which would allow any of the parties to ask the autonomous body to interfere. As a result, after the signing of the agreements and with the provision being there, the position of the party not willing to participate in the process would be against the spirit of the agreement or contract signed and they would be in violation of it.

26. The parties involved in the pipeline could bring to the agency's notice the expansion proposal blocked by one of the stakeholders in the pipeline which is causing a loss for the others, the transit country using its position as a bargaining chip to gain greater access to the consortium, lack of legal commitment from one of the key stakeholders. This is highlighted in detail in Ch. 6.

27. The CPC is made up of three countries and ten private companies and both sides own 50% of the pipeline. The private companies invested money while the states provided infrastructural facilities and the resource.

28. One of the problems Azerbaijan had was Turkey not honouring its contract to buy certain amounts of gas from the country. This did not cause any disruption in the pipeline chain but caused friction between the two which might have caused a disruption. Azerbaijan could have brought this to the notice of the agency and they could have then acted appropriately to see whether all the parties were abiding by their various obligations.

29. The next section, especially point 4 of the enforcement of the decision looks at the way a member from a certain region plays its part to help the agency or ensure the enforcement of the agency's guidelines.

country to have some kind of regional connection or link in order to help the agency.[30]

### 8.4.8.    ENFORCEMENT OF THE DECISION

The enforcement of the decision of the dispute settlement panel could be carried out in one of the following ways:

(1) Depending upon where the dispute takes place the state member from that region on the Board of Directors would be given the responsibility to oversee the implementation of the decision through the Director General of the autonomous body.

(2) Failure to abide by the decision would lead to sanctions being brought on the respective violating member and this could be in the form of economic or diplomatic sanctions. Any economic sanction would have to be in the form of some energy related issue.[31] For example, if the violating member did not abide by the panel's decision that their actions were discriminatory[32] because they charged additional and excessive transit fees or they were holding the pipeline hostage for their own economic or geo-political gains, then the other members who also have some sort of business arrangement with the violating member can cut off their business ties to put pressure on them.[33,34]

---

30. The Board of Governors of the agency is made up of members from countries in all the regions of the world. If a situation does arise that affects a pipeline situated in another region which is not represented in the agency, then the country closest to the region as a member of the agency could help. However, there is no formal requirement for having some kind of geographical link between the Member States and the affected pipe as the interests of all the actors are intertwined.

31. The reason for implying it has to be energy related and nothing else because if it is any sort of economic measure, then the framework would be similar to that of the WTO dispute settlement mechanism where member countries can take any sort of retaliatory measure for their discriminations. As a result to be different from that framework, this is proposed.

32. Discriminatory here means that one of the countries is not abiding by their contractual obligation or what is negotiated between them and increases the tariff unilaterally for their own benefit. Discriminatory here has nothing to do with competition law.

33. Business ties here for the importer means lowering their export from that particular country to hurt it economically or, if the country has any other energy related business in the country, the government can clamp down on those businesses for not abiding by their agency's decision. If the country is an exporter they can lower their export to make the country fulfil its obligations. If it is a private company then the government from where that company originates would be pressured in to forcing it to rein in the company in order to fulfil its obligations. If the country fails to do so then they might have to suffer sanctions from other member countries in projects it is involved in.

34. The reason the other members are also bound to cut off their business relationship is because the other countries are also part of the agency and it is part of their obligation. Although the dispute might not affect them since they are part of a regime, they have a collective responsibility to abide by the rules and regulations of the regime and ensure that the rules are complied with by all the members.

(3) The decision of the dispute panel has to be enforced in the shortest possible time.

(4) The state member of the Board of Governors from the region where the dispute has taken place will be given the task of enforcing the decision and can also ask for the help of other influential Board members to help them to enforce the decision of the panel.

(5) Enforcement can also be done through discouraging and coercing companies and states that provide subsidiary services for the successful operation of the pipeline to stop providing those services due to the discriminatory acts by one of the parties of the pipeline regime towards the others. This act would further put pressure on the discriminating state or party to accept the decision of the dispute panel.

8.5.    THE LEGAL BASIS OF THE INTERNATIONAL PIPELINE AGENCY'S WORK IN CROSS-BORDER PIPELINES

The members of the agency and any country through which the pipeline passes or individual countries from where private companies involved in pipeline projects originate[35] can sign a treaty called 'The Convention of Cross-Border Pipelines'. This treaty would allow the IPA to get involved when one of the parties asks them to do so. The members who have signed the treaty are also obliged to carry out the various rules and regulations of this regime as a whole. The signing of the treaty would allow the agency to enforce the various rules and regulations of the agreement signed by the parties involved in the pipeline project. As a result, all the cross-border pipelines in different parts of the world could come under its jurisdiction if the players ask for its help and guidance.

However, in a situation where one of the countries involved in the project is not a signatory or the country from where the private company originates is not a member of the agency or a signatory to the treaty, then that particular country or company would still have to abide by this obligation of the treaty if there are other actors in the pipeline project who are members and signatories and their obligation would have to be enforced through those members. For example, in the case of the CPC pipeline, if Russia, Oman and Kazakhstan were members of the agency and signatories to the treaty and if one of the countries from where the private oil companies originates is not a member and a signatory then they cannot get away from any liability because of their non-membership. In that circumstance, Russia and Kazakhstan could enforce the obligations or decision of the pipeline agency.[36]

---

35. This means the international oil companies like Shell, Total, Chevron or BP. The companies here mean the shareholders or stakeholders who are involved in the operation and ownership of the pipelines and are major actors in the functioning of the pipeline.

36. See the 'enforcement of decision' part of the International Pipeline Agency regarding what these countries can do to make the non-compliant and non-signatory company or country abide

This treaty would be the basis upon which the sanctions for various disputing parties could be enforced. The agency could also use this to enforce its various rules and regulations as well as through the parties which are its members. This treaty would not affect the right of any member to sign other regional treaties to lessen cross-border pipelines disputes in that particular region but it has to be with conformity with this treaty. The basic objective of this treaty has to be covered by those regional treaties as well. The treaty would also allow the agency to carry out the following because of its regulatory stature:

(i) The IPA would adopt a regulatory management system which is based upon quality management practice and which has to implement its various goals through thorough investigation and surveillance.[37]
(ii) The IPA would engage with the various members and non-members of the agency to demonstrate that they are transparent and approachable in their work and they would also have to build confidence in their regulatory and other decision-making processes.
(iii) The IPA would also establish and maintain cooperation with regional, sub-regional and international partners and other professional bodies, and exchange information and experience.[38]
(iv) The IPA would also work with other enforcement and regulatory agencies in the field of cross-border pipelines and try to ensure some form of consistency.
(v) The IPA would also coordinate its activities with that of the industry in order to get feedback with regard to cross-border pipelines.

## 8.6.    THE OBLIGATIONS OF THE MEMBERS OF THE IPA

The main obligations of the members of the IPA are to abide by the rules and regulations of the contract signed between themselves and the various stakeholders in order to protect their legitimate expectations in the pipeline regime. This involves the IGAs, HGAs and other third party agreements which help in the operation of the pipeline. Any breach of this would result in them being obligated to let the agency inspectors investigate the cause of the disputes in the pipeline and

---

by its obligations. Each cross-border pipeline agreement is unique and different as there is no uniform legal framework for cross-border pipelines but by being a member of this agency and also a signatory to this treaty, the parties who are involved in the cross-border pipeline would automatically have to abide by their treaty obligations.Non-signatory countries or members would also have to abide by it if they are part of the project unless or until these countries specifically mention that they are not obligated by the treaty signed by the other countries that are part of the project.

37. See M. Elbaredi, *Physical Protection of Nuclear materials*, 2006, available at <www.iaea.org/Publications/Documents/Infcircs/1999/infcirc225r4c/rev4_content.html>.
38. See D. Fischer, at <www-pub.iaewa.org/MTCD/publications/PDF/Pub1032_web.pdf>.

report back to the agency that would then form a tribunal which could come to a quick decision to settle the dispute.

The agency members are also obliged to cooperate in the enforcement of the various decisions of the IPA, in that if a state does not abide by the rules under the various pipeline treaties it is part of, then it has to abide by the decision given by the IPA panel and the other members are obliged to cooperate through the enforcement of the IPA rules in this regard.

The members are also obligated to report any dispute arising between the stakeholders that can disrupt the flow of resources through the pipelines. There is a possibility that in a pipeline regime there might be some countries that are members of the agency and others that are not and, in that scenario, the members of the agency are obliged to report any conflict they have to the agency for initial investigation, in order to find out the reasons for the dispute impartially before taking any retaliatory measures which might disrupt the flow of resources through the pipeline.

The members of the agency are also obligated to share any information they have about the pipeline which could be a possible source of conflict between the stakeholders. Governments that are also stakeholders in a pipeline regime cannot interfere in the running of the pipeline to protect their own interest and if they do have to interfere in order to protect their national security, then they are obligated to inform the agency beforehand. They also have to let the agency investigate before taking any unilateral decisions which might disrupt the flow of the pipeline.

All the obligations mentioned above are mandatory and all the signatories to the treaty have to abide by the rules and regulations of the agency. The private companies are also bound by these rules and regulations if their country is a member of the IPA. The IPA acts as a unifying mechanism and any pipeline regime having stakeholders that are not members of the agency would have to abide by its rules and regulations if the pipeline agreement has provisions which allow the IPA to get involved in times of any dispute.


8.7.        SOME IMPORTANT ASPECTS OF THE IPA

One of the arguments that can be put forward against the role of the agency is, if private parties are part of the pipeline project, it is not clear what the agency could do to regulate those companies or enforce the decision of the panel. It would be difficult to force the decision of the panel on a private company which does not have any affiliation with the state. In these circumstances, all the IPA panel decisions could be enforced through the concept of 'direct effect'[39] and this would enable even the private parties to abide by the decision of the panel. The state from

---

39. The concept of direct effect was first established in the case of Van Gend & Loos. The case was about whether Art. 12 of the EC was directly effective or not. The Court was of the opinion that: 'The wording of Article 12 contains a clear and unconditional prohibition which is not a positive but a negative obligation. This obligation, moreover, is not qualified by any reservation on the

where the company originates would be encouraged to take action against the company involved in the pipeline and if the state is a member of the agency then they are obligated to take action even if the country is not directly involved in the pipeline.

There could also be instances when some of the private companies involved in the pipeline project might not be registered in any particular country and may be situated in places outside the jurisdiction of the IPA. In that event, the company's assets in countries where it is involved in the pipeline project could be attached in order to enforce the decision of the IPA. For example, if the company is registered in the Cayman Islands and has business ventures is in Kazakhstan, the US or Russia and its alleged violation took place in Azerbaijan, then either Kazakhstan or the Russian government could be asked to take action against the company in order to force them to accept the decision of the IPA. These countries, if they are part of the agency, would be obliged to carry out the enforcement on behalf of the agency.

Another argument which could be put forward is the capability of the IPA to deal with different regimes with different sets of problems. The agency would be equipped to deal with different regimes because once there is a conflict the agency would nominate inspectors who are expert in their fields and have extensive experience in the area. Any dispute would be investigated by the panel of experts who would give their final verdict regarding the matter, if the state wishes. The purpose of the agency would be multidimensional and flexible just as the problems in cross-border pipelines are and it would also be more proactive in reducing disruption in the supply chain.

The three main goals of the agency would be: (i) the detection of non-compliance with the agreements signed by the parties; (ii) reporting any disruption and conflict in the cross-border pipelines; and (iii) enforcement of the various clauses of the agreement. All these goals would help the agency to constrain government intervention in the event of geo-political, legal or economic issues arising. The verification and compliance regime of the agency would be robust in ensuring that the key stakeholders and members of the agency abide by their obligations. However, non-members would also come under surveillance if they had any pipelines going through their country or they are part of any pipeline projects.

8.8.        THE DIFFERENCE BETWEEN THE IPA AND THE IAEA

Although the IPA would try to adapt the regulatory, verification and enforcement aspects of the IAEA, it goes further than the IAEA and will work in a different manner. The IPA would be enforcing the various rules and regulations of the regime themselves rather than delegating to some other agency or regime. As a

---

part of states which would make its implementation conditional upon a positive legislation measure enacted under national law. The very nature of this prohibition makes it ideally adapted to produce direct effects in the legal relationship between Member States and their subjects'.

result, from this aspect it is different from the IAEA, which has to refer a country to the Security Council once a country is found in breach of its obligations. This aspect of the IPA makes it stronger than the IAEA as it would allow the IPA to ensure that the actors within the regime are abiding by their obligations. Moreover, the IPA is a unifying mechanism and any pipeline regime wishing to use it can use the IPA mechanism and it automatically becomes part of the IPA regulatory structure which is not the case with IAEA.

Another important difference would be the role of the different members of the IPA. In the IAEA structure, there has to be a broad consensus among the board members in order for IAEA to take any action. The IPA would not have a similar system as it would not need to have any consensus for the agency to act. When there is a dispute in the pipeline, the agency can get involved once any of the countries come to it for help and it would send inspectors to verify the claims and find out the cause of the problems. Therefore, even if one of the parties is strong within the agency and is a member they cannot stop the agency from finding out and dealing with the problem being suffered by one of the members of the pipeline regime. In this aspect, the IPA regime would go further than the IAEA and take a different approach.

The IPA would have a quick dispute resolution mechanism and this would start when the inspectors report back to the agency. A panel would be set up to settle the matter in the quickest possible time so that pipeline disruption does not damage the interests of the stakeholders. In this respect, the IPA is also different from the IAEA, as the nuclear watchdog does not have any immediate mechanism by which to stop the members who are violating their NPT obligations.[40] This makes the IPA regime more robust in terms of dealing with the dispute quickly and immediately, which is not the case with the IAEA, as the latter uses a long process to identify and then deal with members who violate their obligations.[41]

8.9.    REGIME AND THE NEW INTERNATIONAL
        PIPELINE AGENCY

The new agency set up to deal with cross-border pipeline issues could also be called a regime because it fulfils all regime qualities and criteria. The agency would have rules and principles which would enable it to be referred to as a regime.[42] The membership criteria for this regime have been discussed above, as all the countries that have pipelines going through their countries, meaning the exporting, importing and transit country together with the other private parties

---

40. In this sense, the IPA is also different from the ECT, as the treaty currently does not have any immediate mechanism to deal with disputes arising out of cross-border pipelines. However, there is now discussion about having emergency arbitration provisions within the ECT.
41. See J. Choe, 'Problems of enforcement: Iran, North Korea, and the N.P.T.', *Harvard International Review* (2006).
42. There is a detailed discussion regarding regime theory in Ch. 2 of this book. The definitions of rules and principles are also provided in Ch. 2. For the pipeline agency, the rules are described in s. 8.4 (8.4–8.4.8) of this chapter while the main principle of the agency would be to enforce the

involved in the cross-border pipeline project, could be members through their respective countries.

The previous chapters discussed the various aspects of a regime and also the different pipeline regimes that have been classified under a strong, moderately strong or a weak regime. This pipeline regime would be given strong enforcement powers together with various other regulatory features in order to ensure that the actors involved in the pipelines comply with the rules and regulations of the agency together with their own commitments in the pipeline chain. The pipeline agency would have all the capabilities to be termed as a strong regime but precedence would have to be set by it in order to be termed as a strong regime.[43] The main aim of this regime would be to enforce and ensure compliance of the rules and regulations of the regime and also the individual obligations entered into by members.

Membership of this regime would be quite diverse as all the states together with other entities in a cross-border pipeline chain could be its member, as the regime is open to all the pipeline countries together with the service providers. Because of its open status there could be both strong and weak members within the regime but all will have equal access to the benefits of joining the regime. The purpose for this is to ensure that the regime has an equal standing among all the members but, in order to be a strong regime, there also is a need for all parties to have access to the regime so that they can take advantage of all its facilities.[44] Krasner pointed out that the strength of the regime not only depends upon the parties joining it but also on the perception of the actors joining that there is equality among all its members.[45]

An example of the role of the new pipeline regime could be given from the case studies in the previous chapter. In the CPC pipeline, the dispute regarding the extension of the pipeline between the different actors could be dealt with by this new pipeline regime. The members of the pipeline, including Russia, Kazakhstan and Oman together with other private companies through their governments, would be the members of the new pipeline regime and the regime would first try to find out the real cause of the problem once it had been reported by one of the parties. The regime would quickly send its inspectors to investigate and prepare a report and based on that report would start the dispute settlement mechanism available within the regime if the parties agreed. They would then quickly pass

---

various obligations of cross-border pipeline stakeholders and to protect their legitimate expectation.

43. This means that if the new regime is to be termed as a strong regime then it has to act in that manner by enforcing the various rules and regulations of the regime on its members. The new regime has not done this yet so precedence means it has to set examples before it can be termed as a regime.

44. This means that the new pipeline regime set up has to ensure that all the members have equal access to it; meaning that all the members can call upon it to act in times of conflict despite the strength of any one member within the regime. This is required in order to be a regime with strong credentials and will ultimately decide the strength of the regime.

45. See S. Krasner, 'Sovereignty, Regimes, and Human Rights', in *Regime Theory and International Relations*, ed. Rittberger, V., et al. (Clarendon: Oxford University Press, 1991).

their opinions or decision through expert arbitrators in this field.[46] The regime would then also enforce its decisions through the enforcement mechanisms discussed previously.[47] If the new regime was able to function in this manner it could be termed as a strong regime especially if all the parties in the CPC pipeline were made to abide by its decisions.

This new regime or mechanism in the form of an agency would be able to address the problem of intervention from regime members for geo-political, legal and economic reasons. The case studies have shown that depending upon the strength of the regime, the level of intervention differs. A strong regime would be better equipped than a moderately strong or weak regime to deal with the various interventions by governments or other members in the regime.[48] The new agency would be equipped with all the regulatory features to ensure that all the members abide by their respective obligations so that any form of intervention by the regime members as part of their own geo-political or legal agenda does not affect the functioning and interests of the other members.

The IPA would by multidimensional in the sense that it would not only try to ensure that the pipeline regimes are able to deal with intervention from different members but also ensure that any disagreements or interventions do not result in any form of disruption. The agency could step in to deal with any intervention by a government for geo political, legal or economic reasons by providing their expertise to the conflicting parties or advising and reminding the government of its obligations.[49] It could also act as a safety net for the other vulnerable members of the regime as a place to go to for impartial opinion and settlement of disputes with regard to problems causing disruption and disagreements among the stakeholders involved in the pipeline.

For example, in the WAGP, Ghana could approach the body regarding the country not receiving an uninterrupted supply of gas from Nigeria, as expected under the pipeline agreement signed by the country. Nigeria, being the stronger party in the pipeline regime, has failed to supply the required gas due to a lack of infrastructure and other security problems but they have gotten away with not fulfilling their obligation and also received no penalty for it. As a result, there is a stalemate between the two countries regarding this[50] as both governments have

---

46. See the previous sections of this chapter for an in-depth discussion on this area.
47. See the 'enforcement' section of this chapter for an in-depth discussion on this area.
48. The reason for this is because the case studies have shown that strong regimes have a stronger regulatory mechanism than moderately strong and weak regimes. It shows that the level of intervention differs because the government or any other member would have to follow more steps and regulations to intervene depending upon the regime strength and they cannot just intervene according to their wish.
49. The previous section of this chapter highlighted the various activities of the agency.
50. There could be an argument that Ghana could have held the Nigerian government responsible for not abiding by its contractual obligation and could have taken them to court but that would not solve the situation because a lot of other parties are involved in the pipeline regime and taking this route would not necessarily mean that they would be able to force Nigeria to pay fines because of the geo-political and time factor involved.

intervened to protect their own interest by blaming the other, while the regulatory body within the pipeline regime failed to take any decision to deal with the problem. The pipeline agency in this scenario could independently assess the liabilities accrued by each party, provide an evaluation and settle the dispute between the two parties which could break the stalemate and stop frequent disruption of the pipeline as well as limit the level of government intervention. As it stands, Ghana, by itself, has so far not been able to protect its interest due to the geo-political scenario in that region.[51]

The pipeline regime would be a mechanism which would try to constrain intervention from governments or other actors in a regime and try to protect the interests of all the actors in the pipeline regime. It would also aim to ensure that all the actors in a pipeline regime understand their collective responsibility to ensure that they abide by their obligations in order to make the pipeline operate without any hindrances and that they do not infringe on any sovereignty issue which individual countries enjoy. They exist to provide regulatory oversight, together with the body acting as a safety net, for vulnerable members in a pipeline regime.

Although it is open to argument whether the benefits would be shared equally by all members of the pipeline agency, the fact remains that some of the members might want to achieve relative gains while others absolute gain.[52] The former is advocated by neo-liberals while the latter by neo-realists. Members of this new regime would be both neo-liberals and neo-realists. For example, the stronger countries like the US, Russia and the EU countries can be considered realists as they will try to maximize their benefits using their regional or political dominance, while other countries like Kazakhstan, Azerbaijan or Georgia are neo-liberals and will be willing to get as much benefit as they can by joining the regime. However, despite the different strengths of the parties within their regime, this new pipeline regime will try to ensure a balance of interests between all parties by providing and giving access to all its members in the same manner.

8.10.    THE REGIONAL OR INTERNATIONAL DEBATE WITH
         REGARD TO THE PIPELINE AGENCY OR MECHANISM

It can be argued that since pipelines are situated in many different regions of the world the geo-political, legal and economic problems they face differ in nature. This will make the work of an international agency or a mechanism following the affairs of the pipeline difficult or potentially impossible. There is also a debate about whether an international agency can interfere in regional pipeline matters when it does not have the expertise to do so and whether this would be a part of international law.

---

51. See Ch. 5, under the 'issues affecting the pipelines' under the WAGP case study for a discussion on this area.
52. See Ch. 2 of the book to understand more about the neo-liberal and neo-realist schools of thought in the regime theory.

The mechanism or the agency that this book is proposing is an international regulatory mechanism which can constrain government policy or the policies of other actors in a regime in ensuring that they abide by their current position. It is not intended that a new branch of international law be created nor does it propose that all the actors involved in the pipeline regime become a part of this agency. It is a mechanism which could be implemented by all the pipelines, both regionally and internationally. The pipelines in a particular region could also use this mechanism to ensure that all the actors benefit from joining the pipeline regime and where no one feels vulnerable to government intervention or intervention from other actors due to economic, geo-political or legal considerations.

This international regulatory mechanism could also be implemented internationally in the form of creating an agency where all the pipeline countries could be a member of the agency and, through greater cooperation and understanding, the amount of disputes disrupting pipelines could be reduced. However, if some of the countries in a particular region are averse to being a member of an international agency then they could also implement this regulatory mechanism in their particular region to ensure that the parties abide by their various obligations within the regime.

Regional can also mean international in the sense that when a pipeline passes into another country it has international status. Although it can be in one particular region there is still an international dimension to it. The role of this regulatory mechanism is to benefit all the parties within a pipeline regime and its international or regional dimension does not change its actual goal, which is to reduce pipeline disruption and to provide a safety net for all the members of a pipeline regime in order to protect them from government intervention or from other strong actors within the regime.

## 8.11.    CONCLUSION

This new pipeline agency would try to deal with the various factors affecting cross-border pipelines and would try to resolve any conflicts as quickly as possible.[53] This new regulatory body, through the signing of a treaty called 'the convention of cross-border pipelines', would be able to help disputing parties in cross-border pipeline projects and would also take into account the economic, geo-political and legal dimensions involved while dealing with disputes.

This unique body, tasked with the job of overseeing the activities of the various actors involved in the pipeline project, would also provide its members and non-members with any technical help required and share information with all the actors involved to prevent any disruption in the flow of hydro-carbon resources. This new agency would be an autonomous body and derive its powers from its

---

53. Certain features of this agency like its enforcement capabilities, the role of inspectors and its compliance procedures have been modelled along IAEA lines, discussed in the previous chapter.

members and the treaty signed by them which would enable it to work independently, impartially and transparently. The main goal would be to strengthen its credibility among the member countries and to constrain the level of interference from governments or other members in a pipeline regime in order to protect the interest of all the actors in a pipeline.

The agency or the unifying mechanism would be able to deal with the economic, geo-political and legal problems which cause the government, as a member of the pipeline regime, to intervene. The agency would act independently in a regulatory capacity enhancing the compliance and enforcement features of a pipeline. It would also deal with a pipeline dispute promptly and would be able to provide the expert analysis required to deal with the dispute. The agency, from this aspect, would go further than either the ECT, WTO DSM or IAEA, as it would be more proactive in ensuring that the actors involved in the pipeline regime are abiding by their various obligations.

The ECT provides the guidelines and the legal framework based upon which the investors and the energy exporting and importing countries carry out their energy trade. It also deals with the transit issue which is relevant to cross-border pipelines and has various dispute settlement mechanisms. The WTO DSM also has dispute settlement measures which are not directly relevant to energy but they do have provisions which are related to energy transport and trade. The IAEA model has no connection with energy but has a stringent compliance and verification method, which is required in cross-border pipelines, and is not provided by the other two institutions.[54] Although the agency has a few similarities with the IAEA model, it goes further than the IAEA, as the agency would act as a unifying mechanism which would have the capability to deal with the geo-political, legal and economic dimensions of cross-border pipelines.[55] As a regulatory agency its role would not only be to ensure that the rules and regulations of the agreements signed by the party are followed but also to facilitate the cooperation of the various actors and act as a safety net for weak members in a pipeline regime.

The agency would deal with frequent government intervention due to geo-political, legal and economic reasons, which is not provided by the ECT, WTO or even the IAEA. All the governments are part of these agencies and all these institutions and treaties work depending upon the strength and leverage of each individual government. Since these institutions do not have the capacity to ensure that the members carry out their various rules and regulations, the government with greater bargaining power will be able to protect its own interests and ambitions. However, the agency would act outside this mould and would work to ensure that all the members', including the weaker members', interests are protected. They would also provide the balance and safety net required which is the incentive for countries to join this regime.

The agency also goes further than the ECT, WTO Dispute Settlement Mechanism and the IAEA in that it is a unifying mechanism which could be incorporated

---

54. The previous chapter has an in-depth discussion of this area.
55. See the section 'the difference between the IPA and IAEA' in this chapter for further clarification.

by any pipeline regime without being a member of the agency.[56] Being a member of the agency has the added benefit of being a part of the regime which could help in the building and operational aspects of the pipeline but by incorporating the ethos of the agency, which in itself is a unifying mechanism, the pipeline regime can have a better regulatory and enforcement capacity which is its most important aspect.

In fact, by incorporating the unifying mechanism in a pipeline regime even a non-member of the agency becomes a de facto member as it then has to abide by the various rules and regulations prescribed by the agency. This kind of flexibility is not offered by any of the institutions mentioned above as one has to be a member of the ECT, WTO or the IAEA in order to incorporate or even follow provisions which might be relevant to a particular country.

The IPA would have both neo-liberal and neo-realist traits. It is neo-liberal in the sense that it would seek the cooperation of all its members in the enforcement of the various rules and regulations. The purpose of the agency is to balance the interest of all the stakeholders in an individual pipeline regime through its involvement so that there is relative gain for all the parties involved in the pipeline. The IPA would also have neo-realist traits in that it would not compromise on the enforcement of the rules and regulations of the regime and would expect the governments involved in the pipeline to respect the legitimate expectations of all the stakeholders involved in the pipeline. The fact that the IPA would be able to send inspectors to find out the cause of the problem and take necessary actions through quick settlement of disputes despite reservations by stakeholders within the pipeline shows its hegemonic capabilities and its ethos of compliance with the regime's rules and principles.[57]

There could be arguments about the possibility of a strong hegemony joining the IPA when it would be better off protecting its interest through neo-realist means rather than sharing its sovereignty and powers with a regulatory regime. However, although in the short term a hegemony might be worse-off by joining a regime, in the long run it might be beneficial because, in cross-border pipelines, interdependence is the key and all the exporting, importing and the transit countries have to cooperate in order for the pipeline to operate without any disruption.[58] Moreover, despite neo-realist intentions,

---

56. There could be an argument that the importance of the nuclear issues that the IAEA handles are more important than the oil and gas issues that will be handled by the proposed IPA and hence states would be less inclined to join the agency. However, the whole purpose of choosing the IAEA as mentioned before in the book is because of its enforcement and compliance mechanisms which could have an impact on cross-border pipelines. The issues of cross-border pipeline management might not be as important as stopping a nuclear bomb exploding, but the argument is that the issue of cross-border pipelines is equally important for the energy security of a country and it also has the capability to cause damaging problems to countries dependent upon energy. As a result, energy exporting, importing and transit countries would be equally inclined to join the proposed agency to safeguard their interest.

57. The main principle of the IPA would be to act in a regulatory capacity in the enforcement of the various rules and regulations of cross-border pipelines. This is in order to protect the legitimate expectations of the stakeholders involved while also trying to balance the disputes between the parties in a pipeline without causing disruption in the pipeline.

58. The reason a hegemony would suffer in the short term is because it has to make concessions which would give it leverage to have a better bargaining position in the future in order to protect

a state 'participates in a regime and signs treaties because it believes its interests would be protected and a successful regime or treaty is one which fosters cooperation among states beyond their political and economic alignments'.[59]

For example, a country like Russia will be tempted to join the IPA in order to further its interests, despite having neo-realist ideals.[60] The recent gas disputes between Russia and Ukraine despite both parties being signatories to the ECT and both favouring political negotiations rather than resolution through ECT mechanisms shows the treaty's lack of effectiveness.[61] The IPA, in this kind of scenario, would send its inspectors promptly to find out the real cause of the problem and try to provide a quick solution to the problems through a fast tribunal decision. In the Russia–Ukraine dispute, both parties were blaming each other and the first monitors did not reach the area until the eleventh day of disruption.[62]

Moreover, in 2009, President Medvedev proposed 'new universal international legally binding instruments, which unlike the existing energy charter base system, would include all major energy producing countries, countries of transit and energy consumers as its parties and cover all aspect of energy'.[63] This shows Russia's attitude to cooperation. Further, the signing of the recent deal with BP to explore the Arctic area despite having previous problems shows its willingness to cooperate despite having neo-realist intentions. A neo-realist state would also be tempted to join the proposed IPA if they saw an opportunity to further their interests in the form of being a benign hegemony. A benign hegemony exercises positive leadership and ensures that the others help it in order to fulfil its interests.[64] A strong country joining the proposed IPA could have a similar role which would only enhance the regulatory aspects and ensure that the legitimate expectations of all the stakeholders in a pipeline are protected.

Regimes tend to change over time and, as a result, they lose some of their enforcement power.[65] For example, the IAEA was created during the 1950s to

---

its interests and make absolute gain. Also read V. Agarwal, *Liberal Protectionism: the International Politics of Organized Textile Trade* (Berkeley: University of California Press, 1985).

59. See A. Konolpayanik, 'Energy Security: the role of Business, Governments, International Organizations and International Framework', IELTR 6 (2007).

60. According to Axelrod, countries tend to cooperate with each other and join a regime if there is some sort of reciprocity present. As a result, Russia could have neo-realist traits but the temptation to gain something in return from joining the regime, meaning other countries also reciprocating Russia's cooperation with their own; furthers the argument of a country with neo-realist traits joining a regime; in this case the IPA. See R. Axelrod, *The Complexity of Cooperation: Agent–Based Models of Competition and Collaboration* (Princeton: Princeton University Press, 1997).

61. See J. Westerhof, 'The Transit Conflict between Russia and Ukraine from a Legal Perspective', in *European Energy Law Report VII*, ed. Roggenkamp, M., et al. (Intersentia, 2010).

62. See *ibid.*

63. See *The Conceptual Approach to the New Legal Framework for Energy Cooperation (Goals and Principles)*, 21 Apr. 2009 available at <www.eng.kremlin.ru/text/docs/2009/04/215305>.

64. See O. Young, *The Effectiveness of International Environmental Regimes: Causal Connections and Behavioural Mechanisms* (Cambridge: MIT Press, 1999).

65. See R. Butler, 'Improving Non-Proliferation Enforcement', *The Washington Quarterly* (2003): 133–145.

provide and enhance knowledge and technology in the field of nuclear technology.[66] The agency's objective was not enforcement and or to investigate whether any country was trying to use nuclear technology for non-peaceful purposes.[67] However, due to the signing of the NPT in 1968, its role totally changed, and as a regime its work was also that of an enforcer and a watchdog.[68]This happened due to the US, the UK and France's strength within the IAEA regime. Over the years China and Russia also became powerful and their interests also had to be accommodated resulting in the IAEA becoming less powerful due to the lack of consensus within the regime.[69] In fact, 'international regimes are created, established and modified or terminated as a result of shifts in the distribution of power which brings to the fore new coalitions with different interests'.[70] The same could be said of the IAEA regime.

The proposed IPA regime would be different in that its main purpose and goal would be to deal with disputes in cross-border pipelines and although there could be flexibility over time regarding ways of enforcing and dealing with cross-border pipeline disputes, it will not change its objective over time like the IAEA. The proposed IPA regime will be set up to balance the interests of the parties despite their strength and no single member or pair of members would be able to sway its function according to their wishes. There could, however, be an argument about whether a strong regime member or a group of neo-realist regime members could be stopped if they wished to block certain actions of the proposed the IPA. The fact remains that in cross-border pipelines the interest of the parties are interlinked and there is a need for cooperation and reciprocity between a weaker transit country and a strong exporting or importing country for the pipeline to be operational. Further, the interests of all the investors and other oil companies would also be interlinked creating a difficulty if a group of strong members tried to intervene in the functioning of the pipeline.

The concept of reciprocity is also crucial in making the proposed IPA free from the grip of strong members, as the strong members would think twice about derailing the activities of the IPA, as they themselves might have to face its scrutiny at a certain stage due to the nature of interdependence in cross-border pipelines.[71] As a result, neo-realists would want to 'teach reciprocity to those with whom they will interact so that they can build a mutually rewarding relationship'.[72] In this case, it is the proposed IPA.

---

66. See *ibid.*
67. See Choe, *supra* n. 41.
68. See *ibid.*
69. See Butler, *supra* n. 65.
70. See J. Peterson, *Managing the Frozen South: The Creation of the Antarctic Treaty System* (Berkeley: University of California Press, 1988).
71. See R. Axelrod, *The Evolution of Cooperation* (New York: Basic Books, 1984).
72. See *ibid.*

# Chapter 9

# Conclusion

The case studies in the previous chapters show that agreements are used as a refuge by governments and other strong members of a pipeline to further their own interests resulting in a breach of legitimate expectation of the stakeholders involved. Currently, the treaties and agreements relevant to cross-border pipeline regimes do not make governments or other members in a regime to take corrective decisions during problem situations,[1] causing frequent interruptions which result in losses for all the partners involved in the pipeline project. The solution was discussed in the last chapter where the proposed agency would be there to make those decisions quickly and decisively, which would have the effect of constraining the government intervention frequently experienced in past years due to geo-political, legal and economic reasons. The agency or unifying mechanism would also ensure that the actors comply by enforcing the rules and regulations of the pipeline regime and ensure that the legitimate expectations of the stakeholders are respected.

An analysis of each pipeline was carried out from a regime perspective in order to understand whether they can be termed as a regime and, if they are a regime, what kind of enforcement and compliance capabilities they have which also showed that all seven pipelines had certain limitations to their regime capabilities. The entire pipeline chain was considered as a regime because all the actors came together with the common intention and interest of building a pipeline.[2] As a consequence, although the actors involved in the pipelines did not want to create some form of regime, the very fact that they have come together in order to achieve a common goal has given cross-border pipelines a regime dimension. Moreover, the functions carried out by the different actors also had regime credentials.

---

1. This means the intervention of the governments or any other members in the regime due to economic, geo-political or legal reasons.
2. See Ch. 2 for an in-depth discussion of this area.

However, despite having regime credentials the case studies have shown that all of the pipelines lacked the most important aspect of a regime, that of having an enforcement and compliance capability which would enable them to constrain constant government intervention due to geo-political, legal and economic reasons. The strength of a regime depends upon its capability to ensure that the actors abide by their obligations and that all the actors have access to the regime facilities and derive gains from joining it. Although all the regimes under different categories had certain qualities they were not able to deal with all the problems faced by the actors in cross-border pipelines.

The role of the agency mechanism or pipeline regime would ensure that the stakeholders involved in that pipeline regime would abide by the position agreed at the signing of the pipeline agreements and would not change that position for economic, geo-political or legal reasons. The agency would do this by constraining interference from governments or powerful actors of the regime by ensuring that all the actors' legitimate expectations are respected and that parties abide by their obligations. The agency would act as a form of safety net, which would operate proactively to diffuse any dispute concerning the pipeline regime which might disrupt the flow of hydro-carbon resources in the pipeline.

The case studies have shown that depending upon the strength of the regime, the level of interference from the government or other actors differs because of changing economic, geo-political and legal interests. A change in one government policy or the policy of some companies can lead them to influence regime dynamics. Consequently, the regulatory capacity of the pipeline regime has to be robust and independent to tackle this sort of pressure from regime members, in order to stabilize the balance in the pipeline regime and ensure uninterrupted supply of gas or oil. In a strong regime like the FSU or Interconnector, if the government or any other members want to interfere to protect its own interest, it has to go through certain steps and procedures and has to take other members into its confidence or even persuade them to support it before it can even contemplate intervention. If it did intervene, the regulators would try to scrutinize their actions. Despite being strong, the chances are that the regulatory body could still be influential because the body is made up of the stakeholders involved in the pipeline.[3]

In a moderately strong regime like the WAGP and the BTC, the chances of intervention by interested parties is slightly increased because the regulatory capacity of the pipeline regime is not as strong as the Interconnector or FSU pipelines. The case study of the WAGP has shown that the regulatory body was not able to act, as governments tried to solve their problems directly instead of going through the regulatory body. This leaves out the weaker parties like Benin and Togo, whereas the two stronger partners, Ghana and Nigeria, benefit. In the case of a weak regime like the CPC, Shah-Deniz and Maghreb–Europe pipelines, the lack of regulatory oversight means that the level of intervention would be

---

3. This means that the parties who are members of the regime decide the formation of the regulatory capacity regulating the pipeline. As a result, the regulators would also have to take into account the interest of the parties involved in the pipeline.

higher as governments, or some other strong members, do not have to go through any steps or policies before an intervention and they can change the structure or the rules and regulations of the pipeline according to their own interest resulting in the breach of a stakeholder's legitimate expectation. As a result, the level of intervention is more direct and widespread.

It is also important to take into account that not all breaches of legitimate expectations will result in a disruption in the pipeline. However, pipelines in moderately strong and weaker regimes deal with a breach of legitimate expectation through negotiation and diplomacy rather than going through the mechanisms available within the agreements signed between the parties. An example of this is the Shah-Deniz pipeline and the WAGP pipeline, where the government, despite not being able to abide by their obligations under the agreement, negotiated with the parties who suffered the breach rather than following the mechanisms available in the agreement.[4]

In terms of the members intervening due to economic reasons, the proposed agency could see whether the parties are abiding by their original position. For example, in the FSU pipeline there were disagreements between Russia and Ukraine with regard to Russia not paying enough transit fees, while the former alleged that Ukraine was unilaterally stealing gas from the pipeline. The agency, in this sort of situation, could send in experts or inspectors to review the actual situation on the ground and give an impartial interpretation of the position of the two parties and, if needed, provide expertise which could diffuse the situation and stop disruption in the pipeline. However, due to lack of any regulatory oversight, most members' allegations result in a unilateral decision by one of the members which harms the interests of others in the regime, especially if the intervening member is strong.

The agency would also look into geo-political and legal problems by providing expertise in the form of experts helping regime members with independent verification as to whether all the members are abiding by their obligations. The agency could also ensure that the decisions taken in the pipeline regime are not taken solely on political grounds, as it might make the vulnerable members in a pipeline regime nervous about losing their benefit. The independent nature of this regulatory body would allow members of the regime to approach the body, which could not only provide them with assistance in order to diffuse any stand off between regime members but also work towards ensuring that the situation never reaches the point where it might disrupt the flow of hydro-carbon resources.

The agency or unifying mechanism proposed is also flexible as it is both international and regional. The system could be adopted by any pipeline regime throughout the world and if a particular region does not want to be part of an international agency and does not like that agency enforcing the various rules

---

4. The government is liable to pay compensation and fines for not honouring the agreements signed between them and the stakeholders involved in the pipeline but they would rather avoid that and go for negotiation and diplomacy, which is outside the bounds of the agreement signed between the parties. See the 'nature and characteristics of the regime' and the 'issues affecting the pipelines' section of the WAGP and the Shah-Deniz pipeline for greater details on this matter.

and regulations in their region they could still implement the work of the agency by modelling themselves a similar regulatory body.[5] This is simply a unifying mechanism but it has enough flexibility to suit everyone's needs. The main objective is to create a regulatory framework or an agency which could constrain the frequent interruption of pipeline activities by governments or other members of a regime in order to protect and diffuse any dispute or conflict which might cause pipeline disruption.

This autonomous body or pipeline agency might not be the answer to all the problems involved in cross-border pipelines but it would be a unifying mechanism which, for the first time, would be able to deal with cross-border pipeline issues in a systematic way. It would also help to tackle frequent government intervention due to geo-political, legal and economic reasons and restrict their intervention through its regulatory capacity.

The agency or unifying mechanism would try to ensure the cooperation of all members within a pipeline regime and would also help with the enforcement of the various rules and regulations of the pipeline regime. The maxim of the agency would be to achieve relative gains for all the partners in a pipeline regime, so that all the members could get some benefit from joining the pipeline regime, as would the agency. The current neo-realist traits shown by some actors or governments in a pipeline regime, where absolute gain or intervention to fulfil the government's own interest, would be able to be constrained and limited as the agency would work for the benefit of all the actors within the agency and the pipeline regime and ensure that their legitimate expectations are protected.[6]

The agency would constrain a government's intervention in the pipeline regime without trespassing into a country's sovereignty. Neither is it advocating for a new piece of international law. The agency also would not decide on the route of the pipeline as routeing is an issue for states to decide, whether to share their sovereignty with other pipeline states.

Despite all the different geo-political, legal and economic problems which cause a government to intervene, resulting in disruption to pipelines, the frequency of and opportunities for these disputes are more rampant in a regime with a weak regulatory and enforcement capacity. A strong regime might not need to trigger the unifying mechanism because of the strength of its regime capabilities over a weak regime, but each of the strong, moderately strong and weak regimes could still benefit from it,[7] although the need for a unifying mechanism is greater in weaker regimes. Irrespective of all these problems, the solution is to get everyone involved in the pipeline working towards the operation of the pipeline. The solution is the same irrespective of the problem.

---

5. See the 'International and regional debate' part of Ch. 9 for an in-depth discussion of this area.
6. The IPA regime would be a mixture of neo-liberalism and neo-realism as it will try to balance the interests of all the actors within the agency as both the neo-liberals and neo-realists have interests which could be implemented through greater cooperation and reciprocity.
7. Chapter 8 of the book has a discussion regarding 'the purpose of joining the regime', which is relevant to this and provides the reasons that could be beneficial to all the parties involved.

## 9.1. OTHER ALTERNATIVES TO THE AGENCY OR UNIFYING MECHANISM

The unifying mechanism, in the form of a pipeline agency or in any other form, acts to ensure that the members in a pipeline regime abide by their various rules and obligations but is not the only alternative available to deal with the geo-political, legal and economic problems in a pipeline regime caused by frequent government intervention. There could be other regulatory bodies that could do the same and have the same powers and principles and membership structure as the pipeline agency or the unifying mechanism proposed.

The ECT or the WTO could implement certain features of the unifying mechanism in that it could act as a regulatory body and ensure that the actors are abiding by their various obligations in the pipeline regime. They would also have to balance the interests of the parties in a pipeline regime and act proactively to deal with any forms of dispute which might take place. However, the problem is with the nature of the ECT, WTO or the BITs. All these treaties and organizations were implemented to facilitate the economic aspects of the investors and some of them might not even be relevant to energy, although the ECT is energy related while the WTO has recently focused on energy related trade.

The biggest challenge of incorporating the unifying mechanism within these treaties and institutions is whether it could deal with the geo-political, legal and economic problems in cross-border pipelines. In most instances, it would be difficult to deal with geo-political problems because most of the countries would prefer the status quo rather than taking the risk to protect a weak member's interest over the interest of other strong members. The response of the ECT members to coordinating a response to the Russia–Ukraine gas crisis in 2009 showed that each country's interest is different and few believed in collective interest.[8] As a result, even if the unifying mechanism was incorporated within the ECT framework, the chance of implementation would be the same as before.[9] However, Russia's termination of the provisional application could create a space for the reconstruction of the ECT.

Currently the ECT is trying to formulate a new dispute settlement mechanism following the 2009 gas dispute.[10] In fact, commentators have proposed a 'speedy reliable and predictable system adapted to the specific requirements of gas trade'.[11] Some other options include emergency arbitration provisions which would

---

8. It could be argued that the same thing could happen in a pipeline agency. However, the chances are low as the sole role of the pipeline agency would be to diffuse and avoid situations where the pipeline gas is disrupted for days resulting in a loss for all the parties involved in the pipeline. The agency would also have features like sending in inspectors and try to deal with any situations which might arise in a pipeline dispute in the quickest possible time because it would be dedicating its entire time to pipeline related problems or other matters.
9. This means the situation would be the same as now, resulting in pipeline disruption.
10. See F. Slaoui, *Emergency Arbitrator – The Proposed New Procedure of the SCC Rules*, 2009, available at <www.kluwerarbitrationblog.com>.
11. See *ibid.*

'provide an efficient protection at a very early stage, short circuiting the possibly lengthy phase of filing a request for arbitration and constituting an arbitral tribunal'.[12] All these options are being currently discussed to make the ECT adept at dealing with future energy disputes.

Although the unifying mechanism option is not the only option available, incorporating it with any current treaties or institutions might not have the desired effect[13] as it will not be able to deal with the geo-political, economic and legal dimension all at once. However, the mechanism is pipeline specific and any pipeline regime could try to implement it or use it for their benefit to ensure that the actors involved in the pipelines are complying with their obligations and that the interests of all the members in the pipeline regime are protected from government intervention due to the three factors mentioned before.

From a regime theory perspective, the ECT, WTO or other institutions are regimes which have already been set up for a particular purpose. Incorporating the unifying mechanism into their system will increase their enforcement capabilities to ensure that the actors in cross-border pipelines abide by their obligations, which is an important regime trait. However, the members within these institutions and treaties will not like their regime focusing on the regulatory aspects of cross-border pipelines as they did not join the regime for that purpose.[14]

Although there could be an argument that by incorporating the unifying mechanisms into their system the interests of the regime members will be protected, the fact remains that they will be shifting their focus to an area which was not the original reason for the setting up of the regime. This might cause the regime to weaken which, in other words, will not help with the enforcement of the rules and regulations in cross-border pipelines or stop government intervention, which is the main problem the unifying mechanism will deal with.[15]

---

12. See *ibid.*
13. 'Desired effect' here means the current institutions being able to deal with the problem promptly and having the regulatory capacity and the mandate to do so.
14. Although there is no precedence for the mechanism that is being proposed, it has similarities with the IAEA in style and with Art. 5 of GATT in content. Also read K.W. Grewlich, 'International Regulatory Governance of the Caspian Pipeline Policy Game', JENRL 29, no. 1 (2011). Here the author talks about using the ECT as a regulator in dealing with the problems in cross-border pipelines. He also uses the term 'ordo liberals' in explaining how the ECT could strengthen the rule of law between both ECT Member States and the stakeholders involved in the pipeline. For further reading also read I.A. Siddiky, 'Towards a New Framework for Cross-Border Pipelines: The International Pipeline Agency', *China and Eurasia Forum Quarterly* 8, no. 3 (2010).
15. It is important to note that the unifying mechanism is not a regime, here the ECT or WTO is considered as the regime.

# Bibliography

I.          PRIMARY SOURCES

1.          AGREEMENTS, TREATIES AND DIRECTIVES

Agreement on Common Conditions for Transit through the Territory of the Custom Union Member-Countries, between Belarus, Kazakhstan, Kyrgyz Republic and the Russian Federation, 1998.

Agreement on the Exploration, Development and Production Sharing for the Shah-Deniz Prospective Area in the Azerbaijan Sector of the Caspian Sea, between The State Oil Company of the Azerbaijan Republic et al., 1996.

Directive 2003/55/EC concerning the rules for the internal marketing natural gas and repealing directive 98/30/EC, can be accessed via <www.europa.eu.int/comm./energy/gas/legislation/amending_legislation_en.htm>.

Directive 2009/73/EC, can be found at <www.ec.europa.eu>.

Directive 98/30/EC, can be found at <www.ec.europa.eu>.

Energy Act 2004, Part3, *Chapter-2: Interconnections for Electricity and Gas* at <www.opsi.gov.uk/acts/acts2004/20040020.htm>.

Host Government Agreement between and among the Government of the Azerbaijan republic and the State Oil Company of the Azerbaijan Republic, BP Exploration (Caspian Sea) LTD, Statoil BTC Caspian as RAMCO Hazar Energy Ltd, Turkiye Petrolleri A.O., UNOCAL BTC Pipeline, Ltd, Itochu Oil Exploration (Azerbaijan) Inc, Delta Hess (BTC) Ltd.

Intergovernmental Agreement among The Republic of Turkey, The Azerbaijan Republic and Georgia relating to the transportation of petroleum via the Baku–Tbilisi–Ceyhan Main Export Pipeline, 1999.

Intergovernmental Agreement between the Republic of Turkey and the Azerbaijan Republic Concerning the Delivery of Azerbaijan Natural Gas to the Republic of Turkey.

Pipeline Consortium Agreement among the Government of the Republic of Kazakhstan, the Government of the Sultanate of Oman and the Government of Russian Federation, 1992.

The agreement between Sonatrach, Engas and Transgas and also the host government agreement between Spain and Sonatrach. Can be accessed via <www.sonatrach-dz.com>.

The Argentina–US Bilateral Treaty.

The Decree of President of the Russian Federation, No. 1403, of 17 November 1992 and the Ordinance of the RF Council of Ministers 810 of 14 August 1993.

The Draft EC Treaty of 2004, could be found at <www.euabc.com>.

The Energy Charter Treaty, 1994.

The Gas sale Agreement between Engas, Sontrach and Transgas, available at <www.sonatrach-dz.com/NEW/>.

The IAEA Statute, 1956.

The Intergovernmental Agreement between the Kingdom of Spain, People's Democratic Republic of Algeria and the Kingdom of Morocco concerning the supply of gas from Algeria to Spain through Morocco, 1992.

The Legislative Act on Foreign Investment in Russian Federation, 1999.

The Lisbon Treaty, 2007. Can be accessed at <http://europa.eu/lisbon_treaty/index_en.htm>.

The Treaty on Non-Proliferation of Nuclear Weapons, 1968.

Treaty on the West African Gas Pipeline Project between the Republic of Benin, Republic of Ghana, Federal republic of Nigeria and The Togolese Republic, 2003.

2.        CASES

Case COMP/E-4/38.075, IP02/401 of 13 March 2002.

*CMS Gas Company Transmission Company v. Argentine Republic*, ICSID Case No. ARB/01/8, 2005.

Compania De Augus Del Aconquija, S.A. & Compagnie General des Eaux V Argentine Republic, ICSID ARB/97/3, Final Award, at para. 32.

*LG&E v. Argentina*, ICSID Case No. ARB/02, 2006.

MTD Equity Sdn.Bhd. and *MTD Chile S.A. v. Republic of Chile*, decision on Jurisdiction, at para. 104.

Nykomb Synergetics Technology Holding AB V Latvia, Stockholm Rules Award. 16 December 2003, Stockholm International Arbitration Review, 2005.

*SGS v. Philippines*, Decision on Jurisdiction, January 2009, 2004, at para 116.

*Yukos Universal Ltd v. Russian Federation*, PCA Case Nos AA 226.

II.        SECONDARY SOURCES

1.         BOOKS

Agarwal, V. *Liberal Protectionism: the International Politics of Organized Textile Trade*. Berkeley: University of California Press, 1985.

Aissaoui, A. *Algeria: the Political Economy of Oil and Gas*. Oxford: Oxford University Press, 2001.

Axelrod, R. *Conflicts of Interest, A theory of Divergent goals with application to Politics*. Chicago: Markham, 1970.

Axelrod, R. *The Complexity of Cooperation: Agent –Based Models of Competition and Collaboration*. Princeton, NJ: Princeton University Press, 1997.

Axelrod, R. *The Evolution of Cooperation*. New York: Basic Books, 1984.

Barton, B. et al. *Energy Security: Managing Risk in a Dynamic Legal and Regulatory Environment*. NY: Oxford University Press, 2004.

Cameron, P. *Competition in Energy Markets: Law and Regulation in the European Union*. Oxford: Oxford University Press, 2007.

Cassese, A. *International Law in a Divided World*. New York: Oxford University Press, 1986.

Chuah, J.C.T. *Law of International Trade*. London: Sweet and Maxwell, 2001.

Cornish, R. *Linking the European Gas Pipeline*. London: World Gas Yearbook, 1998.

Crandall, M.S. *Energy, Economics, and Politics in the Caspian Region: Dreams and Realities*. Westport: Praeger Security International, 2006.

Dore, J. & R. De Bauw. *The Energy Charter Treaty – Origins, Aims and Prospects*. London: Royal Institute of International Affairs, 1995.

Grieco, J. *Cooperation among Nations: Europe, America and Non-Tariff Barriers to Trade*. Ithaca: Cornell University Press, 1990.

Hasenclever, A. et al. *Theories of International Regimes*. New York: Cambridge Studies in International relations, Cambridge University Press, 1997, 27.

Kandiyoti, R. *Pipelines: Flowing Oil and Crude Politics*. London New York: I B Tauris and Co Ltd, 2007.

Kennedy, J.L. *Oil and Gas Pipeline Fundamentals*. Tulsa: Pennwell, 1993.

Kenneth, W. *Theory of International Politics*. New York: Random house, 1979, 179.

Keohane, R. *After Hegemony: Cooperation and Discord in the World Political Economy*. Princeton, New Jersey: Princeton University Press, 1984.

Lagoni, R. 'Pipelines'. *Encyclopedia of Public International Law* 3 (1997).

Ledeneva, A. *How Russia Really Works: The Informal Practices That Shaped Post-Soviet Politics and Business*. Ithaca, NY: Cornell University Press, 2006.

Miesner, T.O. & W.L. Leffler. *Oil and Gas Pipelines in Non-technical Language*. USA: Penwell Corporation, 2006.

Mugaroby, M. *Permanent Sovereignty over Oil Resource*. Beirut, Lebanon: The Middle East Research and Publishing Centre.

Osborne, P.G. *Osborne's Law Dictionary*. London: Sweet and Maxwell, 2009.

Paulwelyn, J. *Global Challenges at the Intersection of Energy, Trade and Environment*. Centre for trade and Economic Integration (CETI), 2010.

Peterson, J. *Managing the Frozen South: The Creation of the Antarctic Treaty System*. Berkeley, CA: University of California Press, 1988.

Qureshi, A.H. *The WTO: Implementing International Trade Norms*. Manchester and New York: Melland Schills Studies in International Law, Manchester University Press, 1996.

Roggenkamp, M. et al. *Energy Law in Europe: National, EU and Internal Regulation*. 2nd edn. Oxford: Oxford University Press, 2007.

Smith, G. *Reforming the Russian Legal System*. Cambridge, UK: Cambridge University Press, 1996.

Sonarajah, M. *The International Law on Foreign Investment*. Cambridge, UK: Cambridge University Press, 2004.

Stern, J.P. *Competition and Liberalization in European Gas Markets: A Diversity of Models*. London: Royal Institute of International Affairs, 1998.

Stern, J.P. *International Gas Trade in Europe: The Policies of Exporting and Importing Countries*. Aldershot: Gower, 1986.

Vernon, R. *Sovereignty at Bay: The Multinational Spread of U.S Enterprises*. New York: Basic Books, 1979.

Victor, D.G. et al. *Natural Gas and Geopolitics: From 1970–2040*. Cambridge: Cambridge University Press, 2006.

Walde, T.W. *The Energy Charter Treaty: An East-West Gateway for Investment and Trade*. The Hague: Kluwer Law International, 1996.

Walde, T.W. & K.M. Christie. (eds). *Energy Charter Treaty: Selected Topics*. Dundee: Centre for Energy Petroleum and Mineral Law and Policy, 1995.

World Trade Organization. *The WTO Dispute Settlement Procedures – A Collection of the Legal Texts*. WTO Geneva, 1995.

Young, O. *International Cooperation: Building Regimes for Natural Resources and the Environment*. Ithaca and London: Cornell University Press, 1989.

Young, O. *The Effectiveness of International Environmental Regimes: Causal Connections and Behavioural Mechanisms*. Cambridge: MIT Press, 1999.

Zacher, W. & A. Sutton. *Governing Global Networks: International Regimes for Transportation and Communications*. Cambridge: Cambridge University Press, 1996.

2.     Reports, Working Papers and other Documents

Andoura, S. et al. *Towards a European Energy Community: A Policy Proposal*. Notre Europe Studies and Research 76, Notre Europe, Paris, 2010.

Appellate Body Report, European Communities – *Regime for the importation, sale and Distribution of Bananas* (EC-'Bananas III'). WT/DS27/AB/R, adopted 25 September 1997, DSR 1997: II, 591.

Appellate body report, USA – *Measure affecting shirts and blouses from India*, WT/DS33/AB/R and Corr.1, adopted 23 May1997, DSR1997: I,323.

Appellate Body Report. *EC Measures concerning Meat and Meat Products* (Hormones) (EC-Hormones'). WT/DS26/AB/R, WT/DS48, adopted 13 February1998, DSR 1998: I 135.

Caspian Development and Export. *Economic, Social and Environmental Overview of the Southern Caspian Oil and Gas Projects*. Briefing Paper, February 2003.

Chufrin, G. *Russia's Caspian Energy Policy and Its Impact on the US–Russian Relationship*. study conducted by the James A. Baker III Institute for Public Policy, Rice University, 2004. Can be found at <www.rice.edu/energy/ publications/docs/PEC_chufrin_10_20041.pdf>.

Dellecker, A. *Caspian Pipeline Consortium, Bellweather of Russia's Investment Climate*. 2008. This can be accessed on the IFRI website at <www.ifri.org/ files/Russie/ifri_RNV_Dellecker_CPC_ENG_juin2008.pdf>.

Driemer, H.M. *Do Bilateral Investment treaties Attract Foreign Direct Investment? Only a Bit . . . and They Could Bite*. Policy Research Working Paper, The World Bank, 2003.

DTI Consultation URN 01/1099. *Concerns about Gas Prices and Possible Improvements to Market Efficiency*. November 2001. Can be found at <www.dti.gov.uk/energy/domestic_markets/gas_market/gascondoc.pdf>.

European Commission Enquiry into Anti-competitive Use of Interconnector, March 2002. Can be found at <europa.eu.int/rapid/reference=IP/02/401>.

Ezequiel, M. *Nuclear security and the IAEA*, The International University Vienna, 13 February 2006, 1–26.

Futyan, M. *The Interconnector Pipeline: A Key Link to Europe's Gas Network*. Oxford: Oxford Institute of Energy Studies, 2006.

Gas transit tariffs in Selected ECT Countries, Energy Charter Secretariat, January, 2006.

Gelb, B.A. *Russia's Oil and Gas Challenges*. CRS report for Congress, 2006. Can be found at <http://fpc.state.gov/documents/organization/58988.pdf>.

Gelder, W.V. *The Financing of the Baku–Tblisi–Ceyhan Project*. A research paper prepared for Focus on Finance, available on the internet via <www. banktrack.org/fileadmin/user_upload/documents/6_profundo-AIDE_research/ BTC0302.pdf>.

Global Insight. *Ensuring Effective and Efficient Forward Gas Markets*, 2005. Can be found at <www.webarchive.nationalarchives.gov.uk/>.

Goodland, R. *Oil and Gas Pipelines: Social and Environmental Impact Assessment*. International Association of Impact Assessment, 2005.

Heslin, S.N. *Key Constraints to Caspian Pipeline Development: Status., Significance and Outlook* in the working paper series titled *Unlocking the Assets: Energy and the Future of Central Asia and the Caucasus*, in The James Baker III Institute for Public Policy, Rice University, April 1998.

ISODEC (Integrated Social Development Centre), *The West African Gas Pipeline Project A Critical Perspective*, vol. 2, no. 1, 2003. Can be accessed via <www. isodec.org.gh>.

Love, P. *The Changing Face of Energy Politics*. The OECD Observer, Summer, 1999, No. 217/218, 2 available online at <www.ciaonet.org/olj/00/00_99lop02.html>.

Pauwelyn, J. *Trade in Energy: WTO Rules Applying under the Energy Charter Treaty*. ECS, Brussels, Belgium, 2001.

Peterson, L.E. *Bilateral Investment Treaties and Development Policy Making*. International Institute for Sustainable Development, 2004.

Pirani, S. *Ukraine's Gas Sector*. Oxford: Oxford Energy Studies, 2007.

Response to consultation on Interconnector licenses, 2004 at <www.Interconnector.com/mediacentre/presentations.htm>.

Selivanova, Y. *The WTO and Energy: WTO Rules and Agreements of Relevance to the Energy Sector*. Energy Charter Secretariat, ICTSD, Issue Paper No. 1, August 2007.

Soligo, R. & A. Jaffe. *The Economics of Pipeline Routes: the Conundrum of Oil Exports from the Caspian Basin*. Baker Institute for Public Policy, Rice University, Working Paper, April 1998.

Sornarajah, M. Affidavit in Ontario Superior Court Of Justice case between The Council of Canadians, et al., and Canada, Court file No. 01-CV-208141, at para. 13.

Stern, J.P. *The Russian –Ukrainian Gas Crisis of 2006*. Oxford Energy Studies, 2006. This can be accessed via <www.oxfordenergy.org>.

Stern, J.P. et al. *The Russian–Ukrainian Gas Dispute of January 2009*. Oxford: Oxford Energy studies, 2009.

Stevens, P. *A History of Transit Pipelines in the Middle East: lessons for the future*. Dundee: University of Dundee, CEPMLP Seminar Paper SP23, 1996.

Stevens, P. *Cross-Border Oil and Gas Pipelines: Problems and Prospects*. ESMAP Technical Paper 035, UNDP/World Bank/ESMAP, 2003.

Stevens, P. *Transit Troubles: Pipelines as a Source of Conflict*. A Chatham house Report, 2009, available at <www.chathamhouse.org.uk/files/13571_r0309_pipelines.pdf>.

Stocktaking of Indian Bilateral Agreements for the Promotion and Protection of Investment, Communication from India to the Working Group on trade and Investment, 3 April 1999, WT/WGTI/W/71.

The Conceptual Approach to the New Legal Framework for Energy Cooperation (Goals and Principles), 21 April 2009 available at <www.eng.kremlin.ru/text/docs/2009/04/215305>.

The Critical Reassessment of the West African Gas Pipeline, 25 Degrees in Africa, vol. 3, no. 3, 2008 at <http://25degrees.net/index.php>.

The World Bank. *Russian Oil Transport and Export Study, Stratetigic Export expansion options and Legal. Contractual and Regulatory framework*, 1997.

The WTO Secretariat. *Guide to Dispute Settlement*. The Hague: Kluwer Law International, 2002.

UNCTAD. *Trade Agreements, Petroleum and Energy Policies*. UNCTAD/ITCD/TSB/9. United Nations, 2000.

Van Grasstek, C. *Why Demands on Acceding Countries Increase Over Time: A Three-dimensional Analysis of Multilateral Trade Diplomacy* in WTO Accessions and Development Policies, UNCTAD, United Nations, 2001.

Vinogradov, S. *Cross-Border Oil & Gas Pipelines: International and Regulatory Regimes.* Dundee: CEPMLP, University of Dundee, 2001.

Vinogradov, S. *Cross-Border Oil and Gas pipelines: International Legal and Regulatory Regimes.* AIPN study, 2001.

Vladimir, S. *Shah-Deniz gas buttressing Georgia, Azerbaijan economically and politically.* The Jamestown Foundation, 2007. Can be accessed at <www. jamestown.org/single/?no_cache=1&tx_ttnews%5Btt_news%5D=32396>.

Walde, T. & A. Gunst. *International Energy Trade and Access to Competing Networks* in Energy and Environmental Services: Negotiating Objectives and Development Priorities, UNCTAD, United Nations, 2003.

Webb, J.C. *Russia – Belarus Oil Trade Dispute Underscores Need for Long Term Crude Transportation Alternatives.* CERA Report, 2007, can be accessed via <www.cera.com>.

Webb, J.C. et al. *From East Siberia to Pacific: Putin's Oil Pipeline Project of the Century.* CERA private Report, March 2008. Can be accessed via <www.cera. com>.

World Bank Project Appraisal Document on 'WAGP' Report no. 30335, 2 November 2004.

Zarilli, S. *International Energy Trade and Access to Competing Networks* in Energy and Environmental Services: Negotiating Objectives and Development Priorities, UNCTAD, United Nations, 2003.

3.      JOURNAL ARTICLES

Adu, O. 'Competition or Energy Security in the EU Internal Gas Market: An Assessment of European Commission Decisions on Long-Term Gas Contracts'. OGEL 9, no. 1 (2011).

Albers, M. 'Energy liberalization and EC Competition Law'. *Fordham International Law Journal* (2002).

Andrews-Speed, P. 'The Politics of Petroleum and the Energy Charter Treaty as an Effective Investment Regime'. *Journal of Energy Finance and Development* 4, no. 1 (June 1999): 117–135.

Axelrod, R.S. 'The European Energy Charter. Reality or illusion?', *Energy Policy* 6 (1996): 497–505.

Azaria, D. 'Energy Transit under the Energy Charter Treaty and the General Agreement on Tariffs and Trade'. *Journal of Energy and Natural Resources Law* 27, no. 4 (2009).

Bahgat, G. 'Pipeline Diplomacy: The Geopolitics of the Caspian Sea Region'. *International Studies Perspectives* 3 (2002): 310–327.

Belyi, A. 'Institutional Weakness of intra-FSU Gas Trade'. OGEL (2006).

Belyi. A. 'New Dimensions of Energy Security of the Enlargining EU and their impact on relations with Russia'. *Journal of European Studies* 25 (2003): 351–369.

Bhala, R. 'The Myth about Stare Decisis and International Trade Law'. *American University International Law Review* 14 (1999a): 845.

Brewer, T.L. & S. Young, 'International Trade WTO Disputes and Developing Countries'. *Journal of World Trade* 33, no. 5 (1999): 169–182.

Butler, R. 'Improving Non-Proliferation Enforcement', *The Washington Quarterly* (2003): 133–145.

Cameron, P. 'The Consumer and the Internal Market in Energy: Who Benefits?'. ELR 31 (2006).

Choe, J. 'Problems of enforcement: Iran, North Korea, and the N.P.T.', *Harvard International Review* (2006).

Curtis, C.T. 'The Legal Security of Economic Development Agreements'. *Harvard International Law Journal* 29 (1998): 317–318.

Davey, W. 'The WTO Dispute Settlement System', *Journal of International Economic Law* (2005): 15.

Dinan, D. 'Institutions and Governance: A New Treaty, a Newly Elected Parliament and a New Commission'. *Journal of Common Market Studies Annual Review* 48 (2010): 95–118.

Emeka, D. 'Permanent Sovereignty and Peoples Ownership of Natural Resources'. *Washington Law Review* (2006).

Fatouros, A.A. 'Energy Transit and Investment in the Energy Charter Treaty'. *Greek Journal of International Law* 2 (1996): 185–221.

Feakin, T. 'Old Interests, New Interdependencies – the Increasing Strategic Importance of Energy Pipelines'. *RUSI Journal* 52, no. 6 (2007).

Flynn, C. 'Russian Roulette: The ECT, Transit and Western European Energy Security'. IELTR 12 (2007).

Footer, M. 'Developing Country Practice in the Matter of WTO Dispute Settlement'. *Journal of World Trade* (2001): 55–98.

Freedenberg, P. et al. 'BTC Explosion and the Russian and Georgian War: How Big a Threat to Caspian Oil Exports?'. CERA (2008).

Ginsburg, R.B. 'Remarks on Writing Separately'. *Washington Law Review* 65, no. 133 (1990): 48.

Goh, G. 'The World Trade Organization, Kyoto and Energy Tax Adjustments at the Border', JWT 38 (2004).

Gregory, P.R. 'Developing Caspian Energy Reserves: The Legal Environment'. *The Emirates Centre for Strategic Studies and Research* (2000): 25.

Grewlich, K.W. 'International Regulatory Governance of the Caspian Pipeline Policy Game'. JENRL 29, no. 1 (2011).

Grieco, J. 'Realist Theory, and the Problem of International Cooperation: Analysis with an amended Prisoner's Dilemma'. *Journal of Politics* 50 (1988): 600–24.

Guzman, A. 'Why LDC's Sign Treaties that Hurt Them: Explaining the Popularity of Bilateral Investment Treaties', *Journal of International Law* 38 (1998): 639–654.

Hassan, E. & Y. Yazar. 'Whither Turkey's Energy Policy'. *Insight Turkey* 9, no. 4 (December 2007).

Hickox, R. 'The Caspian Pipeline Consortium Project'. *Pipeline and Gas Journal* (February 2007). Can be accessed via <www.undergroundinfo.com>.

Ibrahim, A.S. 'The EU Russian Gas Interdependence and Turkey'. *Insight Turkey* 9, no. 4 (December 2007).

Iwayemi, A. 'Nigeria's Dual Energy Problems: Policy Issues and Challenges'. IAEE, 2008.

Kemp, G. 'Iran and Caspian Energy: Prospects for Cooperation and Conflict'. *The Emirates Centre for Strategic Studies and Research* (2000): 55.

Konolpayanik, A. 'Energy Security: the role of Business, Governments, International Organizations and International Framework'. IELTR 6 (2007).

Konoplyanik, A. 'Gas Transit in Eurasia: Transit Issues between Russia and the European Union and the Role of Energy Charter'. JENRL (2009): 445–486.

Konoplyanik, A. 'Russian Gas to Europe: From Long term contracts, on cross-border trade, Destination Clause and Major role of transit to . . . ?'. JENRL (23 2005): 282–307.

Konoplyanik, A. 'Common Russia–EU Energy Space: The New EU Russia Partnership Agreement, Acquis Communautaire and the Energy Charter'. JERL, 27 (2009): 258 291.

Krysiek, T. et al. 'Cracks In The Bridge: The Uncertaintaies of Turkish Gas Transit'. CERA Report, 2008.

Lacarte-Munro, J. & Gappah, P. 'Developing countries and the WTO Legal and Dispute Settlement system: A view from the bench'. *Journal of International Economic Law* (2000): 395–401.

Macaulay, S.R.A. et al. 'West African Gas Pipeline Project: Associated Problems and Possible Remedies'. In *Appropriate technologies for Environmental Protection in the Developing World.* edited by Yanful, E. (Springer, 2009).

Maier, B. 'How Has International Law Dealt with the Tension between Sovereignty over Natural Resources and Investor Interests in the Energy Sector? Is there a Balance?'. IELR (2010).

Malececk, S. *Pipeline Tranist States: How can the legal regime meet investor objectives and Internal Development needs? The Case of Georgia and Caspian Exports* (2001).

Masuda, T. 'Security of Energy Supply and the Geo-politics of Oil and Gas Pipelines'. *European Review of Energy Markets* 2, no. 2 (December 2007).

McLellan, B. 'Transporting Oil and Gas – the Background to the Economics'. *Oil and Gas Finance and Accounting* 7, no. 2 (1992).

Miles, C. 'The Caspian Pipeline Debate Continues: Why Not Iran?'. *Journal of International Affairs* 53, no. 1 (Fall 1999).

Monti, M. *The Single Energy Market: The Relationship between Competition Policy and Regulation*, Speech/02/101 of March 2002.

Ogutcu, M. *Kazakhstan's expanding Cross-Border Gas Links: Implications for Europe, Russia, China and Cis Countries*, paper presented at Windsor Energy Group's regional pipeline roundtable, Almatay, Kazakhstan, 2006.

Olcot, M. 'Pipelines and Pipe Dreams: Energy Development and Caspian Society'. *Journal of International Affairs* 53, no. 1 (1999).

Omonbude, E.J. 'The Economics of Transit Oil and Gas Pipelines: A Review of the Fundamentals'. *OPEC Review* (2009): 125–139.

Pilat, J. et al. 'The Future of the Nuclear Non-proliferation Treaty Regime'. *Los Almos National Labortary* (2009). Available at <www.lanl.gov/orgs/nso/docs/fy07/LA-UR-07-1574_The_Future_of_the_NPT_Regime.pdf>.

Popov, A. et al. 'Russia and the Energy Charter Treaty: Common Interests or Irreconcilable Differences'. IELTR 7 (2006): 189.

Roberts, J. 'The Turkish Gate: Energy Transit and Security Issues'. *Turkish Policy Quarterly* 3, no. 4 (2004).

Schaefer, L. 'The BTC Pipeline: a beacon of Hope or Suffering for the People?'. *Covalence SA* (2006).

Scharpf, F. 'Decision Rules, Decision Styles and Policy Choices'. *Journal of Theoretical Politics* 1, no. 162 (1989): 149–176.

Seener, M. 'Can the IAEA be Saved?'. *Focus Quarterly* (2009).

Shan, W. 'Towards a Common European Community Policy on Investment Issues'. *Journal of World Investment* 2 (2001).

Shihata, I. & A. Parra. 'The Experience of ICSID'. *ICSID Review* 14, no. 2 (Fall 1999): 319–336.

Siddiky, I.A. 'The Caspian Energy Scenario and its Pipelines: Amalgamation of Interests?'. IELR 2 (2009).

Siddiky, I.A. 'Towards a New Framework for Cross-Border Pipelines: The International Pipeline Agency'. *China and Eurasia Forum Quarterly* 8, no. 3 (2010).

Sinuraya, T. 'Possible International Forums for the Resolution of Legal Conflicts Over Pipeline Transit in the Former Soviet Union'. *Leiden Journal of International Law*, 14 (2001): 445–454.

Slaoui, F. *Emergency Arbitrator – The Proposed New Procedure of the SCC Rules*, 2009. Available at <www.kluwerarbitrationblog.com>.

Smith, K. 'Russian Energy Pressure Fails to Unite Europe'. CSIS 13, no. 1 (2007).

Stauffer, T.R. 'Caspian Fantasy: The Economics of Political Pipelines'. *The Brown Journal of World Affairs* VII, no. 2 (2000).

Stevens, P. 'Pipelines or Pipe dreams? Lessons from the History of Arab Transit Pipelines', *Middle East Journal* (2000).

The WTO Dispute Settlement System, Journal of International Economic Law, 2000, 15.

Thomas, J.C. 'A Reply to Professor Brower'. *Columbia Journal of Transnational Law* 40, no. 3 (2002).

Vasconcelos, J. 'Towards the Internal Energy Market: How to Bridge a Regulatory Gas and Build a Regulatory Framework'. *European Review of Energy Markets* (2005): 81–103.

Vayrynen, R. 'Economic Sanctions and the Enforcement of Nuclear Non-Proliferation'. *African Defence Review* 19 (1994).

Waern, K.P. 'Transit Provisions of the Energy Charter Treaty and the Energy Charter Protocol on Transit'. JENRL 20 (2002): 172–183.

Walde, T. & S. Dow. 'Treaties and Regulatory Risk in Infrastructure Investment – The effectiveness of International Law Disciplines versus Sanctions by Global Markets in Reducing the Political and regulatory Risk for Private Infrastructure Investment'. *Journal of World Trade* 34 (2000).

Walker, M. 'Russia v. Europe: The Energy Wars'. *World Policy Journal* 1 (2007).

Werner, J. 'Making Investment arbitration More Certain – A Modest Proposal'. *Journal of World Investment* 4, no. 5 (October 2003).

4.      CHAPTERS AND ARTICLES IN BOOKS

Cossy, M. 'Energy Transport and Transit in the WTO'. In *Global Challenges at the intersection of Energy, Trade and Environment.* edited by Centre for trade and Economic Integration (CETI), 2010, 113–121.

De Burca, G. & J. Scott. 'Neutrality or Discrimination? The WTO, the EU and External Trade'. In *The EU and the WTO: Legal and Constitutional Aspects.* Oxford: Hart Publishing, 2001.

Fischer, D. 'Chapter 1: The Creation of the IAEA, 1939–1953: Eisenhower Proposes a New Agency'. In *History of the International Atomic Energy Agency: The first forty years.* edited by Fischer, D., Vienna: IAEA can be found in <www-pub.iaewa.org/MTCD/publications/PDF/Pub1032_web.pdf>.

Fischer, D. 'Chapter 2: The Creation of the IAEA, 1939–1953: The Dual Challenge of Nuclear Energy'. In *History of the International Atomic Energy Agency: The first forty years.* ed. Fischer, D., Vienna: IAEA can be found in <www-pub.iaewa.org/MTCD/publications/PDF/Pub1032_web.pdf>.

Hober, K. 'Russia Energy Policy and Dispute Settlement: An Overview'. In *European Energy Law Report VII.* edited by Roggenkamp, M., et al., Intersentia, 2010.

Hurrell, A. 'International Society and the Study of Regimes: A Reflective Approach'. In *International Rules: Approached from International Law and International Relations.* edited by Beck, R.J., et al., Oxford: Oxford University Press (1996): 206–223.

Jensen, T.J. 'Natural Gas – The Problem Child of Energy Transport and Trade'. In *Global Challenges at the intersection of Energy, Trade and Environment.* edited by Centre for trade and Economic Integration (CETI), 2010, 127–131.

Keohane, R. 'The Demand for International Regimes'. In *International Regimes.* edited by Krasner, S.D., Ithaca, NY: Cornell University Press, 1983, 150.

Koehane, R. 'Neoliberal Institutionalism: A Perspective on World Politics'. In *International Institutions and State Power: Essays in International Relations Theory.* edited by Keohane, R., Boulder. Colo: Westview Press, 1989.

Krasner, S. 'Structural Causes and Regime Consequences: Regime as Intervening Variables'. In *International Regimes.* edited by Krasner, S. Ithaca: Cornell University Press, 1983.

# Bibliography

Krasner, S. 'Sovereignty, Regimes, and Human Rights'. In *Regime Theory and International Relations*. edited by Volker Rittberger, et al., Clarendon: Oxford University Press, 1991.

Peterson, L.E. 'All Roads Lead Out of Rome: Divergent Paths of Dispute Settlement in Bilateral Investment Treaties'. In *International Investment for Sustainable Development: Balancing Rights and Rewards*. edited by Zarsky, L. Earthscan, 2004.

Rakhmanin, V. 'Transportation and Transit of Energy and Multilateral Trade Rules: WTO and Energy Charter'. In *Global Challenges at the Intersection of Energy, Trade and Environment*. edited by Centre for Trade and Economic Integration (CETI), 2010, 123–131.

Roggenkamp, M.M. 'Transit of Network Bound Energy: The European Experience'. In *The Energy Charter Treaty – An East–West Gateway for Investment and Trade*. edited by Walde, T.W. London: Kluwer Law International, 1996, 495–515.

Seck, A. 'Pipelines from Central Asia and the Transcaucases: A Maze of Alternatives', in *Boundaries and Energy: Problems and Prospects*. edited by Blake, G., et al., London: Kluwer, 1998.

The Energy Charter Protocol on Energy efficiency and Related Environmental Aspects, 17 December 1994, 33 *International Legal Materials* (1995): 445–454, reprinted in Walde, T.W. (ed.). *The Energy Charter Treaty – An East–West Gateway for Investment and Trade*. London: Kluwer Law International, 1996, 660–670.

Westerhof, J. 'The Transit Conflict between Russia and Ukraine from a Legal Perspective'. In *European Energy Law Report VII*. edited by Roggenkamp, M., et al., Intersentia, 2010.


5.     Conference Papers, Presentations, E-Journals
       and Internet Sourced Articles


Akpan, G.S. et al. 'The West African Oil and Gas Pipeline Project: Problems and Prospects'. OGEL 2, no. 1, February 2004. Can be accessed via <www.gasandoil.com>.

Alcock, J. *Developing European Gas Markets: Strategic Importance of the Interconnector*, AIC Conference, 3–4 April 1995.

Alexander's Gas and Oil connections, *Shah Deniz Gas Pipeline expected to Cost $1bn*, News and trends, 6, no. 14, in <www.gasnadoil.com/goc/news/ntc13120.htm>.

Anderson, O. *Risk: Emphasizing Political Risk*. CEPMLP Course materials, Contracts used in the International Oil Industry Development, slides p-18-19 CEPMLP, University of Dundee, 2004.

Baran, Z. *The Baku–Tbilisi–Ceyhan Pipeline: Implications for Turkey*. Central Asia–Caucasus Connections, <www.gasandoil.com/gol/news/ntr41095.htm>.

Das, B.L. 'The WTO Agreements: Deficiencies, Imbalances and Required Changes'. *Third World Network*, 1998.

Elbaredi, M. *Physical Protection of Nuclear materials.* 2006. Available at <www. iaea.org/Publications/Documents/Infcircs/1999/infcirc225r4c/rev4_content. html>.

Energy Charter Treaty: the Reader's Guide, at <www.encharter.org>.

Friends of Earth International (FOEI). *The Myths of West African Gas Pipeline*, 2006. Can be accessed via <www.foei.org/en/publications/pdfs/wagp-inet. pdf/view>.

IAEA website. *Promoting Nuclear Security: What the IAEA is doing.* in the IAEA information Series 1/03/E, 2006. Available at <www.iaea.org>.

Institute, Silk Road Studies Program, available on the Internet via <www. silkroadstudies.org/BTC_6.pdf>.

Karikpo, M. *Negotiating Resource Sovereignty, Fueling Conflicts: The Case of West African Gas Pipeline Project.* can be accessed via <www.eraction.org/ publications/presentations/negotiating_resource_sovereignty.pdf>.

Karipko, M. *The West African Gas Pipeline Project.* Testimony for the Public Hearing on the World Bank, 15 October 2007.

Micola, A. & D. Bunn. *Two Markets and a Weak Link.* Presentation at the 3rd International Conference on Applied Infrastructure Research, Berlin, 9th October 2004.

Middle East Economic Survey (MEES). *US Opposed to Any Pipeline Crossing Iran.* vol. XL, no. 43, 1997.

Moraleda, P. *How the Major Barriers to Cross-Border Gas Trade were Overcome in the Case of Maghreb Pipeline*, IEA Cross-Border Gas Conference, Paris, March 26, Paris International Energy Agency, 2002.

Mulcare, A. *The Impact of the UK–Belgium Interconnector.* can be accessed via <www.Interconnector.com/PDF/The_Impact_of_the_Interconnector.pdf>.

Ogutcu, M. 'Kazakhstan's Expanding Cross-Border Gas Links: Implications for Europe, Russia, China and Other CIS Countries'. *CEPMLP Internet Journal*, vol. 17, Article 8.

Rogers, W.D. *Emergence of the International Centre for Settlement of Investment Disputes(ICSID) as the Most Significant Forum for Submission of Bilateral Investment Treaty Disputes*, Presentation to Inter-American Development Bank Conference, 26–27 October 2000.

Speech by Ian Macdonald, General Director of the CPC in the International Energy Agency Roundtable on Caspian Oil and Gas Scenarios, Florence, 14th April 2003. Can be accessed via <www.iea.org/Textbase/work/2003/caspian/ macdonald.pdf>.

The IAEA's Director General. *Nuclear Security – Measures to Protect Against Nuclear Terrorism, Progress Report and Nuclear Security Plan for 2006– 2009*, Forty-ninth regular session of the General Conference, GC(49)/17, 2005.

Watkins, E. 'Kazakhstan, Azerbaijan to transport Kazakh Crude Through BTC Pipeline'. *Oil and Gas Journal Online*, 6 June 2003. Available online at <http:// ogj.pennet.com/articles/article_display.cfm?Section=ARCHI&C=Trasp& ARTICLE_ID=178376&KEYWORDS=Kazakhstan%2C%20azerbaijan% 20to%20transport>.

Bibliography

Weir, F. *Oil Pipeline Sparks Controversy in Poor Georgian Village*, in Alexander's Gas and Oil connections, <www.gasandoil.com/gol/news/ntr41095.htm>.
Winrow, G.M. *Turkey as an Energy Transit State*, Black Sea: Energy and Environment Conference, Marine Law and Policy Research Centre, 15th May 2003.
WTO Dispute settlement procedure, WTO, Switzerland, available <www.wto.org>.


6.  MAGAZINES, NEWS BULLETIN, NEWSPAPERS, OFFICIAL WEBSITES AND OTHER INTERNET-BASED SOURCES

Alexander's Gas and Oil connections, *Shah-Deniz Gas Pipeline expected to Cost $1bn*, News and trends, vol. 6, no. 14, in <www.gasnadoil.com/goc/news/ntc13120.htm>.
Daly, J.C.K. *Analysis: BTC Pipeline Explosion*. UPI.com, 2008. Can be accessed via <www.upi.com/Energy_Resources/2008/08/06/Analysis-BTC-pipeline-explosion/UPI-36081218062760/>.
Energy Information Administration (EIA) official website, <www.eia.doe.gov/emeu/cabs/wagp.htm>.
Eurasia Daily Monitor. *Turkey and the Problems with BTC*. vol. 5, no. 155, August 2008.
IAEA website at <www.iaea.org>.
IAEA website. *Nuclear Security*. 2006. Available at <www.ns.iaea.org/security/>.
Khripunov, I. 'Nuclear Security: Attitude Check'. *Bulletin of the Atomic Scientists* (2005): 58–64. Available at <www.thebulletin.org/article.php?art_ofn=jf05khripunov>.
Peterson, L.P. *Croatian Firm Invokes Investment Treaty to Challenge Czech Eviction Notice*. INVEST-SD News Bulletin, 1 October 2004. Available at <www.iisd.org/pdf/2004/investment_investsd_oct1_2004.pdf>.
Petroleum Economist. *UK Rushes in where Rest of Europe Fears to Tread*. Article 17, 25th March 1997.
Semmel, A.K. *Future Goals and Challenges of the IAEA Nuclear Security Programme*. In the US Department of State, 2005. Available at <www.state.gov/t/np/rls/rm44213.htm>.
Stratfor, 2008. Can be accessed via <www.stratfor.com/analysis/turkey_implications_blast_btc_pipeline>.
The Interconnector website at <www.Interconnector.com>.
Vladimir, S. 'Azerbaijan–Georgia Corridor: Growing Transit Volumes Bolster Security'. *Eurasia Daily Monitor* 5, no. 221, November 2008. Can be accessed via <www.jamestown.org/single/?no_cache=1&tx_ttnews%5Btt_news%5D=34135>.
Vladimir, S. 'Transneft Squeezing Western Oil Majors in Caspian Consortium'. *Eurasian Daily Monitor* (July 2007).
WAGP website at <www.wagpoco.com>.

7.  DISSERTATIONS

Aniekan, A. *What are the Potential for Developing the Domestic Gas Markets in Nigeria.* CEPMLP, University of Dundee, unpublished dissertation, 2006.

Babajide, A. *How Do Developing Countries React to the Economic Problems that Come with Resource Abundance: The Case Study of Nigeria and Algeria,* CEPMLP, University of Dundee, unpublished dissertation, 2006.

Banego, I. *The Development of Downstream Gas Market in Nigeria.* CEPMLP, University of Dundee, unpublished dissertation, 2005.

Omonbude, E. *How Feasible is a West African Market for Natural Gas?.* CEPMLP, University of Dundee, unpublished dissertation, 2002.

# Index

# ENERGY AND ENVIRONMENTAL LAW & POLICY SERIES

1. Stephen J. Turner, *A Substantive Environmental Right: An Examination of the Legal Obligations of Decision-makers towards the Environment*, 2009 (ISBN 978-90-411-2815-7).
2. Helle Tegner Anker, Birgitte Egelund Olsen & Anita Rønne (eds), *Legal Systems and Wind Energy: A Comparative Perspective*, 2009 (ISBN 978-90-411-2831-7).
3. David Langlet, *Prior Informed Consent and Hazardous Trade: Regulating Trade in Hazardous Goods at the Intersection of Sovereignty, Free Trade and Environmental Protection*, 2009 (ISBN 978-90-411-2821-8).
4. Louis J. Kotzé and Alexander R. Paterson (eds), *The Role of the Judiciary in Environmental Governance: Comparative Perspectives*, 2009 (ISBN 978-90-411-2708-2).
5. Tuula Honkonen, *The Common but Differentiated Responsibility Principle in Multilateral Environmental Agreement's: Regulatory and Policy Aspects*, 2009 (ISBN 978-90-411-3153-9).
6. Barbara Pozzo (ed.), *The Implementation of the Seveso Directives in an Enlarged Europe: A Look into the Past and a challenge for the Future*, 2009 (ISBN 978-90-411-2854-6).
7. Henrik M. Inadomi, *Independent Power Projects in Developing Countries: Legal Investment Protection and Consequences for Development*, 2010 (ISBN 978-90-411-3178-2).
8. Nahid Islam, *The Law of Non-Navigational Uses of International Watercourses: Options for Regional Regime-Building in Asia*, 2010 (ISBN 978-90-411-3196-6).
9. Yasuhiro Shigeta, *International Judicial Control of Environmental Protection: Standard Setting, Compliance Control and the Development of International Environmental Law by the International Judiciary*, 2010 (ISBN 978-90-411-3151-5).
10. Katleen Janssen, *The Availability of Spatial and Environmental Data in the European Union: At the Crossroads between Public and Economic Interests*, 2010 (ISBN 978-90-411-3287-1).
11. Henrik Bjørnebye, *Investing in EU Energy Security: Exploring the Regulatory Approach to Tomorrow's Electricity Production*, 2010 (ISBN 978-90-411-3118-8).
12. Véronique Bruggeman, *Compensating catastrophe victims: A Comparative Law and Economics Approach*, 2010 (ISBN 978-90-411-3263-5).
13. Michael G. Faure, Han Lixin & Shan Hongjun, *Maritime Pollution Liability and Policy: China, Europe and the US*, 2010 (ISBN 978-90-411-2869-0).
14. Anton Ming-Zhi Gao, *Regulating Gas Liberalization: A Comparative Study on Unbundling and Open Access Regimes in the US, Europe, Japan, South Korea and Taiwan*, 2010 (ISBN 978-90-411-3347-2).

15. Mustafa Erkan, *International Energy Investment Law: Stability through Contractual Clauses*, 2011 (ISBN 978-90-411-3411-0).
16. Levente Borzsák, *The Impact of Environmental Concerns on the Public Enforcement Mechanism under EU law: Environmental protection in the 25th hour*, 2011 (ISBN 978-90-411-3408-0).
17. Tarcísio Hardman Reis, *Compensation for Environmental Damages under International Law: The Role of the International Judge*, 2011 (ISBN 978-90-411-3437-0).
18. Kim Talus, *Vertical Natural Gas Transportation Capacity, Upstream Commodity Contracts and EU Competition Law*, 2011 (ISBN 978-90-411-3407-3).
19. Wang Hui, *Civil Liability for Marine Oil Pollution Damage: A Comparative and Economic Study of the International, US and Chinese Compensation Regime*, 2011 (ISBN 978-90-411-3672-5).
20. Chowdhury Ishrak Ahmed Siddiky, *Cross-Border Pipeline Arrangements: What Would a Single Regulatory Framework Look Like?*, 2012 (ISBN 978-90-411-3844-6).